böhlau

Einheit & Vielfalt im Recht / Legal Unity & Pluralism

Edited by
Ulrike Ludwig and Peter Oestmann

Volume 5

Die Reihe versteht Rechtsvielfalt als ein überzeitliches und überregionales Strukturmerkmal von Recht schlechthin. Es kann demnach von einem relationalen und historisch wandelbaren Zusammenhang von Einheit und Vielfalt im Recht gesprochen werden. Die Schriftenreihe möchte diesen Zusammenhang in seiner kulturellen Vielgestaltigkeit umfassend beleuchten: interdisziplinär, räumlich übergreifend und interepochal. Die Bände erscheinen in deutscher und englischer Sprache und sind überwiegend im Open Access zugänglich.

The book series conceptualises legal pluralism as a structural characteristic of law itself. We can therefore speak of a relational and historically changeable association between unity and pluralism in law. The book series intends to comprehensively illuminate these connections in their cultural polymorphy interdisciplinarily, transspatially and interepochally. The volumes are published in German and English and will be predominantly open access.

Die Herausgeber / the editors

Gregor Rohmann / Ulla Kypta (eds.)

How to Ensure Predictability in Legal Pluralism

Merchants and their Interaction in Late Medieval Europe

BÖHLAU

This publication was made possible by the Käte Hamburger Kolleg "Legal Unity and Pluralism" at the University of Münster, funded by the Federal Ministry of Research, Technology and Space (BMFTR).

With funding from the:

KÄTE HAMBURGER KOLLEG MÜNSTER
EINHEIT & VIELFALT IM RECHT
LEGAL UNITY & PLURALISM

Federal Ministry of Research, Technology and Space

Bibliographic information published by the Deutsche Nationalbibliothek:
The Deutsche Nationalbibliothek lists this publication in the Deutsche Nationalbibliografie; detailed bibliographic data available online: https://dnb.de.

Cover image: Illustrated Manuscript of the Hamburg Town Law (1497), Miniature B, Hamburg, Hauptstaatsarchiv der Freien und Hansestadt Hamburg Cl. VII. Lit. LaNr. 2 Vol. 1 c.

Cover design: Michael Haderer, Wien
Proof reading: Bird und Hübner, Berlin
Typesetting: le-tex publishing services, Leipzig
Printed and bound: Elanders Waiblingen GmbH, Anton-Schmidt-Straße 15, 71332 Waiblingen
Printed in the EU

Vandenhoeck & Ruprecht Verlage | www.vandenhoeck-ruprecht-verlage.com
E-Mail: info@boehlau-verlag.com

ISBN 978-3-412-53376-2 (print)
ISBN 978-3-412-53377-9 (digital)

Contents

Gregor Rohmann

How to ensure Predictability in Legal Pluralism

Merchants and their Interaction in Late Medieval Europe. Some introductory Notes to this Volume

1. Introduction

Premodern trade was characterised by legal pluralism. Taken as a starting point, this may sound all too self-evident. However, within the context of the Käte Hamburger Kolleg "Einheit und Vielfalt im Recht" ("Legal Unity and Pluralism"), we want to show that the concept may still be useful to understand some characteristic features of economic life in late medieval Europe. Vice versa, a focus on mercantile practice might be especially helpful in understanding the ways legal pluralism in late medieval Europe worked. This is because wherever they met, merchants had to face a high degree of variability of the normative frameworks within which they acted. How did they manage to cope with this? How did they manage to cope with each other? How did they ascertain the predictability of other's actions? These are the questions the following case studies will try to answer.

Legal pluralism does not mean anomy, that is: the absence of any predictability. In fact, predictability is possible also within legal pluralism. There are however, always overlapping normative framings being negotiated to fulfil expectations. For merchants, this challenge was especially important since they needed a certain degree of predictability to other's behaviour in order to profit. They had to be at least fairly certain that their trading partner was going to pay for their goods, to provide shipping as promised, or pay back money borrowed. Thus, to let trade flourish, some degree of predictability was required even in a setting shaped by legal pluralism such as premodern Northern and Central Europe. So, how did people decide according to which framing they should act? Which patterns of behaviour were used to bargain this? Which practices of communication were used to ensure that others acted as expected? And finally, how did actors cope with unexpected behaviour?

2. What is Legal Pluralism?

Putting aside all terminological debates[1] a sort of minimal working definition of legal pluralism that most scholars would presumably agree upon was formulated by the American legal anthropologist Sally Merry Engle in 1988:

> What is legal pluralism? It is generally defined as a situation in which two or more legal systems coexist in the same social field.[2]

The "social field" in this definition is best understood in a regular ethnographic way, as a social setting within which agents and their positions are located and which an observer can describe.[3] Within such a setting, "legal systems" are said to be overlapping. Accordingly, within a defined group of persons and/or within a defined space more than one normative matrix must apply, so that we can ascertain "legal plurality". In this last sentence at least seven words: group, person, space, normative, matrix, legal, and plurality, would need further clarification, which we cannot pursue here, however.

For now, we will follow Richard Scott's definition, according to whom social "institutions" can be "rules", "norms", or "beliefs".[4] These three differ regarding their degree of obligation, but they all contribute to the reproduction of an "institution", that is, a social constellation which makes people's behaviour expectable. Given that within the same social setting rules, norms, and beliefs of different origin work to constitute institutions, normative plurality is not the exception, but the regular state of human society.

However, how do institutions emerge, basically? In general, normative orders should not be considered as simply engendered by social institutions (as "law" is engendered by a "state"), but also vice versa as institutions are constituted by rules, norms, and beliefs. For example, people go to court because they expect their problem to be solved there. Or, more generally, they act according to the implicit rules and with some level of probability experience successful transactions. If all goes well, other people will also use the expectably successful procedure. If not, they will choose other ways to enforce their claims, within the boundaries of path dependency and situational social dynamics. Thus, the very validity of the institution is dependent on its functioning in the eyes of actors, and vice versa. Such a circle of

---

1 Tamanaha, Legal Pluralism, pp. 375–411; Seinecke, Legal Pluralism, pp. 13–29.

2 Engle, Legal Pluralism, p. 870.

3 Hilgers and Mangez, Theory.

4 "Institutions are comprised of regulative, normative and cultural-cognitive elements, that, together with associated activities and resources, provide stability and meaning to social life." Scott, Institutions, pp. 48 f.; cf. Kypta, Konkurrenzverbot, pp. 369–392, here: pp. 368–370.

mutual constitution allows for a diachronic conceptualisation of how institutions produce predictability. For we have to conceive of society not synchronically as a given structure, but as a dynamic process of continuous reproduction (and iteration) of institutions. A "social field" is thus not a given entity, but something marked by powers and their dynamic interplay, as are the normative orders within it.

A definition like this, borrowed from sociology and economics rather than from legal history, would surely not work as a passport out for all problems of normative plurality; but it could possibly help us to achieve a common understanding of what we are talking about. At least we could avoid loaded terms such as "law" or the German "*Recht*",[5] the specific connotations of which do in fact impede every interdisciplinary debate. Not every human society may have laws or a legal system, but every society surely has rules, norms, and beliefs, the heterogeneity of which we can detect and further analyse to understand how actors tried to cope with this.

Medieval long-distance traders experienced this plurality in a particular way because they regularly crossed different territories, had to do their business according to different rules, and with partners belonging to different social groups. Given this fact, how did people ensure security, and how did they cope with potential breaches of predictability within their mercantile relationships? In a social setting marked by normative plurality, one would, at first glance, expect contract enforcement to be comparably difficult and the corresponding costs to be comparably high. Yet, as far as we know, most of the time, premodern trade worked remarkably well. So, in their everyday life, merchants must have been able to come to terms with the obstacles described – if indeed plurality primarily caused obstacles, rather than providing leeway for creative ways of handling business.

And this is not only about conflict management, but also about all the deals which functioned well. Many of our sources only tell us about problems, since especially, and maybe only in cases of conflict, did actors need to use pen and paper. Only the conflicts became notorious, but they by no means shaped everyday life. As long as we focus on contested claims and lawsuits, we will only see the exceptions, not the rule. For everyday transactions, account books may possibly be the better source to look at than court proceedings. That said, the exceptional cases are especially useful because during these, actors may have explicated their normative expectations so that default could tell us more about normal conditions than the regular case. In any event, we should try to combine the approaches of legal history and economic history – normative plurality and institutional economics. Yet, we should also keep in mind the respective boundaries of these approaches.

One could argue that focusing on long-distance trade just reproduces a misleading tendency in economic history to overrate the interests of mercantile and social

5 Loos/Schreiber, Recht, vol. 5, 1984, pp. 231–311.

elites.[6] What about the everyday practice of grocers, not to mention all other social actors? One could argue that, since they usually stayed where they were, their life was not shaped by legal pluralism to an extent comparable to long-distance traders; but as we know, even the urban landscape of towns was divided into different legal spaces.[7] All the more, the fundamental corporative order and the so-called personality principle of premodern law rendered any social sphere inherently pluralistic. Long-distance traders had to cope with this in their hometowns as well as at the destinations they visited. Hence, the case studies in this volume will hopefully also encompass these problems. Regardless, due to the existing evidence, long-distance traders, their mercantile practice and normative frameworks, provide a good setup for analysing the intersection of legal pluralism and economics.

3. What is "Predictability"?

The "social field" of mercantile business in late medieval Europe did in fact have "laws", that is, written legal texts issued by authorities and at least theoretically claiming bindingness within a scope of validity. However, these laws were, in practice, only relatively enforceable; they were not homogenous but mostly competed against each other. Additionally, there were several forms of social norms and cultural beliefs which very often contradicted each other as well as the mentioned laws. Different rules, norms, and beliefs applied to different groups and persons within the same space. Finally, different institutions of jurisdiction (courts/forums) vied for competence within the same social field. Thus, at least, there were social institutions providing a measurable degree of reliability and predictability for social actors. Yet, if these institutions very often competed each other, and were constituted by heterogenous rules, norms, and beliefs, how did they work to secure expectable behaviour of persons belonging to different social groups? How did people respond to this plurality?

"Reliability" and "predictability" might best be understood as somewhat weak translations of a typically strong category of German social theory: "*Erwartungssicherheit*" (expectation security), as informed by Niklas Luhmann. "Predictability" is the relative security that a counterpart will act according to my expectations.[8] It is generated by social institutions, and it leads to "system trust" (*Systemvertrauen*), as Luhmann termed it. This exceeds personal confidence because the more complex social relations become, the less people can rely

6 This argument was put forward by Louis Sicking during the discussion at the Münster workshop. Cf. Ogilvie, Institutions, pp. 197 f.

7 Arlinghaus, Inklusion.

8 Luhmann, Recht, pp. 148 ff.

on merely individual ties.[9] Only institutions will enable people to shift from particularised to generalised trust, as Ogilvie put it.[10] This security is never absolute but only relative.[11] It must always cope with a considerable degree of breaches, and "trust" is also always relative, since it is about how to calculate and manage the said degree of betrayal.

Usually, we tend to assume that predictability increases the more formalised an institutional setting becomes. We expect strong norms, organisations, and hierarchies to foster expectation security. Yet, at the same time we know that premodern social settings were very often shaped by a remarkable tendency to eschew formalisation. This observation has been the starting point of debates within the field of new institutional economics, which have focused especially on mechanisms of mercantile self-regulation off the beaten tracks of state-building theories.[12] Indeed, the focus on formalisation and strong hierarchical organisations may only be a modernist shortcoming, and synthesising new institutional economics and systems theory might allow for a better understanding of the problems under scrutiny here.

As we know, in their communications merchants referred to "trust" and "trustworthiness" again and again, but we should not perceive this as an interpersonal relationship, instead rather as one fostered by and focused on social interactions within institutions.[13] Late medieval merchants did not need to trust each other as long as they trusted the institutions they engaged with.[14] In fact, economic exchange does not necessarily need trust. An actor can be forced to cooperate with another even if he does not trust him, when due to circumstances he simply has no choice. He can even knowingly continue trading with a fraudulent partner, as long as the risk of being cheated again is lower than the possible gain or as long as for any reason he lacks an alternative. Within this sphere of mistrust, through repetition and routinisation a feeling of security may arise, which actors then might call "trust". Mercantile practice could thus be best described as being about balancing mistrust and trust by always calculating the risk of being cheated or harmed,[15] and about the communicative mechanisms used to produce "trust" in

---

9 Luhmann, Trust, pp. 48–60; cf. idem, Vertrauen, pp. 60–79.

10 Ogilvie, Use and Abuse, pp. 15–52, here: pp. 18 f.

11 Cf. Luhmann, Vertrauen, p. 29; idem, Trust and Power, p. 24: "Trust reflects contingency". Generally, Luhmann discerns between open-ended "trust" (*Vertrauen*) and instrumental "controlling events" (*Ereignisbeherrschung*) or "mastery over things" (*Sachbeherrschung*) respectively, cf.: Luhmann, Vertrauen, pp. 19 f.; Luhmann, Trust and Power, pp. 14 f.

12 Greif, Institutions.

13 Wubs-Mrozewicz, Concept; Wubs-Mrozewicz, Mercantile Conflict Resolution, pp. 417–440.

14 Ogilvie, Use and Abuse, p. 18.

15 Luhmann, Trust, p. 29: "[…] whoever trusts has to keep watch over his own preparedness to accept the risks involved. He must make it clear to himself, if only to reassure himself, that he is not trusting unconditionally but rather within limits and in proportion to specific, rational

such an inherently unstable relationship. To analyse these, we should differentiate between the degree of predictability as a social factor (be it measurable or not) on the one hand, and "trust" as a communicative performance, in Luhmann's terms as "maintained semantics" (*gepflegte Semantik*) used by a society to render a risk manageable, on the other.[16] In communicative practice, expectation security and trust (as always relative categories) may be inextricably intertwined in a form of dynamic reciprocity, but they are not the same.[17]

If they were, the general argument – actors trust each other because they experience security, so they trade with one another according to the rules – would be in great danger of becoming circular. Every merchant will meet counterparts he does not know yet, which means that he cannot evaluate their reliability by simply referring to acquaintance. This implies a good deal of insecurity and the means to cope with this was presumably an unending task of risk calculation. A clever merchant would not simply "trust" the other, but regard profits in relation to potential losses as unavoidable transaction costs. Since he could not simply exclude risks absolutely, he would try to make them manageable.[18] This book deals with the "rules", "norms", and "beliefs" – "institutions" in Scott's sense – which premodern merchants stuck to in a social setting framed by normative plurality.

According to recent research on "securitisation", at the dawn of modernity varieties of formalised or even organisational mechanisms to cope with all the risks inherent to mercantile life emerged.[19] Insurance and new administrative and normative frameworks were developed to make potential losses scalable and manageable and thus foster trade. We tend to perceive this trend to formalisation as progress, an important step in economic growth and social advancement. But was it really

---

expectations." Cf. Idem, Vertrauen, p. 36 f.; Ibid., p. 33; "The clues employed to form trust do not eliminate the risk, they simply make it less. [...] They simply serve as a springboard for the leap into uncertainty, although bounded and structured." Cf. Idem, Vertrauen, p. 40; on the polarity of "trust" and "mistrust" in general cf. Luhmann, Trust, pp. 71–77; Idem, Vertrauen, pp. 92–101.

16 In fact, Luhmann does not use the distinction between semantics and structure in his argument on "trust"; for his concept of "semantics" cf. Luhmann, Gesellschaftsstruktur, vol. 1, pp. 17–21.

17 Cf. Ogilvie's distinction between trust as a "sentiment" or as an observable "propensity"; Ogilvie, Use and Abuse, pp. 17 f: "Such a propensity may or may not derive from an inward sentiment of trust." Ibid., p. 18.

18 But cf. Luhmann, Trust, p. 88; Idem, Vertrauen, p. 116, who explicitly states that "trust" as a communicative medium always exceeds simple risk calculation. This may be due to the external, non-economic factors every actor will consider when evaluating a situation. If, according to Luhmann, Trust, pp. 88 f., the rationality of "trust" always refers to the specific sub-system "system rationality", then in an economic context, risk calculation will possibly be the functional equivalent of "trust". To understand the limits of a "trust economy", it still seems reasonable to re-introduce cost-benefit ratios and risk calculation then as a factor.

19 Scheller, Geburt, pp. 305–330.

an improvement of trading conditions in general? Did merchants strive for this because they had become discontent with the old regime, maybe due to an overall higher degree of complexity of social relations? Or was it rather something primarily implemented by the emerging authorities, that is – the modern state and its rulers against their resisting subjects? In any case, here we come to detect historical change, and we hope that the case studies in this book will help to describe this basic trend in European history in greater detail. Call it "systemic trust", "expectation security", "reliability", or "predictability", the relationship between actors and society is not static but dynamic, a continuous process of institutional reproduction.

4. The Hanse as a Starting Point

Following Luhmann, in social systems of low complexity, "trust" and "justice" are inextricably intertwined, if not identical. As complexity grows, the two categories differentiate, and societies start to develop external institutions to provide expectation security.[20] In general however, the high value of "trust" as a means to reduce complexity in comparison to "control" lies in the relatively low efforts needed to provide it. Control produces transaction costs which any merchant would like to save.[21] It could thus be attractive for him to "trust" his business partners instead of controlling them.[22] Avner Greif and other protagonists of New Institutional Economics have referred to late medieval guilds, and especially to the Hanse, as examples of what they conceived of as proofs for an autonomous, not state-induced normative order of the mercantile sphere.[23] The very emergence of guilds was explained by Greif as a means to guarantee a power equilibrium between the ruler and the mercantile class.[24] According to him, medieval merchants, as inhabitants of a pre-state society, more or less managed to rule their life completely on their own by using personal networks, collective liability, and social exclusion. Stefan Selzer and Ulf Christian Ewert have shown that, concerning the Hanse, this mercantile system was not fostered by interpersonal trust, but rather by incentives.[25] For a merchant or for an agent at a remote destination it was simply more attractive to stick to the rules of reciprocity than to cheat his partner or principle. Sheilagh Ogilvie in contrast criticised Greif's interpretation as being not only shaped by

20 Luhmann, Trust, pp. 34 f.; cf. Idem, Vertrauen, p. 43.

21 Luhmann, Trust, pp. 88 ff.; Greif, Institutions, p. 311.

22 Jahnke, Handelsnetze, pp. 189–212.

23 Greif, Institutions, pp. 105–108; Höhn, Kaufleute, pp. 31–37; cf. very recently: Brunori, Simon, Touchelay and Wijffels, Dynamique.

24 Greif, Institutions, pp. 92 f.

25 Selzer and Ewert, Institutions.

recent claims for an independence of international trade from political intrusion, but also as empirically wrong from a historian's point of view. According to her, late medieval guilds did not operate in a stateless setting but interacted with public order institutions on all levels of the social hierarchy. These authorities thus functioned as guarantors of private and mercantile contract enforcement already in premodern times.[26] This leads to the core of recent debates in economic history. It therefore seems worthwhile to focus on the Hanse and its environment as an example for how economics and normative plurality interacted. What rules did merchants stick to instead of cheating their partners? How did these rules emerge? Who enforced them, and how did people cope with transgressions?

Ogilvie has also criticised that the techniques of a trust economy such as that described by Greif, and especially those by Selzer/Ewert, could only have worked within an integrated group of merchants.[27] Reputation, personal affinity, and networking could possibly solve the principal-agent problem in reciprocal trade within close knit milieus; but as profits tend to grow if trading partners come from different social settings, it is inherently attractive for merchants to search for partners as dissimilar as possible. When doing so, they always have to take into account the expectation insecurities engendered by normative plurality. Relying on collective liability, as Greif has proposed, would only work as long as two guilds or at least two defined social groups met for trade. Here, again, the very institutions of long-distance trade are at stake, and we must focus on what happened when merchants from different normative settings met. To do so, we should look at the margins of the Hanse or even at spaces beyond its scope, and we have to scrutinise how the Hanse was perceived from outside.

Simultaneously, one should also scrutinise the inner structuring of the Hanse and the functioning of its institutions in detail. Even Ogilvie tends to reproduce an all to global concept of the Hanse as a sort of centralised meta-guild[28] where recent research would rather see a weak "community of interests" und "cooperation between egoists".[29] Accordingly, the Hanse did not strive for a unification and harmonisation of laws according to modern statehood. Within the Hanse and by using the imagination of a powerful community, individual actors attempted to enhance their own position in a social field with multiple norms. In most cases, it was not the entire Hanse acting, but a group of merchants, a *Kontor*, or one or more cities, which rhetorically claimed to be the whole. The Hanse could thus indeed

---

26 Ogilvie, Institutions, pp. 230 f., 268 ff., 286 f.

27 Ogilvie, Institutions, pp. 250 f., 268 f., 320; But cf. also Greif's own discussion of reputation as a possible factor in impersonal exchange, Greif, Institutions, pp. 314 f.

28 For example: Ogilvie, Institutions, pp. 321–330, 342 on the alleged monopoly and centrality of the Hanse.

29 Pichierri, Città stato, p. 111: *"communità d'interessi"*, p. 112: *"cooperazione tra egoisti"*.

be understood as a means to cope with what we call legal pluralism.[30] Meanwhile, however, the Hanse itself remained institutionally heterogenous because all efforts to harmonise its own norms and structures failed due to the conflicting individual interests of its members.[31]

However, while trade and distribution seem to have been shaped by normative plurality and informal institutions for a long time, in the field of production and transport, centralisation and formalisation prevailed much earlier: beer,[32] herring,[33] and cloth,[34] three of the main commodities of Hanse trade, became subject to constant quality control and classification. These were further guaranteed by introducing standards of quantity and trademarks of either individual providers or locations of production and distribution.[35] These mechanisms of unification were attractive for buyers and sellers alike because they also worked as early marketing factors.[36]

Thus, as for quality and quantity of the most important commodities, a relatively high degree of predictability could be provided by means of standardisation and its enforcement. Material objects, one can presume, were easier to unify than individual behaviour and social norms. Or rather, all actors in the market may have agreed on standardising commodities and their transport, but not on institutionally regulating each other's actions. Only temporarily did leading factions of the Hanse manage to enforce strong measures to a higher degree, because in this field all relevant actors benefited from a persistency of informal and open structures which gave them leeway to pursue their own interests. Formalisation and standardisation were possible in premodern markets – as soon as actors evaluated them as useful for their business and authorities considered it useful to enforce them.

5. Written Law, Customary Law, or Equity?

In spite of what older university handbooks may tell us, the Hanse was not a state-like institution producing its own laws. There were indicators for legal harmonisation, such as the so-called Hanse statutes of 1417, which may have resulted in a common normative framework had not the diverging interests of the actors

30 Wubs-Mrozewicz, Hanse as an institution, pp. 59–84.

31 Jahnke, Hanse; Hammel-Kiesow, Hanse.

32 Blanckenburg, Hanse.

33 Jahnke, Das Silber des Meeres.

34 Huang, Textilien; Huang and Jahnke, Textiles.

35 Selzer and Ewert, Institutions, pp. 93; Kümper, Traum, pp. 165 f.; Witthöft, Zeichen, pp. 203–224.

36 Huang, Marke, pp. 211–256.

hindered them. Hence, until the mid-sixteenth century at least, the Hanse was determined by a remarkably weak structure. In search of a substitute, scholars often supposed the wide dissemination of the town statutes of Lübeck and Magdeburg in Central Europe to have constituted a common legal sphere interfering with the Hanse.[37] Yet, empirically, both *Rechtsfamilien* and the Hanse were not congruent even in terms of geography. Even more, the founding of towns according to "German" law did by no means constitute legal unity in a territory or even within the said towns. True, authorities as far east as Poland, Ruthenia, and the Rus' very often referred to "German" (that is Magdeburg) law, when they gave their towns a legal status. Due however to the ethnic and social heterogeneity of the region, this did not lead to a unified normative sphere.[38]

The quest for a legal system which premodern merchants supposedly gave themselves has also led to the scholarly revival of an alleged *lex mercatoria*. However, apart from some general usages, such a mercantile common law did not in fact exist.[39] As for a common maritime law, there is at least a detectable tradition of respective texts, encompassing several interdependent law codes, especially derivates of the so-called *Rôles d'Oléron*.[40] Yet, even if different legal collections in Northern Europe belong to this tradition, we should certainly not assume that mariners around the North Sea and the Baltic generally solved their conflicts by explicit or implicit reference to one of these, even if lawyers and town clerks could have expected them to do so.[41]

Debates in economic history have tended to reproduce the idea that mercantile actors must have striven for a homogenisation and rationalisation of their normative framework. In contrast, we should describe how actors moved and acted within an environment marked by normative plurality, how they reacted to or even used these circumstances.[42] Obviously, there was no overwhelming written law code used by tradesmen in Northern Europe. There was only Roman Law, the laws of the merchants' homelands and their destination areas, and the manifold statuary laws of the cities involved. For all these competing norms, since the twelfth century legal savants had developed rules of gradual application.[43]

---

37 Selzer and Ewert, Institutions, p. 93; Dusil, Stadtrecht, pp. 85–108; Dusil, Legal Transplants, pp. 161–180.

38 Höhn, Pluralismus, pp. 268 f.; Karpaviciene, Frage, pp. 247–266, here p. 261.

39 Ogilvie, Institutions, pp. 265 f.; Cordes, The search, pp. 53–67; Greif, Institutions, pp. 314 f.; cf. the recent project "Migrating Commercial Law and Language", funded by the European Research Council: URL: https://www.micoll-erc.eu/, accessed 10/31/2024.

40 Graßmann and Jahnke, Seerecht; Jahnke, Maritime Law, pp. 572–583; Landwehr, Seerecht; Frankot, Maritime Law, pp. 151–172.

41 Ogilvie, Institutions, p. 266; Frankot, Of laws, esp. pp. 155 ff., 164 f., 195 ff.

42 Höhn, Pluralismus, pp. 261–289.

43 Oestmann, Gemeines Recht, pp. 1–50, here: pp. 11–16.

Usually, local courts were lay juries, privileged by the authorities.[44] Similar, but not identical were extra-legal arbitration tribunals recruited from local elites.[45] Local courts in their jurisdictional practice, however, appear to have only rarely referred to law books, relying instead on considerations of equity and justice.[46] It was far less the strict rules and the written laws that shaped legal conflict management, but instead the norms and implicit expectations of how one should behave and how misdemeanour should be judged that mattered. Such expectations were based on a common understanding of right and wrong – a set of commonalities which, in fact, fostered predictability in a world shaped by legal pluralism.[47] One would expect such forums to have tended to disadvantage strangers,[48] all the more so since culprits had to be judged according to the laws of their home jurisdiction, but there were strong incentives for towns to supply impartial forums.[49] The personality principle was very often explicitly abandoned by foreign merchant groups in their privileges, especially if they were given balanced manning of the court in return.[50] Long-distance traders also very often simply appealed to the courts of their destination commune or used extrajudicial arbitration by local brokers instead of trying to draw suits to their hometowns or to the courts of their communities.[51] Vice versa, harbour towns and fair sites provided special market forums to solve the merchants' problems "with dusty feet" ("piepowder") courts that were quick and simple.[52] Sometimes, travelling merchants appear to have preferred a prompt iniquity instead of protracted justice. Time was money, and again, this was not about "trust", but about balancing loss and gain.

The question remains, how did merchants manage to cope with normative plurality? A first hypothetical answer would be that very often they simply didn't care but referred to principles of equity and abandoned losses as soon as possible. In other cases, however, actors sustained legal claims for decades, they even handed

44 Ogilvie, Institutions, pp. 258 ff.

45 Ogilvie, Institutions, pp. 297–300; Höhn, Verflechtungen, pp. 19–40; Fieremans, Arbitration, pp. 439–480; generally: Roebuck, Mediation.

46 Cordes and Höhn, Conflict Management, pp. 509–528; concerning arbitration tribunals, at least in Flanders, there was a difference between "arbiters", who usually oriented their decisions around written law, and "arbitrators", who mostly referred to equity and searched for dilatory compromises rather than for final solutions, cf. Fieremans, Arbitration, pp. 456 f. In practice, both approaches were usually combined, cf. ibid., p. 464.

47 Johnson, Law.

48 Greif, Institutions, pp. 318 ff.

49 Ogilvie, Institutions, pp. 304–306, 309; Wubs-Mrozewicz, Mercantile Conflict Resolution, p. 438.

50 Cordes, Litigating abroad, pp. 11 ff.

51 Ogilvie, Institutions, pp. 262 f., 307–309; Frankot, Of laws, pp. 146–149.

52 Cordes, Litigating abroad, p. 14; Cordes/Höhn, Conflict Management, p. 523.

them down to their descendants – while carrying on communicating with the opponent in everyday life. This worked because all actors on the scene agreed upon the overarching principle that all sides had the right to pursue their interests, as long as those of the others were not too blatantly harmed. Without any form of unified law, there were functioning institutions people used and "trusted" in. Predictability was provided by a normative framing common to all actors which was based not on rules, but on arbitration and common norms of equity.

6. What about Violence?

But what if the institutions failed, an actor transgressed the normative order, or an actor perceived himself as being victim of such a transgression and had tried all peaceful options to enforce his claim unavailingly? According to Greif, especially until the end of the thirteenth century, on the level of communication between communities and their members, in this case reprisals against compatriots of the supposed perpetrator would have worked to implement collective liability and thus enable impersonal exchange.[53] Such acts of retaliation not only against the accused, but also against his compatriots and/or guild brothers, would increase the transaction costs of all actors in the field and thus necessarily lead to a sanctioning of the perpetrator, on the one hand. On the other, actors would have to calculate the expense caused by using force in comparison to other forms of contract enforcement, so that maybe violence would be only a last resort.

It seems highly debatable whether this system really fell out of fashion before the fourteenth century, as Greif has argued.[54] As even Greif concedes, in the Holy Roman Empire the community responsibility system remained in action.[55] Its concise legal definition was laid out as late as 1354 by Bartolus de Saxoferrato (1313–1357) in his *Tractatus repressalium*,[56] Meanwhile, in maritime contexts, it would lead to the emergence of the "letter of marque", a written legal instrument in use well into early modern times.[57]

At least we should take violence into account as an option merchants and mariners had, and used, individually and even more in their communities. Even

53 Greif, Institutions, pp. 310, 328–337; critically: Ogilvie, Institutions, pp. 270–274.

54 Greif, Institutions, pp. 338 ff.

55 Greif, Institutions, pp. 343 f., referring to a somewhat traditional concept of the decline of Imperial power.

56 Tai, Honor, pp. 145–149.; Heebøll-Holm, Piracy, pp. 2 f., 14 f.; Rubin, The Law, pp. 5 f., 15 f.

57 Tai, Marking Water, pp. 205–220.; Idem., The Legal Status, pp. 838–851; Carr-Riegel, Letter of Marque.

if these claimed executive rights very regularly, their actions were primarily determined by their own interests.[58] Most economic historians, however, still tend to describe their actors and their communes as inherently peaceful, only striving for advantages through locational politics.[59] Accordingly, Ogilvie has argued that merchants and their guilds had basically tried to abolish collective liability and to reduce the acceptance of reprisals against third parties, because in economic terms, the use of force was inherently inefficient.[60] But if this were so, why then did violent contract enforcement remained a regular practice long into early modern times? Hanse merchants in particular tended to decry collective liability, reprisals, and the use of force, if others sought to employ these methods. As soon as their own interests were to be enforced, however, they used force very blatantly.[61] In the end, even embargoes as the core instrument used by premodern guilds to pursue their economic and political claims imply the use of force to coerce the will of the community on its members and its environment, even if only as a last resort.[62] Sheilagh Ogilvie has argued that reprisals remained usual, though they were not efficient, because they provided good profit to individual actors.[63] On the other hand, according to her, it was simply the particularity of maritime trade and its heterogenous normative system which fostered "inter merchant piracy" long into the times of the global expansion of European powers.[64] Admittedly, the fact that we can detect merchants using force does not necessarily mean that all merchants indiscriminately or "the merchants" did so. On the other hand, one should avoid reproducing the old cliché of the peaceful tradesman threatened by isolated rogues. If there really was a gradual pacification of the mercantile sphere during early modern times, this can only be argued for within the European centres and was achieved by externalising violence as a means to gain profit at the peripheries of the global expansion.[65]

In any event, violence should not be understood as a mere remnant of the primordial stages of social organisation. As a means to provide security, it is not necessary

58 Ogilvie, Institutions, pp. 216, 219 ff.; Cordes and Höhn, Conflict Management, pp. 524 ff.; Heebøll-Holm, Höhn and Rohmann, Introduction, pp. 9–32.

59 For example: Greif, Institutions, pp. 94 f., when describing the lack of protection from violent attacks merchants had to face at their destination places, without mentioning that all too often these riots against alien traders were instigated by their local competitors: "Merchants abroad needed protection from coercive power." (p. 96); similarly: Gelderblom, Cities of Commerce.

60 Ogilvie, Institutions, pp. 276–281.

61 Höhn, Kaufleute.

62 Ogilvie, Institutions, pp. 222 f., 225–227; cf. Rohmann, Politischer Alltag, pp. 574–585.

63 Ogilvie, Institutions, pp. 281–285.

64 Ogilvie, Institutions, pp. 216–218, 223. Since reprisals were also common on land, this argument does not seem to work, basically.

65 Kempe, Fluch der Weltmeere.

in simple systems within which trust and justice are identical; but it becomes an "ultimate means" the more the complexity of a social system leads to a distinction between these and raises the need for external sanctions.[66] Apparently, a normative system as open as the one described here needed the use or threat of force as a last resort to keep things going, at least if all non-violent institutions had failed to solve a conflict. For an actor who had lost a major part of his liquidity it could simply be necessary to try to regain his outstandings in order to keep his credit by all means possible. Generally, the monetary and social costs of resorting to force seem to have been a matter of calculation, notwithstanding the fact that the use of violence is inherently not only about rational consideration.

However, different to how Philipp Höhn, Thomas Heebøll-Holm, and I have argued in 2019, not simply "the merchants" employed violence in the Late Middle Ages. But – besides individual reprisals – very often their hometowns, their lords, and even their guilds used force to improve their economic and political situation. We have to differentiate these agents, their motivation and intentions when looking at violence as an inherent factor in economic history.[67] In historical evidence, this shift from communal to state institutions and their preferred ways of enforcing predictability turns out to have been a highly heterogeneous and inconsistent process that seemingly took much longer than Greif imagined. To describe these complexities exemplarily is our main task in this volume.

7. Plurality as a Resource

But are these superior agents of mercantile concerns to be associated with public order, as Ogilvie does, or even with "the state" in a modern sense?[68] Or are they rather only powerful actors in a competitive field who sometimes managed to fulfil their claims and become authorities in the long run? Are the harbour towns acting on behalf of their merchants "the state", or simply collective agents for their elites within a political order still pre-state in its structuring? Avner Greif has pointed to the role of the communes, the towns as autonomous corporations, as intermediaries between individual actors and state-like instances, and to the transition from the "community responsibility system" to an "individual responsibility system" nurtured by a growing institutional demand of developing markets.[69] As a matter of course, the territories our merchants travelled to and from had princes, kings, and the like, who, according to their own ideological background functioned as guarantors of

66 Luhmann, Trust, p. 34; cf. Idem, Vertrauen, p. 42.

67 Cf. Ogilvie, Institutions, pp. 224, 227 f., on rulers and polities profiting from guilds' conflicts.

68 Ogilvie, Institutions, pp. 230 f., 245 f., 272–274.

69 Greif, Institutions, pp. 309–349; cf. Ogilvie, Institutions, pp. 235 f.

peace and justice. Indeed, even if they were competing, there were authorities, or at least actors claiming to be such.

Maybe normative plurality as a concept helps us to comprehend this basic competition between claims to authority since it allows for a neutral description of how multiple social groups and institutions produced heterogenous aspirations and vied for their enforcement. What we can describe, following Douglass North's concept of the "natural state",[70] is how some actors managed to be the last man standing, and how these came to be called "the state" in retrospect, having built the institutions which then functioned as a pivot to the development of modern codified law. Historically speaking however, the emergence of the "natural state", as described by Douglass North, is always a dynamic process of competition, which itself inherently and necessarily fosters heterogeneity, at least until one group of actors prevails and becomes able to position themselves as the authority. The "natural state" itself achieves legal unification only at the end of its dynamic emergence. What we come to detect here is, thus, presumably not a premodern institutional regime synchronically speaking, but rather diachronically the extremely contentious process of enforcement of an overall trend to formalisation, the result of which we usually call "the state". The very distinction of "state" and polity respectively on the one hand and "company" or "guild" on the other is misleading since it blurs the fact that often enough communities acted as if they were "states", or polities and merchants coordinated their actions so that both sides profited.

Regardless, during this play-off competition, actors on all levels used the options offered by normative plurality. They chose to which forum they would appeal, or whether they would rather refer to extra-judicial arbitration.[71] When at court, they pleaded for the application of any rule, norm, or belief beneficial for the enforcement of their claims, and they denied the validity of any detrimental ones. For the historical actors, the plurality of norms was an asset rather than a problem. Plurality was simply preconditional, as it shaped the social world they lived in, and this would be the second hypothetical answer to our overarching question.

In the end, maybe the very claim of predictability, even as a relative category, could be an anachronistic concept. Maybe premodern actors simply did not strive for security, but accepted living in a world of fundamental insecurity since they knew no other. Yet, when they traded, to survive, they must have kept in mind the final balance. Predictability remained a matter of calculation, in the end, and as far as we see, this world was not anomic or completely insecure. True, legal unity enabled the predictability of decisions in a doubtless superior way, but before the emergence of modern law, there were already institutions grounded in rules,

70 North, Wallis and Weingast, Violence.

71 Ogilvie, Institutions, pp. 303 f., 310, 314.

norms, and beliefs which made behaviour expectable and thus generated "systemic trust", or rather – predictability.[72] How these institutions worked is discussed in the following case studies.

8. Setup of the Volume

One could argue that in settings of legal pluralism, interaction was typically shaped by four factors:

- Trust: In recent years, economic historians of the Late Middle Ages have stressed the impact of credit, honour, and confidence as basic mechanisms for producing predictability between merchants. This "trust" however, is to be understood merely as a category for communicating one's situational estimation of relative predictability.
- Violence: On a political level, as well as in everyday life, the threat and use of force were eminent options, ranging from trade blockades and the mutual taking of goods and ships to open war or feud. Actors needed to perform the ability to enforce their claims. They showed that they were able to defend themselves and thus to make their partners fulfil their expectations. Hence, violence was not socially disruptive, but functional, as long as it was embedded in a relative equality of military means and the overwhelming consensus of economic exchange. Trust and violence were thus two sides of the same coin. When they agreed upon a contract, merchants bore a sword.
- Diplomacy: Simultaneously, merchants needed stable political preconditions as provided for by the mutual privileges their authorities agreed upon. Here, very different interests and intentions had to be balanced, so the diplomatic negotiation of the general conditions was a highly dynamic process.
- Institutions: Shaped by these factors and by repeated communication, rules, norms, and beliefs emerged which were used to produce and reproduce predictability. In spaces of legal pluralism, however, these institutions remained contested and subject to re-negotiation.

Merchants and their communities did not strive for a unification and harmonisation of laws according to the ideals of modern statehood, but for an enhancement of their individual positions in a pluralist legal field. These communities, for example the Hanse, could possibly be understood as a means to cope with legal pluralism in four steps:

- Actors from different authorities came together in communities.

72 Cf. the mechanisms discussed by Ogilvie, Institutions, passim.

- They did so to secure trading routes (on land or at sea) which crossed pluralist legal spaces.
- They also strove to gain advantageous trading conditions within the pluralist spaces of their destination areas, nota bene, this was done for themselves, not for all merchants trading at the place.[73]
- While doing so, these communities themselves remained heterogenous because all efforts to harmonise their norms failed in practice.

Obviously, the actors did not do all this in order to overcome legal pluralism, but to improve the position of their own respective group in heterogenous legal spaces:

- In their home countries, heterogenous authorities were not contested, but a new collective factor was installed, which crossed the existing particular powers.
- On their traffic routes, exclusive conditions were achieved through agreements with neighbouring authorities, which did not end pluralism, but constituted exceptions through the use of privilege.
- Simultaneously, individual towns within their vicinity strove to supersede legal pluralism through their own hegemony.
- In their destination countries, competing merchant groups tried to improve their positions, especially by producing an exclusive legal space for their members, within which local justice did not apply.
- Finally, efforts for internal institutionalisation were fostered by the ambitions of particular actors to gain a hegemonic position within their respective communities. This is why these efforts were regularly thwarted by other members.

We asked contributors for case studies analysing different aspects of how merchants dealt with legal pluralism, either confirming or challenging the model drawn up here. Topics were not restricted to the Hanse, but could also concern neighbours, partners, and competitors in late medieval Europe, on land as well as at sea. Potential approaches could be:

- How did merchants and other actors deal with legal pluralism and heterogenous authorities in their home countries?
- How did towns and harbours foster their connectivity in a pluralistic environment?
- How did actors deal with legal pluralism on trading routes?
- How was legal pluralism arbitrated in destination areas?
- How was legal pluralism negotiated within and between the merchants' groups?

73 Ogilvie, Institutions. pp. 430 ff.; Greif, Institutions, p. 122, who only acknowledges this for the later period of Hanse history.

9. Contributions

All this may hopefully become clearer, if the Hanse realm is compared with and related to adjacent regions in Central Europe on the one hand and the British Isles on the other.[74] Because of this, we opened the geographical scope of our volume for some exemplary studies. Two contributions concern Poland-Lithuania, Ruthenia, and the Black Sea region, an area where Hanse merchants were present, but outsiders at best. Then we go to Gdansk, a major Hanse town on the Baltic, were locals and especially the English competed for market share. A more systematic view of the Hanse as a legal community leads to the Netherlands, where, again, Hansards and other merchant communities met. Finally, the British Isles come into sight.

An important trade route connected the Near East with Northern Europe via the Black Sea and the Baltic. In "Red Rus" (Galicia, Volhynia, Ruthenia), merchants from all adjacent lands met: Tartars, Armenians, Ruthenians, Poles, Hungarians, Bohemians and Germans. Olga KOZUBSKA shows how the Princes of Ruthenia and later their heirs, the Kings of Poland, tried to channel this trade and settle conflicts, in particular by privileging towns under "German law" and implementing staple rights in favour of the locals, especially Polish merchants. Alexandr OSIPIAN scrutinises how members of the Armenian trading diaspora communicated with each other and with their neighbours, thus bridging vast distances and strong cultural and normative differences through ethnic affiliation. Facing local authorities, they often drew on forum shopping, for example, going to the Magdeburg law courts in Ruthenian and Polish towns. Their courts and the way they organised their caravans might fruitfully be compared to guilds in Western Europe and even more closely to the Hanse *Kontors*. Taken together, both chapters open the way for a re-examination of the relationship between ruler and merchants in East Central Europe.

At the northern end of this trading corridor of global impact, where the Vistula River reaches the Baltic, Gdansk is situated. During the fourteenth and fifteenth centuries, the local authorities there tried to mitigate the growing influx of English merchants and shippers, which led to fierce quarrels in Prussia, and in other Hanse towns as well as England. Philipp HÖHN shows how in these conflicts, legal plurality, but also normative commonalities, were used to enforce self-interests.

By means of a rigorous analysis of historical semantics, Tobias BOESTAD shows that "*der dudeschen recht*" in Hanse parlance did not usually mean "German law",

74 An approach similar to this is proposed by the authors of a special issue of the journal "Urban History" published very recently: FRANKOT and TVEIT, Crossing Urban Legal Boundaries, cf. the introduction: doi:10.1017/S0963926824000105, accessed 05/09/2024. Some of the participants were also present in Münster at the conference this volume is the result of, so one should best read both collections as dear siblings.

but rather belonging to one of the amorphous in-groups later on tied together within the Hanse and their privileged jurisdiction. Here again, in a pluralist environment, normative settings were associated with the construction of an ethnic community, while the means of defining who was in and who was out turn out to have been highly arbitrary and complex. The emergence of the Hanse as a particular legal community could thus be described as a means to cope with the inherent normative plurality of the environment, not by implementing a unified law, but by developing a community of insiders profiting from privileges.[75]

Since the vast, if not the greatest, array of Hanse traffic was conducted at sea, maritime law has been an issue of research for a long time. Taking the problem of General Average as an example, Gijs Dreijer shows that there was no unified judicial code effective in Northern Europe, but that a heterogenous and flexible set of maritime rights emerged out of normative practice during the Late Middle Ages, being a synthesis of older written rules and their situational application that merged with concepts of equity in constant arbitration.

One of the core problems discussed by the new institutional economics approach in economic history is the principle-agent problem. In order to organise trade relations of even basic complexity, merchants necessarily need proxies.[76] But how could they make these other persons stick to the rules with great likelihood, how could the principal "trust" the agent? As Ulla Kypta shows, in Antwerp, merchants from southern and northern Germany alike used the instrument of the *procuratio*, a written appointment of an agent (or sub-agent) for a particular action. This legal instrument developed out of communicative practice, and it was acknowledged all over Northern Europe even though it lacked any form of state guarantee and the towns participating in trade by no means had a unified legal system. "Predictability" thus emerged out of mercantile practice, not out of formalised legal institutions because for merchants it usually made sense to simply play by the rules.

But what if a business partner for some reason did not comply with the moral expectations of today's economic historians and took to cheating? If all judicial means had been pursued in vain, aggrieved parties had the option to use force, that is, to arrest the goods of the perpetrator or of one of his fellows. The threat to legitimately use force was thus an inherent part of the normative and even the legal system, keeping things going and enforcing predictability by means of deterrence. Leslie Carr Riegel scrutinises cases where this law of reprisal failed to lead to conflict settlement, where violence did not end the dispute but fostered its escalation.

---

75 Ogilvie, Institutions, pp. 214 f. (for guilds in general).

76 Lopez, Proxy, pp. 187–194; Ogilvie, Institutions, pp. 316–321.

For a long time, historians have focused on emerging towns and their inhabitants as spearheads of progress. Only in the last two decades have the princely courts and the manor economy of the nobility come to be understood as movers of legal and economic advancement. For example, as Mathias BERLANDI shows, to reorganise their economic relations, the Scottish nobility developed new forums and new rules during the fifteenth century. Again, it is not a central authority, and not the proto-bourgeoisie of the towns, but the economic actors themselves who communicatively engender new legal instruments.

About 200 years earlier, the newly installed dominion of the Anglo-Norman kings in Ireland had, in fact, installed a new legal system in order to favour English merchants over the local inhabitants. Anna MALESZKA compares this to analogous processes in Prussian towns after the coming to power of the Teutonic Order. Here, different layers of norms come into play as defined by ethnic and political boundaries. How they interacted within a given space, and whether they constituted a common legal system or remained distinct; these are problems very well known to scholars of legal pluralism.[77]

To conclude, there may be four points where this volume contributes to debates on the premodern economy and legal pluralism:

1. Competition: Merchants must always cope with competition. As individuals and as members of communities they acted in a contested field. They may have referred to the "common good" again and again,[78] but, in fact (apart from individual requirements of any sort), they strove for advantages for themselves and their particular community. Normative plurality gave them leeway to do so more than legal harmonisation would have helped them.

2. Compromise: As competitors in a market, merchants communicated with each other and negotiated the terms of their exchanges. When doing so, "trust" was first and foremost a semantic means for calculating the risk of being cheated. What made actors stick to the rules might presumably have been the everyday experience that trustability and trust made things work better, while breaches produced

---

77 Unfortunately, some participants of the workshop in Münster were not able to have their papers printed in this volume. Very hopefully, the reader will find them published elsewhere: SZENDE, Katalin (CEU Budapest): Trust and Distrust in the Legal Framework of Urban Life in Late Medieval Hungary.; SICKING, Louis (Leiden): A Microcosm of the Hanse? Legal Pluralism at Scania, 1350–1550.; FRANKOT, Edda B. I. (Bodø): Administering Justice to Foreigners: International Merchants and Mariners before the Late Medieval Aberdeen Courts.; WUBS-MROZEWICZ, Justyna (Amsterdam): The Trouble with Legal Pluralism: a Danzig Case.; LAMBERT, Bart and WINK, Jurriaan (Brussels): Legal Pluralism and the Hanseatic Zuiderzee Towns: Conflict Management in a Multi-layered Legal Landscape between North and Baltic Seas.; FÉLICITÉ, Indravati (La Réunion): Considerations of Legal Unity and Pluralism in Early Modern Hanse Diplomacy.

78 LECUPPRE-DESJARDIN and VAN BRUAENE, De bono communi.

costs. Respectability and credit provided strong incentives to act predictably. Simultaneously however, competition and self-interest latently biased any merchant's perception of a given situation so that they always had to balance their mutual positions. Compromise may thus be the proper concept for understanding the way market actors managed to understand each other's expectations and to bridge differences, be they legal, normative, or social.

3. Coordination: Very often, when trading, merchants were able to rely on the help of external authorities, be it the polities they came from and travelled to, or the rulers of their homelands or their destination countries. Individual traders came together in communities (guilds, communes, and the like). These started to act as polities, to interact with each other, and to gain privileges and help from local rulers and external authorities. As long as all these different actors expected a profit for themselves, they were able to collaborate in providing a normative framework which helped everyone – against their competitors.[79]

4. Coercion: Mutual deterrence and optional coercion – be it individually or collectively – were part of the game. This is not to say that all merchants and their communities were rogues, but that the dagger in the sheath made all market participants calculate the high increase in costs an infringement might possibly cause. The mutual threat of physical force, especially of reprisals, which always touched questions of collective responsibility, clarified the cost-benefit ratio, and thus, in the end, made the normative system function. We would thus, in contrast to Ogilvie, not describe violence as inherently dysfunctional in economic terms (even if in the particular action the gain of using force may have only seldom covered the expenses). Further, in contrast to Avner Greif, we would presume that this productive function of violence in the mercantile world did not diminish until at least the sixteenth century.

In the long run though, some of the most powerful polities in the field would manage to transform their self-referring use of force into an official one, and thus acquire "state" positions. For them, the violence of their competitors gradually became dysfunctional, so they started to exclude it discursively and legally. How this historical process, the emergence of the modern state with its claim to a unified legal system, arose is yet to be fully described, and will surely remain controversial. Nevertheless, we hope that this volume will offer some new insights into its trajectories and its complexities.

---

79 However, institutions, as soon as they have become habitual, tend to develop a life of their own, which leads to path dependencies and institutional continuities even if efficiency is long gone. Co-ordination could thus also weaken actors, if it kept them from reacting to market changes, as in the case of the Bruges Kontor being sustained by the Hanse, while the major point of trade had already moved to Antwerp.

Acknowledgements

What we have learned: successful business needs a secure environment, where one can meet and deal with partners acquainted and unacquainted. Inimitably, such an environment was provided by the Käte Hamburger Kolleg "Einheit und Vielfalt im Recht" ("Legal Unity and Pluralism") at the Westfälische Wilhelms-Universität Münster, funded by the Bundesministerium für Bildung und Forschung. The editors would thus like to thank the entire team of the Kolleg, especially the speakers Ulrike Ludwig and Peter Oestmann. Lennart Pieper, Andre Dechert and Claudia Lieb organised two wonderful days in Münster in October 2022 and helped us to get this volume published. All fellows and the participants of the workshop made us understand premodern legal pluralism. Vera Teske provided a conference report much more concise than what we have produced.[80] Leslie Carr-Riegel not only jumped in to write an intriguing article on very short notice, but also copy-edited all other contributions, including useful notes beyond those concerning language. Finally, we owe the idea for all this to a small talk we had with Angela Huang one evening at a conference. Thank you all for your help and inspiration!

Bibliography

Arlinghaus, Franz-Josef, Inklusion – Exklusion. Funktion und Formen des Rechts in der spätmittelalterlichen Stadt. Das Beispiel Köln, Köln/Weimar/Wien 2008 (Norm und Struktur, vol. 48).

Brunori, Luisa/Simon, Victor/Touchelay, Béatrice/Wijffels, Alain A. (eds.), La dynamique juridique des réseaux marchands. Hanses, nations, agences, filiales et comptoirs, Centre toulousain d'histoire du droit et des idées politiques, Toulouse 2023.

Carr-Riegel, Leslie, Letter of Marque, EViR Working Papers, Münster Glossary on Legal Unity and Pluralism (2023), pp. 60–62. [https://doi.org/10.17879/90089657999], accessed 10/31/2024.

Cordes, Albrecht/Höhn, Philipp, Extra-Legal and Legal Conflict Management among Long-Distance Traders (1250–1650), in: Heikki Pihlajamäki/Markus D. Dubber/Mark Godfrey (eds.), The Oxford Handbook of European Legal History, Oxford 2018, pp. 509–528.

Cordes, Albrecht, Litigating abroad: merchant's expectations regarding procedure before foreign courts according to the Hanseatic privileges (12th–16th c.), Frankfurt am Main 2014 (LOEWE research focus "Extrajudicial and judicial conflict resolution", Working Papers, vol. 4).

80 Teske, Tagungsbericht.

CORDES, Albrecht, The search for a medieval Lex mercatoria, in: Vito PIERGIOVANNI (ed.), From lex mercatoria to commercial law, Berlin 2005 (Vergleichende Untersuchungen zur kontinentaleuropäischen und anglo-amerikanischen Rechtsgeschichte, vol. 24), pp. 53–67.

DUSIL, Stephan, Legal Transplants of Town Law and Historiographical Challenges. Some Reflections on the Dissemination of Town Law in the Late Middle Ages, in: Jesús Ángel Solórzano TELECHEA/Jelle HAEMERS (eds.), Normativa y autoridad en la ciudad medieval atlántica, y más allá, Logroño 2022, pp. 161–180.

DUSIL, Stephan, Stadtrecht und Rechtsraum. Historiographischer Wandel im früheren 20. Jahrhundert am Beispiel der Erforschung von Stadtrechtsfamilien, in: Hansische Geschichtsblätter 123 (2005), pp. 85–108.

ENGLE, Merry, Legal Pluralism, in: Law and Society Review 22 (5) (1988), p. 869–896.

GRAẞMANN, Antjekathrin/JAHNKE, Carsten (ed.), Seerecht im Hanseraum des 15. Jahrhunderts, Lübeck 2003 (Veröffentlichungen zur Geschichte der Hansestadt Lübeck. Reihe B, 36).

FIEREMANS, Niels, "In the hope to have judged a good sentence as merchants": Arbitration as a litigation strategy in late medieval Bruges, in: Tijdschrift voor rechtsgeschiedenis 89 (2021), pp. 439–480.

FRANKOT, Edda B. I./TVEIT, Miriam (eds.), Crossing Urban Legal Boundaries in Northern Europe: Merchants and the Law, 1350–1600, Urban History 51 (2024), No. 3 (doi:10.1017/S0963926824000105), accessed 09/05/2024.

FRANKOT, Edda B. I., Medieval Maritime Law from Oléron to Wisby: Jurisdictions in the Law of the Sea, in: Juan PAN-MONTOJO/Frederik PEDERSEN (eds.), Communities in European History. Representations, Jurisdictions, Conflicts, Pisa 2007, pp. 151–172.

FRANKOT, Edda B. I., "Of laws of ships and shipmen". Medieval maritime law and its practice in urban Northern Europe, Edinburgh 2012 (Scottish Historical Review monographs series, no. 20).

GELDERBLOM, Oscar, Cities of Commerce. The Institutional Foundations of International Trade in the Low Countries, 1250–1650, Princeton, NJ 2013 (The Princeton economic history of the Western world).

GREIF, Avner, Institutions and the Path to the Modern Economy. Lessons from Medieval Trade, New York 2006.

HAMMEL-KIESOW, Rolf, Die Hanse, München ²2002.

HEEBØLL-HOLM, Thomas/HÖHN, Philipp/ROHMANN, Gregor, Introduction, in: idem (eds.), Merchants, Pirates, and Smugglers. Criminalization, Economics and the Transformation of the Maritime World (1200–1600), Frankfurt am Main/New York 2019 (Discourses of Weakness and Resource Regimes, vol. 6), pp. 9–32.

HEEBØLL-HOLM, Thomas, Ports, Piracy and Maritime War. Piracy in the English Channel and the Atlantic, c. 1280–c. 1330, Leiden 2013 (Medieval Law and its Practice, vol. 15).

HILGERS, Mathieu/MANGEZ, Eric, Bourdieu's Theory of Social Fields: Concepts and Applications, London 2014.

Höhn, Philipp, Kaufleute in Konflikt. Rechtspluralismus, Kredit und Gewalt im spätmittelalterlichen Lübeck, Frankfurt am Main/New York 2021 (Schwächediskurse und Ressourcenregime, vol. 11).

Höhn, Philipp, Pluralismus statt Homogenität. Hanse, Konflikträume und Rechtspluralismus im vormodernen Nordeuropa (1400–1600), in: Roland Deigendesch/Christian Jörg (eds.), Städtebünde und städtische Außenpolitik. Träger, Instrumentarien und Konflikte während des hohen und späten Mittelalters, Sigmaringen 2019, pp. 261–290.

Höhn, Philipp, Verflechtungen der Streitschlichtung. Zum Austrag kaufmännischer Interessenkonflikte im Hanseraum, 1365–1435, in: Albrecht Cordes (ed.), Mit Freundschaft oder mit Recht? Inner- und außergerichtliche Alternativen zur kontroversen Streitentscheidung im 15.–19. Jahrhundert, Köln 2014 (Quellen und Forschungen zur höchsten Gerichtsbarkeit im Alten Reich, 65), pp. 19–40.

Huang, Angela, Die Marke vor der Marke: Beschaffenheit und Verbindlichkeit des Markenwesens im mittelalterlichen Textilgewerbe, in: Thomas Ertl (ed.), Ars Vendendi: Werbung und kommerzielle Praktiken im Mittelalter, Ostfildern 2024 (Vorträge und Forschungen, vol. 97), pp. 211–256.

Huang, Angela, Die Textilien des Hanseraumes. Produktion und Distribution einer spätmittelalterlichen Handelsware, Köln/Wien/Weimar 2015 (Quellen und Darstellungen zur hansischen Geschichte, 71).

Huang, Angela/Jahnke, Carsten (eds.), Textiles and the Medieval Economy. Production, Trade, and Consumption of Textiles, 8th–16th Century, Oxford 2015.

Jahnke, Carsten, Das Silber des Meeres. Fang und Vertrieb von Ostseehering zwischen Norwegen und Italien (12.–16. Jahrhundert), Köln [u. a.] 2000 (Quellen und Darstellungen zur hansischen Geschichte, 49).

Jahnke, Carsten, Die Hanse, Stuttgart 2014.

Jahnke, Carsten, Handelsnetze im Ostseeraum, in: Gerhard Fouquet/Hans-Jörg Gilomen (eds), Netzwerke im europäischen Handel des Mittelalters, Ostfildern 2010 (Vorträge und Forschungen, vol. 72), pp. 189–212.

Jahnke, Carsten, The maritime law of the Baltic Sea, in: Michel Balard (ed.), The Sea in History. Vol. 2: The Medieval World, Woodbridge 2017, pp. 572–583.

Johnson, Tom, Law in Common. Legal Cultures in Late-Medieval England, Oxford 2020.

Karpaviciene, Jolanta, "Nach unserem Magdeburger Recht". Zur Frage der stadtbürgerlichen Identität im Großfürstentum Litauen, in: Gabriele Köster/Christina Link/Heiner Lück (eds.), Kulturelle Vernetzung in Europa. Das Magdeburger Recht und seine Städte, Dresden 2018, pp. 247–266.

Kempe, Michael, Fluch der Weltmeere. Piraterie, Völkerrecht und internationale Beziehungen 1500–1900, Frankfurt am Main 2011.

Kümper, Hiram, Der Traum vom ehrbaren Kaufmann. Die Deutschen und die Hanse, Berlin 2021.

Kypta, Ulla, Konkurrenzverbot und Kontorsverlegungen, oder: Wie das institutionelle Setting den Vertragsbruch erklärt, in: Georg Jostkleigrewe (ed.), Der Bruch des Vertrages.

Die Verbindlichkeit spätmittelalterlicher Diplomatie und ihre Grenzen Berlin/New York 2018 (Zeitschrift für Historische Forschung, Beihefte, 55), pp. 369–392.

LANDWEHR, Götz, Das Seerecht der Hanse. 1365–1614, Hamburg 2003.

LECUPPRE-DESJARDIN, Élodie/VAN BRUAENE, Anne-Laure (eds.) De bono communi. The Discourse and Practice of the Common Good in the European City (13th–16th c.), Turnhout 2011 (Studies in European urban history, vol. 22).

LOOS, Fritz/SCHREIBER, Hans-Ludwig, Recht, Gerechtigkeit, in: Otto BRUNNE/Werner CONZE/Reinhart KOSELLECK (eds.), Geschichtliche Grundbegriffe. Historisches Lexikon zur politisch-sozialen Sprache in Deutschland. Arbeitskreis für Moderne Sozialgeschichte, 8 vols., Stuttgart 1972–1997, vol. 5, 1984, pp. 231–311.

LOPEZ, Robert, Proxy in Medieval Trade, in: Bruce MCNAB/Teofilo F. RUIZ/William C. JORDAN (eds.), Order and Innovation in the Middle Ages. Essays in Honor of Joseph R. Strayer, Princeton NJ 1976, pp. 187–194.

LUHMANN, Niklas, Das Recht der Gesellschaft, Frankfurt am Main 1993.

LUHMANN, Niklas, Gesellschaftsstruktur und Semantik. Studien zur Wissenssoziologie der modernen Gesellschaft, 4 vols., Frankfurt am Main 1980–1995.

LUHMANN, Niklas, Vertrauen. Ein Mechanismus der Reduktion sozialer Komplexität, Konstanz ^{5}2014.

LUHMANN, Niklas, Trust and Power, Cambridge 2017.

NORTH, Douglass C./WALLIS, John Joseph/WEINGAST, Barry R., Violence and Social Orders. A Conceptual Framework for Interpreting Recorded Human History, Cambridge/New York 2009.

OGILVIE, Sheilagh, Institutions and European Trade. Merchants Guilds, 1000–1800, Cambridge 2011.

OGILVIE, Sheilagh, The Use and Abuse of Trust. Social Capital and its Deployment in Early Modern Guilds, in: Jahrbuch für Wirtschaftsgeschichte 46 (1) (2005), pp. 15–52.

OESTMANN, Peter, Gemeines Recht und Rechtseinheit. Zum Umgang mit Rechtszersplitterung und Rechtsvielfalt in Mittelalter und Neuzeit, in: Eva SCHUMANN (ed.), Hierarchie, Kooperation und Integration im Europäischen Rechtsraum, Berlin 2015 (Abhandlungen der Akademie der Wissenschaften in Göttingen. Philologisch-Historische Klasse, vol. 38), pp. 1–50.

PICHIERRI, Angelo, Città stato. Economia e politica del modello anseatico. Venezia: Marsilio (Saggi Marsilio) 1997.

ROEBUCK, Derek, Mediation and Arbitration in the Middle Ages. England 1154–1558, Oxford 2013.

ROHMANN, Gregor, Wegnehmen, Verhandeln, Erstatten. Politischer Alltag im Hanseraum um 1400, in: Geschichte in Wissenschaft und Unterricht 65 (2014), No. 9/10, pp. 574–585.

RUBIN, Alfred P., The Law of Piracy, Irvington-on-Hudson, NY, ^{2}1998.

SCHELLER, Benjamin, Die Geburt des Risikos. Kontingenz und kaufmännische Praxis im mediterranen Seehandel des Hoch- und Spätmittelalters, in: Historische Zeitschrift 304 (2017), 2, pp. 305–330.

SCOTT, W. Richard, Institutions and Organizations. Ideas and Interests, Los Angeles/London ^{3}2008.

SELZER Stefan/EWERT Ulf Christian, Institutions of Hanseatic Trade. Studies on the Political Economy of a Medieval Network Organisation, Frankfurt am Main 2016.

SEINECKE, Ralf, What is legal pluralism, and what is it good for?, in: Marju LUTS-SOOTAK (ed.), Legal Pluralism: Cui bono?, Tartu 2018, pp. 13–29.

TAI, Emily Sohmer, Honor among Thieves. Piracy, Restitution, and Reprisal in Genoa, Venice, and the Crown of Aragon, 1339–1417, PhD Diss. Harvard 1996.

TAI, Emily Sohmer, Marking Water. Piracy and Property in the Pre-Modern West, in: Jerry BENTLEY/Renate BRIDENTHAL/Karen WIGEN (eds.): Seascapes, Littoral Cultures, and Trans-Oceanic Exchanges. Honolulu 2007, pp. 205–220.

TAI, Emily Sohmer, The Legal Status of Piracy in Medieval Europe, in: History Compass 10 (2012), No. 11, pp. 838–851.

TAMANAHA, Brian Z., Understanding Legal Pluralism: Past to Present, Local to Global, Sydney Law Review 30 (2008), pp. 375–411.

TESKE, Vera, Tagungsbericht: How to Ensure Predictability in Legal Pluralism. Northern Europe in the Later Middle Ages, in: H-Soz-Kult, 08/02/2023 [http://www.hsozkult.de/conferencereport/id/fdkn-133663], accessed 09/10/2024.

VON BLANCKENBURG, Christine, Die Hanse und ihr Bier. Brauwesen und Bierhandel im hansischen Verkehrsgebiet (Quellen und Darstellungen zur hansischen Geschichte, 51), Köln 2001.

WITTHÖFT, Harald, Zeichen, Verpackung, Maß/Gewicht und Kommunikation im hansischen Handel, in: Stuart JENKS/Michael NORTH (eds.), Der hansische Sonderweg? Beiträge zur Sozial- und Wirtschaftsgeschichte der Hanse (Quellen und Darstellungen zur hansischen Geschichte NF, 39), Köln [u. a.] 1993, pp. 203–224.

WUBS-MROZEWICZ, Justyna, Mercantile conflict resolution and the role of the language of trust: a Danzig case in the middle of the sixteenth century, in: Historical Research 88 (2015), pp. 417–440.

WUBS-MROZEWICZ, Justyna, The late medieval and early modern Hanse as an institution of conflict management, in: Flavio MIRANDA/Justyna WUBS-MROZEWICZ (eds.), Merchants and Commercial Conflicts in Europe, 1250–1600, Continuity and Change, vol. 32, Cambridge 2017, pp. 59–84.

WUBS-MROZEWICZ, Justyna, The concept of language of trust and trustworthiness. (Why) history matters, in: Journal of Trust Research 1 (2019), no. 3, pp. 1–17.

Olga Kozubska

The Merchant and the Ruler

Strategies for Ensuring Predictability on Trade Routes in Late Medieval Red Rus'

1. Introduction

This article focuses on the development of a new commercial axis in East-Central Europe during the second half of the thirteenth and the fourteenth century, on the changes to the economic landscape it produced, and on the main actors – merchants and rulers – who made the commercial activities possible. On this background, I will try to answer the questions of how did the actors provide for predictability? How did the necessary legal framing and institutions evolve to enable and facilitate the functioning of long-distance trade? What was the role of legal exceptions (privileges) in this process? And how did the privileged enforce their rights and cope with non-compliance? Geographically, the focus is on the two westernmost principalities of Rus' – Galicia and Volhynia – which were advantageously positioned in the middle of the exchange route between the Black and Baltic Seas.

2. Historical Background

The chronological framework considered here roughly corresponds to the time defined as the "commercial revolution" (tenth to mid-fourteenth centuries), when, according to Robert Lopez, "commerce [...] became the most dynamic sector of the economy in one country after another, and merchants were the main promoters of change."[1] It was long-distance trade and a class of professional merchants that functioned as "the chief instrument of the economic revival of the 11th and 12th centuries" in Europe.[2] Trade was important for the emergence of Rus' too,[3] though the formation of routes through the eastern European river systems started before

1 Lopez, Commercial revolution, p. 86.

2 Pirenne, Economic and social history, pp. 142–143.

3 To the extent that its very beginning (the first hundred years of Rus) was compared to a commercial corporation like the East India Company of early modern times, "founded to make money but compelled by the absence of any administration in the area of their operations to assume quasi-governmental responsibilities"; Cf.: Pipes, Russia; Толочко, Очерки, pp. 108–109; Tolochko Kievan Rus', 131.

its creation as a polity, fostered by Scandinavians' quest for silver, furs, and other trade goods from the late eighth century onwards.[4] Over the next two centuries, Rus' lands linked the Islamic world and the Baltic region, with the river Volga acting as the primary axis and artery of this trade. However, during the tenth century, the supply of silver from the Middle East began to dry up, and the economy of Rus, built on that silver, was forced to refocus in order to survive. The long-distance trade axis shifted westwards, changing from the Volga to the Dnipro, now focusing on Constantinople, and creating the foundations for the rise of Kyiv.[5]

Discussing the emergence of Rus, scholars have noted that the opening-up of a sea link between the middle Dnipro and Constantinople was a remarkable feat, requiring a substantially higher degree of organisation from the Rus' (as merchant-warriors) than their former trips to the middle Volga. Yet, these actors were ultimately no less dependent upon the goodwill of rulers for profitable trading than the Rus' visiting the Volga had been.[6]

Throughout the entire pre-Mongol era, the city of Kyiv was unquestionably the major political, economic, and religious centre.[7] At the same time, in the course of the twelfth century, the Baltic exchange zone underwent profound transformations as with the rise of Lubeck, Germans started to replace or at least rival Scandinavians as the main trading partners for Rus' commercial centres in the North. This transformation is also reflected archaeologically by the high percentage of German rather than other foreign goods which have been uncovered in the region. Hoards found in the lands of Rus' consisting of coins and silver bars beginning in the twelfth into the thirteenth centuries, after the decline of dirhams from the Middle East were mostly from the German Empire.[8]

The mid-thirteenth century brought the next shift westward in the trade axis, as the Mongol invasion and destruction of Kyiv in 1240 manifested the beginning of a new period in north-south exchange. It was anchored with its immediate southern node in the territories under Mongol (Tatar) control, namely the Black Sea shores, where Italian trading emporia emerged. The other end ran north to the Baltic region, as well as to the west via Kraków and Wrocław. Galicia and Volhynia, assuming the role of Kyiv as mediators, became parts of the broader Black Sea commercial zone together with Moldavia and Walachia, Saxonian towns in Transylvania and, naturally, Genoese maritime colonies (Caffa and Tana most prominently amongst others).[9]

---

4 Raffensperger, Reimagining Europe, pp. 119–120.

5 Ibid., p. 120.

6 Franklin and Shepard, Emergence of Rus, p. 3.

7 Noonan, Monetary history, p. 384.

8 Даркевич, Художественное ремесло.

9 Myśliwski, Wrocław in economic space, p. 64.

Medieval chroniclers from Latin and Orthodox Europe alike depict the horrors of the Mongols, but the conquest soon resulted in the creation of a vast Eurasian empire stretching from the Black and Mediterranean Seas to the Pacific. This had a huge impact on the reconfiguration of international trade routes between Europe and Asia.[10] The historic period (c. 1280–1360) when the Mongol rulers controlled the Eurasian commercial routes is often termed the *Pax Mongolica*,[11] with the Khan as the main actor to ensure the conditions the professional merchants needed to practise their trade.[12] In the thirteenth and fourteenth centuries, the Black Sea benefited from an economic boom, since in this period more than in any other, the region fulfilled the function which the Romanian historian G. Brătianu has aptly described as a "*plaque tournante*", a crossroad of Eurasian trade. The *Pax Mongolica* was fundamental to this process.[13]

Equally significant was the presence of Italian (Genoese and Venetian) colonies on the Black Sea shores between the 1270s and the mid-fifteenth century and their role as components of a commercial as well as political mechanism that connected Mediterranean markets to the great landmass of Eurasia.[14] The exceptionally favourable regime of the Nymphaion treaty concluded by the Genoese negotiators with Byzantium in 1261 indicates these Italian's knowledge of the valuable resources of the Black Sea trade. This included an appreciation for both regional resources as well as those resulting from the establishment of trading routes with inner Asia made possible through the connection of the two parts of the Mongol Empire

---

10 Cristea and Pilat, From Pax Mongolica, p. 2.

11 Di Cosmo, Black Sea Emporia, p. 3.

12 The Khans' approach in favouring foreign merchants not only went beyond the traditional limits of trade policy strictly speaking, but also stressed that merchants fulfilled a central function in the Chinggisid state. They were seen as the saviours of state finances due to both the volume, and the nature, of their payments towards the budget. Ilkhan Aḥmad Teguder expressed an opinion which was surely widely shared by the other Chinggisids, when he called merchants the "foundation of the state." See: Ciociltan, The Mongols, pp. 6 and 11. This conclusion follows from the work of Heyd for whom the word "trade" has a much wider and more complex meaning, and it cannot be understood in its true scale outside of the geopolitical context created by the Mongol conquests, the determining framework for the concrete conditions under which goods were produced and traded. The state of the roads, security and ease of transport, customs duties and many other 'peripheral' matters all entered this extended definition of trade. Heyd, Histoire du commerce.

13 Quoting this view of G. Bratianu, V. Ciociltan remarked, however, that he missed two factors: shifts within the great web of long-distance trade routes controlled by the Chinggisids, and the Khans' own concrete initiatives in the realm of Black Sea trade. Both were of supreme importance for the truly exceptional economic development of the Black Sea region. See: Ciociltan, The Mongols, p. 1.

14 Di Cosmo, Black Sea Emporia, p. 3.

neighbouring the Black Sea – the Golden Horde in the north, with its centre in Sarai on the Volga, and the Iranian Ilkhanate in the south, with its centre in Tabriz.[15]

3. The Times of Rus

The economic situation in the principalities of Galicia and Volhynia during the thirteenth century (later called Red Rus' or the Rus'/Ruthenian Voivodeship) was determined by the poverty of the tax base, which was still dominated by a barter economy with duties waged in kind and labour. The local princes demonstrated an understanding of the overwhelming importance of trade as well as of the necessity to turn to a monetary economy. They also adopted a policy of maximal support for the merchants. The first to profit from the new situation were those with cash at hand, that is, mainly foreign merchants, but also other groups of free people not necessarily of alien origin. Their presence was perceived as a factor which could invigorate the economy and raise the income of rulers by paying taxes in coin. Many of these individuals came from Wrocław, Kraków, and the lands of the Teutonic Order on the Baltic shore, especially from Toruń. These people were invited to settle as separate communities. In the case of the Germans, the community was headed by an *advocatus* or *locator* and was granted jurisdictional autonomy as well as exemption from taxes for a specified period of time. This autonomy or immunity came to be known as *ius theutonicum* or German law. Since an essential element of the foreigners' privileges was their being allowed to exercise "low justice" regarding minor suits according to their own customs ("high justice", especially in cases of murder, was usually reserved for the ruler), there was a trend to create separate groups of merchants and craftsmen based on their origin.[16] The possibility of being judged according to one's own law was certainly an important factor in ensuring predictability. Generally, setting the rules for eventual disputes was one of the matters in numerous agreements concluded by the towns in the North of Rus' and their German and Scandinavian counterparts. One of the earliest was the Treaty of Smolensk from 1229 between Smolensk, Vitebsk and Polotsk together with Riga and Gotland, which became a foundation for later treaties. It included rules and procedures for resolving disputes and for defining jurisdiction, stating that the local authorities should not intervene in internal disputes among foreign merchants and that court decisions in one jurisdiction were binding and not subject to retrial in the other.[17] It also defended a merchant from being tried on foreign

15 Cristea and Pilat, From Pax Mongolica, p. 16.

16 Zientara, German Law, p. 182.

17 Franklin, Writing, p. 167.

ground if the dispute had to be resolved with a fight stating that "a *Rusin* shall not call a *Latin* […] to fight in Rus' land; and a *Latin* shall not call a *Rusin* to fight in Riga or on Gotland shore."[18] This tendency to resolve conflicts at home and/or according to one's customs manifested itself particularly clearly in later agreements between Polotsk and Riga from 1405–06 which declared that "[…] if a merchant of Riga accept [apologized for] his guilt in Polotsk, he shall be sent to Riga and councillors [there] had to judge him according to his right". The practice was applicable to a Polotsk merchant in Riga.[19] The possibility to have their own law court in a foreign land according to "German law" and to manage the internal affairs of their community proved to be an attractive option to German merchants settling in the towns of Galicia and Volhynia.

As is evident from the sources, the grant of *ius theutonicum* could also bring profit to a Ruthenian ruler. For instance, before 1301, the *advocatia* of Przemyśl and a stone church of St Nicolaus were "sold in the '*ius theutonicum*'" for two *marcs* of gold and 40 rolls of cloth to certain Johan by the Ruthenian prince Leo".[20] Situated in the middle of the trade axis, various references concerning foreigners in the towns of Galicia and Volhynia from the second half of the thirteenth century reflect the commercial attractivity of this region, particularly in the town of Wolodymyr, the capital of Volhynia. The Galician-Volhynian chronicle describes a banquet organised by a rich German named Markolt (*Markolt-niemchyn*) for the Ruthenian princes in Wolodymyr in 1268.[21] For 1288, the same chronicle narrates the death of the Volhynian prince, mentioning "*Wolodymyrians, […] Germans and Surozhans,*[22] *Novgorodians*[23] *and Jews.*"[24] It is safe to assume that these people were, in fact,

18 Смоленские грамоты XIII–XIV веков, p. 22.

19 "*…аще которы немьчин изъвиниться у Полочьсце, того немьчина отослати у Ригу, ратьмане его судять по своеи правде.*" [Аже полочанин извиниться у Ризе, ино его послати у Польтеск, и тамо его свои и казнять по своеи правде]. See: ХОРОШКЕВИЧ, Договоры Полоцка 1405–1406, p. 81.

20 "*Ego dux Leo vendidi advocaciam in Premislia Johanni et lapideam ecclesiam s. Nicolai in jus Theutonicum et ipse mihi pro isto dedit duas marcas auri et quadraginta stamina panni flavei.*" See: Купчинський, Акти, pp. 144–145.

21 *Марколтъ же Нѣмѣчинь. зва к собѣ. всѣ кнѧзѣ на wбѣдъ. Василка. Лва Воишелка* [Markolt Nemchyn called all the princes Valysko, Leo and Voyshelk to his place for dinner] see: Полное собрание русских летописей, издаваемое Археографической комиссиею, [The Complete Collection of Russian Chronicles published by the Archeographical commission], vol.2. Ипатьевская летопись [Hypatian Chronicle], p. 868.

22 "*Surozhanie*" came from *Surozh* or *Soldaia* – a town in the Crimea, now Sudak (Tatar *Sudaq*). Founded in the third century as a small, fortified settlement, it became a trading centre under Italian control from the thirteenth century onwards.

23 "*Novgorodtsy*" – apparently merchants from Novgorod.

24 *и тако плакавшесѧ над нимь. все множество. Володимерчевъ. моужи и жены и дѣти. Нѣмци. и Соурожьцѣ и Новгородци. и Жидове плакоусѧ. аки и во взѧтье Иерусалиму егда ведѧ-*

groups of merchants staying in Wolodymyr, though it is not clear who exactly the "Surozhans" were – Italian merchants from the Crimean Peninsula or possibly Armenians settled in Sudak? Still, it is symptomatic that the text of the Galician-Volhynian Chronicle did not qualify these people in any way, be it as "merchants" or "guests" (the latter usually meaning foreigners coming for commercial purposes) and tended to silence the presence of merchants on some other occasions, in contrast to written sources from other principalities of Rus, for instance, Polotsk Principality (*Polatsk* in modern Belarus). Here, the term "merchants" (*kuptsy*) was widely spread and designated a group protected by a Polock Prince in their commercial activities, while "guests" (*gosti*) appeared as long-distance traders or foreigners.[25] In connection with the trade and peace treaty concluded with Latin partners in 1212, there was talk of Polocker "*mercatores*" who had gone to Riga together with their Prince; in another contract between Riga and Polock around 1340, the "*Rusche coopman to Righe*" was named.[26]

Who the Germans mentioned in the chronicle might be is indicated by a privilege of Prince Władysław Łokietek from 1286, granting permission to the citizens of Toruń and Chelmno (Kulm) travelling to the land of Rus, to cross the Polish territories with their goods.[27] Merchants from Toruń had visited Wolodymyr in Volhynia, bringing Flemish and English cloth, manufactured iron goods, and herring, while buying in return oriental wares as well as local commodities like wax, fur, and timber. Wolodymyr is also one of the first Ruthenian towns where the existence of an urban community and a town council is testified to in the sources. A town council, as a representative organ, was formed around 1324, as becomes evident from a letter written by the town councillors of Wolodymyr ("*consules ac uniuersitas civitatis Ladimiriensis*") to the councillors and inhabitants of Stralsund ("*viris honorabilibus et discretis dominis consulibus ac uniuersitati in Stralsund*").[28] The letter was written on behalf of two brothers, "*Bertramus Ruthenus et Nicolaus*", citizens of Wolodymyr, who had suffered a shipwreck within the Principality of Rügen ("*in terminis principis Rugianorum*") in the Baltic Sea, and lost 34 rolls of cloth bought in Flandres. The text demonstrates that it was the task of the coun-

хоуть œ во полонъ Вавилоньскии ["and so all the people of Volodymyr wept over him, men, women and children, German, and Surozhans, and Novgorodians, and Jews wept, as if at the capture of Jerusalem, when they were led into Babylonian captivity"] see: Hypatian Chronicle, p. 920.

25 Rohdewald, Kollektives Handeln, p. 41.

26 Ibid.

27 "*cives de Thorun et de Culmine mercatores videlicet, qui sunt in terra Russiae per terram nostrum cum suis mercibus navigio sine impedimento transire permitteremus.*" Magdanski, Handel Torunia, p. 47.

28 Höhlbaum, Hansisches Urkundenbuch, p. 178.

cil, not of an individual merchant, to settle such problems of mercantile business. Negotiations were taking place not among separate merchants, but between the two corporate bodies – the town councils of Wolodymyr and of Stralsund. Thus, from the very beginning of its formation, this long-distance trade axis was operated not by individual itinerant merchants, but by actors organised into corporations or communities, especially if we are talking about those coming from the western and northern regions of Europe.[29] The fact that princes of Galicia and Volhynia were inviting and protecting foreigners could also serve as a sign of the absence of autochthonous merchants, or at least of their insignificant number, or to the difficulties they encountered representing themselves.

We do not know exactly the conditions granted to the Germans living in Wolodymyr in the 1260–80s, although, according to later evidence it is possible to assume that these were based on the *ius theutonicum*, as in the neighbouring Polish principalities. These conditions might have differed greatly from one principality of Kievan Rus' to another. Therefore, it was probably not possible (and maybe even not necessary) for foreign merchants to obtain uniform trading conditions in different territories. In Novgorod, German merchants established the *Petershof* and aimed at securing the same standing their compatriots enjoyed in other regions of Europe. The Novgorodians however, remained firm in pursuing their own commercial interests: they eventually accepted some of the German's demands, but rejected or modified others.[30] This stands in contrast to Galicia or Volhynia, where foreign merchants were invited to settle permanently in towns. Germans in Novgorod were only seasonal visitors (i. e. coming for summer or for winter) and were not allowed to stay there longer than one year.[31] Novgorodians, whose presence was already attested in Wolodymyr, themselves demonstrated extensive activity in long-distance trade.[32] In Kyiv, they supposedly had their own "guest court" (probably a *Kontor* like the *Petershof* of the Germans) with the church of the Archangel Michael.[33] At home, they intended to dominate trade with the Germans by forbidding immediate commercial contacts between "guests" (that is foreign merchants). Moreover, in an agreement with Prince Yaroslav of Tver, invited to the

29 Not that numerous, but equally important for trade in oriental goods were Armenians and Jews. These merchants also did not operate individually at that time, but as members of their respective religious communities located in the towns of the above-mentioned Black Sea zone.

30 See: Goetz, Handelsverträge, p. 164.

31 Янин, Очерки истории средневекового Новгорода, p. 369. Indeed, the agreement between Novgorod, Gotland, and Lubeck from 1262–1263 mentioned winter and summer "guests", that is [foreign] merchants coming in winter and summer. In German, these were called *wintervart* and *somervart*. See: Валк, Грамоти великого, p. 57 and 60.

32 We do not have evidence of equally active local merchants in the towns of Galicia and Volhynia during the period.

33 Янин, Очерки, p. 360.

Novgorodian princely throne in 1266, Novgorodians also prohibited the prince from trading directly with German "guests" at the *Petershof*, allowing contacts only through "our brotherhood".[34] The people of Novgorod were involved in commerce and strove to monopolise this sphere for their own advantage by limiting possible competitors and negotiating tough trading conditions with Lubeck and other German towns. Thus, the presence of large groups of German merchants in the town did not lead to the foundation of a local/permanent urban community, as was the case in Wolodymyr.[35]

This also points to the agency of urban dwellers in northern Rus' Principalities in their relationships with foreign merchants and their ability to advance their own agenda in these relationships. The list of persons, political institutions, and social groups that represented Novgorod in their agreements with the German towns and the Livonian Order typically included "*all Novgorodians*" in the formulary from the end of the twelfth to the early fourteenth century, while later documents referred to "*the merchant elder [Sidor], and all merchants of Novgorod, as well as all Novgorodians*" (1342) or "*the merchant Elders [Yakim and Fedor], all merchants and the whole of Novgorod*" (1372).[36] Another suitable illustration can be the agreement concluded in 1263/64 between the Magister of the Livonian Order and the Town Council of Riga on the one side and the towns of Polotsk and Vitebsk (both in present-day Belarus) on the other, mediated by the Lithuanian Duke Gerden.[37] Representatives of both towns were defined simply as "*Polochany*" and "*Vitebliany*" (*полочаны и видьб|ляны*) who in the absence of princely power did not hesitate to deal on their own with the matters of settling a peace and resuming trade, though with the help of Duke Gerden.[38] In terms of trade, the agreement stated: "*a German guest is free to travel to Polotsk, to buy and to sell; equally the Polochans and*

34 Novgorod, in the agreement of 1266, was represented by the "*wladika*" (bishop), "*posadnik*" Michail, "*tysiatskii*" (military leader) Kondrat, and by "whole Novgorod, all seniors and juniors". See: Валк, Грамоти, pp. 12–13. It is also interesting to note the involvement of the ruler in long-distance trade. The document also demonstrates the limited legal and political power of the prince, stressing that he was not allowed to judge, give away lands, or issue a privilege without a *posadnik* (a high-rank official who was originally appointed by the prince, but later became elected by the Novgorodian *boyars*).

35 Russian scholars estimated that "a general number of merchants simultaneously living in *Gotenhof* and *Petershof* amounted to 150–200 persons during the heyday of Hansa trade." See: Янин, Очерки, p. 369.

36 Казакова, Начальный текст, pp. 161–175.

37 See: Fontes historiae Magni Ducatus Lithuaniae, http://starbel.by/dok/d048.htm. (Last accessed 09/21/2024).

38 Хорошкевич, Полоцкие грамоты, p. 8.

Viteblians [can be freely] guesting in Riga and on Gotland's shore."[39] In contrast to the "German side", constituted by the Master of the Livonian Order and the town councillors of Riga (*местерѧ и | с ратьманы рижьскыми*), it is not clear from the documents what social groups stood for the people of Polotsk and Vitebsk; all we know is that they participated in the long-distance trade. We do not find much evidence of similar initiatives in pursuing commercial interests from the side of the autochthonous inhabitants of towns in the Galician and Volhynian Principalities, and, in case of Volodymyr, it was the German community (not the Volodymyrians) and its institutions that dealt with matters of trade.

In any event, commercial contacts with Rus' urban centres – be it Novgorod or Wolodymyr – became fundamental for the prosperity of Hansa towns. For Toruń, for instance, it has been stressed that revenues from the commercial contacts with Ruthenia and the profits from trade in Hungarian copper greatly contributed to the wealth of the patricians of that city's Old Town: Tomasz Jasiński has noted that these patricians (many of whom were of Westphalian origin) were the richest group of burghers in the Polish lands by the middle of the fourteenth century.[40] Commercial links from Toruń to Wolodymyr, and later to Lviv, opened new horizons of expansion for Hansa merchants,[41] and at the same time stimulated the economic development of the Polish kingdom, connecting Mazovia, Upper Hungary (now Slovakia), Prussia, Flanders, and England. Moreover, the monopolisation of trade with Hungary and Rus' by Toruń citizens of Westphalian origin (supported by their former compatriots from Dortmund and Soest) gave rise to the Prussian-Westphalian quarter (*Quartier*) within the Hansa, which in 1347 took an institutional form as a circle of Westphalian-Prussian towns in the Bruges Kontor.[42]

The Teutonic Order was also involved in trade via Ruthenia, as numerous agreements concluded between the Princes of Galicia and Volhynia and the Teutonic Order demonstrate.[43] These included protection of Prussian land against "Tatars and other enemies" by the Ruthenian side and favourable political conditions for

---

39 *Верху того, немечькому гостю в Полочьскую волно ехат(и) и торго|ват(и), купити и продат(и). Також полочаном и видиблѧнину во|лно гостити в Ригу и на Готьскы берегъ.* See: http://starbel.by/dok/d048.htm.

40 Jasiński, Handel, p. 99.

41 Weczerka, Hansische Handelsstraßen.

42 Jasiński, Handel, p. 118.

43 The agreement of 1316 was promoted by the Order's official *"frater Sygerhardus de Swarzburg"*, whom the Ruthenian Princes called *"consanguineus noster dilectus"* in the charter. Genealogical studies have demonstrated that a daughter of Daniel of Galicia, Sophia, was married to the Thuringian Count Günter IV (died 1285); they had nine children and two of their sons entered the Order. One of the sons appears to have been the Sigerhardus mentioned in the charter. See: Войтович, Тевтонський орден, in: Український історичний журнал 6 (2010), pp. 4–17; von Isenburg, Stammtafeln, Taf. 157.

trade.[44] Moreover, access to local markets, especially Lviv,[45] as well as ensuring safety on the roads towards the Black Sea were apparently important for the Order as it expressed a wish for their renewal in 1316.[46] The above mentioned agreements with Ruthenian rulers coincide in time with the beginning of the Order's collaboration with merchants from Prussian and Livonian towns as confirmed by respective sources dating from 1315, 1326, and 1330.[47] The Teutonic Order further owned an amber depot in Lviv, and by 1400 its assets in the town, in property and outstanding debts, represented a value of 3,200 Prussian marks.[48]

For the Ruthenian princes, on the other hand, these contacts were a chance for the improvement of their territories (*melioratio terrae*) by "*assisting foreigners who intend to come to our land with cloth or other goods*", as was expressed, for instance, in a document addressed to the "*honourable councillors, judges, and all the citizens in Toruń*" in 1320.[49] Prince Andreas of Galicia and Volhynia (died 1323), who issued this privilege, ordered that none of his tax collectors or officials should burden or confiscate the goods of merchants. Another privilege issued in the same year for Kraków ensured compensation for losses resulting from injustices wrought by his officials or tax collectors, so that for every *denarius* the merchant had lost, they should be compensated with two.[50] Such support offered to foreigners should be viewed as remarkable, since the chronicle of Johannes Vitodurandi explained that the reason for the assassination of the last Ruthenian prince, Yuriy II Boleslaw, by

44 "*terras vestras fideliter praemunire curabimus prae Tataris, dummodo nobis constiterit, et ab hostili quolibet invasore*". See: Купчинський, Акти, p. 151.

45 Its role as a mediator on the trade route from the Black Sea was recognised on one of the medieval maps-portolans (1339) by Angelino Dulcert, who described "*Civita de Leo*" in the following way: "to this town were coming merchants with spices that later headed via the Dutch Sea (Baltic) to Flanders, mainly to Brugges."[45] Lviv (civitat de Leo) and Kyiv (Chiva) can be seen on the Catalan map of 1375 as well. Ровенчак, Львів, Вісник геодезії та картографії, 2(2013), pp. 45–49. After: Carr-Riegel, Italian Traders, p. 167.

46 Initiated by Daniel of Galicia, these contacts continued under his successors, as is evident from charters issued by the Ruthenian princes in 1316, 1325, 1327, 1334, 1335 and addressed to the Grandmaster of the Order (*Magistro generali in Prussiam*). See: Купчинський, Акти, no. 8–11.

47 Trade contacts of the officials of the Teutonic Order in Eastern and Central Europe included Novgorod, Lviv, Livonia, Scandinavia, Polish lands (Mazovia, Kujavia), the lands of the Czech Crown, and Brandenburg. See: Czaja, Economic, p. 65.

48 Dollinger, German Hansa, p. 134.

49 Яковенко/Кравченко, Торгівля на Україні, p. 17.

50 "*Item si alicui injuria, molestia vel violentia per aliquos nostros officiales, ministeriales vel theloneatores illata fuerit in terra nostra, pro uno denario sibi injuste ablato, quod ostendere poterit, duos refundemus.*" It is necessary to mention that in contrast to the privilege for Toruń, here also some customs duties were mentioned that were to be paid by Krakowians. Ibid, no.1, p. 16.

local *boyars* in 1340 was ostensibly due to the rising number of foreigners.[51] This assumption is stressed by information in another chronicle, which mentions the prince's exceptional favour towards "*Bohemos et Alemanos*".[52] The violent death of this last Ruthenian prince started the war of succession between Lithuania and Poland, which lasted until Casimir III ("the Great") managed to annex Galicia and a part of Volhynia in 1349, while the rest of Volhynia fell under Lithuanian control.

Due to a lack of sources however, it is difficult to know for certain whether the conflict was really caused by the clashing spheres of interests of Ruthenian "*boyars*" on the one side and Germans on the other (the prince being the protector of the latter). In terms of law, the operations of foreign merchants in Ruthenia were based on privileges (in written or oral form) granted by the ruler, which guaranteed immunity from local customs and local officials, together with the possibility to appeal directly to the ruler in case of violation.[53] The grant of *ius theutonicum*, seen as "*a freedom*", signified a new [legal] reality: a breach in the existing social relationships based on local customs (defined as Polish or Ruthenian "laws or customs") which from now on had to be removed ("*removentes ibidem omnia iura Polonicalia, Ruthenicalia et quovis alia*") because of the contradictions they presented when faced with the "German law" ("*que ius Theutonicum perturbare consueverunt*").[54]

---

51 He was a son of Prince Trojden II of Mazovia and grandson of the Ruthenian Prince Yurii Lvovych, thus a member of both the Polish Piast dynasty and the Rus' Romanovych dynasty. As a Ruthenian ruler he issued most of the above-mentioned agreements with the Teutonic Order, being at the same time dynastically related to the Order's officials. In this way, political and dynastical ties logically mirrored commercial interests revolving around one of the most important long-distance trade axes of the thirteenth–fourteenth centuries. How these ties were applied to overcome obstacles could be seen, for instance, by reading Jasinski's article on copper trade, where he argues that the total destruction of Gdańsk/Danzig by the Order in 1308 resulted in Toruń's monopoly on the copper trade. In order to secure this, an alternative route that ran via Mazovia and Warsaw towards Rus' and Hungarian copper mines near Košice, now in Slovakia, was established in 1309, so that the road through the territory controlled by the Krakow ruler Władysław Łokietek was left aside. We know that in 1306, Łokietek had granted the staple right on copper to his town Krakow. Copper was carried here from the Hungarian mines near Kosice, and then from Krakow using water- or land-routes to Toruń and further to Flandres. See: Jasiński, Handel, pp. 110, 116–117. The staple right of 1306 was clearly designed against merchants of Toruń and aimed at breaking their direct contacts with Hungary. See: Kutrzeba, Handel, p. 28.

52 Rocznik Traski [Traska's Chronicle], in: Bielowski, Monumenta Poloniae historica, p. 860.

53 The same is applicable to the formation of urban communities in general.

54 It became a typical formula in Magdeburg law privileges. This particular quotation is from a charter issued by King Wladyslaw Jagiello in 1397. See: Akta grodzkie i ziemskie z czasów Rzeczypospolitej Polskiej z archiwum tak zwanego bernardyńskiego we Lwowie, ed. X. Liske, T.2, (Lviv, 1870), no. 24, p. 40.

In a charter to the "*famosis viribus et mercatoribus in Thorun*", issued after the death of Prince Yuriy II in 1341, Dmytro Detko, a governor (*capitaneus Russiae*), promised for those who would like to settle in the town of Lviv, free hereditary right under the annual tax payment, "*as used to be before*", indicating a longer tradition of this practice.[55] He also expressed his readiness to compensate for damages caused after the death of the prince, which indicates some disorder and eventual hostility by the local population against Toruń merchants.[56] Apparently, by inviting and settling these people and protecting them and their possessions with immunity, Ruthenian rulers demonstrated that they fully recognised the role of trade and towns in the whole complex of measures to reorganise their realms.

One of the last charters issued by Yuriy II had been a Magdeburg law privilege for the town of Sanok in 1339. More precisely, the prince had granted *advocatia* "*with all the power and jurisdiction of the German law, which is the law of Magdeburg*" to a certain Bartko from Sandomierz with the right to judge all and everyone, be it a German, Pole, Hungarian, or Ruthenian (*Theuthonicus, Polonus, Ungarus et Ruthenus*), within the boundaries of Sanok.[57] Despite accusations of favouring foreigners, the charter clearly gave the same status also to local Ruthenians.

In addition, the familiarity of a legal framework, a similar organisation of urban courts and legal procedures were factors which mattered in terms of predictability at that time. The commercial organisation based on towns enabled the development of permanent urban governments for the administration and facilitation of trade, and aided the evolution of bodies of law shaped to adjudicate disputes that arose between merchants.[58] However, all this would not have been possible without a conscious policy adopted by the Ruthenian princes (and later Polish kings), who created the possibility for merchants (probably not exclusively, but predominantly of foreign origin) to settle and to be organised as communities in their towns.

The eastward expansion of the Polish Kingdom after 1340 signified future changes in the geography of commercial contacts for Rus' and simultaneously a gradual withdrawal of Hansa (mainly Toruń) merchants from the region. Toruń, for its part, wanted to maintain access to Ruthenian lands and turned to the Lithuanian Dukes

---

55 "*Qui vero ad commansionem ibidem venire proposuerint, haereditaten liberam concedimus et donamus, prout pristini exaccionem nobis annuatam [...]*". See: Купчинський, Акти, pp. 194–200.

56 "*Dampna vero post obitum domini nostril felicis memoriae ducis Russiae quicunque Lemburgenses intulerunt, duntaxat excipimus litteris in aliis et in istis.*" Ibid, p. 199.

57 "*Dedimus [...] fideli nostro Bartkoni de Sandomiria advocatiam in Sanak nostra civitate ... cum plena potestate et omni jurisdictione Theutonico iure id est iure Magdeburgensi, sibi et suis pueris legitimis heredibusque universis perpetuo iure libere [...]*". See: Купчинський, Акти, pp. 190–192. Sanok (now in Poland) situated some 160 km north from Košice (now Slovakia, then Upper Hungary) and medieval Hungarian copper mines, and undoubtfully belonged to the sphere of interest of Torun merchants.

58 See: Kallioinen, Long-Distance Trade, 2020 .

for help. Thus, upon appeal from Toruń merchants, the Dukes Lubart and Keystut issued a privilege in 1341. Written in Ruthenian and addressed to citizens of Toruń (*У Торунь к мѣстычемъ*), the document specified the roads (via Dorohychyn, Melnyk, Brest) to be used by Hansa merchants on their way to Lutsk, located in Volhynia some 70 km east of Wolodymyr.[59] Determining the roads to be used by merchants certainly had a fiscal dimension, because they were directed towards customs stations. There is a list from ca. 1349 of such stations called *Theolonea antiqua de Thorun in Ladimiriam* and vice versa *de Lademiria versus Thorun* listing sums to be paid there, as well as also listing goods usually carried to Wolodymyr (cloth from Toruń, Poperinge, and Brugge, fox fur, sheepskin, linen, a particular sort of expensive purple textiles called *panni scharlatici* and towards Toruń (wax, silk, and spices).[60] Starting from the second half of the fourteenth century, documents contain more and more details concerning toll stations, amount of payments, customs given in rent, customs duties, confiscations of goods for non-payment of tax, etc. can be traced. In this context, the formulations of the Tatar Khan Tokhtamysh's edict (*jarlig*) issued in 1393 – "*as [used to be] before, free roads for the guests, for our and your traders*"– did not at all mean the absence of any financial burden or control along the trade routes.[61] Not only that, the quantity of surviving records related to monetary affairs increased significantly,[62] which also demonstrates a great leap in the economy of Ruthenian lands in terms of monetarisation, as compared to the situation some hundred years before. This went in parallel with the increasing presence of [foreign] merchants in the lands of Galicia and Volhynia, judging from the number of privileges granted to them. Moreover, sources attest to the role of Wolodymyr as an important meeting point on the trade route connecting the Baltic and Black Seas and demonstrate the multi-religious and multi-ethnic character of

---

59 Яковенко/Кравченко, Торгівля на Україні, no. 4, p. 19. Interestingly, the charter addressed to Toruń was written in Ruthenian. Could this mean that because of the intensive contacts with Rus, Hansa merchants were able to read the Slavic language?

60 Яковенко/Кравченко, Торгівля на Україні, no. 7, pp. 21–22.

61 Пещак, Пам'ятки no. 58, p. 109. The source also points to the role of Tatar khans as mediators and promotors of long-distance trade. More than a century earlier, Mengu-Timur, a khan of the Golden Horde, a division of the Mongol Empire, in 1266–1280 mediated the renewal of commercial contacts between Riga and Novgorod. In his "Word" (1266–1270) to Prince Yaroslav, he ordered him to "give way to German guests in your *volost*" That is in the territory under your control [*даи путь немецкому гости на свою волость*]. See: Валк, Грамоти великого, no. 30, p. 58. This document was one episode in the conflict between the prince and the Novgorodians (called also "feudals of Novgorod" in Russian historiography), in which "the Germans of Riga" supported the latter, and appealed to the khan for help in conflict resolution. See: Хорошкевич, Из истории русско-немецких отношений XIII в., in: Исторические записки, 78 (1965), pp. 219–233.

62 Naismith, Money and Coinage in the Middle Ages, Brill 2018, p. 124.

this town, which from then onwards became a typical feature of any commercial centre in the region.[63]

To what extent did merchants coming from Toruń and settling in Wolodymyr regard themselves as Hansa merchants? Did their presence make Wolodymyr a centre of Hanseatic trade?[64] Although individual Hanseatic merchants had trade relations to the south, and reached overland as far as the Black Sea, the Hanseatic League was not active as an organisation in these regions, and its activity seems to have declined greatly from the middle of the sixteenth century.[65] Still, these were not usual trade relations for seasonal visitors ("guests") with "collective privileges made accessible to a wide and (until the middle of the fifteenth century) inclusive group of traders coming from various towns."[66] We also do not have examples of "collective privileges" from this region. Usually, charters were granted to merchants of concrete towns, often upon the request of their town councils. Being invited by local rulers, these citizens of, among others, but not exclusively Hansa towns, began settling here for good, and in the absence of autochthonous merchants contributed greatly to the development of the "commercial stratum" in Galicia and Volhynia. The following section will possibly demonstrate how individual merchants settling here and forming communities were dealt with the issues of long-distance trade

63 Soon, culturally heterogeneous inhabitants (typically resulting from involvement in long-distance trade) became a sign of a successful urban foundation and attractivity of a settlement. Thus, in 1438, a Magdeburg law privilege for Kremenets was issued to a certain Jurek Niemec (that is "George the German") by Lithuanian Duke Švitrigaila. Jurek "the German" himself came from the town of Bus'k, some 30 km from Lviv. The duke appointed Jurek as *advocatus* (*Vogt*) "under the German law […] from Marborg, as it was [usually] given to all royal towns of the Polish Crown" and granted him the right to judge within the urban boundaries all the people: "Ruthenians, Poles, Germans, Wallachians, Armenians, Jews, Tatars, or of any other origin," thus listing almost all ethnic groups participating in local trade. See: Юго-Западной России, Part 5, vol. 1:, , p. 3.

64 In fact, it is difficult to determine what was the decisive factor for a town to be regarded as a Hansa town. Judging from the available lists, there were no Hansa towns in the territory of present-day Ukraine. See: https://www.hanse.org/en/discover-the-hanseatic-cities/hanseatic-cities (accessed 06/01/2025).

65 Hammel-Kiesow, Die Hanse, p. 11. Regarding commercial contacts between Toruń and Wolodymyr, we have sporadic evidence of local burghers travelling with their goods to Toruń as late as the seventeenth century. Law court records of Lutsk castle (*iudicium castrense*) from 1635 mention a certain Syrevych, "a burgher and merchant of Wolodymyr", who reported "in his own name and in the names of his friends, neighbours and servants" an assault on their convoy of carts heading to Toruń. See: Юго-западной России Part 1, vol 6: pp. 585–587.

66 Wubs-Mrozewicz and Jenks, The Hanse, p. 11.

4. The Polish Times

The most profound changes on the trade axis between the Baltic and Black Seas came with the incorporation of the Ruthenian territory under Polish rule in the second half of the fourteenth century. It is necessary to remember that the Polish kingdom was located in the middle between two trade axes: the first leading from the Black Sea colonies via Ruthenian lands and Lesser Poland to Silesia and from there to Central Europe; the second connecting the copper ores in Upper Hungary and, again, Rus' with the Hansa towns on the Baltic. Therefore Kraków, which emerged at the crossing of these roads, had two major rivals – Toruń in the north, and Wrocław in the west. Wrocław was one of the central exchange places between the western and eastern regions of Europe. The Netherlands, Prague, Vienna, and Nuremberg sent cloth, while eastern Europe offered spices, silk, salt, wax, honey, and later oxen.[67] Similar to Toruń, it was vital for Wrocław to have stable access to Ruthenia, a connection which the Polish king came to control and scholarship already described the "trade-road war" conducted by Wrocław on the one hand, and Kraków supported by Casimir III (the Great) on the other.[68] In 1344, when still not yet fully in control of the Ruthenian lands, Casimir issued a decree which laid the fundaments for Kraków's monopoly on trade with Rus' by determining the roads that merchants had to take via Kraków, Wiślica, and Sandomierz to Lviv; and via Lublin to Wolodymyr in Volhynia.[69] In response, citizens of Wrocław appealed to the Roman King and King of Bohemia, Charles IV, for help in 1348 and in 1349 asked him to negotiate the matter of opening the road to Rus. How badly it affected the town could be seen from the information about a Silesian knight, Krige de Rydenburg, who supposedly offended the Polish king with "spoken and written

67 Klemenski, Przywilej Kazimierza Wielkiego, p. 327.

68 See for instance: Kutrzeba, Handel, pp. 75–79.

69 Ibid.; Wolodymyr retained its commercial importance until the end of the fourteenth century. In 1380, Krakow still cared for a privilege from the local duke in the matter of customs duties, but Lviv soon took over, directing the flow of goods to its own market. Wolodymyr never regained its position in long-distance trade. Around the same time, in the early fifteenth century, the trade between Lviv and Prussia also began to decline. See: Kutrzeba, Handel, pp. 107 and 114. Still, the account books of the *Grossschäfferei* of the Teutonic Order in Königsberg mention the presence of its "*Wirt*" Gerike Smithuzen in Lviv in 1400–1402. See: Sattler, Handelsrechnungen, pp. 136 and 137. The account books also mentioned Armenian merchants from Lviv probably as contracting parties: "*Dymitr Armenier*" in Lemberg, and "*Iwan der Kleine*", see ibid., p. 254. According to Sattler, Armenians were exporting amber from Lviv to "the Orient" stating that "from the very beginning, Lemberg (Lviv) came into question in the case of amber, which was the pillar of all the trade of Grossschäffer in Königsberg, where it was bought by Armenians and directly exported to the Orient." See: ibid, p. XXXIII.

words" on the subject of the road blockade.[70] Presumably out of despair, Emperor Charles IV wrote to Wrocław in 1352 that he was going to repress Polish merchants in the territories of Bohemia and the Roman Empire – this must have been his reaction to being cut off from direct access to Ruthenian markets.[71] Still, in the year 1353, a royal decree was issued that forbade foreign merchants from using the roads via Poland to Ruthenia, thus creating a monopoly for Kraków.[72] On an appeal to open the road towards Rus' for Wrocław in 1354, King Casimir famously answered "*that he had conquered this land for his own people.*"[73] In this way, by eliminating its competitors, Kraków secured its monopoly on trade with the whole Black Sea region. Merchants from Toruń were mentioned many times as one of the first [German] burghers in Wolodymyr and Lviv, but the records in the town books of Lviv, namely the *Album civium Leopoliensium* (1388–1783) demonstrates that in the late fourteenth to the early fifteenth century the majority of new burgers were coming first of all from neighbouring towns (Yaroslaw, Halych, Przemyśl, or Sanok) and only secondly from outside of Rus' territories; the new settlers were arriving from Kraków and Silesia (Wrocław, Nyssa, Głogów, or Świdnica).[74] People from Toruń, meanwhile, were few and mostly came at the beginning of the fourteenth century.

The death of Casimir the Great did not change the sharpness of the competition between Wrocław and Kraków regarding access to Rus'. A privilege granted to Kraków by his successor in 1371 clearly expressed a prohibition for merchants from Czech lands to travel to Rus' with their goods stating that "*to all foreign merchants, such as the Bohemians, Moravians, Silesians, and any others to whom [...] the same passage towards Russia and any places in Russia for the purpose of obtaining goods or merchandise [...] is permanently forbidden.*"[75] Later, a privilege for a full staple right was granted to Kraków in 1387 which explicitly mentioned those groups of foreigners who were forbidden to pass the town with their merchandise: "*Thorunenses, Prutheni, Ungari, Moravi, Bohemi, Slesite.*"[76]

In response to this, records of a Hansa gathering in Marienburg in 1389 indicate that there was even a plan to talk to "*our lord*", the Grand Master of the Teutonic

70 Ibid., p. 326.

71 Ibid.

72 Wróbel, Kwestia krzyżacka, pp. 136–187, 138. Because this also affected Toruń, it is not surprising that the two towns cooperated with each other later.

73 "*Rex dixit, se terram Russye propriis suis hominibus expugnasse et quod illa solum suis hominibus et mercatoribus patere debet [...]*". See : Korn, Breslauer Urkundenbuch, p. 170.

74 Janeczek, Album civium Leopoliensium, vol. 1.

75 Foreign merchants with their goods could not pass Krakow, and this decree de facto introduced the staple right : "*Sed mercatores iidem extranei... cum eorum rebus et mercibus [...] ad nostram civitatem Cracoviam et non ulterim [...] transire potuerint.*" See: Myśliński, Lublin a handel, p. 6.

76 Codex diplomaticus civitatis Cracoviensis, pp. 76–77.

Order, about organising a trade blockade against Poland with the support of other towns.[77]

Interestingly, the very same document also contains information on a diplomatic mission to Novgorod with the aim to establish equal rules and rights for all Hansa merchants travelling to that town. The necessity to remain "*equal in trade*" was clearly emphasised in the text calling for unanimity among the Hansa towns in that matter.[78] Apparently, to establish a similar uniformity of rules in the trade with Ruthenia was not deemed necessary. On the contrary, we see how Wrocław, Kraków, and Toruń, all Hansa towns, were competing directly for access to Ruthenia. The staple right Toruń received in 1403 was interpreted as "the beginning of the end" of the great epoch of its long-distance trade.[79] The main purpose of obtaining it was to gain leverage in the negotiations with Kraków and revenge for being cut off from the Hungarian mines and Ruthenian markets, Lviv first of all, as well as for the restriction of movement in Polish lands. According to the literature, Toruń most likely did not need the staple law; the idea was to return to the previous status of trade contacts without limitations, because experienced Toruń merchants were not afraid to compete on the free market.[80] However, this strategy failed to bring the expected results not least because the Krakówians did not comply with Toruń's claims, and the latter had no particular means to enforce it.

In one of the most recent definitions, the Hanse was an organisation of traders (specifically traders speaking Low German and engaged in foreign trade) and an organisation of towns in which these traders were burghers.[81] Since the ultimate motive of traders was profit, they only played the Hanseatic game as long as it was profitable. When it was no longer enticing for traders of a town to conduct trade jointly with merchants from other Hanse towns, they (often silently) gave up their membership and their participation in common rights.[82] Considering that Toruń, Wrocław, and Kraków were all Hansa towns (at least occasionally), they only prove the statements expressed above. It looks like as soon as individual "Hansa"

---

77 "*Item das man rede mit unsirm herren, dem homeister, das man den anderen stetin ouch gebite, das sie das gebot myte halden, das man keyn gut in das land czu Polen fure.*" See: Koppmann, Hanserecesse, Band 3: 1387–1390, no. 439, §10, p. 453.

78 "*Item von der Nowgarduschin reysyn, das sullin unsir sendebotin so vor- antwortin, wenne uns dy gemeynen stete bekennen, das wir glyche mit in [in]d deme rechte syn czu Nowgardin und in allin andirin dyngin mit unsirm aldermanne, und keyn gebot noch gesecze machin, is sf mit unsirm wyssin und willin: wes sf denne mit uns und wir mit yn eyns werdin czu nucze und vromen deme kouf-manne, das welle wir allecziit glych mit in haldin, und des sullin unsir sendebotin mechtig syn, was sy mit den stetin eyns werdin in der sachin.*" See: Hanserecesse, no. 439, §3, p. 452.

79 Magdanski, Handel Torunia, p. 152.

80 Ibid, p. 153.

81 Wubs-Mrozewicz and Jenks, The Hanse, p. 5.

82 Ibid.

merchants lost their citizenship and settled in towns of Galician Rus' or Poland, they did not seem to care much for their Hanseatic ties. Instead, they fought tooth and nail for better conditions only for themselves and attempted to monopolise the market at the expense of other cities (including their "towns of origin"). Can we say that this "deviation" could be observed only on the periphery of Hansa activity? Should this be regarded as a kind of "localisation" of German merchants (if not assimilation), who, after settling in Lviv, Wolodymyr, or Kraków focused on their own interests and lost any thought for Hanseatic solidarity? Indeed, when, in the absence of strong groups of "autochthonous" merchants, the rulers of Poland, Ruthenia, or Mazovia invited Germans (and others) and treated them as "their people", these merchants actually became "their people", demonstrating loyalty to a new homeland and taking care of its (and now, thus, their own) interests. If so, here again, the local rulers were the ones who changed the "rules of the game" causing a "dissolution" of Hansa ties by offering citizenship to German merchants and better protection of their commercial activities than did cooperation with other Hansa members.[83]

5. Staple Right: Producing an Exclusive Legal Space for Lviv

The "staple right" (*ius emporii* in Latin, *Stapelrecht* and *Niederlagerecht* in German), which was sometimes used to the extreme by the urban communities in the region, securing a trade monopoly for local merchants and limiting the transit through a town, became a way to ensure predictability (and profitability). As with every exclusion, it brought further fragmentation to a legal sphere within which commerce and commercial centres of the country operated. It was also another strategy for which the cooperation between ruler and merchants was crucial, and at the same time especially profitable for both sides. As part and parcel of this privilege, external merchants were obliged to stay in a town for a certain period of time selling their goods to local citizens. Typically, the staple right further comprised the prohibition for "guests" to trade with each other. This policy was oriented towards imported goods like cloth, wine, or "oriental wares". Moreover, retail trade was as a rule forbidden for foreign merchants. Despite its various forms and manifestations, we can speak about a partial staple right when after a week or two spent in town merchants were able to move further with unsold goods; and a full staple right

83 One can notice a sharp difference with Novgorod, where the duration of stays was limited in time (seasonally), so that it was profitable for German merchants to gather in groups and to conduct trade jointly. Here, they continued to rely on a common solidarity in an all too often hostile surrounding and thus remained interested in the uniformity of rights regardless of their origin and their destination.

when "guests" had to sell everything to local merchants, who themselves would carry the merchandise further down the trade route.[84] A variety of forms of staple right resulted from a lack of uniformity of its application, since the strictness of rules and prohibitions was different from one place to another, depending on a town's position in the urban hierarchy, its political importance, relationship with the ruler, geographical location, etc. Growing competition on the trade route made the staple right a suitable means to secure better trading conditions and to overcome competitors.

Thus, staple right became the main source of Lviv's prosperity and turned the town into one of the biggest emporia for "oriental goods," and arguably into the most important town in East European trade.[85] Lviv was, in many aspects, special in terms of the strictness of its staple right, especially regarding "Tatar goods" (*mercibus de Thartaria*). Political changes in the kingdom, for example the succession of rulers, time and again stimulated the council to confirm the staple right as one of the most important prerogatives of the town. Thus, in a document issued in 1379 by Duke Lubart-Demetrius (*groser Furste von Ladymir und von Luczk*)[86] addressed to the council and "the whole town of Lviv" the staple right here (as well as in Wolodymyr and Lutsk) was confirmed. The duke promised that no merchant coming from Poland or Germany and heading towards the "Pagan lands" (i. e. Black Sea shores controlled by the Tatars) through his territory should be able to avoid "*Niederlagerecht*" in those three towns.[87] In the same year (1379), the Hungarian King Louis I ("the Great"), who after the death of King Casimir III had taken control of Galician Rus, promised to keep Lviv "in all rights and freedoms, namely in the deposition of all goods."[88] Still, already in the next year, the king

84 On Lviv *Stapelrecht* see: LEWICKI, Prawo składu w Polsce.

85 For F. Lutge, Lviv at that time belonged to the most important commercial towns in the world: "*Doch wenden wir uns wieder Lemberg als der seit dem 14. Jh. aufblühenden großen Zentrale des Osthandels zu. Es ist tatsächlich – um es zu wiederholen und zu unterstreichen – jetzt die für den osteuropäischen Handel wichtigste Stadt, ja – das kann man ohne Übertreibung sagen – eine der wichtigsten Handelsstädte der damaligen Welt.*" See: LÜTGE, Strukturwandlungen, p. 16.

86 Liubartas or Lubart (Demetrius was his Christian name) was the youngest son of Gediminas Grand Duke of Lithuania. He started a struggle against Poland and Hungary for the lands of Galicia and Volhynia after the assassination of the last Ruthenian prince in 1340 and became a Volhynian duke in 1340–84 making Lutsk his capital. His attempts to conquer Galicia remained unsuccessful.

87 "*Gelobin den erbarn Luyten dem Ratę und den gemeynen Burgern und der ganczen Stat czu der Lemburg, das Wir keynen Koufman nicht wellen losen czyn mit zyme gute, her zey von Polen oder von Duyczhen Landen durch unzer lant ken Heydenlant, das dy Nyderloge blybe czu Ladymir czu Luczk und czu der Lemberg, als is von alders her vormols gewest ist.*" Торгівля на Україні, no. 8, p. 22.

88 "*in omnibus iuribus et libertatibus, videlicet, deposicione omnium mercanciarum [...].*" See: Privilegia civitatis Leopoliensis XIV–XVIII saec., KAPRAL, no. 7, p. 43.

had to specify this privilege when his subjects in Hungary and Poland complained about the difficulties and prohibitions along "the Tatar way" (*racione preclusionis et prohibicionis vie Tartarice*). Lviv had apparently defended its privileged position against the outsiders.[89] The king ordered merchants from Hungary and Poland (and of whatever other origin) on their way from or to (*Tarthariam et ad quasvis Thartarie partes*) to stay and sell their goods in the town for 14 days in order to satisfy the desires of Lviv's inhabitants. Unsold goods could be freely carried further after paying customs taxes.[90] The next Polish ruler, Queen Jadwiga, confirmed the previous privileges in 1387 and in addition to the deposit of oriental goods established also a "salt deposit" (*deposicio salis et mercimoniorum in civitate nostra Lemburgensi*).[91] The fact that Lviv did not allow Kraków merchants free transit towards *Tataria* led to the issuing of yet another document in 1403 that undermined Lviv's monopoly. This document freed merchants of Kraków from the obligation to sell their merchandise for 14 days.[92] The Polish capital of Kraków was more successful in "closing roads" for all "outsiders" defined as "all and every guest, stranger, or foreign merchant" (*universi et singuli hospites, advene seu mercatores extranei*), and in securing better conditions of trade, such as freedom from customs duties along Polish roads.[93]

In general, the conflict between Lviv and Kraków belonged to the whole range of struggles and negotiations among the major trading centres Wrocław, Toruń, and Kraków for controlling exchange between Upper Hungary and the Levantine colonies on the one hand and Flanders on the other.[94] Being located closer to the source of "oriental goods" and with the help of its staple right, Lviv was able to gain in commercial weight and, together with Kraków, made up the two genuinely important trading centres of the medieval Polish kingdom. Transit of goods from South to North enriched Kraków, while transit from East to West (important to Kraków as well) enriched Lviv.[95] A great role in their commercial success was the ability to secure the necessary privileges, like exceptions for their merchants from paying customs duties on the trade roads, or favourable commercial conditions leading to a monopoly of the market.[96] The introduction of staple rights along the

89 Ibid., no. 8, p. 44.

90 Ibid.

91 Ibid, no. 9, p. 46.

92 Ibid no. 17, pp. 58–59.

93 The town council of Kraków eagerly supervised the observation of the staple right.

94 See: Kutrzeba, Handel, p. 35.

95 Ibid, p. 108.

96 Commenting on the flow of goods via Lviv, F. Lütge mentioned the exceptional privilege of Nuremberg, which managed to overcome Krakow's staple and thus reach Lviv: "Von Lemberg gingen die Güter weiter nach Breslau und Krakau, später auch gerade nach Nürnberg. In diesem Handel ist Nürnberg mit einem besonders weitreichenden Privileg ausgestattet worden, das ungeachtet

trade axis was probably the final blow that ended the free flow of goods known from the thirteenth century by shutting down markets for external merchants, thus securing a monopoly for locals versus outsiders.

For Lviv, however, the most important development took place in 1444, when King Wladyslaw III of Poland established the full staple right there (*depositum generale Leopoliense*), and, above all, intending to regulate different "*iura et consuetudines*", subjected all foreign merchants visiting Lviv to the jurisdiction of the local town court "which followed Magdeburg law" (*in iure civitatis Maydburgensi*).[97] In a context of legal unity and pluralism, this was an attempt to bring some uniformity to the legal regulation of trade for both external and internal participants, taking into account the constant influx of numerous merchants, traders, and sellers (*maxime advenis mercatoribus, institoribus, venditoribus*) from different lands to the town. The king ordered that all merchants, be they Greeks, Armenians, Saracens, Jews, *Bessermens*, or of any status or origins (*Greci, Armeni, Saraceni, Iudei, Bessermeni et cuiuscunque generis, condicionis sive status*), either Christians or Pagans, coming from the Polish kingdom, or from any other land to Lviv, with or without goods, in all cases (*in quibuslibet causis magnis et parvis*) had to be judged by local judges. Indeed, this must surely have brought more predictability to commercial operations; taking into account that Lviv was the end destination for many foreign merchants, it would have been convenient to solve eventual disputes on the spot and by people competent in long-distance trade.

Furthermore, the charter declared that "Italian merchants and some others, pagans or Christians, from the lands over the sea" (*mercatores Italici vel alii quicumque pagani vel Christiani de transmaritimis partibus*), who were coming to Lviv with their merchandise, should not dare to go past "*depositum Leopoliense*", but had to sell everything in the town. Further, goods bought to Lviv could not be sold in neighbouring Walachia, in order to prevent interference with the staple right of Lviv, its inhabitants and merchants (*ne incolis, mercatoribus et deposito Leopoliensis civitatis preiudicium causarent vel quovismodo inferrent*).

The Italians from the Black Sea shores were mentioned in the first line, as it seems that Lviv remained an important destination for them, but at the same time it became their last station on this trade route. The charter further stated that if these Italians, pagan or Christian merchants violated the royal decree and sold their

---

der dadurch berührten und bisher immer geschützten Stellung von Krakau König Kasimir auf Ansuchen Kaiser Karls IV. gewährt hatte. *Ad instantes petitionum voluntates Karoli Romanorum Imperatoris*, heißt es, bekamen die Nürnberger das Recht, *per civitatem Cracoviensem ad terras Russie usque ad Lemburgam transeundi, standi, mercandi et omnia oportuna faciendi*; solche Handelskonzessionen hatte bis dahin keine Stadt in Polen erlangt." See: Lütge, Strukturwandlungen, p. 19.

97 Ibid., no. 31 and 90.

goods in Walachia, the Lviv city councillors had the right to punish the violator, taking half of the penalty for the use of their community (*pro utilitate ipsorum reipublice*) and giving the other half to the king.[98] Consequently, on the one hand confiscating goods was a way to deal with non-compliance and on the other, it meant financial gains for both the ruler and the town.

It is not by chance that Walachia appeared in the context of Lviv's staple right. Merchants from the town of Lviv spared no effort to gain access to the markets of the Romanian principalities of Moldavia and Walachia, and of the Transylvanian region of the Kingdom of Hungary, as well as to the newly formed road towards the Black Sea (*via moldavica*). Similar to Lviv, towns in this region benefitted greatly from acting as intermediaries in long-distance trade between the Levantine colonies and Central Europe. Since the fourteenth century, trade laid the foundation of urban development here and continued to be a major economic nexus until the dawn of modern times.[99] The importance of opening this new route towards the Black Sea shore is hardly to be overestimated, since until the end of the fourteenth century, the old *via tatarica* had been the only route that supplied "oriental goods" to Lviv and further west.[100]

The Lviv register of incomes and expenses for 1404–14 contains many references related to diplomatic contacts between the town council of Lviv and rulers of the Romanian principalities, especially Walachia.[101] Starting from 1406, we can see numerous expenditures made "*pro reyssa in Walachia*", for delivering letters "*ad Walachiam in facto civitatis* or *ad Woyewodam*", and for presents in honour of the Woyewode of Walachia (*Woyewode Walachiensi honorato*) as well as the "*Woyewode Moldawie et eius Capitaneo*".[102] Diplomatic efforts of the town council

---

98 Thus, the king would also gain immediate profit from Lviv's *ius emporii*. More on that: LEWICKI, Prawo składu (supra note 69), p. 6. It was connected to the so-called "compulsory roads" or "road enforcement," when merchants were forced to travel along certain specified roads, where customs duties were to be paid. These customs payments along a road were mentioned, for instance, in a well-known document from ca. 1350–60: "*thelonea antiqua de Thorun in Ladimir[iam]; de Thorun versus Lemburgam; versus Wratislaviam de Thorun via nova*", etc. See: HÖHLBAUM, Hansisches Urkundenbuch. Band 3: 1343–1360, no. 559.

99 As L. Radvan demonstrated, from the fourteenth to the sixteenth century the medieval urban economy in Wallachia was based mainly on trade, and towns in this area became true intermediaries between the centres of Central Europe, Transylvania, and the South-Danubian lands, while crafts were only of secondary importance. See: RADVAN, On the Medieval Urban Economy p. 489. For the connections between Lviv and Moldavian towns in the second-half of the fifteenth century, see: KAPRAL, Lviv.

100 KUTRZEBA, Handel, p. 108.

101 The original title is: *Inventarium perceptorum et expensarum annualium cassae civilis, necnon exactionum et debitorum ab a. 1404 ad 1414.* Published as: CZOLOWSKI, Księga przychodów.

102 This meant payments for servants who delivered letters, as well as travel expenses for town councillors (*domini*) and the coachmen who brought them to their destination (*Vectori, qui currum*

were supported by the Polish king, aiming at gaining access to the route through Moldavia, which came to be more secure than the older "Tatar way", as well as commercial prerogatives for Lviv merchants at local markets.[103]

These efforts brought the expected results. In 1408, Alexander the Good, *Woyewode* of Moldavia, issued a separate privilege for Lviv listing in detail, goods, customs, and roads to be used by merchants making his town of Suceava the main centre for commercial activity and customs payments.[104] This privilege listed silk, *kamka* (damask, patterned textile of silk or wool), cotton, pepper, thyme, and Greek acid (lemon juice?) among the "Tatar goods" as well as livestock (sheep and pigs), and Moldavian and Hungarian horses and cattle "from Tatar lands" to be imported to Lviv. In the other direction went cloth (*Tuch*), hats and trousers, iron goods (specifically swords) and also silver from Hungary, wax, furs, skins, and fish.[105] Even though the Moldavian ruler declared in the privilege that "*we have done this to the merchants of our lord, the Polish King, from all the Rus' and Pyodolian lands*",[106] merchants from Lviv were apparently the main initiators and recipients of this privilege. They were not only often mentioned in the text, but also listed among the witnesses as "*envoys from Lviv who accomplished this matter with us*".[107] Moreover, merchants from Lviv received exclusive permission to establish a "guest house" (something like a *Kontor*)[108] in Suceava, but were prohibited from turning it into a tavern, to sell beverages, have a butchery, or bake bread. These items had to be obtained in the town. To a great extent, this and other commercial privileges were the result of diplomatic efforts undertaken by the citizens of Lviv, who were also the main beneficiaries. Even if a similar document by the Transylvanian Woyewode Mircea from 1390 was meant for "*all merchants from the land of Wladyslaw the*

---

duxit dominorum). In 1408, a sum of money was spent "for the final agreement in the matter of trade" (*pro finali vnione in facto mercatorum*) with Walachia. See: Księga przychodów, pp. 20, 26, 48, 54, 61, 63, 68, 78.

103 Moldavia gained access to the Black Sea shore in the second half of the fourteenth century, when a Genoese citadel Moncastro (Akkerman, Белыгородъ, now Bilhorod-Dnistrovskyi) on the mouth of the river Dniester represented the main commercial centre for delivering goods from Western Europe to Crimea, Anatolia, and Constantinople, as well as importing "Tatar goods" to Hungary, Ruthenia and Poland. Charewiczowa, Handel, pp. 9–10.

104 Ibid., p. 10.

105 Privilegia civitatis Leopoliensis, no. 210. p. 520. The privilege given to Lviv merchants secured at the same time the prices for cloth imported to Moldavia, stating that it should be sold at the same price in Suceava as in Lviv.

106 *А то єсмы оучинили купцємъ господара нашего, короля полского, изъ оусєи рускои зємли и съ подолскои*. See: Privilegia civitatis Leopoliensis, p. 521.

107 Ibid.

108 H. Weczerka noted that the merchants of Lemberg (Lviv) were the only ones to establish a Kontor: "In Suczawa durften sie sogar ein Haus als Handelsniederlage errichten – der einzige Fall, wo in der Moldau ein Handelskontor fremder Kaufleute erwähnt wird." See: Weczerka, Herkunft, p. 509.

King, from Lviv and from the land of Great Duke Witold," merchants from Lviv were the only ones mentioned explicitly.[109] And again, in 1409, the same ruler addressed his privilege to the "*judges and jury and all the merchants of the town of Lemberg, present and future*".[110] Furthermore, in 1434, citizens of Lviv approached the Moldavian ruler Stephan, the successor of Alexander the Good, in order to have their privilege of 1408 confirmed.[111] The same procedure could be seen on similar occasions, when citizens of Lviv were involved in diplomatic relationships to secure better conditions for trade.[112] Thus, in addition to the staple right, diplomatic contacts were also undertaken by the Lviv town council in what appears to have been an effective strategy for securing beneficial trading conditions, or in other words, for ensuring predictability for their operations in a foreign land. In general, the town council of Lviv became the institution which dealt with different tasks related to long-distance trade on behalf of the urban community: organising trade and production in the town, supervising the market, controlling the execution of their privileges, conducting all necessary communication with rulers, other towns, etc.

What is more, the staple right in Lviv prompted further institutional developments with the aim to control the ever-growing flow of wares through the town and to ensure compliance with the norms and requirements expressed in the related privileges. Already the first known charter of 1379 implied a great variety and quantity of goods to be deposited in the town for the period of its staple right; since external merchants were forbidden to deal with each other and instead had to sell their goods to local citizens exclusively, a logical solution was to establish warehouses (known from later sources as *testitudines*) where goods would be stored and exchange controlled.[113] Such warehouses were closed with two keys, one of which remained in the hands of the goods' owner, the other kept by a local citizen appointed by the magistrate.[114] Additionally, in order to ensure that the rules and regulations of the staple right were observed, a special commission called *custodes depositorii* was elected annually from among the citizens of Lviv.[115] To the urban personnel serving the needs of the staple right also belonged an interpreter (called *tolmacz* in documents, which is related to the German *Dolmetscher*) who acted as

---

109 Privilegia civitatis Leopoliensis, no. 209, p. 518.

110 Ibid no. 211, pp. 522–523.

111 *iudicibus, iuratis ac universis mercatoribus civitatis Leonburgensis, presentibus et futuris, salutem et omnis boni continuum incrementum*. Ibid no.212, pp. 523–526.

112 Ibid no. 213, p. 526.

113 Moreover, the sources indicate that this institution also existed in Krakow, and that it became a model for Lviv: *Iuxta praxiam Civitatis nostrae Cracoviensis*. See: Lewicki, Historja handlu, p. 75.

114 Ibid., p. 35.

115 Ibid.

a mediator in dealing with foreign merchants who had to pay for their services.[116] Interpreters in medieval Lviv are attested in the early town books 1382–1389 (e. g., "*Atlabey tolmacz, Kaczarys tolmacz, Noradyn tolmacz*"), many of whom were Armenians living in town, being familiar with languages (like Kipchak) used by traders with oriental goods.[117] At the same time, as sources from later times reveal, there was an office of a "general interpreter", being appointed by the "royal representative" (*starosta*) in Lviv and sworn in by the town council. The holder was expected to have good knowledge of "oriental languages" (Kipchak, Greek, Armenian). His duties included control of "oriental foreigners visiting the towns, especially those located on the border in order to identify possible spies."[118]

All these changes, which took place in Lviv after the mid-fourteenth century, can be seen as the next major step in the development of institutions related to long-distance trade. Hence, did the emergence of these institutions lead to the growth of trade, or did increased trade volumes provide incentives to generate institutions that facilitated it?[119] In general, it is difficult to find an answer to this question.[120] Sources related to medieval Lviv do not allow for further speculations on the matter either. What remains indisputable is that "markets rest upon institutions", as Avner Greif put it,[121] and the growth of Lviv as a major commercial centre can only affirm this statement. The necessity to administer the staple right, and to ensure compliance, resulted in the further development of a legal and institutional framework within which long-distance trade had to be conducted, while the importance of policing the economy allowed diplomatic activities to expand the area of commercial influence. However, at the end of the medieval period, a growing administrative capacity and higher complexity of mechanisms for monopolisation, control, and coercion,

116 For more on the topic see: Janeczek, Tłumacz lwowski.

117 Czolowski, Najstarsza księga miejska.

118 Lewicki, Historja, p. 68.

119 This question was posed by Kallioinen, who also stressed that the shift in medieval economic history from business techniques or merchants' networks, for example, to institutions, has revived the debate related to the roots of early economic growth in Europe. See: Kallioinen, Long-Distance trade, p. 15. If we take this as a dichotomy (merchants' networks vs. institutions) it may possibly explain (or at least illustrate) the differing approaches of Hansa merchants in dealing with Novgorod on the one hand and Krakow on the other, as revealed by the earlier quoted document of the Hanserecesse. The case of Novgorod exemplifies operations based on a network of merchants, while the case of Krakow demonstrates an institution-based approach, thus showing the flexibility and adaptability of strategies the Hansa applied to its commercial relationships with different regions.

120 These causalities are inherently difficult to identify and even more difficult to prove. See: Kallioinen, Long-Distance trade, p. 15.

121 Greif, Commitment, , p. 727. He has suggested that the institutions created in medieval Europe, and especially those that supported long-distance trade, may explain the rise of the West.

demonstrated a tendency to halt the free flow of goods, to curb the market, and to block economic competition, which would become apparent in the early modern period.

6. Conclusion

The timespan described here, covering slightly more than 100 years (the late thirteenth century to the late fourteenth century) started with the development of a long-distance trading route crossing the lands of Galicia and Volhynia. This brought a profound transformation to the region which paralleled "the long 13th century" in Europe with its equally large-scale economic, demographic, and social changes. The shift of the axis that ran through Kyiv and along the Dnipro River to the west, to Galicia and Volhynia, also brought changes in conducting long-distance trade when organised groups of merchants started to act as a corporate body with "intercommunal conciliation mechanisms" to resolve conflicts. The end of the thirteenth century was the time when a land route connecting the Baltic and the Black Seas became frequented by merchants from Hansa towns. They contributed to the formation of urban communities in the main commercial centres like Wolodymyr and Lviv.

Urban institutions, first of all town councils and urban courts, facilitated and controlled trade, dealt with disagreements between individual merchants, and conducted diplomatic activities in commercial matters. Intercommunal conciliation mechanisms evolved to support trade between a large number of distant communities. Thus, the development of trade paralleled the emergence of fully-fledged towns under Magdeburg law (towns in a legal sense), which provided an appropriate legal and institutional framework familiar to merchants from other urban communities. This could be another piece of proof supporting the assumption that commerce was indeed the most dynamic sector of the economy, and that merchants had become the main promotors of change.

Concerning the early, formative years, it is difficult to talk about specific aspects of legal pluralism, since the lack of written sources from the late thirteenth and the first half of the fourteenth centuries does not allow for reconstructing a legal "landscape" in which merchants could have operated. Yet, the very existence of the early communities of foreign merchants – typically exempted from the local laws and customs – pointed to legal pluralism. We can only trace the main features of the new emerging order, of the above mentioned legal and institutional framework which was built with the help of granted privileges. These, however, were not aimed at individuals, but they became the foundation for a new type of social relationship, the new social group of free people organised in urban communities and dealing, inter alia, with matters pertinent to long-distance trade.

Once established, these communities and their urban institutions might start to search for the means to make further advances, privileges, and exceptions that could guarantee better conditions than those of neighbouring towns, and it is probably at this point that we can talk about the first traces of legal pluralism. Facing the growth of competition, urban governments tried to secure more comprehensive prerogatives, like the staple right, which enabled Lviv and Kraków to monopolise trade and to become the two most important commercial centres in the Polish kingdom.

That said, there was no uniformity in the application of staple rights in Polish towns. Every town possessing a staple had its own variation in terms of duration, nomenclature of goods, and exceptions from it, thus further contributing to legal plurality. Coercive power also differed from place to place depending on the political and economic weight of the particular town and the development of its institutions.

The period in question here thus demonstrates how the legal and institutional frameworks for long-distance trade emerged and matured, and – with increasing rivalry on the one hand and the growing political and economic weight of the main commercial centres on the other – started to show more exclusionist and restrictive arrangements. Merchants, however, did not operate in a vacuum. In order to promote change, they needed support from a ruler who was able to recognise their potential and to use it for the good of their land. As has been shown, many of the rulers from the Mongol/Tatar khans and the Ruthenian princes to the Polish kings were highly aware of the opportunities and perspectives opened by the emergence of a new commercial axis, which connected the Eurasian zone via the Black (and Mediterranean) Sea and the Baltic with Central and Northern Europe. The princes of Galicia and Volhynia looked for new ways to enlarge their monetary income, so it is no surprise that they welcomed merchants, offering them all the necessary support and compensation for eventual losses. For merchants in a foreign country, on the other hand, protection from a ruler, who at the same time could be a source *of* local law and someone who could offer immunity *from* local law, granting privileges and possessing the necessary power for its enforcement, would certainly be the easiest way to ensure predictability.

In the case of Lviv and its merchants, profits from cooperating with the central power (that is the king) becomes especially apparent when we take into account the staple right. If strictly observed, this instrument effectively interrupted the flow of long-distance trade, cutting it into isolated segments under the control of privileged urban communities such as Kraków or Lviv. It was the enforcement of Kraków's staple right that cut Hansa merchants from Toruń off from their sources of copper and oriental goods and thus ended their presence in the region. This would not have been possible without consequent policy by the Polish king. Generally speaking, the development of sophisticated and institutionalised ways of doing business, raising profits, and monopolising markets would not have been possible without the involvement of a central power, be it in the Mongolian steppe or in the towns of East-Central Europe. Most of the successful cases were achieved by systematic cooperation between a ruler and merchants. This cooperation was of paramount importance. In the end, both needed predictability and profitability.

Bibliography

Антонович, Володимир (ed.), Архив Юго-Западной России, издаваемый Временной комиссией для разбора древних актов [Archive of South-West Russia, published by the Temporary Commission for the Survey of Ancient Acts] Part 1, vol. 6: Acts of the Church and Religious Relationships (1322–1648), Kyiv 1883.

Антонович, Володимир (ed.), Архив Юго-Западной России, издаваемый Временной комиссией для разбора древних актов, [Archive of South-West Russia, published by the Temporary Commission for the Survey of Ancient Acts] Part 5, vol. 1: Acts of towns (1432–1798), Kyiv 1869.

Аванесов, Рубен, (ed.), Смоленские грамоты XIII–XIV веков [Smolensk Charters of the 13th–14th centuries], Moscow 1963.

Валк, Сергей, (ed), Грамоти великого Новгорода и Пскова, [Charters of Veliky (the Great) Novgorod and Pskov], Leningrad 1949.

Bielowski, August (ed.), Rocznik Traski [Traska's Chronicle], Monumenta Poloniae historica, [vol. 2], Lviv 1872.

Войтович, Лентій, Тевтонський орден у політиці Галицько-Волинського князівства [The Teutonic Order in the Politics of the Galicia-Volhynia Principality], in: Український історичний журнал 6 (2010), pp. 4–17.

Carr-Riegel, Leslie, Italian Traders in Poland 1300–1500, PhD Thesis, Budapest 2021.

Charewiczowa, Lucia, Handel Lwowa z Moldawją i Multanami w wiekach średnich [Trade of Lviv with Moldavia and Muntenia in the Middle Ages], Lviv 1924.

Ciociltan, Virgil, The Mongols and the Black Sea Trade in the Thirteenth and Fourteenth Centuries, Brill 2012.

Codex diplomaticus civitatis Cracoviensis 1257–1506, Franciszek Piekosiński (ed.), Krakow 1879.

Cristea, Ovidiu/Pilat, Liviu, From *Pax Mongolica* to *Pax Ottomanica*: War, Religion and Trade in the Northwestern Black Sea Region (14th–16th Centuries), Turnhout 2020.

Czaja, Roman, Economic, social and political aspects of the trade of the Teutonic Order in Prussia, in: Iris Shagrir/Benjamin Kedar/Michel Balard (eds.), Communicating the Middle Ages. Essays in Honor of Sophia Menache, London 2018, pp. 64–75.

Czolowski, Aleksander (ed.), Pomniki dziejowe Lwowa z archiwum miasta. T. 3: Księga przychodów i rozchodów miasta 1404–1414 [Historical records of Lviv from the urban archive. T. 3: The book of incomes and expenditures of the town 1404–1414], Lviv 1896.

Czolowski, Alexander (ed.), Pomniki dziejowe Lwowa z archiwum miasta. T. 1: Najstarsza księga miejska 1382–1389 [Historical records of Lviv from the urban archive. T. 1: The oldest town book 1382–1389], Lviv 1892.

Даркевич, Владислав, Художественное ремесло средневекового Запада (X–XIV вв.): по материалам раскопок в Восточной Европе [Applied arts of medieval West 10–14th century: after the materials of excavations in Eastern Europe], Moscow 2010.

Di Cosmo, Nicola, Black Sea Emporia and the Mongol Empire: A Reassessment of the *Pax Mongolica*, in: Journal of the Economic and Social History of the Orient, vol. 53: Empires and Emporia: The Orient in World Historical Space and Time, 1/2 (2010), pp. 83–108.

Dollinger, Phillipe, The German Hansa, London 1970.

Franklin, Simon/Shepard, Jonathan, The Emergence of Rus 750–1200, London 1996.

Franklin, Simon, Writing, Society and Culture in Early Rus, c.950–1300, Cambridge 2002.

Fontes historiae Magni Ducatus Lithuaniae. (http://starbel.by/dok/d048.htm Last accessed 09/21/2024)

Goetz, Leopold, Deutsch-russische Handelsverträge des Mittelalters, Hamburg 1916.

Greif, Avner, Commitment, Coercion, and Markets: The Nature and Dynamics of Institutions Supporting Exchange, in: Claude Ménard/Mary M. Shirley (eds.), Handbook of New Institutional Economics, New York 2005, pp. 727–786.

Hammel-Kiesow, Rolf, Die Hanse, Munich 2014.

Heyd, Willhelm, Histoire du commerce du Levant au moyen âge, [vol. 2], Leipzig 1923.

Höhlbaum, Konstantin, Hansisches Urkundenbuch, [vol. 2], Halle 1879.

Höhlbaum, Konstantin, Hansisches Urkundenbuch, [vol. 3], 1343–1360, Halle 1882.

Isenburg, Wilhelm Karl von, Stammtafeln zur Geschichte der Europäischen Staaten, [vol. 1], Marburg 1953.

Janeczek, Andrzej (ed.), Album civium Leopoliensium. Registers of admissions to the municipal law in Lviv 1388–1783, vol. 1, Poznan 2005.

Janeczek, Andrzej, Tłumacz lwowski. Z zagadnień komunikacji językowej w wieloetnicznym mieście późnego średniowiecza [Lviv interpreter. Aspects of linguistic communication in a multi-ethnic town of the late Middle Ages], in: A. Karpiński, E. Opaliński, T. Wiślicz (eds.), Gospodarka, społeczeństwo, kultura w dziejach nowożytnych. Studia ofiarowane Pani Profesor Marii Boguckiej. Warsaw, 2010, pp. 203–222.

Jasiński, Tomasz, Handel miedzią węgierską a restytucja rządów Władysława Łokietka w Polsce (1304–1312) [Hungarian copper trade and the restoration of Władysław Lokietek rule in Poland (1304–1312)], in: Roczniki Historyczne, LXXXIV (2018), pp. 116–117.

Kallioinen, Mika, "Long-Distance Trade in Medieval Europe", in: Oxford Research Encyclopedia of Economics and Finance (doi: https://doi.org/10.1093/acrefore/9780190625979.013.558).

Kapral, Myron, Lviv and Towns of the Moldavian Principality in the Second Half of the 15th Century: Economic and Social Contacts, in: Historia urbana (Sibiu), 29 (2021), pp. 5–20.

Kapral, Myron, Privilegia civitatis Leopoliensis XIV–XVIII saec., Lviv 2010.

КАЗАКОВА, Наталия, Начальный текст новгородско-немецких договоров XII–XV вв [Initial text of Novgorodian-German agreements of the 12–15th centuries], in: Вспомогательные исторические дисциплины. Leningrad 1974, vol. 6, pp. 161–175.

Klemenski, Marcin A., Przywilej Kazimierza Wielkiego o wolnym handlu z Rusią dla Świdnicy z 1345 r. [The privilege of free trade with Rus' for Świdnica of Casimir the Great from 1345], in: V. Nagirnyy (ed.), Colloquia Russica. Series I, vol. 9, Rus' and Poland (10th–14th centuries), Krakow 2019, pp. 321–327.

Koppmann, Karl (ed.), Hanserecesse Abt. 1, Band 3: 1387–1390, Leipzig 1875.

Kutrzeba, Stanisław, Handel Krakowa w wiekach średnich na tle stosunków handlowych [Trade of Krakow in the Middle Ages on the background of commercial relationships], Kraków 1902.

Купчинський, Олег (ed), Акти та документи Галицько-Волинського князівства XIII – першої половини XIV століть [Acts and documents of Galician-Volynian Principality of the 13th–first half of the 14th centuries], Lviv 2004.

Lewicki, Stanisław, Historja handlu w Polsce na tle przywilejów handlowych; prawo składu [History of trade in Poland on the background of commercial privileges; staple right], Warszawa 1920.

Lewicki, Stanislaw, Prawo składu w Polsce (Staple right in Poland), Krakow 1910.

Liske, Xawery (ed) Akta grodzkie i ziemskie z czasów Rzeczypospolitej Polskiej z archiwum tak zwanego bernardyńskiego we Lwowie, [Acts of the castle and land from the times of the Republic of Poland from the so-called Bernardine archives in Lviv] T.2, Lviv 1870.

Lopez, Robert, The commercial revolution of the Middle Ages, 950–1350, Cambridge 1976.

Lütge, Friedrich, Strukturwandlungen im ostdeutschen und osteuropäischen Fernhandel des 14. bis 16. Jahrhunderts, Munich 1964.

Magdanski, Marian, Handel Torunia na morzu w wiekach średnich [Trade of Toruń on the sea in the Middle Ages], Poznań 1935.

Mysliwski, Grzegorz, Wrocław w przestrzeni gospodarczej Europy (XIII–XV wiek). Centrum czy peryferie? [Wroclaw in the economic space of Europe (13th–15th centuries) A centre or a periphery?], Wroclaw 2009.

Myśliński, Kazimierz, Lublin a handel Wrocławia z Rusią w XIV i XV w. [Lublin and the trade of Wroclaw with Rus in the 14 and 15th centuries], in: Rocznik Lubelski 3 (1960), pp. 5–36.

Naismith, Rory, Money and Coinage in the Middle Ages, Turnhout 2018.

Noonan, Thomas, The Monetary history of Kiev in the pre-Mongol Period, in: Harvard Ukrainian Studies Vol. 11, no. 3/4 (1987), pp. 384–443.

Пещак, Марія (ed.), Пам'ятки української мови. Грамоти XIV ст., [Vestiges of the Ukrainian language: Charters of the 14th century], Kyiv 1974.

Полное собрание русских летописей, издаваемое Археографической комиссиею, [The Complete Collection of Russian Chronicles published by the Archeographical commission], vol.2. Ипатьевская летопись [Hypatian Chronicle], St Petersburg 1908.

Pipes, Richard, Russia under the Old regime, New York 1974.

Pirenne, Henri, Economic and social history of medieval Europe, London 1936.

Radvan, Laurentiu, On the Medieval Urban Economy in Wallachia, in: Analele Stiintifice ale Universitatii "Alexandru Ioan Cuza" din Iasi, 56 (2009), pp. 489–501.

Raffensperger, Christian, Reimagining Europe. Kievan Rus' in the Medieval World, 988–1146, Harvard 2012.

РОВЕНЧАК, Іван, Львів на найдавніших географічних картах [Lviv on the oldest geographical maps] Вісник геодезії та картографії, 2 (2013), pp. 45–49.

Rohdewald, Stefan, "Vom Polocker Venedig". Kollektives Handeln sozialer Gruppen einer Stadt zwischen Ost- und Mitteleuropa (Mittelalter, frühe Neuzeit, 19. Jh. bis 1914), Stuttgart 2005.

Sattler, Karl, Handelsrechnungen des Deutschen Ordens, Leipzig 1887.

Tolochko, Oleksiy, Kievan Rus around the Year 1000, in: Europe around the Year 1000, Przemysław Urbańczyk (ed.), Warsaw 2001, pp. 123–140.

Толочко, Алексей, Очерки начальной Руси [Essays on early Rus'], Kyiv/St Petersburg 2015.

Weczerka, Hugo, Hansische Handelsstraßen, Atlas, Köln 1968.

Weczerka, Hugo, Herkunft und Volkszugehörigkeit der Lemberger Neubürger im 15. Jahrhundert, in: Zeitschrift für Ostforschung 4 (1955), pp. 507–530.

Wubs-Mrozewicz, Justyna/Jenks, Stuart (eds.), The Hanse in Medieval and Early Modern Europe, Leiden 2013.

Wróbel, Darius, Kwestia krzyżacka a wschodnia polityka Kazimierza Wielkiego po roku 1343 [The Teutonic Order question and eastern politics of Kazimir the Great after the year 1343], in: Średniowiecze Polskie i Powszechne, 4 (2007), pp. 136–187.

Хорошкевич, Анна, Договоры Полоцка 1405–1406 гг. как источник по истории его внешней торговли и торговой политики [Polotsk agreements of 1405–1406 as a source for the history of its foreign trade and commercial politics], in: Археографический ежегодник за 1962 год, Moscow 1963, pp. 79–87.

Хорошкевич, Анна, Из истории русско-немецких отношений XIII в. [From the history of Russian-German relations in the 13th century], in: Исторические записки, 78 (1965), pp. 219–233.

Хорошкевич, Анна, ed., Полоцкие грамоты XIII – начала XVI в [Charters of Polotsk 13–early 16th centuries], vol. 2, Moscow 2015.

Яковенко, Наталя/Кравченко, Володимир (eds), Торгівля на Україні XIV-середина XVII століття. Волинь і Наддніпрянщина: актові джерела [Trade in Ukraine 14th–mid-17th century. Volynia and Dnipro region: documentary sources], Kyiv 1990.

Янин, Валентин, Очерки истории средневекового Новгорода, [Essays on the history of medieval Novgorod], Moscow 2008.

Zientara, Benedykt, The Sources and Origin of the "German Law" (*Ius Teutonicum*) in the Context of the Settlement Movement in Western and Central Europe (11th to 12th centuries), in: Acta Poloniae Historica, 107 (2013), pp. 179–216.

Alexandr Osipian

Contract Enforcement and Predictability in Long-distance Trade

Armenian Merchant Networks between the Middle East and Eastern Europe, 1350–1650

1. Introduction

For centuries Armenian merchant networks successfully managed long-distance trade in a situation of legal pluralism – between countries with different legal cultures being frequently at war with each other. The history of the Armenian trading diaspora is different from other Armenian diasporas. In the Early Middle Ages many Armenian noblemen and common people were forcefully removed from their country under the Byzantine Empire and settled in Asia Minor and the Balkan provinces. Meanwhile, the twentieth-century Armenian diaspora was caused by the persecution and extermination of Armenians in the Ottoman Empire in 1894–1896 and 1915–1922. Medieval Armenia lost its independence twice – in 1045 when the Armenian Bagratid Kingdom collapsed and again in 1375 when the Armenian Kingdom of Cilicia was conquered by Mameluke Egypt. Since then, Armenia has been divided by competing emperies. On the other hand, Armenia was at the crossroads of the main trade routes between East and West. Armenian merchants were engaged in international trade, competing and cooperating with Genoese and Venetian merchants. However, while these merchants were supported by their maritime republics, the Armenian trading diaspora lacked any such support. After the loss of statehood in the fourteenth century, Armenian merchants settled along the main trade routes and established their communities there.

From the thirteenth to the seventeenth century, networks of Armenian merchant communities gradually expanded as far as Madras, Calcutta, and the Philippines in the east, and Venice, Marseille, Livorno, and Amsterdam in the west. Trading networks of stateless Armenian merchants elaborated their own system of commercial jurisdiction and authentication of commercial documents. The case of Armenian merchant networks in Poland-Lithuania is particularly remarkable. In comparison with many absolutist monarchies, the late medieval Kingdom of Poland and early modern Polish-Lithuanian Commonwealth escaped processes of centralisation and unification of the judicial system. Every social estate and ethno-confessional community in the country was allowed its own body of law and court system.

The great variety of jurisdictions stimulated legal pluralism and affected contract enforcement, particularly in international trade.

In the 1990s, legal pluralism became associated with an emphasis on the instability of the legal order and a "constructionist" understanding of multi-centric legal systems as contingent products of conflict.[1] In legal anthropology, a situation of legal pluralism is considered as "the omnipresent, normal situation in human society" while legal centralism is treated as "a myth, an ideal, a claim, an illusion".[2] The change in perspective from "above" to "below" reveals "[...] that the 'law' which is actually effective on the 'ground floor' of society is the result of enormously complex and usually in practice unpredictable patterns of competition, interaction, negotiation, isolationism, and the like".[3]

Armenian communities in Poland-Lithuania enjoyed the highest degree of judicial autonomy compared to the Armenian diaspora in other countries. Armenians settled between the Carpathian Mountains and Dnipro River in the principalities of Galicia (*Ruthenia Rubra* or *Ruś Czerwona* that is Red Ruthenia), Podolia, Volhynia, and Kyiv, in the western and central parts of present-day Ukraine. From the 1340s to the 1360s, these lands were conquered and incorporated into the Kingdom of Poland and the Grand Duchy of Lithuania (these two states formed a dynastic union from 1385 and a parliamentary union from 1569 onwards).

The issue of Armenian law in the Ukrainian parts of premodern Poland has a rich historiography. Relations in the triangle between king, municipal authorities (city magistrates), and the Armenian community have already been examined in earlier works.[4] These have been based primarily on research into royal privileges and decrees issued to resolve conflicts between city magistrates, who had adopted Magdeburg Law (and represented the dominant Catholic "nation") on the one hand, and Armenian communities on the other. The functioning of Armenian law in Poland-Lithuania has therefore received a fair amount of attention. However, historians have largely disregarded individual uses of justice. This omission also characterises the research of the past few decades. For instance, the Ukrainian historian Yaroslav Dashkevitch[5] interpreted the jurisdictional conflicts between the city magistrates and Armenian communities in the context of such topoi as the "Polish Catholic expansion", "assimilation", and "denationalisation", in which the

1 Tamanaha, Folly.

2 Griffiths, Legal pluralism, pp. 4 and 39.

3 Ibid., p. 39.

4 Bischoff, Urkunden zur Geschichte der Armenier in Lemberg; Gromnicki, Ormjanie; Łoziński, Patrycjat i mieszczaństwo; Balzer, Sądownictwo ormiańskie; von Brünneck, Magdeburger Recht; Matwijowski, Prawo; Oleś, Armenian Law; Oleś, Casimir The Great.

5 Dashkevitch, Armenian Law; Dashkevitch, Armianskaya koloniya; Dashkevitch, Armianskoe samoupravlenie; Dashkevitch, Ustav armianskoi.

"national" was understood in primordial terms. The accounts of the Polish scholars Mirosława Zakrzewska-Dubasowa[6] and Artur Korobowicz[7] on Armenian court practices in the private town of Zamość also largely omitted the individual strategies employed by Armenian litigants. The Polish historian Krzysztof Stopka[8] meanwhile examined the reduction and decline of Armenian judicial autonomy. He explained such reduction largely through cultural categories – such as the attractiveness of Polish high culture and the readiness of local Armenians to adopt it.[9] In the recent works of the Ukrainian Myron Kapral[10] and the German Jürgen Heyde,[11] the judicial expansion of the city magistrate is considered as the only explanation for the competence reduction of the Armenian court in Lviv. In short, historiography has thus far considered the Armenian urban "nations" as homogeneous and coherent communities opposing the jurisdictional interventions of the city magistrates in order to protect their national or religious identity, and/or economic interests.

Thus, the issue of Armenian judicial autonomy has been examined through prisms of legal and cultural history and such concepts as identity-making, acculturation, and assimilation. Consequently, the issue of how legal pluralism affected predictability in long-distance trade has been left out of the picture. This chapter intends to address this missing link by examining the causal relationships between legal pluralism and contract enforcement in long-distance trade.

Accordingly, this chapter aims to uncover the agency of Armenian merchants operating their transnational long-distance trade in a pluralistic legal environment, dealing with heterogenous authorities and merchants of other legal statuses, negotiating their legal framing, and choosing patterns of behaviour to ensure contract enforcement.

The chapter starts with an overview of the complexity of the late medieval and early modern Polish legal system – particularly concerning the application of the so-called "German" or "Magdeburg" law in the multi-ethnic and multi-confessional cities of the eastern provinces of the kingdom. It analyses how Armenian law courts coexisted with the dominant courts of German/Magdeburg law through comparison of models developed in two royal cities (Lviv and Kamianets-Podilskyi) and a private one (Zamość). It then examines contract enforcement in a pluralistic legal environment through an analysis of corporate responsibility for debts, jurisdictional conflicts between Armenian and municipal Magdeburg courts, commercial disputes

6 Zakrzewska-Dubasowa, Organizacja gminy ormiańskiej; Zakrzewska-Dubasowa, Ormianie Zamojscy; Zakrzewska-Dubasowa, Ormiańska Temida.

7 Korobowicz, Sąd ormiański; Korobowicz, Elementy.

8 Stopka, Ormianie; Stopka, Interakcje; Stopka, Ormianie.

9 Stopka, Migracje; Stopka, Nasza polska; Stopka, Religious Culture.

10 Kapral, Natsionalni; Kapral, Pravovoe; Kapral, Legal Regulation; Kapral, L'viv.

11 Heyde, Polityka Rady; Heyde, Armenier.

at the fairs, as well as contract enforcement in times of war and political turmoil. It goes on to examine how contract enforcement was affected by the interventions of powerful patrons – monarchs, diplomats, and dignitaries – into legal trials. It then investigates the exterritorial jurisdiction of Armenian caravans operating on trade routes between Poland and the Ottoman Empire with its main focus on the office of the Armenian caravanbashi and his judicial power. The final section focuses on how an ecclesiastical institution – the Armenian Consistory Court of Lviv – was used by foreign Armenian merchants for contract enforcement and to solve other commercial issues.

2. Armenian Courts and Multiple Jurisdictions in the Kingdom of Poland

The remarkable complexity of the early modern Polish legal system was informed by at least three historic changes that can be traced back to the Late Middle Ages. First, between the fourteenth and the sixteenth century, territorial expansion resulted in the legal autonomy of Prussia, Courland, and Livonia as well as in the maintenance of Ruthenian law applied by the Orthodox Ruthenians in the Polish eastern provinces – the region of present-day Ukraine. Second, the suburbs of royal cities became the domains of noblemen, bishops, monasteries, and the royal governor (*starosta*, *capitaneus*), independent of the city magistrate and generally known as *jurydyka*. The residents of these domains/*jurydyka*s were under the jurisdiction of Polish or Terrestrial Law (*prawo ziemskie*) – if they were subjects of a nobleman or governor – or under the jurisdiction of Church Law – if they were subjects of a bishop or monastery. Third, bodies of foreign law were imported during the thirteenth and fourteenth centuries concomitant with the influx of foreign settlers, including Armenians, Germans, Jews, Karaites, and Vlachs. These groups were granted legal autonomy by the Polish kings and later by the aristocrats in their domains. Since the invited German Catholic settlers invested hugely in the economic and the legal transformation of urban life in late medieval Poland, German Law (*Jus Theutonicum*) or Magdeburg Law (*Magdeburger Recht*, *Jus Magdeburgensis*) became the dominant legal model in royal and private cities alike. Municipal law in Poland was thus mostly based on the code of law of the city of Magdeburg in Saxony that had been compiled in 1188, and the Saxon Mirror (*Sachsenspiegel*, *Speculum Saxonum*) that had been composed between 1220 and 1235 by Eike von Repkow, a juryman (*Schöffe*) in Saxony.[12]

Initially, Magdeburg law was granted to German settlers in order to protect them from the alleged excesses and corrupt practices of local authorities. Their

---

12 Bily, Carls and Gönczi, Sächsisch-magdeburgisches Recht.

judicial autonomy was to guarantee them comfortable conditions in the foreign environment and, thereby, help to attract more settlers.[13] At the same time, the German settlers brought with them the model of the homogeneous Catholic city community with a Jewish ghetto on the outskirts. In the cities with a large Catholic burgher community, they tried to treat non-Catholics in the same way as they were accustomed to treat Jews, that is, as a subordinate group excluded from the burghers' community and, therefore, from the economic and social privileges granted by the sovereign.[14] As will be seen, however, the sovereign granted judicial autonomy to non-Catholic communities as well, including Armenians, in exchange for diplomatic services and loans.

In the late thirteenth and fourteenth centuries Armenian merchant communities emerged in the lands of present-day Ukraine in the cities of Lviv, Lutsk, Volodymyr, Kyiv, and Kamianets-Podilskyi.[15] By the turn of the seventeenth century, the Armenian communities in Lutsk and Volodymyr had totally vanished, and in Kyiv there were only eight families left, while in Lviv and Kamianets-Podilskyi they constituted between about 7 and 30 percent of the residents respectively. At that time, numerous Armenian communities also emerged in the private towns of the aristocracy and by the mid-seventeenth century, the Armenian diaspora in the Kingdom of Poland could be estimated at 7,000 persons.[16]

Armenian communities were granted judicial autonomy for two reasons: because of distinctiveness of the Armenian Church, and for the various services Armenian merchants provided to the Polish Crown. In the Christological disputes on the divine and human nature of Christ, the Armenian Church follows the Monophysite doctrine believing solely in the divine. Since the Fourth Ecumenical Council of Chalcedon in 451 rejected the Monophysite doctrine,[17] both the Greek Orthodox (Byzantine) and Roman Catholic Churches consider Armenians to be heretics[18] – followers of the heresy of Eutyches and Dioscorus.[19] However, in Poland and the Grand Duchy of Lithuania, Armenians were protected by the monarchs and dignitaries in exchange for diplomatic and commercial services. Armenian merchants frequented the markets of the Golden Horde, the Ottoman Empire, Persia, and later the Crimean Khanate, providing the Polish nobility with fashionable oriental

13 Janeczek, Kolonisationsströmungen; Janeczek, Modernisierung.

14 Charewiczowa, Ograniczenia; Janeczek, Exceptis schismaticis; Janeczek, Żydzi; Janeczek, Listy.

15 Osipian, Armenian Diasporas.

16 Osipian, Long distance trade.

17 Frend, Monophysite Movement.

18 Grumel, Les invectives; Garitte, Les écrits; Ermilov, Satanic Heresy; Sharf, Byzantine Orthodoxy; Nasturel, L'attitude; Najdenova, Anti-Armenian Polemics.

19 For instance, Prochovicius, Relatio, p. 88.

luxury.[20] Because of their fluency in Kipchak,[21] the language of their domestic and business conversations, Armenian merchants were in royal service as royal interpreters, diplomats, and spies.

Armenian communities were dominated by the merchant majority accompanied by clergymen and some artisans. Armenian merchants ennobled for their diplomatic services left the community for the noble estate, though many maintained their religious affiliation with the Armenian Church.

Delineation of Armenian communities from outside – in the host society – was multifaceted and distinctive in the case of every social estate. The king and royal court considered Armenians as a fiscal group responsible for payment of collective taxes. It is also reflected in the interstate treaties, for instance, disputes over collective responsibility of Armenian merchants for debts abroad, accordingly, the property of Armenian merchants who died abroad were to be handed over to other members of the network present at the site.[22] The royal chancellery and dignitaries considered Armenians as a helpful professional corporation whose members were employed as royal envoys, interpreters, infiltrators, and intermediaries in diplomatic relations with the Ottoman Empire, Persia, and the Crimean Khanate. The nobility perceived Armenians as a professional corporation supplying noblemen with oriental goods. This attitude is well-reflected in the Polish legislation passed by the nobility's deputies in the Diet (*Sejm*) and local assemblies (*sejmiki*). For instance, the imported oriental goods were defined as either "Armenian goods" or "Turkish goods", and the toll on cash exports from Poland to the Ottoman Empire was labelled as the "Armenian toll from [exported] money", while the goods manufactured by local artisans in oriental style were named "Armenian work". The Polish Catholic clergy simultaneously considered Armenian communities as suspect heretics enjoying commercial privileges in "*the lands of infidels*."[23] Catholic patricians and burghers considered the wealthy Armenian merchants as competitors in commerce and social advancement whose religious and ethnic distinctiveness was a good pretext to restrict the autonomy of the Armenian community.[24]

Meanwhile, Armenian merchants considered themselves as simultaneously a privileged professional corporation and a religious community. The membership in this merchant corporation implied a high entry tax in terms of financial capital and commercial knowledge. The newcomers – foreign Armenians – had to be adopted

---

20 Osipian, The Ottoman.

21 For more details, see: Macler, Rapport. Deny, L'armeno-coman;. Dachkevytch, Armeno-Kipchaks.

22 Panaite, Trade and Merchants, p. 268; Ivanova, Foreigners, pp. 685–686, 691; Faroqhi, Trade; Faroqhi, Religious Interactions.

23 Solicovii, Commentarius brevis, p. 108.

24 Osipian, Between Mercantilism.

into the "Armenian nation" in a given city and only after applying to the city council and obtaining citizenship there. In order to be recorded in the special register book of the Armenian Nation Brotherhood, an applicant had to pay to the public treasury a sum which varied from 15[25] to 150 Polish zlotys.[26] The applicant was only then accompanied to the city council and represented there by at least two recommenders. Ordinarily the recommenders were Armenian jurymen/elders.[27]

Thus, being formally a confessional community and legally an urban "nation", the Armenian community could be compared with a merchant guild monopolising trade between Poland-Lithuania and the Middle East. However, the Armenian communities of Lviv and Kamianets had much more power than an average merchant guild in Europe. Their interests in the Ottoman Empire were represented by Armenian *caravanbashi* whose office could be compared with that of the French, Dutch, and English consul or the Genoese and Venetian *bailo* (Poland-Lithuania never had a permanent representative at the sultan's court). Furthermore, these two communities elected an Armenian archbishop of Lviv while their elders, along with Armenian clergymen, adjudicated cases in an Armenian Consistory Court there.

Since the Late Middle Ages, urban communities in Poland had adopted a model of self-government generally known as German Law – with a judge (Latin *advocatus*, German *Vogt*, Polish *wójt*) who presided over the law court ordinarily consisting of 6 to 12 jurymen (Latin *seniores*, *scabini*, Polish *radni*, *starsi*, *ławnicy*). At the same time, Armenian courts in Poland operated in accordance with the Codex of Armenian Law (*Datastanagirk*) composed in 1184 in Greater Armenia by the religious scholar (*vardapet*) Mkhitar Gosh (c.1130–1213).[28] Later, the Mkhitar law code was adapted to the judicial realities of the stateless Armenian diaspora. Its Latin translation – *Statuta iuris armenici* – was confirmed with some changes and comments by the Polish King Sigismund I in 1519.[29] The procedural code of the Armenian courts was then codified in Polish in 1604.[30]

Although the various Armenian communities used the same court model and law code, there were differences in their jurisdiction between royal and private

---

25 Dzieje Ormian lwowskich od roku 1649 aż do r. 1713, in: Dział Rękopisów Biblioteki Zakładu Narodowego im. Ossolińskich, Wrocław. Sygnatura oryginału: 1646/II, fol. 64.

26 Ibid, fol. 38.

27 Osipian, Long distance trade, pp. 169–171.

28 Gosh, The Lawcode.

29 Kutrzeba, Datastanagirk; von Brünneck, Magdeburger Recht; Lewicki and Kohnowa, La version; Statut ormiański w zatwierdzeniu Zygmunta I z roku 1519, ed. by Balzer; Kapral, Pryvilei natsionalnykh hromad mista Lvova (XIV–XVIII st.); Garkavets, Kypchakskoe pismennoye nasledie.

30 Balzer, Porządek sadów i spraw prawa ormiańskiego z r. 1604.

towns as well as among royal cities, which could be explained by the relative balance of power between the dominant Catholic community and non-Catholic ones.[31]

2.1 Lviv

The royal city of Lviv represents a case where the city council and the Armenian community repeatedly clashed over their respective jurisdictions. As will be seen, the king was an important actor in these conflicts, whose interventions were largely informed by his own fiscal or political interests. These conflicts and the way they were resolved were decisive for Armenian law and legal practice. The analysis also indicates how decisions by ordinary Armenians were an important factor in the clashes between the city court and the Armenian court. The problematic functioning and limited jurisdiction of the Armenian court often induced Armenian litigants to prefer the Magdeburg court, which in turn aggravated the position of the Armenian court.

After the Polish conquest of Lviv in 1349, local townspeople of German descent (*cives catholici*) became the dominant community, converting Lviv to Lemberg. They constituted the city community (*civitas*) and were granted Magdeburg Law by the Polish King Casimir III in 1356. All members of the city magistrate were Catholics. The rights of other urban "nations" – Armenians, Jews, Tatars, Saracens, and Ruthenians – each had their own separate law courts which were guaranteed and confirmed by the king.[32] In accordance with a royal privilege of 1356, non-Catholic inhabitants had the right to choose between their "national" and the Magdeburg law court. The jurisdiction of the Armenian court headed by an Armenian *wójt* was, however, rather limited. All cases between Armenians and noblemen were judged in the governor's court (*jus castrensis*) in accordance with Polish law (*jus Polonicum*).[33] Many cases between Armenian defendants and Catholic, Orthodox, and Jewish plaintiffs were heard in the city court in accordance with Magdeburg law.[34] Cases were even judged in the city court when both litigants were Armenians. Apart from the Armenian civil and criminal court, there was the Armenian Consistory Court, presided over by the Armenian archbishop and consisting of an archpriest, the clergymen, and the elders of the Armenian civil court. It judged cases of blasphemy and sacrilege, of marriage within forbidden degrees (*khas ev chekhas*) and marriage settlements (*krorenk*), of last wills and inheritance, all in accordance with Armenian canon law.[35] It had jurisdiction over

31 For more details see: Osipian, Legal pluralism.

32 Kapral, Pryvilei mista Lvova (XIV–XVIII st.), pp. 27–28.

33 Balzer, Sądownictwo ormiańskie, pp. 69–74.

34 Ibid., pp. 74–76.

35 Schütz, Ehekontrakte.

all Armenian communities in the kingdom. As will be seen, the parallel existence of these two Armenian courts created opportunities for local and foreign Armenians to avoid some restrictive regulations imposed by the royal and city authorities.

According to Oswald Balzer, Armenians preferred the city court in many cases because the Armenian court had too narrow a jurisdiction – the latter judged cases between Armenians only – and because the very legal status of the Armenian judge (*wójt*) was ambiguous since this office was absent from the privilege of 1356.[36] Some Armenians tried to become full members of the German/Magdeburg community, because their economic rights were restricted and because they were burdened with taxes from which the Catholic burghers were exempt. However, only a few among them succeeded, since the city magistrate reserved such privileged status for Catholics.[37] Only very few Armenians were granted the full Magdeburg status by royal decrees for services and loans they had provided to the king.[38]

By the royal decree of 1469, the office of Armenian *wójt* in Lviv was abolished and the Armenian court sessions were henceforth to be presided over by the city *wójt*, that is, by a Catholic.[39] In accordance with the royal decrees of 1476 and of 1510, the jurisdiction of the Armenian courts was further reduced: cases of manslaughter, bloody and bruised wounds, larceny, and immovable Armenian property (the so-called "four articles"), henceforth fell under the jurisdiction of the city jury, which had to try these cases according to Magdeburg Law.[40]

In accordance with the Armenian law code of 1519, article 120, the Armenian court was supposed to consist of twelve elders, but the presence of at least four elders and the *wójt* sufficed to issue a verdict.[41] In accordance with "the procedural code of Armenian court and law" (1604) two elders and the *wójt* were enough for cases below ten marcs.[42] Yet bringing together even this reduced number of jurymen appears to have been a complicated task, as merchants, involved in long-distance trade, annually spent several months on commercial travels.

The problematic functioning of the Armenian court, which was partly owing to actions by the city council, probably caused many Armenians to have an ambivalent

36 Balzer, Sądownictwo ormiańskie, pp. 77–81.

37 Even Armenians who became citizens (*concives noster*) of Lviv were not granted tax exemptions that *cives catholici* enjoyed. Only a few Armenians were adopted to the Magdeburg community, mainly those who converted to Catholicism – thus leaving the Armenian community – and those granted privilege by the king. The key difference was tax exemption. Both the king and the municipal authorities were interested to keep Armenians paying taxes.

38 Ibid., pp. 69–74.

39 Ibid., p. 137.

40 Kapral, Pryvilei natsionalnykh hromad, pp. 147–149, 169–172.

41 Ibid., p. 217.

42 Porządek sadów i spraw, p. 28.

attitude towards their own forum, thereby encouraging them to bring their cases before the Magdeburg court.

Finally, in the mid-seventeenth century, two royal decrees granted those Armenians who adopted the religious union with the Roman Church equal rights with Catholic burghers.[43] In the next decade, the most prominent Armenians in Lviv were ennobled by King Jan Casimir (r. 1648–1668) and left the Armenian "nation."[44] By the late seventeenth century, the Armenian court had lost most of its judicial functions. It was finally abolished in 1784 by the Austrian authorities, after Lviv became part of the Habsburg province of *Galizien* in 1772.[45]

2.2 Kamianets-Podilskyi

Kamianets-Podilskyi represents a royal town with a specific modus vivendi between its Catholic-Polish and its Armenian communities. It was first granted German Law in 1374 when it belonged to the Grand Duchy of Lithuania. Then, in 1432, the city was incorporated into the Kingdom of Poland. There were three autonomous communities from the fifteenth century onwards: Catholic, Armenian, and Ruthenian-Orthodox, all of which had their own courts and city halls. However, there was only one burgomaster and city council, namely the Catholic-Polish one.[46] The jurisdiction of the communities' ("nations") law courts included both civil and criminal cases. In 1460, King Casimir IV (r. 1447–1492) granted Armenians the right to elect their *wójt*.[47] The competence of the Armenian law court comprised cases in which both litigants were Armenians, or where an Armenian was the defendant.[48] In the mid-sixteenth century, the city magistrate tried to extend its jurisdiction over the Armenian community. In 1550, King Sigismund II (r. 1548–1572) subsequently ordered that when an Armenian had violated the rights of the city or of a burgher of the Magdeburg "nation," he had to be detained by the Armenian *wójt*. He then had to be judged before a court composed of the Magdeburg *wójt* as well as the Armenian *wójt*. If they could not reach a compromise, the case should be referred to the royal court.[49]

43 Kapral, Pryvilei natsionalnyh hromad, p. 334.
44 Osipian, Historical Identity, p. 75.
45 Kapral, Funktsionuvannia organiv, p. 120.
46 Król-Mazur and Stopka, Die Stadt; Stopka, Interakcje etniczne; Heyde, Kamieniec.
47 Stopka, Interakcje etniczne, p. 98.
48 Ibid., pp. 98–99.
49 Ibid., p. 100.

A book of records has been preserved that shows which cases were heard in the years 1559–1567.[50] The records include not only civil and criminal cases but also claims, contracts, and testaments. Most records related to debt cases. Secondly, there were cases based on quarrels and scuffles. A third group constituted sale and purchase contracts and partnership agreements. In addition, the Armenian court was the first instance to which the local, non-resident, and foreign Armenians applied to be granted citizenship.

As a judicial infrastructure, the Armenian court in Kamianets-Podilskyi had at its disposal the city hall and the gaol in its basement, while it hired the officers of justice – or at least some of them – from the Magdeburg court. For instance, in 1577 the Armenian court employed Stas, the Magdeburg court bailiff, as marshal for a yearly salary of 14 florins.[51] The absence of numerous jurisdictional conflicts suggests that in Kamianets-Podilskyi, a kind of modus vivendi had been found. The Armenian court functioned there till 1791, when this particular municipal legal system was abolished by the Polish Diet.

2.3 Zamość

Zamość represents a third type of town with an Armenian community, notably, a private town where the Armenian community enjoyed a fair amount of autonomy, yet in actual practice cooperated successfully with the Polish municipal authorities. When the Chancellor of Poland Jan Zamoyski founded the town of Zamość (1580) in his private domains, he invited Catholics, Armenians, Greeks, Scots, and Sephardic Jews to settle there. Zamoyski granted the Armenian community the privilege to establish its own court on 9 January 1589.[52] In their records, the Armenians of Zamość emphasised their model of self-government and a justice system they had adopted from their compatriots in Kamianets-Podilskyi. Nonetheless, since Zamość was a private town, the Armenians had to appeal not to the royal court or royal governor but to the appeals court (*Trybunał Zamojski*) or court of the town owner.[53] The same model was employed in other Armenian communities founded in private towns during the seventeenth century.

In contrast to the royal cities of Lviv and Kamianets-Podilskyi, Zamość demonstrated a remarkable absence of jurisdictional conflicts. The Armenian court in Zamość administered justice in cases between Armenians as well as when an individual – a nobleman, a Jew, an Armenian from another town or country –

---

50 Dokumenty na polovetskom iazyke XVI v. (Sudebnye akty Kamenets-Podolskoi armianskoi obshchiny), ed. by Grunin.

51 Garkavets, Kypchakskoe pismennoye nasledie, [vol. 1], p. 872.

52 Zakrzewska-Dubasowa, Ormianie Zamojscy; Majewski, Ormianie w Zamościu.

53 Korobowicz, Sąd ormiański; Zakrzewska-Dubasowa, Ormiańska Temida.

filed a lawsuit against an Armenian of Zamość. In the latter case, a temporary change of jurisdiction was practised. In 1637, for instance, the nobleman Stefan Nowosielecki acknowledged the recovery of a debt from an Armenian called Gabriel Ariewowicz. In accordance with the legal formula written down in the court records, Nowosielecki "for the mean time left his proper terrestrial law and jurisdiction and incorporated himself – so far as necessary for the current act – to the present jurisdiction of Armenian law."[54]

A flexible solution was found that reflected not only the level of friendly coexistence of Armenian and Magdeburg courts in the city, but also the open-mindedness of provincial interpreters of law. It was decided that "in an urgent criminal case or case with a foreigner involved ("*sprawa gościnna*"), if no one of the Armenian jurymen would be present, then – for the completeness of the criminal process – the jurymen of the Polish nation have to be adopted as many as necessary according to the law with no derogation of the privileges of the Armenian Nation of Zamość."[55] In reality, however, the court sessions were irregular; sometimes there were no proceedings for several months.[56] One can suppose that along with such eventualities as commercial trips by jurymen and the outbreak of epidemics and wars, another reason could be the inability to pay a salary to a court scribe, an office that was ordinarily occupied by a Pole.

The competence of the Armenian court in Zamość was reduced in actual practice. In the entire seventeenth century, only two criminal cases were recorded. Conceivably, all other criminal cases were judged by the city court. Even in these two cases, a composed court was assembled to administer justice. A composed court included the Armenian *wójt*, the city burgomaster, four Armenian jurymen, the scribe of the city court, the municipal interrogator (*instygator*) and the prosecutor (*delator*). The accused was detained in the city gaol. It appears that the Armenian court completely lacked the judicial infrastructure necessary for a criminal process.

The Armenian community in Zamość was much smaller than that in Lviv or Kamianets-Podilskyi. According to the record of the head tax levied in Zamość in 1678, there were 90 Armenian taxpayers in the city and suburbs.[57] In such a small community the *wójt* and jurymen were the relatives of many members. As a result, litigants sometimes questioned the impartiality of the judgments.[58] As Zakrzewska-Dubasowa has pointed out, this was probably the main reason

54 Wojewódzki Archiwum Państwowe w Lublinie. Księgi prawa ormiańskiego. Acta Armenica Zamosciana, file 1, fol. 97v.

55 Wojewódzki Archiwum Państwowe w Lublinie. Księgi prawa ormiańskiego. Acta Armenica Zamosciana, file 6, fol. 58.

56 Zakrzewska-Dubasowa, Organizacja gminy ormiańskiej, p. 78.

57 Zakrzewska-Dubasowa, Ormianie Zamojscy, p. 56.

58 Zakrzewska-Dubasowa, Ormiańska Temida, p. 28.

for appeals against a judgment.[59] Armenian jurymen gradually introduced some norms of Magdeburg law and "land law" (*ius terrestre*) to the court sentences. In Zamość, Armenians were granted the same rights as other townspeople. Armenians also occupied some offices in the Magdeburg city magistracy. Thus, the evident ineffectiveness of the Armenian court and the apparent absence of segregation in Zamość led to the successful integration of local Armenians into the Magdeburg community. Consequently, the Armenian court in Zamość was abolished in 1738.[60]

3. Legal Pluralism and Contract Enforcement

Trust and security are key factors in predictability in long-distance trade. Trust is based on reputation, transparency in doing business, and accountability, particularly accountability of agents/factors to their principal.[61] Thus, mutual trust, transparency, and accountability increase predictability. Instability and insecurity demand more flexibility from merchants and, in turn, decrease predictability. Flexibility caused by external factors increases the role of contract enforcement mechanisms.

On the one hand, predictability depends on the relations between economic actors – first of all within the broadly understood merchant community. On the other hand, predictability depends on external agents and factors – officials and other representatives of the state, changes in legislation and interstate treaties, insecurity along trade routes caused by robbery, mutiny, wars, and finally, interruption of trade because of epidemics and natural disasters.

3.1 Avoiding Corporate Responsibility for Debts

When trading abroad, the Armenian merchants – Polish, Ottoman, and Persian subjects – were treated by the local authorities as a corporation with a particular name, for instance, *Armenus Persicus* and *Armenus Turcicus* in Poland, or in the Ottoman sources as *Acem Ermeni* (an Armenian of Iran). The members of such a network were sometimes granted collective privileges of safe conduct when travelling within the domains of a given sovereign.[62] They were taxed as a group, and if a member died abroad, his property was to be handed over to other members of the network currently staying in the same place.[63] The Polish-Ottoman treaty of 1525

59 Zakrzewska-Dubasowa, Organizacja gminy ormiańskiej, p. 79.

60 Ibid., p. 80.

61 Osipian, Debt.

62 Osipian, Voting; Troebst, Isfahan.

63 Ivanova, Foreigners; Faroqhi, Religious Interactions.

introduced a clause concerning debt disputes: responsibility for debts and crimes should be deemed individual and not collective. This clause could be a formal consequence of the abuses expected to have arisen by treating merchants coming from the same country as a group with collective responsibility.[64]

Nevertheless, there were cases when Armenian merchants were forced to pay debts of other members of "the nation." For instance, Awak Aksentowicz, an Armenian of Lviv, did his trade in Constantinople in May 1590. A local Jew demanded from Awak to pay the debt of one Holub, an Armenian of Lviv. The Jew claimed that Awak was a guarantor of Holub. Awak was put in jail because he had no money to pay. He was released thanks to Jolczy, an Armenian merchant of Zamość, originally from Caffa (*Jolczey Kaphenczanin Civis Zamoscensis*), who provided Awak with a loan of 840 thalers guaranteed by written obligation (*cyrograf*).[65]

3.2 Jurisdictional Conflicts over Contract Enforcement

Contract enforcement often became quite complicated in cases of competing jurisdictions. Rostakis, an Armenian of Lviv, was indebted 117 florins to Benesch, a burgher of Kraków. Being unable to pay the debt to Benesch and other creditors (*aliorum creditorum*), Rostakis escaped to the Dominican convent which was at the end of Armenian Street in Lviv. Then, on 3 August 1474, Iarosch Mornstein, an authorised representative of Benesch, accompanied by the representatives of the municipal authorities – proconsul, consul, and notary – came to the Dominican convent and negotiated the contract enforcement with Rostakis who was accompanied by his wife. In accordance with the negotiated agreement, Rostakis should pay his debt in three tranches: 37 florins in the next six weeks (14 September) to the city proconsul who would deliver the money to Iarosch; 30 florins in the next six weeks (26 October) to the city consul; finally, 50 florins to Benesch himself by the St Agnes fair in Lviv (21 January 1475).[66] The practice of paying debts at a fair was widespread in premodern times.

When Benesch came to Lviv at the time of a payment – probably on 26 October 1474 – he found Rostakis absent. It is not clear from the available sources if Rostakis had died, escaped, or refused to deal with his creditors. Then, Benesch at the city hall claimed his money from Rostakis' wife. Armenian elders (*Armeni seniores*) of Lviv required that the case had to be adjudicated at the Armenian civil court presided over by the city judge (*advocatus, wójt*) in accordance with the royal decree

---

64 Panaite, Trade and Merchants, p. 268.

65 Central State Historical Archive of Ukraine in Lviv, fond 52, holding 2, file 515, pp. 162–165, 168–169.

66 Akta grodzkie i ziemskie z czasów Rzeczypospolitej Polskiej z archiwum bernardynskiego we Lwowie, ed. by Liske, [vol. 7], p. 134.

of 1469. In late medieval and early modern Poland, a plaintiff, as a rule, applied to the court of the defendant's jurisdiction (*actor sequitur forum rei*). Then a jury was composed of a judge (*advocatus*), jurymen (*scabuni*), and Armenian elders, finally accompanied by two consuls – representatives of the city council. Benesch complained to the court that both Rostakis and his wife had recognised the debt and now the wife was responsible for the payment. The woman did not deny that she had been enrolled in the negotiations, but claimed that she had been compelled to do so by her husband (*compulsa per maritum suum*). The Armenian elders claimed that she should be free from the obligations of her husband. On the contrary, the judge and all the representatives of the city authorities – the Catholics – insisted that when staying in the convent, her husband had had no power to force her and she had come freely to him, so now she had to pay the debt in accordance with her husband's obligations. After this litigation, on 3 December 1474, a decision was made to ask the king for a verdict.

However, the city authorities asked for a sentence for the next time the king would be back in the kingdom, while the Armenian elders suggested a sentence when the king would next visit Lviv. Predictably, Benesch was against the term proposed by the Armenian elders.[67] At the time, the King Casimir IV (r. 1447–1492) was absent from the Kingdom of Poland, busy with a military conflict over Silesia – a province contested by Casimir IV and Matthias Corvinus, King of Hungary. On 15 November 1474, the negotiations began between the kings of Poland, Bohemia, and Hungary in the vicinity of Wrocław in Silesia. On 8 December 1474 the truce was signed.[68] Thus, when the court composed a petition on 3 December 1474, the king's return was expected in early 1475. However, no one could predict when the king would visit Lviv, if ever. Thus, the Armenian elders actually wanted to postpone the sentence indefinitely. This case demonstrates how ineffective the Armenian civil court presided over by the city judge became when adjudicating litigations between an Armenian and a Catholic burgher.

3.3. Resolving Commercial Disputes at Fairs and Beyond

Joseph Pitton de Tournefort, a French botanist who journeyed through the Levant between 1700 and 1702,[69] wrote in a letter to Louis Phelypeaux, Comte de Pontchartrain, Chancellor of France (1699–1714), describing the bargaining behaviour of Armenian merchants he witnessed in the Ottoman city of Erzurum:

67 Akta grodzkie i ziemskie, pp. 134–136.

68 Biskup and Górski, Kazimierz Jagiellończyk, pp. 238–240.

69 Baghdiantz-McCabe, Orientalism, p. 121.

> *We could not but laugh to see the way of trafficking among the Armenians in the caravanseras of Erzeron. They begin by putting money upon the table, as among the Turks; after that they haggle a great while, and add one piece after another, but not without a great deal of noise. We believ'd by their way of talking they were ready to cut one another's throats; but they meant nothing like it. After having pushed one another backward and forward with a great deal of violence, the brokers or mediators squeeze the hands of the seller so very hard as to make them cry out, and don't let them go till they agree that the buyer shall not pay above so much as they think a reasonable price. After that everyone laughs. They say, with reason, that the sight of the money makes them sooner agree.*[70]

Assuredly, Tournefort exaggerated the performativity of bargaining – noise, emotions, and "violence" – to entertain his Frech readers. He was an outsider – as a Frenchman and botanist he understood neither the language nor commercial habits. In reality, the culture of bargaining followed its own strict rules, while merchants had known each other for decades and their emotions were nothing but a part of corporative culture.

Fairs played an enormous role in the commercial culture of premodern trade. Fairs were places where merchants struck deals, borrowed money and goods, paid debts,[71] and exchanged news. Every fair was an important event in the annual cycle for contract enforcement, settling disputes, and reputation-making. Fairs were two to three weeks long – enough time for numerous commercial controversies, quarrels, and criminal offences. There was also a particular "fair court" (Latin – *iudicium nundinale*, Polish – *sąd jarmarczny*) at the most important fairs of Jarosław and Lublin.[72] Ordinarily, the fair court consisted of the mayor-judge (*wójt*) and two jurymen.

Commercial controversies between merchants were often arbitrated at fairs by their business partners without going to court. For instance, in 1599 at the fair in Lublin there was a controversy over a bill of exchange (*membran*) between the Armenian merchant Murath Melenki of Zamość, an issuer, and the endorsees – Norbek Popowicz and Murath Kierymowicz of Lviv. Murath Melenki declared that there was a mistake in their calculations. A new register was written down in the presence of three other Armenian merchants, but arbitration was postponed because of Norbek Popowicz's illness. Then (after the death of Murath Kierymowicz), all these merchants sat together in the house of Bochdan Donowakowicz in Lviv and,

---

70 Tournefort, A voyage, p. 296.

71 For instance, in a book of records of the Armenian court of Kamianets-Podilskyi for the years 1559–1567 there were recorded 37 cases on bills of debt or acknowledgements of debt. Of these 37 cases, in 13 instances a debtor promised to pay it back at a fair. In most cases, reference was made to the fairs of Lviv, Lutsk, and Jazłowiec.

72 Zakrzewska-Dubasowa, Przyczynek do historii.

in the presence of the city court secretary, redid the calculations and proposed an agreement with Murath Melenki. The latter, however, refused to comply and ultimately filed a lawsuit with the Armenian civil court in Lviv the next year.[73]

This case of arbitration demonstrates a high level of merchants' legal flexibility and ability to solve their commercial disputes without litigation through the formal court system. This flexibility helped merchants to save time and money. In most cases, merchants chose an arbitrator from among themselves. Sometimes, Armenians chose non-Armenians as their arbitrators. An arbitrator had to be a man of consequence who enjoyed credibility both within and outside the Armenian community.

3.4 Contract Enforcement in Times of War

Long-distance trade was frequently interrupted by wars. Nevertheless, some honest merchants fulfilled their obligations despite unpredictable circumstances. On 24 April 1475 Jacub, son of Amÿrcza, Armenian of Lviv (*Jacub, Amÿrczin filius, Armenus Leopoliensis*) came to the city council of Lviv and acknowledged his debt of 380 Hungarian florins he had borrowed earlier from Jacub, Armenian of Tokat in Asia Minor (*Jacub, Armeno de Tochat*).[74] When they had made the deal, Jacub of Lviv had promised to pay back his debt when he next travelled to the city of Caffa in Crimea and meet Jacub of Tokat there. Since the late thirteenth century Caffa had been a famous commercial hub on the Silk Road. However, when in Caffa, Jacub of Lviv did not find Jacub of Tokat there. He went back to Lviv and acknowledged to the city council that he would pay his debt as soon as Jacub of Tokat came to Lviv. Then, in autumn 1475 a subscription was made to the record: Jacub of Tokat, when in Lviv on his way to Moldavia, in the presence of the city consuls and notary had acknowledged that Jacub of Lviv had repaid his debt.

Probably, Jacub of Lviv was in Caffa in winter and/or March because he was back in Lviv on 22 April 1475. On 31 May 1475 the Ottoman navy came to Caffa and seized the city as well as other Genoese colonies in the Crimea. It is highly likely that Jacub of Tokat did not go to Caffa (or left it earlier than initially planned) in 1475 because he knew about the Ottoman plans. Major preparations of the army and navy took a long time and were no secret to the Ottoman subjects. One can suppose that Jacub of Tokat came to Lviv via Crimea when it was once again safe, or via Moldavia, and planned to take the Moldavian route back after completing his business in Poland.

---

73 Central State Historical Archive of Ukraine in Lviv, fond 52, holding 2, file 517, pp. 14–15.

74 Liber consulum civitatis leopoliensis (1460–1506), ed. by Kapral and Petryshak, p. 224.

Generally, in the Black Sea region, with its ill-populated buffer areas without clearly defined borders, merchants did their trade under conditions of permanent undeclared war. Commercial trips there, particularly in the Pontic steppe, were dangerous because of the Crimean Tatar and Nogai raids in the lands of Poland-Lithuania and Russia, as well as because of the Cossack naval raids on the Ottoman sea ports and regular brigandage along the trade routes.[75]

4. Partnership of Errors or Bargaining under Conditions of Political Turmoil?

Internal wars and political turmoil made long-distance trade complicated as well. On 24 October 1510, in Kraków, Sigismund I, King of Poland and Grand Duke of Lithuania, ordered his dignitaries to consider litigation between two Armenian merchants – Demian of Kyiv and Beiaty of Caffa.[76] The former was a subject of the Grand Duke, while the latter was a subject of the Ottoman sultan – as since 1475 the city of Caffa in the Crimea had belonged to the Ottoman Empire. Probably in 1507 or 1508, Demian and Beiaty had made a deal. Beiaty had come to Kyiv and given on credit, goods estimated at about 150 *sexagena* to Demian. With these, Demian had travelled as far as to Vilnius – the capital of the Grand Duchy of Lithuania. However, Beiaty had not waited for Demian in Kyiv but had gone to Vilnius as well and demanded the loan back. There, Damian paid 40 *sexagena* to Beiaty and promised to pay the rest of the sum later. Together, they travelled back to Kyiv.

However, at the halfway mark in their travels, in the city of Slutsk, they received news of Prince Mikhail Glinsky's rebellion. Backed by Ivan III of Muscovy, he had raised arms against Sigismund I between February and October 1508 (which helps us date events). Because of the insurgency, the two merchants changed their plans. Demian left his goods and a servant with Beiaty in Slutsk to wait for him and went to the city of Lutsk because it was too dangerous to travel with precious cargo through territories controlled by the insurgents. On 12 June 1508, Slutsk was besieged by the insurgents. Perhaps, because of this, Beiaty then also left the city and travelled to Lutsk as well. What is important is that he travelled not by "commercial routes", as merchants were required to do but along "ambassadorial routes" in order "to bypass customs." However, Beiaty could have chosen the "ambassadorial routes" in the hope that they would be safer. Furthermore, as an Ottoman subject, Beiaty probably

75 Osipian, Restraining-encouraging violence.

76 Litovskaia Metrika, [vol. 1], in: Russkaia istoricheskaia biblioteka, [vol. 20], ed. by Gildebrandt, pp. 635–637.

could have claimed to be an Ottoman/Tatar envoy – at that time, the Crimean Khan had proposed his protection to the insurgents.

Nevertheless, on his way to Lutsk, Beiaty was detained by a customs collector called Shymko, a Jew, who confiscated the goods of both merchants. Because the customs office had been leased to Shymko by Prince Kostiantyn Ostrozsky, after he had reached Lutsk, Beiaty approached Ostrozsky's viceregent through some mediators (there was an Armenian community in the city). The viceregent returned only half of his goods to Beiaty, while he confiscated the other half on behalf of his prince. Then Demian demanded back his goods from Beiaty. After making some calculations they took a compromise decision – Demian would not pay back the debt – presumably 110 *sexagena* – because his loss of goods was due to a fault of Beiaty. Having made this arrangement between themselves, the two merchants went to the city hall of Lutsk and stood before the deputy mayor (*lantvoit*) and eldermen (*burmistry*). There, Beiaty recognised that Demian was no longer in debt to him, and Demian took from the municipal authorities a written confirmation with the city seal.

However, later, Beiaty changed his mind, and probably in 1510 sued Demian at the royal court in Kraków. This time, Beiaty was accompanied by two representatives of the Crimean Khan – Avgustyn and Patestyn (ethnic Italians in the Khan's service). Presumably, when back in Caffa, Beiaty was approached by his creditors demanding the return of their money because in 1510 two envoys of the Crimean Khan acted on behalf of Beiaty. One can suppose that the Khan had leased goods or money to Beiaty in 1507/1508, which was a rather ordinary practice. This time, at the royal court in Kraków, Beiaty declared that in Lutsk he had been forced to discharge Demian of his debt. According to Beiaty's statement, he had been chained in the city hall of Lutsk. The royal judges had asked Beiaty if he had any confirmation for his statement but Beiaty could not provide any evidence and kept silent, so the judges reported the case to the king who declared Demian free of debt to Beiaty.

At first glance, Beiaty's behaviour looks highly unpredictable, if not treacherous. However, a closer look can explain his ever-changing mood. Why had Beiaty credited his goods to Demian in Kyiv and later followed him to Vilnius instead of bringing his goods there himself? The explanation is rather predictable – to pay no customs for the said goods. Armenian merchants of Poland-Lithuania were fluent in the Kipchak/Tatar language and were frequently employed as interpreters for diplomatic relations with the Ottoman sultan and Crimean Khan. For these diplomatic services, Armenian merchants were granted their commercial privileges. Demian could have been one of them. At least, his son – Lenko Demianovich, an Armenian of Kyiv (*орменин киевский Лѣнко Демянович*) – was sent, at approximately the same time, by the Lithuanian dignitaries (*паны-рада*) to accompany the ducal ambassadors to the Khan Mängli Giräy.[77] Ordinarily, in Poland-Lithuania such diplomatic services were conducted by Armenian merchants through two or even three generations. As an interpreter and diplomatic courier in ducal service, Demian might have travelled along the "ambasadorial routes" paying no customs for his goods. That is also why Beiaty had later followed him to Vilnius without goods. However, when Beiaty himself used this trick on his way from Slutsk to Lutsk, he was detained by the customs collector.

Additionally, the two merchants applied to three different courts - of viceregent, municipal, and royal. As a ducal subject and a townsman, Demian took Beiaty to the municipal court of Lutsk. Conversely, Beiaty, as a foreigner and sultan's subject, applied to the viceregent and king – municipal courts were unknown in the Ottoman Empire. Furthermore, as a commercial partner of the Crimean Khan backed by his patron, Beiaty preferred to apply to more powerful persons than to the jurymen. Demian obtained an excerpt from the municipal court records (and paid a tax for it), while Beiaty relied on his mighty patron – the Crimean Khan. This case thus reveals a difference in the judicial cultures of Poland-Lithuania and the Ottoman Empire.

5. The intervention of powerful patrons into legal trials and contract enforcement

Foreign merchants often approached Armenian civil and municipal (Magdeburg) courts to have their claims registered in the court's records rather than to receive a verdict. As a rule, merchants preferred to solve their commercial disputes in their own milieu through the mediation of arbiters – other respectable and trustworthy merchants. However, when commodities had been confiscated or foreign merchants were robbed, they very often asked the monarch in whose domains they had lost their property for justice. In order to do so, they usually asked their own king for a letter of support addressed to the ruler whom they then approached for justice. In many cases, these merchants were accompanied with envoys acting on their behalf.[78]

For example, in their letters, the Sultans Selim I (r. 1512–1520) and Suleiman I (r. 1520–1566) frequently reminded King Sigismund II of property that Ottoman merchants who had died in Poland-Lithuania or had been robbed by the king's

77 On 24 September 1510 King Sigismund I granted to Lenko Demianovich and his descendants a manor, Otochilovichi in Mozyr district, to cover his travel expenses. Sbornik materialov, otnosiashchikhsia k istorii panov-rady Velikogo kniazhestva Litovskogo, ed. by Malinovskii, pp. 307–308.

78 For more details see my article: Osipian, Restraining-encouraging violence, pp. 129–131, 134.

subjects were owed.[79] A significant role was played by the sultan's interpreters. For example, a young Polish nobleman called Joachim Strasz, who had been captured by Tatars, converted to Islam, and made his career at the sultan's court as Ibrahim Beg. In 1551–1571 he held the office of Grand Dragoman and was frequently sent to Poland as the sultan's envoy.[80] In his correspondence with the Polish king's court, Ibrahim Beg mentions an Armenian of Kamianets who had asked the envoy for help obtaining a letter to be put before the sultan. As a sample, Ibrahim Beg attached a letter addressed to the previous sultan. Thus, the Ottoman envoy asked the Polish courtier to produce a letter from the royal chancery addressed to the ruling sultan. Highly likely, the Armenian of Kamianets had asked for this in order to approach the sultan's court and solve his business issues in the Ottoman domains.

Another case in Ibrahim's letter is of no less interest. The Grand Dragoman had proposed to some Armenians of Lviv to pay him money they owed to one of the sultan's merchants. Ibrahim promised them to issue a receipt (*kwit*) under the sultan's or his own name stating that the debt had been repaid. In response, one of these Armenians of Lviv asked Ibrahim Beg for a letter exempting him from paying his debts to the creditors for six months in order to save money and pay his debt to the sultan's merchant.[81] Probably, Ibrahim Beg was expected to ask the king to grant this Armenian an exemption for six months from the judicial claims of his Polish creditors.

There were many legal ways to evade contract enforcement. Some Armenian merchants who were employed by the kings of Poland as royal interpreters, diplomatic couriers, and secret envoys were granted so-called protective letters that went by various names. The first sort was called a "*glejt* or *litteras salvi conductus*" – "letter of safe conduct".[82] The second form was called a "*list żelazny*" – literally the "iron letter" in Polish – or "*litteras moratorias*" – "letters imposing moratoria on a court's verdict". The "iron letter" was given by the king to debtors unable to pay because of the damages caused by war, fire, brigandage, or because they had suffered losses on behalf of the public or royal good. It could help to delay the execution of a court sentence against a debtor for three years.[83] Similar letters from Polish dignitaries protected wealthy Armenian merchants who supplied them with oriental commodities, provided them with loans, and managed their manors. These letters exempted the holder from the jurisdiction of a municipal court in royal

79 Katalog dokumentów tureckich. Dokumenty do dziejów Polski i krajów ościennych w latach 1455–1672, ed. by Abrahamowicz, [vol. 2], pp. 107, 109, 122, 165; vol. 3, pp. 187, 220.

80 Kroll, Polish Converts to Islam, https://www.wilanow-palac.pl/print/polish_converts_to_islam_in_the_service_of_the_sultan.html, last access 02/06/2024.

81 Katalog dokumentów tureckich, [vol. 3], p. 196.

82 A German loanword *"Geleit"*, which means "convoy, escort, safe conduct, safeguard."

83 Gloger, Encyklopedia staropolska, p. 382.

or private domains. For the most part, they were granted to merchants who had already had a debt case brought against them in a court. As a countermeasure, in some cases, a particular stipulation was included in a "warranty letter" (*membron*) that the debt was to be paid despite any *litteras moratorias*.[84]

Grzegorz Iwaszkiewicz, an Armenian merchant of Lviv, traded in the Ottoman Empire and probably also acted as an unofficial royal envoy – his business was frequently protected by the king. In 1594, Grzegorz and his brother Zacharyasz were robbed in Moldavia, and were subsequently attacked by their creditors. Under these complicated circumstances, the Iwaszkiewicz brothers received royal support. On 26 August 1596, King Sigismund III (r. 1587–1632) sent a letter to the Armenian civil court of Lviv instructing it to adjudicate the claims of only the Ottoman creditors and dismiss the pleas of all other claimants.[85] Later, in 1600–1602, the Iwaszkiewicz brothers made deals with merchants of Constantinople and Ankara for the massive amount of 25,000 ducats.[86] The brothers could not meet their obligations and were imprisoned in Lviv. However, Sigismund III ordered the city council to release Zacharyasz and Grzegorz Iwaszkiewicz on bail.[87]

Due to the decline of royal power in the Polish-Lithuanian Commonwealth since the late sixteenth century, many merchants tried to obtain letters of support from their powerful patrons in order to influence court decisions. In September 1592, Chrzystoph Zachnowic, an Armenian merchant of Lviv, died in Constantinople. His last will was recorded there by another Armenian – Iwaszko Mikołaiowicz. In his will, Chrzystoph Zachnowic bequeathed 200 złotys to his uncle Jendrzej Kosczewic of Zamość. At least, this was claimed by Jendrzej Kosczewic with reference to Iwaszko Mikołaiowicz, who allegedly had delivered the will to his relatives in Lviv. However, Awedik, Gabriel, and Jakob – brothers of the late Chrzystoph Zachnowic – refused to pay the 200 Złotys. This being the case, in 1593 Jendrzej Kosczewic sued his nephews at the Armenian civil court of Lviv. He also brought a letter of support from the owner of Zamość – Jan Zamoyski, the Grand Chancellor of the Crown (1578–1605) and Great Hetman of Poland (1581–1605). However, the letter did not help. A servant of the late Chrzystoph Zachnowic – who had accompanied his master until his final moments – testified at trial that no such last will had been left.[88]

The powerful magnates sought to protect the merchants in their service even far beyond the borders of their domains in remote cities. For instance, in 1651 the

84 Łoziński, Patrycyat i mieszczaństwo, pp. 58, 291.

85 Akta grodzkie i ziemskie z czasów Rzeczypospolitej Polskiej z archiwum bernardynskiego we Lwowie, wydal X. Liske [et al.], [vol. 10], p. 178.

86 Łoziński, Patrycyat i mieszczaństwo, p. 274.

87 Akta grodzkie i ziemskie, [vol. 10], pp. 186, 187.

88 Central State Historical Archive of Ukraine in Lviv, fond 52, holding 2, file 515, pp. 557, 567, 754.

magistrate of the city of Lviv arrested the commodities of the Armenian merchant Chrystof Baleiowicz of Zamość, who had refused to pay tolls when crossing the city borders. As a rule, in such cases, merchants argued that the commodities under question were not theirs, but the property of a magnate, since the nobility was officially freed from fees and tolls. In this case, Jan Sobiepan Zamoyski (1627–1665), the owner of Zamość and some domains remote from Lviv, in a letter to the municipal authorities of Lviv, demanded that the merchant and his merchandise be freed. Otherwise, he threatened to detain in his domains the merchants of Lviv.[89]

In some cases, aristocrats and dignitaries adjudicated litigations between merchants and even considered the claims of business reputation. For example, in 1614 Kirkor Hołubowicz, an Armenian merchant of Lviv, brought a claim to the local municipal court (*iudicium advocatiale, sąd wójtowski*) against Simon Rabiczka, an Armenian merchant of the same place. However, the judge (*advocatus*, *wójt*) refused to adjudicate the claim, because Simon Rabiczka was a servant of Prince Janusz Ostrozski (1554–1620) – the most powerful aristocrat in the Polish Kingdom. Then, on 30 July 1614, Kirkor Hołubowicz brought his case to the seniorial court (*sąd zadworny*) of Janusz Ostrozski, who resided in the village Wałowice on the Vistula – some 300 km away from Lviv. Both litigant and defendant were present in person and accompanied by their representatives (*plenipotent*). These were both noblemen, because the prince adjudicated the case in accordance with the land law (*ius terrestre, prawo ziemskie*). Both litigant and defendant, as burghers, were ignorant in the land law and thus hired noblemen as their plenipotentiary representatives. Kirkor Hołubowicz claimed that Simon Rabiczka publicly – in the presence of other Armenian merchants – had labelled him as a dishonest person (*zlodziej*). According to the offensive words (*de verbis iniuriosis*) of the defendant, Kirkor Hołubowicz for six years had operated as factor of Kasper Zadykowic – the father of Simon Rabiczka – and had never delivered an account to his principal. In the meantime, Kirkor Hołubowicz's fortune had increased from 20 thalers to 18,000 zlotys. Under such circumstances, Hołubowicz's commercial success was considered suspect by Simon Rabiczka. Thus, the litigant's business reputation (*dobra sława*) was publicly questioned. After an exchange of arguments between litigant and defendant, Prince Ostrozski delivered his verdict: The litigant's fame and reputation (*sława y reputatia*) were not to be damaged, and both parties must embrace one another, excuse one another, and forget all their old offences. Finally, on 5 August 1614 Kirkor Hołubowicz brought the princely verdict to the jurymen

89 Central State Historical Archive of Ukraine in Lviv, fond 132 (Letters of dignitaries, statesmen, and religious hierarchs), holding 1, file 545, p. 1.

court of Lviv (*iudicium scabinale, sąd ławniczy*) to insert the verdict into the court records.[90]

6. Justice on the Move: The *caravanbashi* as a Judge with Exterritorial Jurisdiction

Armenian trade in the Early Modern period passed in great part over land routes, mostly as caravan traffic. Armenian merchants from the Polish kingdom organised into large well-armed parties or convoys (*caravans*), regularly travelling as far as Adrianople/Edirne and Constantinople/Istanbul. They sometimes also reached Iran's capital city of Isfahan. When doing so, they, and their property, were protected by treaties between the Ottoman sultans and the Polish kings. These treaties emphasised the particular role and significance of Armenian merchants in trade between the two states. The capitulations sent by Sultan Murad III (r. 1574–1595) to the Polish King Stefan Bathory (r. 1576–1586) in 1577 read:

> *When Armenians and other infidel merchants living under the royal hand [i. e. the subjects of the Polish king] want to come to Moldavia and my other well-protected dominions and practise trade, they should not travel through deserted and wild areas or use hidden roads, but they should come by the direct public road which has been customarily travelled by merchants.*[91]

Every caravan was led by a *caravanbashi*. The very term *caravanbashi* is derived from the Turkish – *karban başi, kervan başi*, or a head/headman of a caravan. The *caravanbashi* was responsible for the management of safe and comfortable travel.

The election of a *caravanbashi*, his power and functions are mentioned in a lawsuit between the litigant *caravanbashi* Owanisowicz and one Iwaszko Sepherowicz, merchant of the same caravan, adjudicated by the Armenian civil court in Lviv on 25 February 1642. According to the court records

> *[…] the litigant Owanisowicz was chosen by the company of merchants, travelling to the Turkish land, as the head of this caravan, as a caravanbashi, thereby voluntarily giving [him] legal and supervisory power over them during their travels. All will obey his orders, since in accordance with the ancient merchant custom a caravanbashi is authorized to adjudicate the disputes that emerge during the travel and to punish the recalcitrant.*[92]

---

90 Central State Historical Archive of Ukraine in Lviv, fond 52, holding 2, file 258, pp. 476–480.

91 Kołodziejczyk, Ottoman-Polish Diplomatic Relations, p. 278.

92 Central State Historical Archive of Ukraine in Lviv, fond 52, holding 2, file 526, p. 718.

The *caravanbashi* was ordinarily assisted by two persons – a steward/purser and secretary/scribe. The English merchant Robert Bargrave, who joined an Armenian caravan from Constantinople to Lviv in 1652, described a *caravanbashi's* functions and staff in this way:

> *And here I first learnd the manner of Caravans in the Field: which is thus. A Man is agreed upon to take the Office on him of Caravan-Bassi; who like the Commander of a Partie, orders our going to, or quartring at, this or that Place; appoints the houre of our setting out, and corrects those who stragle from the Company, or otherwise disobey his Orders. [...] This Caravan Bassi chuses to himselfe a Keiah (or Steward) who with his Assistants is to buy in provisions for Men & horses: as also his Yazigee (or Clerke) who takes all mens' names, appoints whom to watch, & when: and in the evening calls over the names of all the Company, to find if any be wanting.*[93]

The *caravanbashi* was either elected by the merchants or nominated by the council of Armenian elders in Lviv and Kamianets. During travel, he executed the functions of a notary. There is a letter or inquiry certificate (*attestatio*) written in Constantinople on 26 July 1618 by Armenian merchants from the Polish kingdom and given to their associate and fellow traveller Iwaszko Warteresowicz. In the first line, there is a note that the inquiry certificate had been issued after "we arrived in Constantinople on 12th June, in the time of caravanbashi Christoph Serepkowicz [who was] elected [to this office] by the whole company".[94] This certificate of inquiry was issued to be used in ongoing litigation between two Armenian merchants, Iwaszko Warteresowicz and his uncle Holub Iwaszkowicz, in the Armenian civil court in Lviv. The certificate was signed by Christoph Serepkowicz and four other Armenian merchants from his caravan as eyewitnesses.

Jean-Baptiste Tavernier, a Frenchman who travelled with Armenian caravans from Constantinople, Aleppo, and Smyrna to Persia six times between 1630 and 1676, noted that:

> *these Merchants choose among themselves a Caravan-Bashi, who orders them how they shall march, assigns the places of lodging at night, and who with the chief of the Caravan, is a kind of Judge of the differences that fall out by the way.*[95]

In some cases, there could be two *caravanbashis* in a single caravan. One possible explanation can be made by analogy with contemporary merchant and artisan

93 Bargrave, Travel Diary, pp. 127–128.

94 Central State Historical Archive of Ukraine in Lviv, fond 52, holding 2, file 521, p. 1061.

95 Tavernier, Six voyages, pp. 45–46.

guilds, which very often had two heads (*zechmistrz*), who oversaw each other. Another option is that the caravan at some point could divide into two parts. For instance, Armenian caravans travelled from Poland to the Ottoman border on the Danube where merchants had two options – to take the land route through the Balkans or to embark and continue their trip to Constantinople via the Black Sea. There is note in the records of the Armenian Consistory Court in Lviv on 6 October 1606 which states that:

> *as the caravan set out, the Council of Elders called upon the people and reminded them that great disorder and great discord happens in the caravans, and that much loss is caused [...] as a result of this discord. Therefore, the Council of Elders [points out that] in order for them to run better, there must be a head of the caravan, to whom [those] in the caravan should obey. For the outgoing caravan, the Council of Elders appointed, by common agreement, two heads of the caravan: Mr. Stecko, son of Misko, and Mr. Haczko, son of Jagop, and for better functioning from among the fellows four assistants: Mr. Aswadur from [the town of] Zamość, and Mr. Stecko, son of Hodżigi, and Mr. Szimko, son of der Mikajel, and Mr. Szimko, son of Kosta. The Elders approved them, gave them the authority to admonish the guilty [of misbehaviour]. For that matter the Elders are wishing them to substitute the caravan heads in everything.*[96]

The *caravanbashi* regularly executed the functions of a judge over all members of a caravan – merchants, apprentices, servants, cart drivers, and fellow-travellers. Accordingly, the Sublime Port, the central government of the Ottoman Empire, officially authorised *karban başis* to solve criminal and civil cases among the Polish subjects participating in their caravans.[97]

However, the judicial autonomy of Polish-Armenian caravans was later questioned by some Ottoman officials. This autonomy was assured however when, on 17 July 1568, Sultan Selim II (r. 1566–1574) – in response to the intervention of the Polish Ambassador Piotr Zborowski – issued an order to the Ottoman governors (*sanjakbei*) and judges (*qadi*) not to interfere in the disputes between Polish merchants:

96 Zapisy sądu duchownego Ormian miasta Lwowa za lata 1564–1608 w języku ormiańsko-kipczackim, ed. by Tryjarski, p. 528.

97 Kołodziejczyk, Ottoman-Polish Diplomatic Relations, pp. 186, 336, 343.

In the case of disputes and quarrels between Polish subjects, let them be settled by the heads of the caravans, and let the town guardians not interfere in them at all. Neither should you give your permission for any person outside of the caravans to meddle in the matter.[98]

Martin Gruneweg, a young Danzig-born ethnic German who served as a scribe and secretary for Armenian caravans in 1582–1588, wrote in his diary that the Armenian merchants had at their disposal charters for free and safe passage,[99] granted to them by the Ottoman sultan, the Polish king, and their permanent city of residence.[100] These charters were kept in the Armenian courts in Kamianets-Podilskyi and Lviv. Before the trip to the Ottoman Empire, a senior member of the caravan – that is the *caravanbashi* – went to the Armenian city hall (*ratusz*) and asked for these charters which guaranteed the caravan safe conduct on its travels. Then the *wójt*, the mayor of the autonomous Armenian community in Kamianets, gave him the so-called "Turkish privileges" on eight sheets of paper in one carrying case. The *caravanbashis* were obliged to use these privileges to defend their companions during the travel and to return them when the trip was finished.[101] The privileges were confirmed by each new sultan in exchange for a special payment.[102]

The young Dutch humanist Georg van der Does (Dousa), who travelled with an Armenian caravan from Lviv to Constantinople in 1597, described a case in which an Armenian merchant was arrested in Ottoman territory by a Muslim judge (*qadi*). Van der Does stated that, in accordance with the privilege given by the Ottoman sultan, an Armenian merchant could not be condemned by any Muslim judge but only by his *senior*. The *qadi* therefore called the Armenian *caravanbashi*, who showed the privileges granted by the Ottoman sultan.[103] Van der Does then describes a dispute between the *qadi* and *caravanbashi*, since the former tried to place in doubt the jurisdiction of the latter in order to extort a bribe.[104]

---

98 Yoldaki elçi: Osmanlı'dan günümüze Türk-Leh ilişkileri = Poseł w drodze. Stosunki turecko-polskie od czasów osmańskich do dnia dzisiejszego, ed. by Yekeler and Wajs, p. 61.

99 Latin *litteras salvi conductus*, German *Pasbriewe*, *Passbortt*, Polish *glejt*.

100 Die Aufzeichnungen des Dominikaners Martin Gruneweg (1562–ca. 1618): über seine Familie in Danzig, seine Handelsreisen in Osteuropa und sein Klosterleben in Polen, [vol. 2], ed. by Bues, p. 686.

101 Central State Historical Archive of Ukraine in Kyiv, fond 39, holding 1, file 20, fol. 50; file 26, fol. 40.

102 In the calculations of the public expenses made by the Armenian civil court in Lviv from 1614 to 1647 there is a note that "For the Turkish privileges were given out 1348 [Polish] zlotys." Dzieje Ormian lwowskich od roku 1649 aż do r. 1713. Dział Rękopisów Biblioteki Zakładu Narodowego im. Ossolińskich we Wrocławiu, file 1646 II, p. 151.

103 Dousa, De itinere suo, pp. 29–30.

104 Dousa, De itinere suo, p. 30.

7. Uses of the Armenian Consistory Court of Lviv by Foreign Armenian Merchants

In the late fourteenth and early fifteenth centuries, Lviv was the main centre of Polish trade with the Golden Horde and Eastern Mediterranean. According to the royal decree of 1444, foreign merchants – actually all non-Catholics (*Greci, Armeni, Saraceni, Iudei, Bessermeni*) – were subjected to the jurisdiction of the city jury of Lviv. The decree further prohibited foreign and local merchants to bring their mutual disputes before the courts of the "Polish Law" exercised by the royal officials.[105] Henceforth, the decree provoked jurisdictional conflict. As can be seen from the royal decrees of 1469 and 1476, the Armenian court of Lviv also adjudicated cases of foreign Armenians. The decrees clarified that fines in the litigations between local Armenians (*Armeni domestici*) had to be paid to the Armenian community, while in litigations between foreign Armenians (*Armeni forensi*) and anybody else, fines had to be paid to the city judge (*advocatus*).[106] Sometimes, however, foreign Armenians used another possible option, notably the Armenian Consistory Court.

The long-distance trade of Armenian merchant networks was based mostly on a form of partnership known as *commenda*.[107] The *commenda* is a type of commercial contract that involves two parties: a principal merchant (*khoja*, *agha*, or *ter*) who entrusts his money or merchandise to an agent (*vakil*) or factor (*enker*) to travel long distances to sell the merchandise entrusted to him. In accordance with a *commenda* contract (*enkeragir*), the investor receives either three-fourths or two-thirds of the profit, while the agent keeps the remainder.[108] It frequently happened that agents could not fulfil a contract, and sometimes they disappeared abroad.

Joseph Pitton de Tournefort in his letter to the French Chancellor Pontchartrain[109] praised Armenians as "the best people in the world, civil, polite, and full of good sense and probity", all the more especially dedicated to "trade, which they follow with the utmost attention and application."[110] He does note, however, a troubling habit:

> *If they succeed ill in any foreign country where they are trading, they never return home again; they say they have not the face to shew themselves after they are become bankrupts:*

---

105 Kapral, Pryvilei natsionalnykh hromad, pp. 90–92.

106 Ibid., pp. 146, 148.

107 Pryor, The Origins; Gonzalez de Lara, Venetian success; van Doosselaere, Commercial Agreements.

108 Aslanian, The Circulation.

109 Pontchartrain made efforts to reintroduce Armenian merchants of New Julfa to Marseille.

110 Tournefort, A voyage, [vol. 2], p. 291.

But their creditors obtain no satisfaction by this. However, this justice must be done them, to own there are very few bankrupts among them.[111]

Thus, in order to get back their money and/or merchandise, wealthy merchants tried to employ various legal facilities of the Armenian diaspora abroad. On 23 September 1628, in the city of Tabriz in Persia, the Armenian merchant Khodja Mahmat Gülipeks authorised another Armenian merchant, Khodja Farukh of Julfa,[112] to act as his attorney on his travels to Europe (*Frangistan*). If Farukh were to meet Gülipeks' commercial agents (*vakil*), he was authorised to take from them all the entrusted commodities. Probably, Gülipeks had already lost connection with his agents and suspected them of being dishonest. Farukh also received a letter of support from Movses, the Patriarch of all the Armenians (1629–1632), addressed to the Armenian archbishop of Lviv – Nigol Torosowicz. Patriarch Movses asked Archbishop Nigol to help Farukh to gain commodities from three Armenian merchants who were Persian subjects. On 20 July 1630, upon arriving in Lviv, Farukh appeared before the local Armenian Consistory Court and submitted both letters, which were then registered in the court records, while Farukh obtained a Polish translation authenticated with the archbishop's seal.[113] Henceforth, in case the agents were detected anywhere in the Polish-Lithuanian Commonwealth, Farukh could demand the royal or municipal authorities to apprehend them. Thus, once again, the Armenian Consistory Court, actually having no jurisdiction over the business cases of foreign Armenians, was turned into their legal representative and appropriated the legal functions – translation and legal confirmation of documents – that had never been granted by the Polish king.

In 1656, Iovhannes, an Armenian merchant and Ottoman subject, travelled from the city of Tokat (in Asia Minor) through Caffa (in the Crimea) to Lviv, where

111 Ibid., p. 295.

112 Armenian merchants successfully adapted themselves to the cultures in their host societies. This is reflected in their names as well. Getting Armenian Christian names as their baptismal names, most of them later used secular names of various origins – nicknames as well as names popular in the host society. They were recorded under these non-baptismal names in the court records, tax lists, censuses, and other written sources. The merchants were known in their transnational professional milieu under these names which functioned as their business names. Armenian merchants of Persia and the Ottoman Empire were mentioned under Arabic, Persian, and Turkic names and nicknames. Only Armenian clergymen were mentioned under their Armenian names. Furthermore, Armenian names in Poland-Lithuania were Polonised, Ukrainianised, and Latinised when recorded in the court books. For instance, an Armenian Khachatur/Chaczatur could be mentioned in the sources as Chaczko (Ukrainianised), Christoph (Latinised), and Krzysztof (Polonised) as well as Chaczeris, Kaczeris or Christko.

113 Zapisy sądu duchownego Ormian miasta Lwowa za lata 1625–1630 w języku ormiańsko-kipczackim, ed. by Tryjarski, pp. 219–220.

he died in early January 1657. When the news reached Tokat, Iovhannes's widow married anew, while his son and daughter were adopted by others. Friends of the late Iovhannes had authorised another Armenian merchant – Aydyn of Caffa in the Crimea – to act as plenipotentiary on behalf of the orphans in order to take back Iovhannes' commodities. Aydyn also asked for support from the Armenian archimandrite and Vicar Bishop of Tokat, Iovhannes. The archimandrite wrote a letter to Nigol Torosowicz, the Armenian archbishop of Lviv, and to the twelve Armenian elders, asking them to help Aydyn. In accordance with the letter, the late merchant Iovhannes was in debt to some non-Armenians, and unless his heirs were willing to pay his debts, there was a risk that they could be forced to convert to Islam. The archimandrite was aware that the restitution of the deceased's estate far abroad was a complicated process, thus he used the religious argument. He also made a reference to the precedents and judicial practices in other western and eastern countries frequently visited by Armenian merchants:

> *Please, your graces, give back [the money and commodities] to the children to free them from the debts, as it is in the cases with those who died in* "Frangistan" *(Europe)*[114] *as well as in the Indies and, nevertheless, their property is restituted to their heirs.*[115]

After obtaining the letters of the attorney and the archimandrite, Aydyn of Caffa arrived in Lviv in March 1658. There, the letters were submitted to the Armenian Consistory Court and translated into Polish. On 11 March 1658, accompanied by four Armenian elders and the licenced municipal interpreter (*dragoman*) Mikołaj Bajdulowicz (also an Armenian), Aydyn appeared before the city jury, which delivered a judgment in favour of the heirs.[116]

Thus, the Armenian Consistory Court acted as an additional but unauthorised judicial mediator between foreign Armenians and the city jury of Lviv. The court not only provided foreign Armenians with authorised translations of the letters of the attorney and letters of support, but also with the legal assistance necessary to apply to the city jury. Actually, it could be considered as a preliminary or introductory judicial instance which considered the claims of foreign plaintiffs and established the authenticity of the submitted documents. The reference to the precedents in Frangistan/Europe and in the Indies could be evidence that the legal support provided to the Armenian merchants abroad by Armenian clergymen was widely used in the seventeenth century.

---

114 In Polish translation: "in Italian lands" (*we włoskich kraiach*).

115 Central State Historical Archive of Ukraine in Lviv, fond 52, holding 2, file 546, pp. 1354–1356, 1358; file 67, pp. 594–597.

116 Central State Historical Archive of Ukraine in Lviv, fond 52, holding 2, file 67, pp. 593–594, 597–598.

8. Conclusion

Premodern merchant communities did not strive for unification and harmonisation of laws. Quite the opposite, they masterfully navigated their businesses in the turbulent waters of legal pluralism. Unlike the Armenian diaspora in other countries, Armenian communities in Poland-Lithuania and the Moldavian Principality succeeded in establishing their own autonomous civil courts along with church courts. The Armenian merchant "nation" approached every new king of Poland and the Ottoman sultan in order to gain confirmation of their privileges granted by previous monarchs.

The existence of multiple jurisdictions within one city periodically resulted in jurisdictional conflicts arbitrated by the king. The king was not interested in imposing a uniform official national law. On the contrary, his main task – as understood by contemporaries – was to defend the rights of all his loyal subjects, and to maintain a balance stabilising the existing legal pluralism and its hierarchy.

In the royal cities of Lviv and Kamianets-Podilskyi, application to the Magdeburg Law court was attractive for many Armenians because of tax exemptions, greater economic opportunities, and the legality of verdicts issued by the court. Moreover, the Armenian court was not as effective as its Magdeburg counterpart: first, the sessions of the Armenian court were not held for many weeks because of the absence of jurymen who were on commercial trips; second, the fairness of the court was in question since the elders were close relatives of each other and of many community members; and finally, criminal and property cases were removed from the Armenian court's competence.

In order to make their long-distance trade successful and predictable, Armenian merchants switched between legal institutions of various jurisdictions, developed new legal institutions, and, finally, adopted for their commercial purposes old institutions which were not originally intended to adjudicate commercial cases, for instance, the Armenian Consistory Court. Given that from 1444, foreign merchants in Lviv could apply only to the city court, foreign Armenian merchants sometimes employed the Armenian Consistory Court as a mediator in their relations with city authorities. Armenian communities in Poland established a particular judicial institution – the extra-territorial adjudicative power of Armenian *caravanbashis*, whose legal status was defined and confirmed by a particular article in the treaty between the sultan and the king.

Merchants made the judicial system more complicated by asking their powerful patrons to intervene in the jurisdiction of municipal courts. Primarily, this strategy was practised by merchants of the non-Catholic communities who experienced restrictions of their rights by the dominant Catholic patricians. This occurred for two reasons.

First, merchants doing trade abroad asked foreign rulers for letters of safe conduct. Some frequently operated on behalf of their own ruler, while some traded abroad with goods and/or money they had received from their own monarch, or purchased commodities commissioned by their monarch. Many cases of violation of a merchant's rights, i. e., debts, robbery, or inheritance entitlement of a merchant who had died abroad, were discussed in the diplomatic correspondence between rulers.

Second, wealthy merchants traded in luxury goods consumed mainly by the nobility. Many statesmen and dignitaries of Poland-Lithuania ordered oriental luxury goods from Armenian merchants going to the Ottoman Empire and Persia. This helped to establish trustworthy relations between Armenian merchants and high-ranking nobility. Merchants and noblemen made business partnerships – merchants exported cattle, grain, timber, potassium, and other goods that they were trusted with by the nobility. Many high-ranking noblemen leased their manors to wealthy merchants. Armenian merchants fluent in Turkic languages were frequently employed by powerful Polish statesmen as interpreters, envoys, and infiltrators in Moldavia, the Crimean Khanate, and the Ottoman Empire. In exchange for their services, many wealthy merchants were granted the status of "servant" (*sluga*) by certain powerful statesmen. A "servant" was provided with letters of support by his patron to protect him in legal trials – municipal judges and jurymen did not dare to fall into disfavour with a powerful dignitary. On the one hand, the intervention of powerful patrons – particularly the letters granting exemption from debt payment – made trade less predictable. On the other hand, it helped to enforce contracts in cases of higher priority. For instance, merchants were granted exemption from debts to their compatriots in order to be able to pay back their foreign creditors.

Thus, merchants themselves chose strategies when dealing with authorities, negotiating legal framing, and changing patterns of behaviour in every particular case. That said, the individual agency of merchants was limited by their belonging to a professional group, which in case of the Armenians was further defined legally, religiously, and ethnically. Corporate ethics and reputation mechanisms were of no less importance for contract enforcement. The Armenian community – the "Armenian nation" – in many ways was equal to a merchant guild. Newcomers had to be adopted into the "Armenian nation" in a given city and then only after applying for citizenship to the local city council. Therefore, when recommending an applicant, the "Armenian nation" in a given town guaranteed that he was a credible and trustworthy person. Thus, belonging to a merchant network or corporation was a guarantee of predictable, honest behaviour.

Bibliography

Abrahamowicz, Zygmunt, Katalog dokumentów tureckich. Dokumenty do dziejów Polski i krajów ościennych w latach 1455–1672, Warszawa 1959, vol. 2.

Aslanian, Sebouh, The Circulation of Men and Credit. The Role of the Commenda and the Family Firm in Julfan Society, in: Journal of the Economic and Social History of the Orient 50, 2/3 (2007), pp. 124–171.

Baghdiantz-McCabe, Ina, Orientalism in Early Modern France. Eurasian Trade, Exoticism and the Ancien Regime, Oxford 2008.

Balzer, Oswald (ed.), Porządek sadów i spraw prawa ormiańskiego z r. 1604, Lwów 1912.

Balzer, Oswald, Sądownictwo ormiańskie w średniowiecznym Lwowie, Lwów 1909.

Balzer, Oswald (ed.), Statut ormiański w zatwierdzeniu Zygmunta I z roku 1519, Lwów 1910.

Brennan, Michael G. (ed.), The Travel Diary of Robert Bargrave, Levant Merchant (1647–1656), London 1999.

Bily, Inge/Carls, Wieland/Gönczi, Katalin (eds.), Sächsisch-magdeburgisches Recht in Polen. Untersuchungen zur Geschichte des Rechts und seiner Sprache, Berlin 2011.

Bischoff, Ferdinand (ed.), Urkunden zur Geschichte der Armenier in Lemberg, Wien 1864.

Biskup, Marian/Górski, Karol, Kazimierz Jagiellończyk. Zbiór studiów o Polsce drugiej połowy XV wieku, Warszawa 1987.

Bues, Almut (ed.), Die Aufzeichnungen des Dominikaners Martin Gruneweg (1562–ca. 1618). Über seine Familie in Danzig, seine Handelsreisen in Osteuropa und sein Klosterleben in Polen, [vol. 2], Wiesbaden 2008.

Charewiczowa, Lucja, Ograniczenia gospodarcze nacyj schizmatyckich i Żydów we Lwowie XV i XVI wieku, Lwów 1925.

Dachkevytch, Yaroslav R., Who are Armeno-Kipchaks? On the Ethnical Substrate of the Armenian Colonies in the Ukraine, in: Revue des études arméniennes 16 (1982), pp. 357–416.

Dashkevitch, Yaroslav R., Armianskaya koloniya v Kamentse-Podolske v 50–60-kh godakh XVI veka, in: Timofei Grunin (ed.), Dokumenty na polovetskom yazyke XVI v. (Sudebnye akty Kamenets-Podolskoy armianskoy obshchiny), Moscow 1967, pp. 65–96.

Dashkevitch, Yaroslav R., Armianskoe samoupravlenie vo Lvove v 60–80 gg. XVII v. (Protokoly armianskogo soveta stareyshin kak istoricheskiy istochnik), in: Banber Matenadarani 9 (1969), pp. 213–240.

Dashkevitch, Yaroslav R., Kipchak Acts of the Armenian Law Court at Kamenetz Podolsk (1559–1567) as a Cultural and Historical Monument, in: Ural-Altaische Jahrbücher 36 (3–4) (1965), pp. 292–310.

Dashkevitch, Yaroslav R., Ustav armianskoi obshchiny v Kamentse-Podolskom 1616 g., in: Rocznik Orientalistyczny 38 (1976), pp. 103–109.

Deny, Jean, L'armeno-coman et les «Ephemerides» de Kamieniec. 1604–1613, Wiesbaden 1957.

Dousa, Georgius, De itinere suo Constantinopolitano, Epistola, Lugdunum Batavorum : Ex Officina Plantiniana, Apud Christophorum Raphlelengium, Academiae Lugduno-Batavae Typographum, 1599.

Ermilov, Pavel, "Satanic Heresy". On one Topic in Anti-Armenian Polemic, in: Antonio Rigo (ed.), Orthodoxy and Heresy in Byzantium. The Definition and the Notion of Orthodoxy and Some Other Studies on the Heresies and the Non-Christian Religions, Rome 2010, pp. 79–97.

Faroqhi, Suraiya, Religious Interactions and Transnational Diplomatic Representation. Protection for Persian Traders (Acem tüccarı) in the Ottoman Lands around 1700, in: C. X. George Wei, Asian Culture, Diplomacy and Foreign Relations, Volume II, Individual Nations and Cases, Leiden/Boston 2022, pp. 199–220.

Faroqhi, Suraiya, Trade between the Ottomans and Safavids. The Acem tüccarı and others, in: Edmund Herzig/Willem Floor (eds.), Iran and the world in the Safavid Age, London 2015, pp. 237–252.

Frend, William H., The Rise of the Monophysite Movement. Chapters in the History of the Church in the Fifth and Sixth Centuries, Cambridge 1972.

Garitte, Gérard, Les écrits anti-arméniens dits du catholicos Isaac, in : Revue d'histoire ecclésiastique 45 (1960), pp. 711–715.

Garkavets, Aleksandr (ed.), Kypchakskoe pismennoye nasledie (2 volumes), Almaty 2002.

Gildebrandt, P.A. (ed.), Litovskaia Metrika, [vol. 1], in : Russkaia istoricheskaia biblioteka, [vol. 20], Sankt Petersburg 1903, pp. 635–637.

Gonzalez de Lara, Yadira, The secret of Venetian success : a public-order, reputation-based institution, in : European Review of Economic History 12, 3 (2008), pp. 247–285.

Gosh, Mkhitar, The Lawcode, translated from Old Armenian by Robert W. Thomson, New Jersey 2000.

Gloger, Zygmunt, Encyklopedia staropolska, Warszawa 1901.

Griffiths, John, What is legal pluralism?, in: Journal of Legal Pluralism 24 (1986), pp. 1–55.

Gromnicki, Tadeusz, Ormjanie w Polsce. Ich historja, prawa i przywileje, Warszawa 1889.

Grumel, Venance, Les invectives contre les Arméniens du "Catholicos Isaac", in : Revue des études byzantines 14 (1956), pp. 174–194.

Grunin, Timofei I. (ed.), Dokumenty na polovetskom iazyke XVI v. (Sudebnye akty Kamenets-Podolskoi armianskoi obshchiny), Moscow 1967.

Heyde, Jürgen, Armenier in Lemberg und Krakau. Städtische Migrationsgesellschaften und Magdeburger Recht, in: Gabriele Köster/Charlotte Link/Heiner Lück (eds.), Kulturelle Vernetzung in Europa: Das Magdeburger Recht und seine Städte. Wissenschaftlicher Begleitband zur Ausstellung "Faszination Stadt", Dresden 2018, pp. 285–297.

Heyde, Jürgen, Kamieniec im späten Mittelalter – Entwicklungslinien sozialer Ordnung in einer Migrationsgesellschaft, in: Zeitschrift für Ostmitteleuropaforschung 71 (3) (2022), pp. 327–358.

Heyde, Jürgen, Polityka Rady miejskiej Lwowa wobec Żydów i Ormian w XV/XVI wieku. Heterogeniczność etniczno-religijna w mieście jako wyzwanie ustrojowe, in: Kwartalnik Historii Kultury Materialnej 63 (2) (2015), pp. 283–292.

Ivanova, Svetlana, The Empire's "Own" Foreigners. Armenians and Acem Tüccar in Rumeli in the Seventeenh and Eighteenth Centuries, in: Oriente Moderno 83, 3 (2003), pp. 681–686, 691, 703.

Janeczek, Andrzej, Die Modernisierung der Städte Rutheniens. Die Reformen des 14.–16. Jahrhunderts, in: Eduard Mühle (ed.), Rechtsstadtgründungen im mittelalterlichen Polen, Köln 2011, pp. 355–372.

Janeczek, Andrzej, Exceptis schismaticis: uposledzenie Rusinow w przwilejach prawa niemieckiego Wladyslawa Jagielly, in: Przeglad historyczny 75 (1984), pp. 527–542.

Janeczek, Andrzej, Kolonisationsströmungen im polnisch-reußischen Grenzgebiet von der Mitte des 14. bis zum 16. Jahrhundert, in: Hans-Werner Rautenberg (ed.), Wanderungen und Kulturaustausch im östlichen Mitteleuropa. Forschungen zum ausgehenden Mittelalter, München 2006, pp. 29–58.

Janeczek, Andrzej, Listy dobrego urodzenia i dobrej sławy w procedurze nadawania prawa miejskiego Lwowa w XV wieku, in: KLIO. Czasopismo poświęcone dziejom Polski i powszechnym 23 (4) (2012), pp. 89–116.

Janeczek, Andrzej, Żydzi i Ormianie – dwie gminy religijno-prawne w krajobrazie etnicznym późnośredniowiecznej Polski, in: Halina Manikowska/Wojciech Brojer (eds.), Animarum cultura. Studia nad kulturą religijną na ziemiach polskich w średniowieczu, vol. 1: Struktury kościelno-publiczne, Warszawa 2008, pp. 271–298.

Kapral, Myron, Funktsionuvannia organiv vlady Lvova u XIII–XVIII st. (narys istorii instytutiv magdeburzkoho prava), in: Ukrainskyi istorychnyi zhurnal 5 (2006), pp. 111–130.

Kapral, Myron, Legal Regulation and National (Ethnic) Differentiation in Lviv, 1350–1600, in: Thomas Wünsch/Andrzej Janeczek (eds.), On the frontier of Latin Europe. Integration and segregation in Red Ruthenia, 1350–1600, Warsaw 2004.

Kapral, Myron, L'viv and its Ethnic Groups in the Second half of the Sixteenth Century, in: Almut Bues (ed.), Martin Gruneweg (1562– after 1615). A European Way of Life, Wiesbaden 2009, pp. 79–110.

Kapral, Myron, Natsionalni hromady Lvova XVI–XVIII st. (sotsialno-pravovi vzaiemyny), Lviv 2003.

Kapral, Myron, Pravovoe ustroistvo armianskoi obshchiny Lvova v XIV–XVIII vekakh. obzor dokumentov, in: Aleksandr N. Garkavets/G. Sapargaliev (eds.), Kypchaksko-pol'skaya versiya Armianskogo Sudebnika Mkhitara Gosha i Armiano-kypchakskiy Protsessual'nyi kodeks. Lvov, Kamenets-Podol'skiy, 1519–1594, Desht-i-Kypchak, Baur, Almaty 2003, pp. 741–754.

Kapral, Myron (ed.), Pryvilei mista Lvova (XIV–XVIII st.), Lviv 1998.

Kapral, Myron (ed.), Pryvilei natsionalnykh hromad mista Lvova (XIV–XVIII st.), Lviv 2000.

Kapral, Myron/Petryshak, Bohdana (eds.), Liber consulum civitatis leopoliensis (1460–1506), Leopoli 2020.

Kołodziejczyk, Dariusz, Ottoman-Polish Diplomatic Relations (15th–18th Century). An Annotated Edition of 'Ahdnames and Other Documents, Leiden 2000.

Korobowicz, Artur, Elementy rodzime i obce w sądownictwie ormiańskim w Zamościu, in: Jerzy Kłoczowski (ed.), Dzieje Lubelszczyzny 6, 1989, pp. 339–351.

Korobowicz, Artur, Sąd ormiański w Zamościu i postępowanie przed nim w świetle ksiąg sądowych, in: Annales Universitates M. Curie-Skłodowska. Sect. G, 11 (1964), pp. 195–212.

Król-Mazur, Renata/Stopka, Krzysztof, Die Stadt, in der Polen Deutsche genannt werden. Zwischenethnische Interaktion in Kamjanec' Podil's'kyj in der Darstellung armenischer Quellen um 1600, in: Stefan Rohdewald/David Frick (eds.), Litauen und Ruthenien. Studien zu einer transkulturellen Kommunikationsregion (15.-18. Jahrhundert), Lithuania and Ruthenia, Wiesbaden 2007, pp. 67–110.

Kroll, Piotr, Polish Converts to Islam in the Service of the Sultan, in: Silva Rerum, Muzeum of King Jan III's Palace at Wilanów, Warsaw 2013, https://www.wilanow-palac.pl/print/polish_converts_to_islam_in_the_service_of_the_sultan.html, accessed 02/06/2025.

Kutrzeba, Stanisław, Datastanagirk Mechitara Gosza i statut ormianski z r. 1519, in: Kwartalnik Historyczny 22 (1908), pp. 658–679.

Lewicki, M./Kohnowa, R., La version turque-kiptchak du 'Code des lois des Arméniens polonais' d'après le ms. No 1916 de la Bibliothèque Ossolineum, in : Rocznik Orientalistyczny 21 (1957), pp. 153–300.

Liske, Xawery (ed.), Akta grodzkie i ziemskie z czasów Rzeczypospolitej Polskiej z archiwum bernardynskiego we Lwowie, [vol. 7], Lwów 1878, pp. 134–136.

Łoziński, Władysław, Patrycyat i mieszczaństwo lwowskie w XVI i XVII wieku, Lwów 1892.

Łoziński, Władysław, Patrycjat i mieszczaństwo lwowskie w XVI i XVII wieku, Lwów 1902.

Macler, Frédéric, Rapport sur une mission scientifique en Galicie et en Bukovine, juillet-août 1925, in : Revue des études arméniennes VII, 1 (1927), pp. 11–177.

Majewski, Marcin Łukasz, Ormianie w Zamościu w pierwszych trzech dekadach istnienia miasta (1580–1610), in : Lehahayer 7 (2020), pp. 5–41.

Malinovskii, Ioannii A. (ed.), Sbornik materialov otnosiashchikhsia k istorii panov-rady Velikogo kniazhestva Litovskogo, Tomsk 1901.

Matwijowski, Leon, Prawo ormiańskie w dawnej Polsce, Lwów 1939.

Najdenova, Desislava Tacheva, Anti-Armenian Polemics in a Slavic Canon Law Miscellany (Ms. Slav. No 461 from the Manuscript Collection of the Romanian Academy), in: Etudes balkaniques 3 (2014), pp. 82–95.

Năsturel, Petre Ş, L'attitude du Patriarcat oequmenique envers les Armenienes des pays Roumains (fin XIVe siècle-debut XVIe siecle), in : L'Armenie et Byzance. Histoire et culture, Paris 1996.

Oleś, Marian, Casimir The Great and The Armenian Privileges, 1333–1370, in : Études Slaves et Est-Européennes/Slavic and East-European Studies 11, 3/4 (1966/67), pp. 67–90.

Oleś, Marian, The Armenian Law in the Polish Kingdom (1356–1519). A juridical and historical study, Rome 1966.

Osipian, Alexandr, Armenian Diasporas between the Golden Horde, Rus', and Poland: Long-Distance Trade and Diplomatic Services, in: Alexander V. Maiorov and Roman Hautala (eds.), The Routledge Handbook on the Mongols and Central-Eastern Europe, London 2021, pp. 405–424.

Osipian, Alexandr, Between Mercantilism, Oriental Luxury and the Ottoman Threat. Discourses on the Armenian Diaspora in the Early Modern Kingdom of Poland, in: Acta Poloniae Historica 116 (2017), pp. 171–208.

Osipian, Alexandr, Debt, Trust and Reputation in Early Modern Armenian Merchant Networks, in: Laura Kolb/George Oppitz-Trotman (eds.), Early Modern Debts, 1550–1700, London 2020, pp. 155–182.

Osipian, Alexandr, Legal pluralism in the cities of the early modern Kingdom of Poland. The jurisdictional conflicts and uses of justice by Armenian merchants, in: Griet Vermeesch/Manon Van Der Heijden/Jaco Zuijderduijn (eds.), The uses of justice in global perspective, 1600–1900, London 2019, pp. 80–102.

Osipian, Alexandr, Long distance trade and Armenian migration to the lands of Poland-Lithuania in 1350–1795, in: Historische Mitteilungen 33 (2022), pp. 155–182.

Osipian, Alexandr, Restraining-encouraging violence: Commerce, diplomacy, and brigandage on the steppe routes between the Ottoman Empire, Poland-Lithuania, and Russia, 1470s–1570s, in: Peter H. Wilson/Marie Houllemare/Erica Charters (eds.), A Global History of Early Modern Violence, Manchester 2020, pp. 124–141.

Osipian, Alexandr, The Construction of Historical Identity among Polish and Armenian Patricians in Lviv, 1570s–1670s, in: Cristian Luca/Laurentiu Radvan (eds.), Social and Political Elites in Eastern and Central Europe (15th–18th centuries), University College London, London 2015, p. 65–83.

Osipian, Alexandr, The Ottoman and Persian Luxury between Fashion and Politics. Armenian Merchant Network and the Making of Sarmatian Culture in the Early Modern Poland-Lithuania, in: Alina Payne (ed.), The Land between Two Seas. Art on the Move in the Mediterranean and the Black Sea, 1300–1700, Boston/Leiden 2022, pp. 311–333.

Osipian, Alexandr, Voting at Home and on the Move. Elections of Mayors and caravanbashi by Armenian Merchants in Poland and the Ottoman Empire, 1500–1700, in: Serena Ferente/Lovro Kuncevic/Miles Pattenden (eds.), Cultures of Voting in Pre-modern Europe, London 2018, pp. 310–328.

Panaite, Viorel, Trade and Merchants in the 16th-century Polish-Ottoman Treaties, in: Revue des Etudes sud-est europeennes 32, nos. 3–4 (1994), pp. 259–276.

Prochovicius, Ioannes Andreas, Relatio Archiepiscopi Leopoliensis ritus latini de status spirituali suae provinciae …; de Ruthenis et Armenis, in: Litterae Episcoporum historiam Ucrainae illustrantes (1600–1900), vol. 1: 1600–1640, Rome 1972, pp. 82–89.

Pryor, John H., The Origins of the Commenda Contract, in: Speculum 52, 1 (1977), pp. 5–37.

Schütz, Edmund, Armeno-kiptschakische Ehekontrakte und Testamente aus dem XVI. Jahrhundert, in: Acta Orientalia Academiae Scientiarum Hungaricae 24 (1971), pp. 265–300.

Sharf, Andrew, Byzantine Orthodoxy and the 'Preliminary Fast' of the Armenians, in: Byzance: Hommage à André N. Stratos, 2. Athens 1986, pp. 650–672.

Solicovii, Ioannis Demetrii, Commentarius brevis rerum Polonicarum a morte Sigismundi Augusti. Dantisci 1647.

Stopka, Krzysztof, Interakcje etniczne w mieście staropolskim. Kamieniec Podolski w ujęciu źródeł ormiańskich od XV do połowy XVII wieku, in: Prace Komisji Wschodnioeuropejskiej Polskiej Akademii Umiejętności 11 (2010), pp. 85–124.

Stopka, Krzysztof, Migracje a przemiany tożsamości ormiańskiej w średniowiecznej Europie Wschodniej, in: Macieja Salamon/Jerzy Strzelczyk (ed.), Wędrówka i etnogeneza w starożytności i średniowieczu, Kraków 2004, pp. 355–365.

Stopka, Krzysztof, "Nasza polska nacja". Kształtowanie się patriotyzmu polskiego wśród Ormian w okresie staropolskim, in: Andrzej Nowak/Andrzej Aleksander Zięba (eds.), Formuły patriotyzmu w Europie Wschodniej i Środkowej od nowożytności do współczesności, Kraków 2009, pp. 37–54.

Stopka, Krzysztof, Ormianie, in: Michał Kopczyński/Wojciech Tygielski (ed.), Pod wspólnym niebem. Narody dawnej Rzeczypospolitej, Warszawa 2010, pp. 115–133.

Stopka, Krzysztof, Ormianie w Polsce dawnej i dzisiejszej, Kraków 2000.

Stopka, Krzysztof, The Religious Culture of Polish Armenians (Church-Public Structures and Relations), in: Acta Poloniae Historica 101 (2010), pp. 163–205.

Tamanaha, Brian Z., The Folly of the 'Social Scientific' Concept of Legal Pluralism, in: Journal of Law & Society 20 (2), 1993, pp. 192–217.

Tavernier, John Baptista, The six voyages of John Baptista Tavernier, London 1678.

de Tournefort, Joseph Pitton, A voyage into the Levant perform'd by command of the late French king, in two volumes, [vol. 2], translated by J. Ozell, London 1718.

Troebst, Stefan, Isfahan – Moskau – Amsterdam. Zur Entstehungsgeschichte des moskauischen Transitprivilegs für die Armenische Handelskompanie in Persien (1666–1676), in: Jahrbücher für Geschichte Osteuropas 41 (1993), pp. 180–209.

Tryjarski, Edward (ed.), Zapisy sądu duchownego Ormian miasta Lwowa za lata 1564–1608 w języku ormiańsko-kipczackim, Kraków 2017.

Tryjarski, Edward (ed.), Zapisy sądu duchownego Ormian miasta Lwowa za lata 1625–1630 w języku ormiańsko-kipczackim, Kraków 2010.

van Doosselaere, Quentin, Commercial Agreements and Social Dynamics in Medieval Genoa, Cambridge 2009.

von Brünneck, Wilhelm, Zur Geschichte des Magdeburger Rechts und der Statuten der Armenier in Lemberg, in: Zeitschrift der Savigny-Stiftung für Rechtsgeschichte. Germanistische Abteilung 35 (1914), pp. 1–40.

Yekeler, Numan/Wajs, Hubert (eds.), Yoldaki elçi: Osmanlı'dan günümüze Türk-Leh ilişkileri = Poseł w drodze. Stosunki turecko-polskie od czasów osmańskich do dnia dzisiejszego, İstanbul 2014.

Zakrzewska-Dubasowa, Mirosława, Organizacja gminy ormiańskiej w Zamosciu w XVI–XVII wieku, in: Rocznik Lubelski 3 (1960), pp. 63–82.

Zakrzewska-Dubasowa, Mirosława, Ormianie Zamojscy i ich rola w wymianie handlowej i kulturalnej między Polską a Wschodem, Lublin 1965.

Zakrzewska-Dubasowa, Mirosława, Przyczynek do historii jarmarków lubelskich, in: Annales Universitatis Mariae Curie-Skłodowska. Sectio F, Nauki Filozoficzne i Humanistyczne 20 (1968), pp. 59–74.

Zakrzewska-Dubasowa, Ormiańska Temida, in: Palestra 24, 7 (1980), pp. 19–37.

Unpublished archival sources:

Central State Historical Archive of Ukraine in Kyiv, fond 39 (City Magistrate of Kamianets-Podilskyi), holding 1, file 20, fol. 50; file 26, fol. 40.

Central State Historical Archive of Ukraine in Lviv, fond 132 (Letters of dignitaries, statesmen, and religious hierarchs), holding 1, file 545, p. 1.

Central State Historical Archive of Ukraine in Lviv, fond 52 (City Magistrate of Lviv), holding 2, file 67, 258, 515, 517, 521, 526, 546, pp. 14–15, 162–165, 168–169, 476–480, 557, 567, 593–594, 597–598, 718, 754, 1061, 1354–1356, 1358.

Dzieje Ormian lwowskich od roku 1649 aż do r. 1713, in: Dział Rękopisów Biblioteki Zakładu Narodowego im. Ossolińskich, Wrocław. Sygnatura oryginału: 1646/II, fol. 64. fol. 38.

Wojewódzki Archiwum Państwowe w Lublinie. Księgi prawa ormiańskiego. Acta Armenica Zamosciana, file 1, fol. 97v.

Wojewódzki Archiwum Państwowe w Lublinie. Księgi prawa ormiańskiego. Acta Armenica Zamosciana, file 6, fol. 58.

Philipp Höhn

The Dogs of Danzig

Semantic Pluralism and Common Legalities in Late Medieval Anglo-Hansard Disputes

1. Introduction

A petition of "English merchants" to the English Parliament, which met in November 1422, gives a fascinating insight into the dynamics of legal pluralism in Anglo-Hanseatic relations.[1] The petitioners complained bitterly that when they had gone to Danzig to trade, the mayors had told them that they would "*slaughter them until the dogs of Danzig would be licking their blood off the city's streets.*"[2] The governor (*guverner*) of the English was captured, threatened, and almost killed. Several other gravamina brought up by these merchants, who plead to suspend the privileges of the Hansards in England which had to be confirmed formally by the new King Henry VI (r. 1422–1461, 1470–1471), ran a similar line. The merchants took great effort to clarify that not only had individuals been treated badly by the Danzigers, but all English merchants, and even the honour of the English king had been impugned. Allegedly, Danzig burghers had thrown English banners into the mud to mock the Crown and nailed the royal coat of arms to the pillory like a thief's.

Similarly, in 1423, four merchants from London, York, Norwich, and King's Lynn complained to Parliament that the Greifswald Council had captured them on their way to Scania, treating them "*as if we were Jews*", accusing them and all other English merchants of being pirates and threatening to behead them. The English prisoners had been tied up, so that they had to sit outside in winter and could not see their feet in the snow for six weeks. The Hanse Kontor in London had not only refused

1 Hanserecesse (HR) I, 7; Given-Wilson, Parliament: Henry VI, November 1422, app. 25, 26. The petition has only survived in German translations in the archives of Gdańsk and Wismar and is not part of the roll which appears to be complete. As Given-Wilson indicates in his introduction, this absence does not mean that Parliament did not tackle these claims. The English merchants apparently presented their grievances orally in Parliament. Also, the correspondence of the Steelyard (the Hanse Kontor in London) indicates that these grievances were brought up in Parliament and that the common lords supported the Hansards against these claims – see HR I, 7, no. 402. This is also indicated by the activities of the Hanse Kontor to protect the privileges by appealing to the Privy Council in July 1423 – Nicolas, Proceedings, pp. 110, 112, 117.

2 HR I, 7, no. 592 § 1.

to help the arrested merchants, but also explained that all Englishmen would be slaughtered, when they came to their lands.[3]

Arguably, these petitions show in a nutshell the dangers, injustices, and arbitrariness which medieval long-distance traders had to face in a legal landscape potentially hostile to them. I will, however, argue that the "dogs of Danzig" were rather ciphers for a particular way to shape episodes of confrontation. The narrative was presented as a conflict in which loyal subjects of the English king, who only traded for the "common wealth" and "profit" of the realm, were terribly mistreated by the brutal Hansards, who dishonoured the king by desecrating his insignia and claiming that he was the head of a gang of robbers. The "dogs of Danzig" are a fascinating example of the semantics, narratives, and framing of conflict in late medieval legal pluralism. The detailed gravamina most probably do not depict the relationship between the mercantile and seafaring elites of the Prussian towns and English ports on the coast of the North Sea, but rather show that sources, such as the petition mentioned, constructed a conflict following the logic of the forum before which they had been brought up, and the semantics connected with it.

Accounts such as the mentioned petition tell us about the evolution of the legal landscape and about the importance of political and legal semantics and discourses for conflict management. At the same time, they point to phenomena of coherence in legal pluralism. The ability of medieval forums to end conflicts was limited. Actors did not strive to resolve conflicts but to improve their position and avoid quarrels escalating to an extent where talking would stop. Conflict communication primarily meant that the parties continued to talk to each other, or at least about each other, in front of a forum.[4] Thus, legal pluralism required factors of social coherence to keep things going. It is exactly this aspect that is the focus of this article.

In his illustrative 2020 monograph, Tom Johnson addresses the question of how forms of coherence emerged against the backdrop of different legal cultures in England.[5] His starting point is the consolidation of the English legal landscape in the fifteenth century in connection with the formation of a "political society" shaped by discourses, a political language, and communicative anchors.[6] He argues that "common legalities" allowed conflicts to be managed within pluralism. Ambiguities and contradictions shaped the legal landscape, but they also created sociability. Johnson identifies four fields in which "legal commonalities" developed: perception of a legal landscape, beliefs about legitimate judicial knowledge, the vernacularisation of law,

3 HR I, 7, no. 592 §§ 7.

4 See: Höhn, Entscheidungsfindung.

5 Johnson, Law, p. 11: "Common legalities represented crucial vectors of communication and solidarity."

6 Watts, Pressure; Harriss, Political.

and common legal documents. His concept is particularly stimulating because it describes elements of coherence within legal pluralism and overcomes powerful dichotomies in legal history by looking not into macroprocesses of harmonisation or unification, but law and conflict management as social practices.[7]

Taking up Johnson's considerations, the aim of this article is to analyse pluralistic legal landscapes as created by social practice, by day-to-day interactions of conflicting actors.[8] While Johnson focuses on legal interactions within a political entity, my approach expands the perspective by asking how foreigners interacted with this political entity and participated in its negotiation. Especially in the third part, I reflect on how far Johnson's terminology related to England might be applicable for the politically multi-layered land- and seascape of North and Western Europe. I try to recalibrate our understanding of mercantile conflict management in two aspects:

(1) By focusing on the semantics which the conflicting parties adopted when they litigated before specific fora, I argue for taking the normative framework of a particular legal landscape more seriously. These frameworks restricted how people could narrate their conflicts and act within them. They were thus part of the social construction of the conflict itself.

(2) These discourses and semantics, however, co-created legal structures. They were brought up and developed by the merchants themselves – not as per se progressive predecessors of free trade, but as an interest group with particular goals, intentions, and scope of action.

My approach thus focuses on actors as members of complex networks, rather than as atomised individuals confronted with judicial institutions. Further, political semantics characterised the practices of mercantile conflict management, since these were not separated from the sphere of politics and political conflicts. The way in which structural conflicts were discursively treated, mattered for individual disputes. Without looking at the underlying structural dimensions, we can hardly expect to comprehend the judicial and political background which shaped conflict management. Vice versa, without looking into practices, structures and their development cannot be fully explained. Thus, the individual narratives and framings of conflict shaped the political and legal landscapes of late medieval Northern and Western Europe.[9]

My argument is built up in three steps. Following the example of the 1422 petition, the first part asks about the impact of the political and legal discourses connected to a legal forum on the framing of conflicts. The second part focuses on the practices

7 Johnson, Law, pp. 7–8.

8 For this approach see: Höhn, Kaufleute, pp. 351–362; Höhn, Criminalization.

9 For a comparative approach see: Jostkleigrewe, Monarchischer Staat.

by which conflicting parties adopted these framings, developed them further and thereby shaped the legal landscape. In the third part, I will discuss how Johnson's "common legalities" might be applicable to the multi-layered conflict landscape of North and Western Europe.

2. Semantics and Framings

Research on late medieval litigation strategies has pointed out that conflicting parties had several options to act, and that they combined different tactics.[10] Quarrels between Englishmen and Hansards were negotiated at both local and regional common law courts, but also using special jurisdictions such as the royal oyer-et-terminer commissions or central courts. There is considerable research on royal and central courts such as the King's Bench[11] as well as the Court of Admiralty. This court in particular expanded its jurisdiction on many matters concerning maritime trade until the end of the fourteenth century, when its power was restricted, responding to pressure by English and foreign merchants.[12] The "*carta mercatoria*" of 1303 and following treaties had determined that conflicts between Hansards and Englishmen should be judged by mixed juries.[13] Until now however, the local level of mercantile and maritime conflict management has been studied only in fits and starts.[14]

Depending on which forum they decided to appeal to, actors had to adopt specific narrative framings of the conflict. If they decided to raise their complaint in a specific forum, they had to narrate and mediate their position in a certain way to underpin their points. In the case of the 1422 petition, this was the English Parliament, within which "'the Commons', as a broad constituency of people and a legitimating idea, came to take a greater prominence in public discourse".[15] By bringing their case here, the English merchants escalated it. Their communicative strategy emphasised confrontation because they communicated with English "political society", not with their Hanse counterparts.

Such petitions show how petitioners had to choose a forum out of the plurality of jurisdictions and norms which characterised the legal landscape of late medieval Northern Europe, which resulted in narrating their conflict in a particular way.

10 Cordes and Höhn, Conflict.
11 Blatcher, Court.
12 See below.
13 Jenks, England, p. 611; Masschaele, Jury, p. 106.
14 Johnson, Law, pp. 101–108.
15 Ibid, p. 13. For its adaption in conflict management see: Fletcher, Communauté.

Actors decided to bring a case before a particular forum because of political calculation. What they intended, however, can only be understood when analysing the precise conflict constellation.

As for the 1422 petition, some structural dimensions of the conflict can be tackled. Formally, the petition was directed against "*de coplude van der hanse van Almanien, geheten oesterlinge*" (the merchants of the German Hanse, called Easterlings), but in fact, nine out of ten of the complaints concentrated on Danzig.[16] That is to say, disputes between the English and the Hanse in general were not the issue here, but rather those among merchants from ports in northern England trading to Prussia on the one hand, and Prussian traders in England on the other. Very probably, the petition had not been initiated by "the English merchants" as such, but by certain interest groups from King's Lynn and London engaged in trade with Prussia. As Terrence Lloyd has shown, merchants from King's Lynn had collected £20 especially for agitation in Parliament.[17] Accordingly, in 1437, Danzig's Mayor Heinrich Vorrath, when submitting information about that year's Parliament session, wrote to his hometown that it was exactly the merchants from the English North Sea coast who intrigued against Danzig, which allegedly caused him many problems because he had to intervene to protect the urban privileges.[18]

What the petitioners in 1422 wanted the English King to do also indicates that their plea was part of a conflict between economic competitors. They asked for a suspension of the privileges of the London outpost of the Hanse, the Steelyard, and the arrest of the Hansards if the Prussians would not guarantee to treat the English traders reciprocally.[19] Danzig and its neighbours stood in fierce competition with English merchants from Hull, King's Lynn, and London who increasingly gained dominance in seafaring between England and Prussia in the first decades of the

16 HR I, 7, no. 592, list of grievances: The Danzig city council threatened to arrest the governor of the English Merchants' outpost within the town, to tell the local hangmen to blockade access to houses in which Englishmen lived, and to force them to reside in hostels run by burghers (§ 1). The council had prohibited burghers and other men in town to sell goods to Englishmen on market days (§ 2) and raised illegal levies and customs (§§ 3, 4). The English were not allowed to buy or sell things in winter, even if they stayed in Danzig (§ 5), and were forbidden to buy wood for arches and other types of wood (§ 6). Four additional claims dealing with causes of maritime violence between the people of Danzig and Greifswald and men from Hull and King's Lynn (§§ 7–10). See also: Jenks, England, pp. 555–558.

17 Lloyd, England, pp. 555–556.

18 HR II, 2, no. 67: "*Sunderlik so ik ju lest schreff, wo de ut der nortcost uns so hartlik entkegen sin, de to Prusen plegen to vorkeren, und by allen herren gestlik und wertlik mit so valscher logen und vor dem parlemente so vorvolgen, sowol myns herren gnade alz ju und de stede, dat my sunderlik vel arbeit mackt und den unsen groten schaden deit.*"

19 HR I, 7, no. 592, pp. 400–401.

fifteenth century.[20] Violence by mariners from ports of the southern Baltic coast, such as Danzig, was often directed against competing merchants from northern England.[21] What the petition framed as a conflict between "the English merchant" and the "merchants of the Hanse of Allemagne", was presumably the escalating competition between the English east coast and the Prussian towns, especially Danzig.

Nathalie Zemon Davies has pointed to the narrative character of pleas as "fictions in the archives".[22] Petitioners told stories which they thought looked promising within the juridical-political framework within which they were raised. The 1422 petitioners shaped their narrative as a series of episodic acts of violence, naming opponents, conflict lines, and assumed causes of the quarrel. The gravamina framed conflicts as harming the honour of king and realm, referring to the broad semantic field of "common good", "common weal", or the "common profit" of the English realm, ideas which were becoming increasingly important exactly in this period.[23]

In the 1422 petition, this is illustrated by the claim of John Bedford of Hull. As he said, his ship, the *Bartholomew* had been seized by the Admiral of the North for warfare against the Scots.[24] With the *Bartholomew*, the admiral had attacked a Prussian ship freighted in Scotland. When another ship from Hull arrived in Danzig, the council seized this one because it was supposed to have committed the taking. Shortly afterwards, the *Bartholomew* was captured by a Prussian ship.[25] Bedford was one of Hull's leading merchants with close connections to John Tutbury, Mayor of Hull, who himself had acquired licences to fight the enemies of the English king at sea. In the shadow of the Anglo-Scottish conflict, a network around Tutbury, Bedford, and other inhabitants of Hull and King's Lynn fought against the Danzig mariners and merchants.[26]

When he mentioned that his ship had been commandeered by the admiral for war, he referred to a typical way in which English merchant elites framed their violent actions at sea as part of "safeguarding" the sea or as warfare against the enemies of the king – although a lot of these conflicts had an individual or regional component. He highlighted that he was not responsible for the attack, but the admiral and finally

---

20 JENKS, England, pp. 740–741.

21 HÖHN, Kaufleute, pp. 294–305; KUNZE, Hanseakten, pp. 199–328.

22 ZEMON DAVIS, Fictions.

23 ORMROD, Common; FLETCHER, Communauté, pp. 116–119.

24 In the petition, the admiral is named as "Schroop van Balthon", who is not identifiable as an English admiral (see RODGERS, Safeguard, pp. 506–507). The mentioned admiral was probably Thomas Beaufort (admiral from 1408–1426).

25 HR I, 7, no. 592 § 8.

26 KUNZE, Hanseakten, pp. 102, 106, 247 fn., 130, 215–220.

the king himself, which implied that the attack had been legitimate. This argument was widespread.[27]

The framing employed by the 1422 petitioners however, served to deny responsibility by claiming to have acted not in their own interest. They contextualised their actions as violence for the "common weal" of the realm. By referring to the alleged dishonouring of the insignia of the reign, the coat of arms and the banner of the English king, the petitions construed a major conflict, within which the English were disadvantaged and disgraced by the Hansards, and which affected England's economic and social capital. Additionally, the supposed disenfranchisement was depicted in dishonouring acts of violence such as the attack on the king's coat of arms.

The claimants had an interest in portraying individual actions as outcomes of broader conflicts involving the king and the realm. They were highly aware of the political situation.[28] Some of their points, for example the one on the Prussian prohibition on buying wood for bows and other weapons, which were necessary for English military success, were frequently referred to in order to frame local conflicts in Parliament.[29]

In general, the very reference to the "English merchant" followed the usual rhetoric of petitions to Parliament. Around 1400, Parliament transformed from a court for private lawsuits into a forum of the consolidating political system, which developed different legal, fiscal, and political functions.[30] In the understanding of contemporaries, a "common petition" differed from individual complaints. It concerned the often-unspecified public – the commons as a whole.[31] Hence, it was a promising strategy for the petitioners to associate their individual claims with the alleged "English merchant" as an anonymous collective.[32] Also naming their opponents not as Danzigers or as subjects of the Teutonic Order, but as "Hansards", lifted the dispute to the most politically general level. It fitted into the distinction of friend and foe often brought up before Parliament, which confronted the loyal subjects and friends of the king and the realm with their alleged enemies.[33]

This specific framing of conflicts also formed the character of these. Parliament was primarily an inner forum, a place where factions of English long-distance

---

27 For comparable examples see: Fletcher, Communauté, pp. 111–116; Saul, English Towns.

28 Sumption, Triumph and Illusion, pp. 1–59.

29 For this argument see: Jenks, England, p. 599 n. 47, 672; Given-Wilson, Parliament.

30 For this aspect see: Johnson, Law, pp. 209–275.

31 Fletcher, Political Language, p. 97; Dodd, Justice; Ormrod, Common, pp. 247–248. For several examples see: Liddy, War, pp. 140–189.

32 For another example from the conflicts between English Prussian traders and their Prussian competitors, see Ormrod, Killick and Bradford, Common, pp. 153–155.

33 Fletcher, Communauté.

merchants and shipowners could make their grievances political.[34] These economic interest groups played a considerable role in shaping political discourses in Parliament.[35] Consider, for example, the recurring references in English sources of the fourteenth and fifteenth centuries to the king exercising "safeguard" over the "narrow seas" or to his duty "to keep the sea", which opened opportunities to fight economic rivals, foreign as well as English.[36] This discourse did not originate in the royal chancery, but was brought to Parliament or to the royal court by precisely the mentioned economic interest groups, often in order to justify their own violent actions.[37]

At first glance, this could be seen as evidence that foreign merchants were confronted with a legal system that was opaque and potentially disadvantageous to them. At second glance, however, it must be stated that the communicative escalation was a usual part of merchant conflict practices in which foreign actors were also involved.[38] This was the case because for the Hansards, there were opportunities to raise their conflicts to a political level, for example at the Hanse Diets. These were, above all, a place where Hansa members communicated and escalated conflicts, again framing them not as individual conflicts, but as ones that were about the "common good" and in the best interests of the "common merchant". Here as well, actors did not necessarily aim at resolving their conflicts. Rather, by declaring individual disputes to be political ones, they tried to gain the right to exercise reprisals or to call in diplomatic help. Comparable to the "common profit" of the English kingdom, the "common benefit" (*gemene nute*) of the "common merchant" (*gemener kopman*) was the leitmotif of conflict communication used to transform individual interests into collective ones.[39]

In fact, however, this was only one step in a multi-step chain of conflict management, from which it was possible to switch back to other, less escalation-oriented procedures such as mediation or arbitration. A common way of reacting to accusations, which the London Kontor chose in 1422,[40] was to reciprocally complain about oppression by the English at the Hanse Diet. Similarly, one could ask the Grandmaster of the Teutonic Order, the Lord of Danzig, to intervene diplomatically.[41] Accordingly, in April 1423 a Prussian Diet decided that the Grand Master

---

34 See for e. g.: Liddy, War, pp. 43–57.

35 Saul, Local Politics.

36 This is part of my current project. Meanwhile, for the discourse on this topic see: Rodgers, Safeguard, pp. 150–152

37 Höhn, Criminalization.

38 Cordes and Höhn, Extra-Legal, pp. 513–521.

39 Höhn, Kaufleute, pp. 192–193; Höhn, Entscheidungsfindung; Boestad, Profit.

40 HR I, 7, no. 594.

41 Ibid., no. 594 § 7.

should write to the English king and Parliament. Simultaneously, the Grand Master was asked to re-establish older Prussian claims against the English, probably a reference to open compensation claims resulting from the treaty of The Hague in 1407.[42] In May, the Danzig council asked the English Council of the Realm not to believe the accusations of the English traders, but to instruct them to bring their complaints before the Grand Master.[43]

Conflict narratives thus often followed dominant political semantics and discourses. From a source-critical perspective, this implies a look at the structural frontlines from the back, configurations which would otherwise probably be concealed by the narratives. From a perspective focusing on conflict practices, it indicates that the structural characteristics of a legal landscape, here the semantics, had a fundamental impact on the social construction of conflicts and should thus be taken very seriously.

3. Creating a Legal Landscape

However, foreign merchants in England also adopted discourses that had emerged within Parliament and developed them further, which in turn influenced the respective forums. Normative frameworks were not simply proposed, but constantly redefined, reinterpreted, and changed by the recurrent practices of conflict communication. In what follows, this reciprocal creation of a legal landscape is studied by focusing on four strategies of conflict management which Hansards and other foreign actors utilised when interacting with the English fora.

3.1 Encoding Political and Judicial Semantics

The petition of 1422 has only survived in a Low German translation, probably produced by the *Hansekontor* in London. In January 1423, the Kontor wrote to unspecified Hanse cities complaining about attacks by English merchants.[44] The edition of this letter follows the Wismar manuscript of the Hanse records, which might suggest that it had been addressed not only to Hanse cities directly involved in the conflicts mentioned. Probably, Wismar was only addressed as one of the Hanse towns on the southern shore of the Baltic Sea. The translations of two petitions edited in the *Hanserecesse* come from the Gdańsk city archives: the one mentioned

---

42 Ibid., no. 595 § 7. See also no. 461 §§ 7, 19, no. 590 § 8.

43 HR I, 7, no. 596.

44 HR I, 7, no. 594.

and a second one, which, as the Kontor noted, contained grievances of the English merchants presented orally to Parliament.[45]

As mentioned above, the "English merchants" pleaded for the suspension of the privileges and the arrest of Hansards in general.[46] Thus, the Kontor had a vital interest in archiving a copy of the petition to find support from the Hanse towns, but also before the fora of royal jurisdiction.[47] The Kontor thus sent copies to Danzig, as the town affected by most of the English complaints. Such written records, their translation, transcription, compilation, and archival collection have recently been discussed in terms of their significance for the management of conflicts.[48] Precisely these forms of conflict writing (*Konfliktschriftlichkeit*) constituted an essential memory, which helped actors to navigate their legally pluralistic environment.[49]

Within the Low German translation, several loanwords and paraphrases indicate that the translator was familiar with the negotiations in Parliament. Apparently, there were actors in the Kontor's environment who helped to gather information even from political circles, or the Kontor had access to legal experts at the royal court or Parliament.[50] The letter, with which the translations were sent, mentions that merchants from London and some other towns had plotted against the Hansards. However, it goes on to say that the ecclesiastical and secular lords in Parliament had shown themselves to be friends of the Hansa, for which the towns should show themselves grateful (whatever this means), and had decided that the Hansards should continue to trade according to the old privileges and customs.[51] This indicates that the Kontor had access to the negotiations inside Parliament, or at least relations close enough to get first-hand information.[52] Very probably, the Steelyard could utilise a network of local actors to pursue the interests of the Hansa.[53]

---

45 HR I, 7, no. 593: "De claghen, de de Ingelsche copluden montliken deden": On the back, the Hansekontor recorded a list of English and Hanse merchants (probably primarily English engaged in trade to Danzig and Prussian councillors involved in trade with England), whose role in the conflict remains unclear.

46 HR I, 7, no. 592, pp. 400–401.

47 For the negotiation of the case in the Hanse towns see: HR I, 7, no. 623.

48 Wubs-Mrozewicz, Kopieergedrag; Boestad, Profit, pp. 49–112; Manger, Behind the scenes.

49 Höhn, Kaufleute, pp. 108–111.

50 Jenks, England, p. 556 n. 28; for loanwords see e. g. HR I, 7, no. 592, p. 396 "remedie", p. 399 "pladeringe"; For the legal experts at the royal council, Chancery, and Parliament, and their role in individual conflicts see: Harriss, Political, p. 35.

51 HR I, 7, no. 594.

52 For the legal experts, especially the scribes and notaries within the *Kontor* who might have collected such information, see: Boestad, Plumes.

53 For Hanseatic "insiders" in Danish political society see: Höhn, Herren, pp. 390–392.

3.2 Adopting and Strengthening Semantics

With their judicial practices, not only the English, but also foreigners, influenced the courts and the discourse inventory used within them. Take for example the Court of Chancery: The chancellor did not judge according to common law, but according to their "conscience", often translated as equity.[54] The basis for his decisions were the petitions addressed to the court by plaintiffs. These were formulated from an individual perspective, but took up narrative patterns and phrases by which the petitioners tried to give their complaints more credibility. During the fourteenth and fifteenth centuries, plaintiffs increasingly turned to the Court of Chancery, asking for correction of purported injustices done to them.[55]

Because the Court of Chancery saw itself as a corrective against the injustice of common law courts and local officials, this is hardly surprising. Foreign merchants actively framed their complaints as conflicts with the local gentry, the judiciary, or corrupt officials, probably relying on the legal experts in the milieu of the Chancery.[56] They used the same key terms as the English plaintiffs to narrate the conflicts in a way which strengthened the role of the monarch, the chancellor, and his entourage vis-à-vis local elites.

In 1463, for example, some Hamburg merchants approached the Treasurer of England, John Tiptoft. A ship chartered by them had been attacked in the Kirkley Roads, an anchorage protected by sandbanks close to Great Yarmouth that was contested by local maritime communities, by "*a kervell of yours, whereof Harry Skawe is mastyr, that waits on warfare [...] not withstanding that he lay in peas at hys need without any moving of warre.*"[57] He had taken their ship to Sandwich, where the spoils had been distributed. The petitioners requested that the treasurer write letters to the mayor of Sandwich so that their goods might be reseized there until the treasurer would arrive. They claimed that they had obtained a commission from the Court of Chancery, which appointed the warden of the Cinque Ports, an association of port towns that had emerged in the thirteenth century, holding jurisdictional rights at their own courts, to take custody of the goods.[58] The petitioners had not received their goods there, however, maybe because local authorities had not followed the commission. They asked the treasurer to decide according to "*ryght and conscience will*".[59] The Hamburgers thus explicitly referred to the governing

54 Haskett, Medieval; Haskett, Conscience.

55 Gardiner, Calendar; for Hansards see Zoomer, Representing.

56 Harriss, Political, p. 35.

57 HUB 8, no. 1222; Calendar of Parliament Rolls, Edward IV, 1461–1467, p. 232. For the Kirkley Roads see Butcher, Medieval Lowestoft.

58 For the Cinque Ports cf. Murray, Constitutional History.

59 HUB 8, no. 1228.

principle of the Court of Chancery. Furthermore, they swore that they had had "safe conducts", which had been registered by the Chancery, and that they had been in a state of friendly peace with the English king. These were topical accusations, which Breton or Portuguese complaints before the Court of Chancery repeatedly emphasised as well.[60] Similar to their English counterparts, they declared their conflicts to be political ones which directly affected the realm and the king.

By claiming that Harry Skawe had been lying in wait in Kirkley Roads, the plaintiffs depicted him as having been the aggressor, who by claiming that he had been waging war for the king, had wrongfully justified what they saw as an unlawful act of violence. Friendly Hamburgers had been attacked by the king's men, who had thus violated the treaties that the monarch had agreed to. The damage done to them was therefore to be understood as a breach of loyalty and, according to the regulations of the "statute of truces", finally as high treason. Probably motivated by foreign merchants, in 1414 the English King Henry V (r. 1413–1422) had announced that maritime violence committed by the king's subjects during truces would be penalised as high treason.[61] As the Hanse in the North and Baltic Sea regions referred to other ways of criminalising maritime violence, a remarkable adaptability to the political discourse in the kingdom is evident here.[62] Furthermore, the Hamburgers claimed that the commission sent was unsuccessful, pointing to the fact that the mayor of Sandwich had not arranged for the return of the goods taken. In response, they took up a topical argument. Frequently, petitioners claimed that commissions had acted corruptly, that perpetrators from the local gentry had been part of these commissions, that local office holders had circumvented the decisions of the commissions, or even attacked the members of these commissions and other office holders.[63] In this respect, in the complaints of foreigners the English countryside appears as a place where one was permanently wronged by local elites, and lawlessness reigned.

3.3 Creating Arguments which could be adopted by the Authorities

Numerous complaints about the lawlessness of the English coastal regions, which were also brought up by English mariners themselves, at first sight seem to illustrate exactly this anarchy.[64] At second sight, they indicate that the allegedly rudderless coastal counties were particularly closely integrated into the legal landscape of royal

60 Gardiner, Calendar, no. 16 with n., 20, 23, 33, 40 n., 52 n., 60 n., 64, 65, 66, 67 n., 71a, 72b-f, 75ab, 76 n., 89acd with n., 95. For Portuguese claims see Viula de Faria, Maritime conflict.

61 Given-Wilson, Parliament, pp. 170–174.

62 Höhn, Criminalization.

63 Gardiner, Calendar, no. 2, 12.

64 Cressy, Shipwrecks, pp. 71–83.

jurisdiction. The king was frequently asked to take action there and, consequently, nominated commissions, which permanently crossed the region.[65] The petitions are thus to be understood as stabilising the king's rule. Complaints about corrupt officials and disloyal subjects were not a critique of the ruler. Instead, local, and foreign petitioners as well, confirmed the king's claim to rule and supersede local jurisdictions and gave the Crown the opportunity to communicate these assertions on the ground.

With their numerous lawsuits, the foreign plaintiffs became an active part in the process of consolidating royal power. In the case of the aforementioned Henry Skawe, the Court of Chancery, officers from Sandwich, Ipswich, Yarmouth, and London were appointed to the commission.[66] Among them was Richard Neville, Earl of Warwick, the warden of the Cinque Ports. According to the petitioners from Hamburg, the plunder had been distributed in Sandwich, one of these towns. Presumably, the petition had been directed primarily against the inability or unwillingness of local actors to ensure justice.[67] Given this, one can ask all the more what the Court of Chancery was pursuing when, of all people, the warden of the Cinque Ports was appointed to investigate the accusations of the Hamburgers against the people of Sandwich.

A comparative view indicates that members of commissions were often drawn from the leading strata of the region in which the incident had occurred. There are, in fact, also cases in which members themselves were accused of having committed sea robbery or even of having been involved in the attack they were supposed to investigate. Thomas Carmynow, who was accused by Lambert Whitynburgh of Danzig of having attacked and then arrested the latter's ship in Plymouth in 1434–1435, was himself a member of numerous commissions investigating maritime violence.[68] In the case of the Dartmouth mariner Thomas Buk, who was sued by a Scottish mariner in 1430, a commission consisting of representatives from Dartmouth around John Hawley Jr., a local magnate who probably also had business connections with the accused, investigated.[69]

It seems that kings and chancellors may have appointed commissioners, probably intentionally, who themselves were involved in the cases that came before them. Obviously, this means of recruitment must have produced conflicts of interest.[70] This should not be interpreted as a sign of royal weakness too quickly. As far as

---

65 Masschaele, Jury, pp. 45–87; for a systematic study of the West Countries see: Tyldesley, Crown.

66 Bosworth and Saunders, Original Documents.

67 HUB 8, no. 1228.

68 Gardiner, Calendar, no. 44; CPR Henry VI, 1429–1436, pp. 469, 474, 475, 519; CPR Henry VI, 1436–1441, p. 409.

69 Gardiner, Calendar, no. 25.

70 For examples see: Masschaele, Jury, pp. 111–113.

we know, the Court of Chancery was not accused by foreign plaintiffs of judging arbitrarily. Indeed, rather the number of foreign complaints might indicate a certain acceptance of the Court of Chancery. The composition of the commissions might rather have been due to an intentional involvement of the local elites into these very conflicts. They were included in the proceedings, which at the same time put them under pressure to find a form of settlement accommodating the petitioners, since otherwise they ran the risk of being criminalised in the proceedings.[71] The appointment of the commissions offered the opportunity to enforce the loyalty of local elites by using particular conflict resolution practices. In this respect, the foreign petitions became an active part in the processes of consolidating royal power.

To sum up, the dynamics of legal pluralism can hardly be reduced to a confrontation of foreign merchants with a judicial system. Through their conflict practices, the parties themselves actively shaped processes of power consolidation, they exerted influence on micro-politics at court, and thus on the negotiation of power positions within competing networks of actors in the formation of English political society.

3.4 Denying Arguments, Denying Forums

So far, we have seen the tactics of adapting discourses, taking them up in the field of the developing "political society", and thus ultimately also changing the characteristics of the legal landscape. Another tactic was to refuse to take up discourses, as the *Bergenfahrer* (merchants going to Bergen, Norway) from Lübeck did in 1465. Merchants from Beverley, Hull, and York had sued two members of the company at the Court of Chancery to get compensation for the seizure of a ship called George of Beverley.[72] According to their interpretation, a certain Olaf Olafson, who had been attacked by the *Bergenfahrer*, had been in the service of the English king "to safeguard the sea" and had tried to protect the George, which had been taken by the Hansards. The *Bergenfahrer* had chased Olaf Olafsson in the North Atlantic until his ship sank, drowning Olaf and his crew. This final clash had been the result of a series of feuds between Olaf's family and the *Bergenfahrer* company, which in 1454 had killed his father Olaf Nilsson, the Norwegian king's bailiff in Bergen. The Lübeck *Bergenfahrer* on the other hand, framed these quarrels as fights against pirates, even drawing on Cicero's concept of the pirate as a "*hostis omnium*" – enemy of all mankind.[73] Unlike in the cases mentioned above, the parties did not refer to

71 For examples of members of commissions who were also ordered to be arrested for other cases see: Gardiner, Calendar, no. 15, 24.

72 Childs, George.

73 Höhn, Lutte, pp. 319–321.

the other side's arguments. The Lübeck merchants only responded to the plaintiffs' account by emphasising that the George of Beverley had first been stolen by Olaf Olafsson, and then taken back by them. They did not even respond to the claim that Olaf had been in the service of the English king.[74] Finally, as Wendy Childs assumes, plaintiff and defendants settled the dispute out of court.[75]

There are also instances in which actors denied the competence of particular forums. Robin Ward and David Cressy have traced the polemics against the emerging and expanding jurisdiction of the English admirals during the fourteenth century. These royal officials, who initially primarily had played a role in the recruitment of fleets, increasingly expanded their jurisdiction in the context of conflicts with the French king from around 1340 onwards.[76] The English monarchy favoured this, since the admirals claimed jurisdiction over everything that happened at sea. This strengthened the royal claim to rule over the "narrow seas", which the English King Edward III (r. 1327–1377) had articulated, with reference to Richard the Lionheart's alleged confirmation of the *Rôles d'Oleron*, a collection of maritime law named after the Isle d'Oleron as it tackles mainly customs for shipping wine from Bordeaux. From a customary claim of the English Crown, jurisdiction over the coasts of France could be derived.[77]

At the beginning of the fifteenth century, several manuscripts were collected, the most famous of which is known as the Black Book of the Admiralty.[78] These books can be associated with individual admirals such as Thomas of Beaufort (brother of King Henry IV (r. 1399–1413) and admiral between 1408 and 1422). They contain disparate texts on maritime law translated into English, as well as royal ordinances relating to the duties and tasks of naval warfare or the sanctioning of breaches of the law at sea, and judgements from various courts from which the jurisdiction of the Court of Admiralty could be derived. Apparently, they did not aim at codifying a coherent legal system, but rather at providing arguments in favour of the admirals' judicial powers.

In one of these manuscripts there is a petition from 1412 by a Danzig merchant, abridged as "*J.B.*" (presumably Johann Broke). In a so called "letter of marque", Henry IV authorised Broke to take Breton goods, up to the amount of damages

---

74 Höhn, Lutte, p. 320.

75 Childs, George, p. 109.

76 As there was usually more than "one" Admiral, several Courts of Admiralty existed. Furthermore, some ports held their own Courts of Admiralty – see: Johnson, Law, p. 100. In this sense, I use the term in singular when I talk about the Court of the Admirals of England, and in plural when I discuss the diversity of courts.

77 Cressy, Shipwrecks, pp. 59–63; Ward, Shipmaster, pp. 29–33; Heebøll-Holm, Origins, pp. 162–166; Johnson, Law, pp. 94–96; Sobecki, Sea, pp. 140–160.

78 Twiss, Black Book, pp. 109–116.

he had suffered when he had been attacked by Bretons in the roadstead off Cape Finistère during a truce between the Duke of Brittany, the English and French Kings, because the courts in Brittany had denied him his rights.[79] That Broke's case became part of this compilation may have been due to the fact that (as indicated by the abbreviation of the name) the documents were intended to function as formula for the issuing of letters of marque. Probably, it also found its way into the book because Broke had claimed that the English king had had jurisdictional rights in this case, which had occurred along the coast of Brittany. Since claims for sovereignty could be derived from jurisdictional rights, this supported the position of the Court of Admiralty. Broke's petition thus not only adapted to discourses on the jurisdiction of the English king; it also legitimised the claims of the king and the admiralty.

Hence, the above-mentioned manuscripts are to be understood in the context of polemics on the jurisdiction of the admirals. From the last years of Edward III's reign onwards, the "commons" increasingly complained about this. These debates followed the logic of the discourses we have seen in the petitions to Parliament or Chancery. They were directed partly against the excessive court fees the admirals and their officials were charging, partly against false judgements or cases of alleged corruption.[80] However, they also had a systemic dimension. The "commons" pointed to the fact that the Courts of Admiralty were undermining the jurisdiction of local or common law courts by taking on cases in areas beyond their competence. Both Richard II (r. 1377–1399) and Henry IV restricted the jurisdictional rights of the Admiralty by limiting it solely to disputes having had occurred at sea. The discourse however continued.[81]

Hansards lamenting the admirals' jurisdiction also resorted to English polemics. In 1437, the Prussian diplomats led by the Danzig Mayor Heinrich Vorrath explicitly took up the English polemics against the Court of Admiralty and referred to the restrictions placed on its jurisdiction by Richard II and Henry IV. Accordingly, Vorrath required the jurisdiction of common law courts for the Hanse.[82] This also appears indirectly in the above-mentioned petition of the "English merchants" of 1422: John Smyth, a Danzig shipmaster who, because his ship had foundered near King's Lynn, had been sued by his English charterers before the Court of Admiralty. He obtained arrests against English merchants in the Teutonic Order's territory accusing the Court of Admiralty to have misjudged the case.[83]

79 Twiss, Black Book, pp. 385–390.
80 Ward, Shipmaster, pp. 44–45.
81 Ward, Shipmaster, pp. 39, 42–46.
82 HR II, 2, no. 74 § 57; Jenks, Roundtable, p. 325.
83 HR I, 7, no. 592 § 10, see also HUB 6, no. 418, 447, 561, 569, 678, 789.

The polemics against the Court of Admiralty have long been interpreted as an expression of an actual deficiency of the admirals' jurisdiction.[84] However, they primarily reflect the invectives of the parties who attempted to question the competence of the Court of Admiralty in very heated disputes. Competing actors discredited forums of conflict regulation; however, they also valorised them through their judicial practices. They played a significant role in shaping the discourse on which forum should be used to settle conflicts. In many of the actions, the claimants did not seek to have the Admiralty repealed. Rather, they aimed at preserving and strengthening local courts, to obtain exemptions from the Courts of Admiralty, or to receive the right to hold a court of admiralty locally.[85] The actors neither called for legal standardisation nor defended legal plurality. They were mostly focused on describing why they considered certain forums to be incompetent. However, this structured the legal landscape, because these arguments were taken up by other plaintiffs.

4. Legal Commonalities?

Until now, we have focused on the pluralism of semantics and the strategies that actors used not only to deal with this pluralism, but where they contributed to the creation of the English legal landscape. Structures and discourses mattered for conflict management, but they also emerged, developed, and changed day-to-day legal practices. Foreign merchants were not simply confronted with a legal system alien to them, but shaped and transformed the legal landscape themselves. Strategies such as the above mentioned, created specific forms of coherence which allowed for communication. In this part, I will prescind my previous considerations and focus on practices and references made by the claimants, which, as "common legalities", allowed to communicate conflict and thus created coherence. According to Johnson, "common legalities" were related to particular environmental spaces or occupations within the forming English political society. Within these legal cultures, these common legalities created the "commons" as a social group. However, apparently not only the legal, but also the conflict landscape of Northern and Western Europe did not harmonise in the fifteenth century. There yet existed specific communicative practices and procedures which allowed individuals to communicate and deal with conflict.[86]

---

84 Ward, Shipmaster, pp. 40–46.

85 For smaller ports which received the right to hold a Court of Admiralty see e. g.: Johnson, Tree, p. 45.

86 For a broader perspective on the spatial implications of my considerations here, see: Höhn, Records.

A point to start with are the political semantics which I sketched out in the first part of this contribution. The language of the petition of 1422 can, at first sight, only be understood within the contemporary English political culture. It was, however, part of a broader entangled vocabulary, in which terms referring to "the commons", the "common good", "use", or "profit" were widespread – also at the Hanse Diets.[87] Still, this does not mean that all actors spoke the same political language. Actors simply did not refer to the same political entities when they used terms such as "common". English and Hansard semantics were, however, so vague that they allowed for the framing of conflicts using terms and concepts which the respective other side was able to adopt.

Particular legalities were connected not to states, but to the spheres between them, and to the relations between war and peace. Maritime economic interactions were shaped by pervasive violence. Individual actors and groups temporarily held legal titles in various forms: privileges, licences, or safe conducts which granted them protection.[88] For the conflicts in the Atlantic, the truces and safe conducts between princes and the Hanse in general, but also between towns on a more local level, created a legal context in which documents associated particular actors with a specific status as friend, foe, or not involved in the conflict.[89] These were not only abstract legal titles, but tangible documents about how conflicting actors should be able to negotiate claims. Although such documents followed different formulae and applied to different legal traditions, the simple material quality of a document made it a point of reference in the widespread practices of collecting and presenting evidence.[90] In petitions to the English king and chancellor, respective documents the petitioners had acquired and carried with them were repeatedly referred to.[91] These documents themselves did not lead to legal security, but they created a way on which all actors, whether or not they shared the same political and legal semantics, could negotiate the legitimacy of claims by discussing the authenticity and applicability of these very documents.

Another arena where coherence was created were the more or less institutionalised forms of associative culture existing in the conflict landscape of Northern and Western Europe.[92] Negotiations repeatedly took place between the English and the Hanse, often in Flanders or the Low Countries, for example in 1407 in Dordrecht and The Hague.[93] There were also legal concepts which shaped the development of

87 Boestad, Profit, pp. 319–369.

88 Höhn, Krieg, pp. 139–140.

89 For several examples see: Höhn, Records.

90 Teuscher, Recht, pp. 260–270.

91 See e. g. the references for safe conduct and licences in: Gardiner, Calendar, pp. xiv–xvi.

92 See e. g.: Hardy, Political; Dirks, Konfliktaustragung.

93 Lloyd, England, pp. 116–120; Jenks, England, pp. 538–549.

conflict management at diets in Western Europe, fitting quite well the distinctive sociability of the Hanse towns (*Hansetage*):[94] Other practices such as the mixed juries, which often formed spontaneously out of foreign and English merchants,[95] the temporary truces the English kings increasingly agreed upon with the Scots, French, and Bretons in the last decades of the fourteenth century, and the idea of marches as spheres characterised by specific procedures and legal norms played an important role. Sohmer Tai, Heebøll-Holm, Grohse, and Armstrong have shown that the law of marches, which was typical for frontier areas, was extended to the sea, and that conflicts emerging in this sphere were regulated by diets at places within the march. A characteristic of this were truces as temporary suspensions of violence which created the basis for negotiating feuds and raids, although these often continued, nevertheless. Conservators were appointed by both sides to judge breaches of a truce and to meet in "neutral" territory or in areas disputed between two parties in order to negotiate mutual claims for compensation.[96] Such was the case, for example, at the *dieta marchiarum* in the Anglo-Scottish march or in Leulinghem, which lay close to English-occupied Calais, where the truce between the French and English kings was concluded in 1389. Other respective negotiations between England and France took place on the island of Guernsey in the Channel.[97]

Besides these documents, a particular way of writing about conflicts within the associative culture facilitated this communication, especially a specific language actors used to negotiate damages. Through their "itemisation",[98] lists of grievances helped confine quarrels to negotiable information and thus reduce their complexity so that the problems could be identified and dealt with. Lengthy compensation claims, such as the gravamina for the negotiations at the Hague in 1407,[99] had a normative function: According to Michael Jucker, lists reflected the authorities' desire to control market access and market displacement as well as resources and their distribution.[100] These grievances show their normativity on several levels: They determine whose quarrels might find their way into arbitration, which information should be included (and which not), what was seen as a negotiable conflict, and what was not.

A letter by the representatives of the Hanse cities gathered in Copenhagen to the Kontor in Bruges dated 30 August 1398 provides information about the prepa-

94 For recent studies on the Hanse Diets see: Kypta, Versammeln, with reference to further literature.

95 Masschaele, Jury, p. 106.

96 Sohmer Tai, Marking; Heebøll-Holm, Ports, pp. 161–190; see also: Grohse, Frontiers; Armstrong, England's, pp. 185–186; Sumption, Divided, pp. 674–677; Dick, Framing, p. 124.

97 Powell, Kingship, p. 203; Rymer, Foedera, pp. 85, 114, 163, 194.

98 For this term see: Nüllen, Civitates.

99 Kunze, Hanseakten, no. 308–364.

100 Jucker, Beute, p. 38.

ration of such lists. As a diet with the Danish queen had been scheduled to take place the following Pentecost, the representatives asked the Kontor to collect the names of the Danish subjects who had harmed Hansards until St Nicholas' Day. Those who had been injured should come to the diet in Vordingborg personally or authorise representatives. Those who could not come or send representatives would no longer be allowed to make claims against the queen's subjects. Everyone was to report this to his friends so that they too could have their claims enlisted.[101] Considering the distance between Copenhagen and Bruges, the deadlines were tight and increased the chances for those who had closer connections to Hanse city councils or the aldermen of the Kontor. The chance to be included thus strongly depended on integration into social networks. This perhaps also explains why we find comparatively little evidence concerning assaults on mariners in the lists. The registers tend to contain primarily complaints by the merchant elites; they focus on aspects which affected precisely this group and their claims.[102]

Lists of grievances were also normative regarding the information they contained. According to Nüllen, the writing down of conflicts by recording the details of the quarrelling parties, their relationship, the damage done and its value provided a specific reduction of complexity.[103] The registers restricted conflicts to basic data: names, places and routes, and standardised formulations about practices. The entries focused primarily on who was liable for the damage. To that end, they show a remarkable interest in describing the quality of the goods taken and their categorisation, but also the material damage and the money the owners would have had to spend to attain restitution.

Gravamina made conflicts communicable because they reduced them to compensation claims in monetary terms. Conflicts were thus perceived as "market-shaped", as is shown by the fact that in 1407 the English representatives and those from Dorpat and Riga agreed upon calculating claims according to the values that would have applied in Bruges at the time of the respective seizures. Accordingly, they asked merchants in Bruges to inform them about market prices at that time.[104] The emotional and social dimensions of conflicts were thus no longer part of the negotiations. Other cases were also settled with ostentatious atonements, such as the endowment of *memoria* for killed opponents.[105] This is not mentioned in the gravamina of 1407, however. It was apparently not part of the negotiations which

101 HR I, 4, no. 498; Höhn, Kaufleute, p. 318; for the negotiations in The Hague see: Stamp, Calendar, p. 501.

102 See Höhn, Schwelle, pp. 402–404.

103 Nüllen, Civitates, p. 63.

104 Kunze, Hanseakten, no. 357, 359.

105 Jenks, Friedensvorstellungen, pp. 429–439; Paravicini, Schuld, pp. 424–429.

took place in The Hague. The reduction chosen here apparently allowed the parties to reduce a complex conflict constellation to monetary "basic data".

Through "itemisation", political, or at least collective conflicts, were also split into individual episodes. Only when the lists of items are viewed together does something like a history of the conflict emerge. The advantage of reducing conflicts to items was that one could recognise the claims of the aggrieved parties and try to negotiate them without considering the general conflict anymore. In societies which tended to see conflicts primarily as personal disputes, this was certainly communicatively productive. Conflicts could now be negotiated without addressing social and political issues, without asking for the reason or a narrative framing of what had caused the conflict. This did not mean that the conflicts were solved. As Stuart Jenks has shown for the negotiations in The Hague, a large proportion of the agreed compensation payments were paid late or never, which caused further disputes.[106] The mechanisms creating coherence I have sketched here did not necessarily end conflicts but opened opportunities for constant negotiations accompanied by political and judicial confrontation as well as ongoing low-level violence. Finally, within a network of different fora and varying norms of conflict management, communication rarely broke down. This might explain why we find many conflicts which were never solved, but very few in which these conflicts escalated so far that communication collapsed completely.

5. Conclusion

In his novel *Hundarna i Riga*, first published in 1992, Henning Mankell has detective Kurt Wallander investigate the murder of a Latvian policeman who had been assisting him in an investigation in post-reunification Riga. Wallander moves around the city clandestinely with the support of the policeman's widow who is close to the independence movement. On the run from still Soviet-minded policemen and corrupt elites, Wallander finds himself confronted with an impenetrable, opaque network. His contacts cajole, hide behind official channels; sometimes they threaten, whisper and murmur. Who is friend and who is foe remains open until the end.[107]

Like the dogs of Riga, the dogs of Danzig, which allegedly lick the blood of the English from the streets of the city on the Mottlau, were ciphers for the insecurity of the English merchants who only wanted to do business. The dogs of Danzig stood for imagined threats the English had to face; for the illegitimacy of the local

106 Jenks, England, pp. 543 and 550.

107 Mankell, Hundarna.

legal system, for the perfidy, violence, and unfairness of the city's elites, and the unfaithfulness of the Grand Master's subjects, who allegedly did not face up to agonal confrontation, but resorted to judicial murder, imprisonment, and lynch mobs.

If we compare the "Dogs of Danzig" to the "Dogs of Riga", differences become apparent which lead us back to the question how actors interacted with legal structures. Until the end, Kurt Wallander does not know who the "dogs" are. The petitioners of 1422, on the other hand, knew very well who held the dogs supposed to lick their blood from the streets, and also when and where to take action to pursue their interests against these opponents – in Parliament just before the coronation of a new king. The impenetrability of the conflict landscape they evoked was part of the narrative strategies they resorted to in order to assert their interests.

These imaginations of a threatening counterworld should be read as part of the discourse inventory with which actors communicated, framed, and externalised their conflicts. Political semantics mattered. The choice of a forum in legal pluralism always meant picking up on particular political discourses and developing them further. Imagined threats, distinguishing friend and foe, the selection of elements to be portrayed, all referred to political discourses and semantics. The actors themselves were part of "polities in the making".[108] This study has focused on how merchants created and shaped the legal landscapes in which they acted, how they reshaped these discourses and provided them with new elements. Conflicts were narrative constructions, framings, and interpretations made by contemporaries. They were not however only a cognitive phenomenon; they had material foundations in premodern economic life.

This has consequences for our understanding of the transformation of legal landscapes. Institutional change has often been located at the level of the emerging state: the establishment of supreme courts, the rise of merchant-friendly legal structures as an advantage in competition between markets, or as a result of commercial self-administration in the form of guilds, specialised jurisdiction, and the supposed *lex mercatoria*.[109] However, the distinction between actors and legal frameworks is based on problematic assumptions. They cannot simply be seen as antagonistic; the kings and their officials or the Hanse town councillors themselves were actors pursuing their own interests in their jurisdiction. They used the administration of justice to also finance war, to recruit fleets, to appropriate resources, to ideologically substantiate their claims to power, to integrate local elites into a system of rule, and to communicate power locally. At the same time, economic actors also appear as

108 Watts, Polities.

109 See e. g.: Volckart, Wettbewerb; Greif, Institutions; Ogilvie, Institutions; for a critical perspective see: Höhn, Kaufleute, pp. 31–56.

political groups that lobbied and shaped major politics. Precisely these groups of actors developed forums and norms in legal pluralism.

Here, the concept of "common legalities" offers new perspectives to consider coherence within legal pluralism not only in England, but also in multi-layered legal landscapes such as those within which the Hansards interacted. There were communicative anchors that had a stabilising and cohesion-generating effect: discourses on the "common good", writing practices, procedures, spatial projections, and the itemisation of conflicts. These made it possible to shift collective conflicts into individual episodes that could be dealt with communicatively. To a certain extent, they created landscapes that made it possible to articulate conflicts, talk about, and negotiate them.

Bibliography

Armstrong, Jackson W., England's Northern Frontier. Conflict and Local Society in the fifteenth-century Scottish Marches, Cambridge 2020.

Blatcher, Marjorie, The Court of King's Bench, 1450–1550. A study in self-help, London 1978.

Boestad, Tobias, Les plumes de la Hanse. Rôle et capacité d'action des notaires municipaux aux diètes hanséatiques (c. 1360-c. 1450), in : Revue historique 325 (2023), pp. 179–204.

Boestad, Tobias, Pour le profit du commun marchand. La genèse de la Hanse, Geneva 2022.

Bosworth, George F./Saunders, Constance D. (eds.), Original Documents Relating to the Monoux Family, Walthamstow 1928.

Butcher, David, Medieval Lowestoft. The Origins and Growth of a Suffolk Coastal Community, Woodbridge 2016.

Childs, Wendy, The 'George' of Beverley and Olav Olavesson. Trading Conditions in the North Sea in 1464, in: Northern History 31 (1995), pp. 108–122.

Cordes, Albrecht/Höhn, Philipp, Extra-legal and legal conflict management among long distance traders (1250–1650), in: Heikki Pihlajamäki/Markus D. Dubber/Mark Godfrey (eds.), The Oxford Handbook of European Legal History, Oxford 2018, pp. 509–527.

Cressy, David, Shipwrecks and the bounty of the sea, Oxford 2022, pp. 59–63, 71–83.

Dick, Bryan D., 'Framing Piracy'. Restitution at Sea in the Later Middle Ages, PhD Thesis, University of Glasgow 2010.

Dirks, Florian, Konfliktaustragung im norddeutschen Raum des 14. und 15. Jahrhunderts. Untersuchungen zu Fehdewesen und Tagfahrt, Göttingen 2015.

Dodd, Gwymlin, Justice and Grave. Private Petitioning and the English Parliament in the Late Middle Ages, Oxford 2007.

Fletcher, Christopher D., De la communauté du royaume au common weal. Les requêtes anglaises et leurs strategies au XIVe siècle, in : Revue française d'histoire des idées politiques 32 (2010), pp. 359–372.

Fletcher, Christopher, La communauté anglaise face à l'étranger. La loi de marque, le bien commun et la dot de Lucia Visconti (†1422), in : Cahiers de recherches médiévales et humanists 19 (2010), pp. 105–122.

Fletcher, Christopher D., What Makes a Political Language? Key Terms, Profit and Damage in the Common Petitions of the English Parliament, 1343–1422, in: Jan Dumolyn et al. (eds.), The Voices of the People in Late Medieval Europe. Communication and Popular Politics, Turnhout 2014, p. 91–106.

Gardiner, Dorothy M. (ed.), A calendar of early chancery proceedings relating to West Country shipping, 1388–1493 (Devon and Cornwall records society 21), Torquay 1976.

Given-Wilson, Chris et al., (eds.), Parliament Rolls of Medieval England, Woodbridge 2005.

Greif, Avner, Institutions and the path to the modern economy. Lessons from medieval trade, Cambridge 2006.

Grohse, Ian Peter, Frontiers for Peace in the Medieval North. The Norwegian-Scottish Frontier, c. 1260–1470 (The Northern World 79), Leiden 2017.

Hansischer Geschichtsverein (ed.), Hansisches Urkundenbuch (cited as HUB). Vol. 6–8, Leipzig 1899.

Hardy, Duncan, Associative Political Culture in the Holy Roman Empire. Upper Germany, 1346–1521, Oxford 2018.

Harriss, Gerald, Political Society and the Growth of Government in Late Medieval England, in: Past & Present 138 (1993), pp. 28–57.

Haskett, Timothy S., Conscience, justice and authority in the late-medieval English court of chancery, in: Anthony Musson (ed.), Expectations of the law in the Middle Ages, Woodbridge 2001, pp. 151–163.

Haskett, Timothy S., The Medieval English Court of Chancery, in: Law and History Review 14 (1996), pp. 245–314.

Heebøll-Holm, Thomas K., Ports, Piracy, and Maritime War: Piracy in the English Channel and the Atlantic, c. 1280–c. 1330, Leiden 2013.

Heebøll-Holm, Thomas K., The origins and jurisdiction of the English Court of Admiralty in the Fourteenth century, in: Anthony Musson/Nigel Ramsay (eds.), Courts of Chivalry and Admiralty in late medieval Europe, Woodbridge 2018, pp. 162–166.

Heebøll-Holm, Thomas K., Towards a Criminalization of Piracy in Late Medieval England, in: Louis H. J. Sicking/Alain Wijffels (eds.), Conflict management in the Mediterranean and the Atlantic, 1000–1800: Actors, institutions and strategies of dispute settlement (Legal History Library 39/Studies in the History of International Law 15), Leiden 2020, pp. 170–174.

Historische Kommission bei der Königlichen Akademie der Wissenschaften (ed.), Hanserecesse (cited as HR). Die Recesse und andere Akten der Hansetage von 1256–1430, Leipzig 1889.

Höhn, Philipp, Auf der Schwelle. Meerestiere, der Strand und die litorale Ökonomie im spätmittelalterlichen England, in: Das Mittelalter 28 (2023), pp. 388–406.

Höhn, Philipp, Criminalization as Practice. Maritime Violence and the Making of Sovereignty in the Late Middle Ages, in: Jésus A. Solorzano Telechea/Marcelo Pereira Lima (eds.), Criminal Cultures in the Atlantic City and Beyond (13th–16th centuries), Rioja (forthcoming).

Höhn, Philipp, Entscheidungsfindung und Entscheidungsvermeidung in der Hanse. Das Beispiel der Sunddurchfahrt um 1440, in: Wolfgang Eric Wagner (ed.), Entscheidungsfindung in spätmittelalterlichen Gemeinschaften (Kulturen des Entscheidens 8), Göttingen 2022, pp. 91–137.

Höhn, Philipp, Herren "vieler Welten"? Bertolt Burammer und die Elitelandschaften des Ostseeraums in der ersten Hälfte des 15. Jahrhunderts, in: Paul Srodecki/Ludwig Steindorff, Viele Welten des Ostseeraumes. Politischer, wirtschaftlicher und kultureller Austausch vom Hochmittelalter bis zum Beginn der Neuzeit, Marburg 2024, pp. 371–391.

Höhn, Philipp, Kaufleute in Konflikt. Rechtspluralismus, Kredit und Gewalt im spätmittelalterlichen Lübeck, Frankfurt a. M. 2021.

Höhn, Philipp, „Krieg und Frieden" in den Praktiken der Konfliktführung um 1370 und der „Friede von Stralsund", in: Hansische Geschichtsblätter 139 (2021), pp. 105–141.

Höhn, Philipp, La "lutte contre les pirates" comme paradigm. Conflit, concurrence et criminalization à Lübeck et dans le commerce nord-européen aux Xve et XVIe siècles, in : Annales. Historie, sciences sociales 77 (2022), pp. 293–327.

Höhn, Philipp, Off the Records. The Spatiality of Maritime Conflicts and the Economic Activities of Hansards South of Bruges, in: Tobias Boestad/Philipp Höhn (eds.), La Hanse et l'Atlantique 1300–1500. Acteurs, commerce, conflits/The Hanse and the Atlantic, 1300–1500. Actors, Trade and Conflicts, Rennes (forthcoming).

Jenks, Stuart, England, die Hanse und Preußen. Handel und Diplomatie, 1377–1474 (Quellen und Darstellungen zur hansischen Geschichte 38), Köln et al. 1992.

Jenks, Stuart, Friedensvorstellungen der Hanse (1356–1474), in: Johannes Fried (ed.), Träger und Instrumentarien des Friedens im hohen und späten Mittelalter (Vorträge und Forschungen 43), Sigmaringen 1996, pp. 405–439.

Jenks, Stuart, Review of Robin Ward, The World of the Medieval Shipmaster, in: International Journal of Maritime History 21 (2009), p. 323–330.

Johnson, Tom, Law in Common. Legal Cultures in Late-Medieval England, Oxford 2020.

Johnson, Tom, The Tree and the Rod. Jurisdiction in Late Medieval England, in: Past & Present 237 (2017), p. 13–52.

Jostkleigrewe, Georg, Monarchischer Staat und 'Société politique'. Politische Interaktion und staatliche Verdichtung im spätmittelalterlichen Frankreich (Mittelalter-Forschungen 56), Ostfildern 2018.

Jucker, Michael, Beute, in: Christof Dejung/Monika Dormann/Daniel Speich Chassé (eds.), Auf der Suche nach der Ökonomie. Historische Annäherungen, Tübingen 2014, p. 17–46.

Kermode, Jenny, Medieval Merchants. York, Beverley and Hull in the Later Middle Ages, Cambridge 1998.

Kunze, Karl (ed.), Hanseakten aus England 1275–1412 (Hansische Geschichtsquellen 6), Halle (Saale) 1891.

Kypta, Ulla, Versammeln, besprechen, beschließen. Der Vergleich verschiedener Tagfahrten des späten Mittelalters und der frühen Neuzeit, in: Hansische Geschichtsblätter 138 (2020), p. 1–23.

Liddy, Christian D., War, Politics, and Finance in Late Medieval English Towns. Bristol, York and the Crown, 1350–1400, Woodbridge 2005.

Lloyd, Terrence H., England and the German Hanse, 1157–1611, Cambridge 1991.

Lyte, Henry C. M. (ed.), Calendar of Parliament Rolls (cited as e. g. "CPR"), Edward IV, 1461–1467, London 1897; Henry VI, 1429–1436; Henry VI, 1436–1441.

Manger, Christian, Behind the scenes. Urban secretaries as managers of legal and diplomatic conflicts in the Baltic region, c. 1470–1540, in: Journal of Medieval History 48 (2022), pp. 571–586.

Mankell, Henning, Hundarna i Riga, Stockholm 1992.

Masschaele, James, Jury, State, and Society in Medieval England, Basingstoke 2008.

Murray, Katherine M. E., The Constitutional History of the Cinque Ports, Manchester 1935.

Nicolas, Harris (ed.), Proceedings and ordinances of the Privy Council of England, [vol. 3], London 1834.

Nüllen, Hanna, Civitates Librorum. Informationsverarbeitung und Wissensproduktion in den spätmittelalterlichen Stadtbüchern der Reichsstädte Friedberg und Gelnhausen, PhD Thesis, Martin-Luther-Universität Halle-Wittenberg 2024.

Ogilvie, Sheilagh, Institutions and European trade. Merchant guilds, 1000–1800, Cambridge 2011.

Ormrod, W. Mark, "Common profit" and "the profit of the king and kingdom". Parliament and the development of political language in England, 1250–1659, in: Viator 46, 2 (2015), pp. 219–252.

Ormrod, W. Mark/Killick, Helen/Bradford, Phil (eds.), Early Common Petitions in the English Parliament, c. 1290–c. 1420, Cambridge 2017.

Paravicini, Werner, Schuld und Sühne. Der Hansenmord zu Sluis in Flandern anno 1436, in: Jan Hirschbiegel/Andreas Ranft/Jörg Wettlaufer (eds.), Edelleute und Kaufleute im Norden Europas. Gesammelte Aufsätze, Ostfildern 2007, pp. 517–559.

Powell, Edward, Kingship, Law and Society. Criminal Justice in the Reign of Henry V, Oxford 1989.

Rodger, N. A. M., The Safeguard of the Sea. A Naval History of Britain, 660–1649, London 1999.

Rymer, Thomas, Foedera, [vol. 9], London 1709.

Saul, Anthony, English Towns in the Middle Ages. The Case of Great Yarmouth, in: Journal of Medieval History 8 (1982), pp. 75–88.

Saul, Anthony, Local Politics and the Good Parliament, in: Tony Pollard (ed.), Property and Politics. Essays in Later Medieval English History, Gloucester 1984, pp. 156–171.

SOBECKI, Sebastian I., Last Words. The Public Self and the Social Author in Late Medieval England, Oxford 2019.

SOBECKI, Sebastian I., The sea and medieval English literature, Cambridge 2008.

SOHMER TAI, Emily, Marking Water. Piracy and Property in the Premodern West, in: Jerry H. BENTLEY/Renate BRIDENTHAL/Kären WIGEN (eds.), Seascapes. Maritime Histories, Littoral Cultures, and Transoceanic Exchanges, Honolulu 2007, pp. 205–220.

STAMP et al., A. E. (eds.), Calendar of Close Rolls, Henry IV, 1402–1405, London 1929.

SUMPTION, Jonathan, Divided Houses. The Hundred Years War, [vol. 3], London 2009.

SUMPTION, Jonathan, Triumph and Illusion. The Hundred Years War, Vol. 5, London 2023.

TEUSCHER, Simon, Erzähltes Recht. Lokale Herrschaft, Verschriftlichung und Traditionsbildung im Spätmittelalter, Frankfurt a. M. 2007.

TURNER, Ralph W., The origins of common pleas and the King's Bench, in: The American Journal of Legal History 21 (1977), pp. 238–254.

TWISS, Travers (ed.), The Black Book of the Admiralty. With an Appendix, 4 vols., London/Edinburgh 1871–1876.

TYLDESLEY, C. J., The Crown and the Local Communities in Devon and Cornwall from 1377 to 1422, PhD Thesis, Exeter 1978.

VIULA DE FARIA, Tiago A., Maritime conflict among Hundred Years' war allies, in: Louis H. J. SICKING/Alain WIJFFELS (eds.), Conflict management in the Mediterranean and the Atlantic, 1000–1800. Actors, institutions and strategies of dispute settlement (Legal History Library 39/Studies in the History of International Law 15), Leiden 2020, pp. 198–216.

VOLCKART, Oliver, Wettbewerb und Wettbewerbsbeschränkung in Politik und Wirtschaft. Deutschland in Mittelalter und Früher Neuzeit, Marburg 2002.

WARD, Robin, The World of a Medieval Shipmaster. Law, business and the sea, c. 1340–c. 1450, Woodbridge 2009.

WATKIN, Hugh R. (ed.), Dartmouth. Vol. 1: Pre-Reformation (Parochial Histories of Devonshire 5), Torquay 1935.

WATTS, John, The Making of Polities. Europe, 1300–1500, Cambridge 2009.

WATTS, John, The Pressure of the Public on Later Medieval Politics, in: Linda CLARK/Chris CARPENTER (eds.), The Fifteenth Century IV: Political Culture in Late-Medieval England, Woodbrige 2004, pp. 159–180.

WUBS-MROZEWICZ, Justyna, Kopieergedrag. De vormen en functies van afschriften in het laatmiddeleeuwse politieke briefverkeer van de Hanzesteden, in: Tijdschrift voor Geschiedenis 127 (2014), pp. 603–624.

ZEMON DAVIS, Natalie, Fictions in the Archives. Pardon Tales and their Tellers in Sixteenth-Century France, Stanford 1987.

ZOOMER, Ester, Representing the Hanse? The Involvement of the London Kontor and Hanseatic Community in Chancery Court Proceedings, c. 1368–1545, in: Jésus A. SOLÓRZANO TELECHEA/Jelle HAEMERS (eds.), Normativa y autoridad en la ciudad medieval atlántica (y más allá), Logrono 2022, pp. 117–138.

Tobias Boestad

"German Law" or "Law of the Germans"?

Plurality and Unity of German Merchant Jurisdictions in the Fourteenth Century

1. Introduction

Before the emergence of the Hanse Diets in the 1350s, the early Hanse consisted primarily of a network of commercial settlements run by German merchants in various marketplaces in Northern Europe. From the early thirteenth century, organisations of "Common Merchants" (Latin: *communes mercatores* or *universi mercatores*; Middle Low German: *(ge)meyne koplude*), bringing together burghers from various cities in northern Germany, were established on the island of Gotland, in Livonia, and in Russia. During the same century, similar organisations arose by merging German merchant communities, called "hanses", active in London and Bruges. Their main function was to represent the German merchants in their dealings with local authorities and to adjudicate disputes among them.[1] The actors who managed these organisations were well-informed about the legal realities of the places in which they operated and could intervene quickly in case of conflict. They were also involved in negotiating trade privileges to secure the German merchants' legal status and position.

Was this enough to make the Hanse merchants' interactions with denizens and local authorities more predictable? It has sometimes been argued – especially in works devoted to the economic history of the Hanse – that these organisations would have helped enforcing a "German law" specific to Hanse merchants. In 2005, for example, Stuart Jenks defined "German law" as "the international [...] Hanseatic (*gesamthansische*) order, which accompanied the Hanse merchant wherever he went and gave him immense advantages over his competitors in long-distance trade".[2] However, such assertions raise two intertwined but distinct questions. First, they remain vague about the nature of this "German law", although this notion willingly or not echoes the "German" (or "Germanic") Law – as opposed to Roman and Canon

1 Among the most recent studies on the history of the thirteenth-century German merchant associations, see: Jahnke, Homines Imperii; Hammel-Kiesow, The Early Hansas. On the concept of "common merchant?" and its connection to these early associations, see: Boestad, Pour le profit, pp. 113–189.

2 Jenks, Transaktionskostentheorie, p. 41. See also Jahnke, Handelsstrukturen, pp. 158 and 184.

Law – whose existence has long been assumed in legal history but is now contested.[3] Second, they build on the assumption that heterogenous legal environments would have been an obstacle to trade.[4] Thus, it has long been assumed that late medieval trade would have benefitted from a process of harmonisation of the commercial norms across Northern Europe. Over the last twenty years, the theoretical relevance of this model has been reasserted based on an application of the theory of transaction costs to Hanse trade.[5] At the same time, other scholars have emphasised the persistent diversity of commercial norms in Northern Europe in areas as far ranging as maritime customs, transaction law, and the rules governing conflict management.[6] Serious doubts have emerged about the often-postulated existence of a medieval *lex mercatoria*.[7] The focus that recent approaches to medieval legal culture have put on the social practices of law has led to an emphasis being placed on local landscapes and networks in which norms were embedded. The subsequent heterogeneity of legal norms neither prevented the actors – merchants or not – from ensuring predictability in agreeing on certain principles or methods to settle their conflicts, nor from taking advantage of them.[8] Under these circumstances, the idea that the medieval Hanse would have consciously sought to limit this legal pluralism – if it was even capable of doing so – is not self-evident.

One important aspect in these discussions is the question of how to understand the mentions of a "German law" (*dat dudesche recht*) or of a "Law of the Germans" (*der dudeschen recht*) in the fourteenth-century sources. Its appearance in documents relating to marketplaces as distant from each other as London, Bruges, and Novgorod could suggest that the Low German traders active there were following trading rules and norms which would have been more or less the same all across Northern Europe. These merchants originated from the north of the Holy Roman Empire – also referred to in some sources as *Almanie*. Although they named

3 This concept underpins the numerous studies carried out on the spread of "German law" (or of specific German town laws). See for example: Koebner, Deutsches Recht; Frahm, Stadtrecht; Ebel, Deutsches Recht; Ebel, Lübisches Recht. Even in more recent studies, the Hanse has sometimes been presented as reflecting specifically German or Germanic legal conceptions: Pitz, Bürgereinung. For an overview of these discussions, see Cordes, Deutsches Recht; Groth, Hanse und Recht.

4 See for example: Munzinger, Profits, pp. 166–167, 180–182; Jahnke, Livonija no skandinavu. See however: Boestad, Pour le profit, pp. 93–101.

5 Jenks, Transaktionskostentheorie, pp. 31–42; Selzer and Ewert, Institutions.

6 On sea law, see: Frankot, Of laws. On transaction law, see Gustafsson, Sale of Goods. On conflict management in North European maritime trade and the role of the Hanse in this respect, see Sicking, Maritime conflict management; Wubs-Mrozewicz, Late Medieval.

7 Cordes, Auf der Suche; Kadens, The Myth; Cordes, Future.

8 Johnson, Law in Common; Höhn, Pluralismus; Höhn, Kaufleute. See also Philipp Höhn's contribution in this volume.

themselves "Germans" (*dudesche*; *teutonici*), this label was mostly language-based and included people originating from Low-German-speaking towns in Prussia and Livonia, as well as from cities now located in the Netherlands, to which they were linguistically very close. One may therefore ask whether the mentions of *"dat dudesche recht"* or *"der dudeschen recht"* referred to a unified and coherent set of legal norms and trading customs known to all Low German merchants, and if so, whether this "German law" was the same from one marketplace to another.

This article examines this question in the context of the early Hanse. It is primarily based on the Common Merchants' correspondence and statutes. It aims to show that this concept did not refer to a process of standardisation of trade norms and practices in the German merchants' zone of activity, but rather to the gradual interconnection of their merchant jurisdictions into a system that would eventually be placed under the authority of the Hanse Diets. The examples I will discuss range from the second half of the thirteenth century to the emergence of the Hanse Diets in the 1350s, but they focus mainly on the first half of the fourteenth century – a period rarely studied for its own sake, but during which the concept of *dudesches recht* was utilised with particular frequency. I will begin by showing that this term did not refer to a set of commercial laws specific to German merchants, but above all, to the autonomous jurisdictions they enjoyed in foreign marketplaces. These courts produced written regulations kept, and published, by the Common Merchants, whose growing interconnection in the first half of the fourteenth century foreshadowed the emergence of the Hanse.

2. German Law or German Jurisdictions?

2.1 "*dat Dudesche recht*" or "*der Dudeschen recht*"?

The expression "*dat dudesche recht*" (German Law) did exist in sources from the thirteenth and especially the fourteenth centuries. At that time, it mainly appeared in documents relating to the activities of associations of Common Merchants. We find it as early as c. 1270 in the *First Novgorod Scra*, the ninth chapter of which applied to "any German who comes from the country and abides by German Law".[9] Half a century later, the *Third Scra* (c. 1320), on the contrary, condemned "anyone who has the boldness to allow into the Yard [i. e. the Peterhof, the German trading post in Novgorod], on his own initiative and without the knowledge and agreement of the alderman and his advisors, a German merchant who has come by land

9 Schlüter, Nowgoroder Schra, p. 64 (I § 9): "*Welic Dhutsche ute dheme lande comet, dhe sic to dhutscheme rechte hølt*". On the dating of the *First Scra*: Ibid., pp. 7–9.

(*"landvare"*) and who does not abide by German Law".[10] Similarly, in 1348, a statute of the German Merchant of Bruges stipulated that "the aldermen may order anyone to take an oath when they question him about issues that pertain to German Law".[11]

However, several synonymous variants of this expression are equally frequently mentioned in the sources, e. g., "*der Dudeschen recht*" (the Law of the Germans), or "*des Dudeschen copmannes recht*" (the Law of the German merchant). Thus, in 1354, another statute of the Merchant of Bruges stated that "no man who has been valet or clerk to a burgher (*"porter"*) of Bruges may enter the Law of the Germans".[12] As for the aldermen of Novgorod, they concluded one of their statutes in 1341 by recalling that "everyone must be careful not to infringe this statute so as not to suffer any harm or to cause any to the Law of the Germans".[13] In 1342, merchants were asked to stop buying Russian furs in batches of 1 000, 500, or 250, "neither in Riga, nor in Dorpat, Reval, Pskov or Polotsk, nor anywhere else where the Law of the German merchant applies, and [they] will [thus] remain under the Law of the German merchant".[14] Likewise, other sources referred to the "Law of Saint Peter" – i. e., the Law of the Peterhof, the German merchants' local outpost (*kontor*).[15] In all these examples, the Low German word *recht* is not associated with an epithet, but with a genitive that links it either to a group or category of people (the Germans, the "German merchant"),[16] or to a specific institution (the Peterhof).

The relatively sparse occurrences of all these terms make it impossible to determine which of them was oldest or most widespread. However, if we accept the hypothesis that all of them were synonymous, as their undifferentiated use in the examples listed above suggests, it follows that "German Law" referred on the one hand to a set of rules specific to a group that identified itself as German merchants; and on the other hand, to bodies exercising autonomous jurisdiction over this same

---

10 Ibid., p. 63 (III § 8). On the dating of the *Third Scra*: Ibid., pp. 18–21. The article already existed in the earlier versions of the *Scra* but did not mention explicitly the *"dudesch recht"*.

11 Koppmann, Recesse, vol. 1, no 147 § 16: *"die olderlude moghen enen elken man vermanen bi sinen eede, die warheit to secghene, des men ene vraghen sal van eliken dinghen, de behoren in dat Dudesche recht"*.

12 Höhlbaum, Hansisches Urkundenbuch, vol. 3 n° 573 § 6: *"Neghen man, de knape of clerk gewesen hevet yenighes mannes to Brucge, de porter es, en mach noch en sal comen in der Duschen recht"*.

13 HUB, vol. 3 n° 589: *"Hirumme so beware sich en jewelich man, dat he dissen wilkore nicht ne breke, upe dat he in nenen scaden ne come unde der Dudeschen reght nicht over en geve"*.

14 HUB vol. 3 n° 592: *"Noch to der Righe eder to Darbete noch to Revele noch to Plescowe eder to Ploscow noch nergene, dar des Dudeschen copmannes reght is unde [de] wil an des Dudeschen copmannes reghte wesen"*.

15 See for example: HUB vol. 3 n° 586.

16 On the use of the expression "common merchant" in singular, see: Boestad, Pour le profit pp. 345–367.

group, such as the trading posts of Bruges and Novgorod.[17] As Carsten Jahnke has pointed out, this "law" – whatever its nature – played an important role in the self-perception of German merchants and the emergence of a collective identity.[18] Two questions then arise: first, was the "Law of the Germans" limited to what was written in the privileges and statutes of the German merchants, or did it refer to a wider set of unwritten commercial customs? Second, was it the same in Bruges, Novgorod, and elsewhere, or did each settlement have its own "Law of the Germans"?

2.2 "*Judicium et libertas Theutonicorum*" – or the Janus-faced "Law of the Germans"

Some answers to these questions may be found in a letter of the alderman of the "Hanse of Germany" (*hansa Almanie*) in England: in 1303, he wrote to the consuls of Rostock to report that several merchants from Stralsund, Wismar, and Lübeck had breached the temporary ban he had declared on visiting the port of King's Lynn, with the result that the case he was then pursuing with the local authorities had been "totally annihilated". In response to this act of disobedience, the alderman announced that "we have placed and excluded the above-mentioned persons, and others who have been acting against the common promise of the Germans, out of our judgement and liberty" (*extra judicium nostrum ac libertatem*).[19] Only two of the offenders were spared: As they had responded to the alderman's summons, "we have asked them whether they preferred to be placed outside the judgement and liberty of the Germans (*extra judicium et libertatem Teutonicorum*) or to pay a fine for their offence" – and they had chosen the second option.[20]

The use of "*judicium et libertas Teutonicorum*" here resembles the previously discussed occurrences of "German Law". It refers to a community of merchants who recognised themselves as "German" and obeyed a specific jurisdiction, from which they could be excluded if they breached the "common promise" and rules. This duality of the "German Law", both justice and liberty, can also be found in other contexts. For example, from 1356 onwards, the aldermen of the Common Merchants in Bruges were required, when taking up their duties, to swear that they would "help, keep, and preserve the Law of the Germans (*der Duschen recht*) according to their privileges and according to their ordinances (*na er privilegie ende*

---

17 On the different meanings of *recht* in Middle Low German, see "Recht", in: Deutsches Rechtswörterbuch. (https://drw.hadw-bw.de/drw-cgi/zeige?index=lemmata&term=recht), accessed 08/27/2023. See especially the sections I.5, VI, and VII (col. 272–274, 290–292).

18 Jahnke, Homines Imperii, p. 52.

19 HUB vol. 2 n° 40.

20 HUB vol. 2 n° 40. On the meaning of *hansa Almanie*, see: Jahnke, Homines Imperii, pp. 22–23; Boestad, Pour le profit, pp. 134–145.

na er ordinantie)".[21] Later on, in 1374, a city diet gathered in Stralsund decided that Brunswick, whose burghers had risen up against their council, should be excluded "from the justice and liberty (*rechtcheid unde vriheid*) of the Merchant in all cities and places where the Merchant has and enjoys justice and liberty".[22]

The twin terms *judicium* and *libertas* draw attention to what appear to have been the two fundamental aspects of *Ius Teutonicorum*, not only in England but also in Flanders and Russia. Its first aspect was *libertas*. In the Middle Ages, this term most often referred to a privilege or set of privileges granted to a group of people or an institution by a sovereign authority.[23] In the present case, *libertas Teutonicorum* would thus refer to the privileges granted by the king of England to German merchants as a whole – as opposed to those available to merchants from isolated towns, e. g. Cologne, or to the more general liberties that King Edward I (r. 1272–1307) had granted a few months earlier to all foreign merchants travelling to England.[24] The second aspect was *judicium*. It referred to the Low German merchants' autonomous jurisdiction abroad, as well as to their ability to produce and implement their own statutes, as evidenced by the Novgorod *Scra* and the later statutes of the German merchants in Bruges, Bergen, and London.[25] It was by virtue of this *judicium* that the London alderman was able to exclude those who did not observe these statutes.

This dual definition of *dudesches recht* calls for two comments. First, the aforesaid dimensions of the *Ius Teutonicorum* should be seen as complementary. The *judicium* itself was almost always a *libertas* that had been granted to the merchants by the local authorities. At the same time, it was a way of imposing collective discipline on the Common Merchants and of punishing those whose attitude compromised the collective liberties and privileges. This concern is manifest in the statutes that the Novgorod aldermen regularly adopted to ensure the quality of goods sold or bought from the Russians; for example, when they decided in 1332 that the *wantvinders* – who were entrusted with the task of assessing the quality of cloth sold to the Russians – would have to do so in both winter and summer, "as many fraudulent cloths have been sold when there were no *wantvinders*, and because of this the Germans have suffered much dishonour (*opprobrium*) from the Russians, which is harmful to the common German merchants who visit the Novgorod

---

21 HR vol. 1 n° 200 § 5.

22 HR vol. 2 n° 80. On the Brunswick uprising and the Hanse's reactions to it, see: Jenks, Einstellung, pp. 77–80; Puhle, Hüter.

23 Fossier, Privilège, 1149–1150. See also Mohnhaupt and Dölemeyer, Privileg.

24 On this "Carta mercatoria", see: Jenks, Carta Mercatoria. However, the German merchants' role in the negotiations that led to its promulgation does not make it a specifically German privilege in 1303: As Stuart Jenks has pointed out, this was the result of a longer evolution.

25 Burkhardt, Ordnungen.

Yard".[26] The Merchant of Bruges went so far as to rule, around 1348, that "if one of them [i. e. the German merchants] infringes the points that are forbidden in our privileges, what he will lose and pay for it to the Lord and the Court, he will also have to pay it in compensation to the Common Merchants".[27] It was thus considered that by infringing the privileges, the merchant in question was not only harming his victim and the local authorities, but also his own fellow merchants, who might face the consequences of his behaviour by being sued or exposed to reprisals.

Second, this definition implies that there was a plurality of "German laws" since the German merchants' liberties and their aldermen's attributions were granted separately by the different sovereigns with whom they dealt. Thus, at the beginning of the fourteenth century the *libertas Teutonicorum* in England was based on the *Carta mercatoria*, a general charter granted by the English king to all foreign merchants trading in his realm, supplemented by some other charters such as that of Edward II in 1317.[28] In Flanders, it originated in the charters that had been granted by Countess Margaret to "all merchants of the Roman Empire" in 1253, and which were regularly renegotiated thereafter.[29] In Novgorod, it was based on treaties concluded with the Russian princes, in particular that of 1269.[30] In fact, when the aldermen of Bruges or Novgorod, or of the Hanse of Germany in England, referred to "German Law", they always meant first and foremost their own local jurisdiction. This does not necessarily rule out the existence of commercial customs specific to German merchants across Northern Europe; yet, such customs are not clearly apparent from the previous examples, and their existence remains unproven. The only exception to this might be the custom to elect or designate judges of their own, which, however, corresponded to usual commercial practices in the Medieval West.[31] In terms of predictability and legal pluralism, the most important was not that the rules were the same from one place to another, but that they were fixed and known.

26 HUB vol. 3 n° 587.

27 HUB vol. 3 n° 573 § 1.

28 HUB vol. 2 n° 356.

29 HUB vol. 1 n° 421, 422; vol. 2, n° 154, 160; HR vol. 1 n° 24. On these charters, see Stützel, Privilegien.

30 For the text and commentary of the treaty of 1269: Goetz, Handelsverträge. On these treaties, see: Boestad, Old Peace.

31 We may quote for example the merchants from Languedoc on the Champagne fairs or those from Florence in Pisa; both "nations" used to appoint *consuls* or *syndici* with attributions very close to those of the Low German aldermen. (Nicolussi-Köhler, Marseille, pp. 437–439; Quertier, Guerres et richesses.)

3. A written "Law of the Germans"

The Common Merchants' judicial authority encompassed the power to adopt temporary or permanent statutes. In the main settlements of the German merchants, the writing down of these decisions, alongside the charters that founded the *libertas Teutonicorum*, constituted the basis of law that was practised from at least the middle of the thirteenth century. The practical relevance of these rules is demonstrated by the concern to publicise them. From the end of the thirteenth century, the *Second Scra of Novgorod* stipulated that "every year the entire law shall be read once to the summer merchants and once to the winter merchants, as it is written, and from the beginning to the end of the book".[32] Similarly, the *Fourth Scra*, which was composed before 1361, stated that the Peterhof aldermen had to read the book of statutes before taking up their duties; they were also expected to "do their best to keep knowledge of all privileges and letters sent to the Merchant of Novgorod".[33] The same rules applied in Bruges, where the 1356 statutes stipulated that:

> *Every year at Pentecost, or even more often, the privileges they have received from the Count of Flanders and the city of Bruges, as well as the ordinances of the Common Merchant of Germany, must be read out before the Common Merchant of Germany, so that each man can stand by them for his rights and offences.*[34]

Another way of publishing these rules was to display them in public places. We know, for example, that the 1346 statutes of the Novgorod aldermen were intended to be "nailed to the wardrobe" in the common room at the Peterhof.[35] All these examples illustrate how the aldermen's written law cemented the German merchant communities abroad.

Consequently, the principles of "German Law" and its practice must be sought in the written collections of letters and statutes that were kept by the associations of Common Merchants. Some of these collections may be reconstructed by examining the provenance of various charters and other documents now kept in city archives.

3.1 An Early Attempt to centralise Charters on Gotland?

During the thirteenth century, the most important of these collections was probably the one kept in Saint Mary's Church in Visby. This place was the seat of the Common

---

32 SCHLÜTER, Nowgoroder Schra, p. 108 (II § 60a).
33 SCHLÜTER, Nowgoroder Schra, p. 165 (IV § 116); cf. also p. 129 (V § 9).
34 HR vol. 1 n° 200 § 8.
35 SCHLÜTER, Nowgoroder Schra, p. 125 (ms. Ri § 9).

Merchants of Gotland – an association known in older literature as the "Gotländische Genossenschaft", which has given rise to much speculation.[36] Although this collection has since then been lost or dispersed, it is possible to partially reconstruct it based on indirect evidence. Its origins may date back to the 1220s, when an original copy of the Treaty of Artlenburg, concluded in 1161 by Henry the Lion, Duke of Saxony, with the Scandinavian merchants of Gotland, was transferred from Lübeck to Visby. Just before this transfer – the exact reasons for which are unknown – an authenticated copy of this charter was made to be preserved in Lübeck. On this copy, a contemporary hand has written: "this privilege has been relocated (*repositum est*) to the Virgin Saint Mary's church in Visby".[37] Other documents were soon added to this collection. In 1231, Bishop Nicholas of Riga offered a commercial privilege to the "merchants of all places and cities" wishing to visit Livonia.[38] This charter was "given in Visby" (*Dat[um] Wisbuœ*), and it was probably still to be found there in the seventeenth century, when the Swedish Bishop Håkan Spegel (1645–1714) copied it during his stay on the island.[39] Similarly, Archbishop Johannes of Riga's charter to the "merchants from all places and cities travelling on the Baltic Sea" (1277) must have been kept on Gotland at least until the fifteenth century, since the religious and municipal institutions of Visby regularly sent authorised copies of it to Lübeck.[40]

The Common Merchants of Gotland's activity in Russia led them to keep several documents relating to this region in particular. For example, they kept a copy of the Treaty of Smolensk (1229), as the so-called "Gotland version" of this treaty states that "this charter was handed over on the Gotlandic coast before the Russian envoy and all Latin merchants".[41] This document may have been identical to the now-lost copy which was kept in the Stockholm archives during the seventeenth century. The following archival note related to the document was found in the nineteenth century: "A law or trade statute between the Russians, the Rigans, and Gotland, in which it is also described how criminal cases between the inhabitants of these countries are punished, given in Visby in 1228".[42] The Gotland aldermen

36 See for example: Kattinger, Gotländische Genossenschaft.

37 Lübeck, Archiv der Hansestadt Lübeck, 07.1–3/27 Suecica, n° 1: "*Privilegium ipsum repositum est in ecclesia beate Marie virginis in Wisby*"; HUB vol. 1 n° 15.

38 Stockholm, Riksarkivet, Skoklostersammlingen E8883, Position 49, n°3, fol. 5r–6r. The text of this charter has been published in my dissertation (Boestad, Pour le profit, pp. 703–704).

39 Ibid.

40 Lübeck, Archiv der Hansestadt Lübeck, 07.1–3/19 Livonica, n° 017–017c.

41 Gonneau and Ivanovs, Les plus anciennes, p. 90: "*Сѧ грамота іесть выдана на Гочкомь березѣ пьрьдъ роускимь посломь и пьрьдъ всеми латинскими коупци*".

42 Schirren, Verzeichnis livländischer Geschichts-Quellen, p. 128 n° 31. Carl Schirren observes that this note did not say anything about the language in which the document had been composed, nor whether it was an original or a copy. Yet, it allows some speculations. First, the date is wrong

were even able to have charters originally written in Russian translated into Low German. Thus, Prince Jaroslav of Novgorod's treaty with the German merchants (1269) seems to have been translated in Visby.[43] It is therefore likely that the lost original of this treaty, on which the German translations were based, was originally kept in Saint Mary's Church in Visby.

According to Wolfgang Schlüter, the translation of the 1269 treaty bears strong palaeographic resemblance to the primary extant manuscript of the *First Novgorod Scra*, which was drawn up "by a common statute of the wisest of all cities in German land" – i. e. under the direction of the Gotland aldermen.[44] It is therefore assumed that both manuscripts were written around 1270 on Gotland. This hypothesis is unverifiable in the present work – as both documents are now kept in Moscow and are inaccessible – but supported by the existence of a third fragment, which was found by Schlüter in the Herzog August Bibliothek in Wolfenbüttel. This parchment leaf, which had been re-used to bind a seventeenth-century manuscript, combined a copy of the *First Scra* with statutes of the German burghers of Visby in a small booklet of about 20 x 15 cm. The text is ornated with blue initials, red chapter headings, and floral motives in the margins; it may have belonged to the Gotland aldermen. It is thought to have been written in the same chronological and geographical context as the other two manuscripts. It thus strengthens the impression that Visby was a major centre for the conservation of charters relating to the German merchants' activities in the thirteenth century.[45]

It is important for our discussion that most of the charters preserved in Visby did not specifically concern trade on Gotland. The links between the Common Merchants of Gotland, Livonia, and Russia in the thirteenth century are well known and easily explained by the fact that the island was located on the main sea route linking the German lands to these regions.[46] However, it is more difficult to explain

---

(the right one is 1229); but this error is consistent with the date that appears in the remaining manuscripts of the "Gotland version" – whereas the "Riga version" is accurately dated to 1229. Second, the charter was not given in Visby. Here again however, this error may depend on a misinterpretation of the Russian wording, according to which the charter had been "handed over (*выдана*) on the Gotlandic coast". As we do not know in what language this copy was written, it is impossible to determine if this mistake was made by the seventeenth-century Swedish archivist or by a possibly German translator. The treaties of Smolensk have given rise to very intricate scholarly discussions, see: PETRUXIN, О датировке списка, pp. 161–178; PETRUXIN, О новом издании, pp. 386–398; GONNEAU and IVANOVS, Les plus anciennes chartes. I have commented on these discussions: BOESTAD, Pour le profit, pp. 679–701.

43 SCHLÜTER, Zwei Bruchstücke, pp. 513–516.

44 SCHLÜTER, Nowgoroder Schra, p. 8 and 50 (I); FRENSDORFF, Das statutarische Recht, pp. 7–8.

45 Wolfenbüttel, Herzog August Bibliothek, Novi 404, 9 n° 17. For an edition of this manuscript, see: SCHLÜTER, Zwei Bruchstücke, pp. 492–501.

46 KATTINGER, Gotländische Genossenschaft.

why one of the four copies of the 1253 privilege of the German merchants in Flanders was addressed to "all merchants of the Roman Empire frequenting Gotland" (*universorum mercatorum Romani imperii Godlandiam frequentantium*).[47] This now lost copy was kept in the Lübeck City Archives in the eighteenth century, and it is therefore not certain that it actually reached the island. In older historiography, it has been seen as evidence of the range of the Common Merchants of Gotland's activities and of their aldermen's attributions.[48] Yet, there is no indication that the latter would have been involved in any way in the negotiations with Flanders. Generally speaking, their capacity of action remained very limited beyond Gotland and the Russian settlements. Given the Lübeckers' involvement in the Flemish negotiations of 1252–1253, this copy can just as easily be seen as further evidence of their concern to collect charters relating to German trade in Visby.[49]

Consequently, there are several indications that attempts were made in the thirteenth century to gather documents relating to the activities of the German merchants in various marketplaces throughout Northern Europe on Gotland. Although one may doubt that these efforts resulted in regular cooperation between the aldermen of Visby and the merchants active in the North Sea, they demonstrate an awareness of the interconnectedness of these different marketplaces and a desire to get an overview of this network. Unfortunately, the sources do not reveal who was behind these attempts – was it only Lübeck or were there other cities or powers involved? – or what their exact motivations were.[50]

3.2 The London Guildhall

Other merchant jurisdictions also kept collections of charters in the thirteenth century. This was the case, for example, for the *hansa Almanie* in London, from which some of the collections relating to England in the thirteenth and early fourteenth centuries now kept in the Lübeck City Archive appear to have originated. Based on information provided by Stuart Jenks, Carsten Jahnke has pointed out that the English King Henry III's (r. 1216–1272) charter to the merchants of Gotland (1237) had remained in the hands of the London Black Friars until the Common Merchants bought it from them during the fifteenth century. It was then provided with a chancery note written in the same hand as the accounts of the Cologne merchants in London in the 1460s. Quite characteristically, this note appears on a parchment label attached to the seal cord and reads: "*Privilegium datum mercatoribus de Gothlandia et suis successoribus per regem Henricum Anglie, Hybernie,*

47 HUB vol. 1 n° 421.

48 Stein, Über die ältesten Privilegien, pp. 53–56.

49 Jahnke, Homines Imperii, pp. 26–29; Boestad, Pour le profit, pp. 128–134.

50 For the context of these attempts, see: Boestad, Hansischer Moment, pp. 31–57.

dux Normannie anno regni 21." (Privilege given to the merchants of Gotland and their heirs by King Henry of England and Ireland, Duke of Normandy, in the 21st year of his reign).[51] As Swedish historian Hugo Yrwing has shown, this charter was transferred to Lübeck in the conflictual circumstances that followed the Peace of Utrecht in 1474.[52]

However, the 1237 privilege may not have been the only charter to have been transferred under such circumstances, as similar parchment labels, all written by the same hand, can be found at the foot of several other English charters from the thirteenth and fourteenth centuries in Lübeck. This is the case, for example, with an original of the *Carta mercatoria* of 1303, as well as with one of the copies of King Edward II's privilege of 7 December 1317.[53] The agreement concluded by the City of London with the *hansa Almanie* in 1282 bears traces of similar labelling as well – remnants of a string and parchment scraps.[54] However, many other documents in the *Anglicana* series in Lübeck do not have such labels: this is particularly true of the charters addressed solely to the city of Lübeck, which must logically have been deposited in the City Archives when received in the thirteenth century.[55] These observations confirm the English origin of these labels and the hypothesis that the documents in question – with the exception of the charter of 1237 – were initially in the hands of the Common Merchants in London, who may perhaps have used them as the written basis of the "Law of the Germans" in England.

3.3 The Collections of the Common Merchant in Bruges

Although German merchants were present in Flanders as early as the twelfth century, the first traces of a written collection of privileges did not appear there until the early fourteenth century. This collection can be reconstructed on the basis of an inventory of the charters of the *Hansekontor* in Antwerp, which was drawn up when the charters were transferred to Cologne in 1591.[56] Given that the Antwerp trading post itself was the result of the transfer of the former Bruges *kontor* at the beginning of the sixteenth century, it can be assumed that the items listed in the inventory had originally been kept by the German Merchant in Flanders.[57]

51 Archiv der Stadt Lübeck, 07.1–3/01, Anglicana, n° 1. Jahnke, Homines imperii, p. 15 n. 81.

52 Yrwing, Visby, pp. 64–66.

53 Archiv der Stadt Lübeck, 07.1–3/01, Anglicana, n° 15/2, 22/1.

54 Archiv der Stadt Lübeck, 07.1–3/01, Anglicana, n° 10.

55 Archiv der Stadt Lübeck, 07.1–3/01, Anglicana, n° 3, 5.

56 This section is based on the publication of this inventory: Höhlbaum and Hagedorn, Das Hansekontor.

57 Kypta, Von Brügge nach Antwerpen.

The Antwerp inventory shows that the Common Merchant of Bruges did not possess any original charters from the thirteenth century; all the documents they kept from that period were in fact copies included in later cartularies. Originals that have survived are mainly to be found in the Lübeck City Archives.[58] This absence is unlikely to be due only to a gap in documentation. We know for example that the copies produced after the negotiations of 1252–1253 were not intended to be preserved locally, but in Lübeck, Hamburg, Gotland, and (probably) Dortmund.[59] From the late 1290s onwards, some original charters preserved in the Lübeck City Archives were doubled by authorised copies sent to Lübeck by religious institutions in Bruges, which could indicate that these charters (or lost copies of them) had originally been preserved locally.[60] However, the real signs of disruption date from the early fourteenth century. From 1307 onwards, the original charters relating to German trade in Bruges were no longer kept in Lübeck but in Cologne, where they had probably been transferred with the other archival material of the Antwerp *kontor*. This suggests that by 1307 at the latest, German merchants had begun to keep their charters in Bruges – either on their own premises or in one of the city's many religious institutions.[61] This observation corroborates Volker Henn's cautious observation that a decisive step towards the emergence of a German trading post in Bruges was taken in 1307–1309. Indeed, it appears that the Common Merchants in Bruges must indeed have come into being in this period or shortly afterwards.[62]

The Bruges collection is perhaps the richest one assembled by German merchants in the fourteenth century. It included numerous originals, most often granted by the Counts of Flanders, but sometimes also by the Duke of Brabant, the Count of Holland or city councils. It also included authorisations of Flemish charters. The Common Merchant in Bruges was even interested in the liberties enjoyed by German merchants on the other side of the Channel. Accordingly, their collection contained several copies of English privileges: for example, a fine replica of the charter granted to the *hansa Almanie* by the City of London in 1282, with a careful representation of the seals appended to it; as well as copies of the *Carta mercatoria*, and of Edward II's charter of 1317, which Konstantin Höhlbaum and Anton Hagedorn describe as contemporary with the originals.[63] This interest in

58 Archiv der Stadt Lübeck, 07.1–3/01, Batavica, n° 7/1, 7/2, 8, 9, 10, 21, 25.

59 Stein, Die ältesten Privilegien, pp. 74–77.

60 Archiv der Stadt Lübeck, 07.1–3/01, Batavica, n° 26a, 26b, 27aa, 28a, 28b.

61 We may think, for example, of the Carmelite monastery, with which German merchants maintained privileged relations. However, they also had links with several other institutions in the city; see: Leloux, Kariche und Caritas, pp. 36–40.

62 Henn, Über die Anfänge, pp. 53–54.

63 The copy of the 1282 charter can still be found in the Cologne archives (Köln, Historisches Archiv Köln, Best. 80, U 1/2). I have not been able to find the 'contemporary' copies of the charters of

the "Law of the Germans" in England is easily explained by geographic proximity, especially as conflicts between German and English merchants could easily escalate with repercussions extending to Flanders.[64]

Thus, the "German Law"/"Law of the Germans" did not only refer to merchant jurisdictions, but also to the collections of written documents that were held and used by these jurisdictions and regulated the German merchants' relations not only with denizens and local authorities, but also with their peers. While the overview of these collections has once again revealed the plurality of jurisdictions claiming to be ruled by the "Law of the Germans" and their independence from one another, the efforts made in several places to gather copies of legal texts relating to other trading posts also bear witness to the interconnectedness of these jurisdictions and an awareness of belonging to one common whole. Such interjurisdictional coordination was yet another way of overcoming the plurality of norms faced by the German merchants when trading between different marketplaces.

4. From "German Law" to "German Hanse"

4.1 A Network of Jurisdictions

From the beginning of the fourteenth century, there are indications of growing contacts between the various jurisdictions of German merchants abroad, particularly between those of Novgorod and Bruges. For example, Stuart Jenks has drawn a link between a clause in the 1309 and 1360 privileges of the German merchants in Flanders, which exempted their goods from inspection by Flemish officers (*dekers* and *vinders*), with the exception of "unsealed wax", and the statutes of German merchants in Novgorod, which stipulated that wax intended for export had to be assessed on the spot by *wasvinders*, whose seal had to attest to the conformity of the product. These procedures suggest that the Common Merchants in Flanders and Novgorod cooperated in order to control the quality of these products.[65] Exchanges between both jurisdictions continued in the following decades. In 1355, after several disputes with the Russians over the quality of cloth imported from Flanders, the alderman in Novgorod wrote to the Council of Reval ordering that:

1303 and 1317 – only other copies or confirmations of these charters, produced in 1352 and 1356 respectively, which are mentioned in the inventory as well (Köln, Historisches Archiv Köln, Best. 80, U 2/3, U 1/19). Cf. Höhlbaum and Hagedorn, Das Hansekontor, p. 21 and 24.

64 See for example the case of the execution of the English shipman Richard Curteys in 1351, for which the Germans were held responsible by the English authorities (HR vol. 1 n° 145, 148, 152).

65 Jenks, Transaktionskostentheorie, p. 38.

> *from the moment this letter is read before the Common Merchant in Bruges, no cut cloth shall be purchased to be sold to the Russians in Novgorod, nor in Gotland, Riga, Reval, Pernau, Dorpat, nor to any lord of this land [i. e., Livonia and Estonia], wherever produced, with the exception of English wools.*[66]

This letter was copied by a Reval notary on a loose leaf, which was then inserted into a book of memoranda.[67] The fact that it was intended to be read out in Bruges testifies to an acute awareness of the interconnectedness of the various marketplaces where the Germans were active in the mid-fourteenth century.

However, at the same time, the letter raises the question of the limits of the alderman's jurisdiction. Indeed, one would expect the application of such a statute in Visby and Livonia to be the competence of the city councils. On the contrary, these decisions "of the alderman of the Yard, his wise men and the common German merchant who was then in Novgorod" give the impression that in the second quarter of the fourteenth century, the Peterhof had authority *ratione materiae,* over all matters relating to German trading relations with Novgorod. In 1343, the Common Merchants in Novgorod prohibited trade with Russian furs and ordered that such trade should be conducted "neither in Riga nor in Dorpat, Reval, Pskov or Polotsk, '*nor in any place where the German merchant's Law prevails*', if he wants to be part of the German merchant's Law".[68] Here again, there is no doubt that this "German merchant's Law" referred to the German "liberties and justice" in Novgorod. A letter addressed to Dorpat during these years ordered in a very similar manner that "nobody should come here with [Poperinge] cloth after Easter, nor to Dorpat, Reval, Fellin, Gotland or anywhere else to the Russians, if he wants to be part of Saint Peter's Law".[69] We can conclude from these examples that the Novgorod aldermen claimed authority for regulating German-Russian trade, regardless of the place where the merchants met.

It is true, however, that some statutes recognised the geographical limits of this jurisdiction. In the 1332 statute on fraudulent wax, for example, the Peterhof aldermen mention that unlawful transactions could have been concluded outside their jurisdiction: "if someone buys fake wax '*outside the Law of Saint Peter*' and comes to Novgorod thereafter, then he shall not be allowed to store his goods in Saint Peter's church nor to be in the Law of the Germans".[70] In this particular case, the nature of the goods involved suggests that the ruling may have been directed

66 HUB vol. 3 n° 321.

67 Salminen, Obscure Hands, pp. 384–386.

68 HUB vol. 3 n° 592. Emphasis added.

69 HUB vol. 3 n° 564.

70 HUB vol. 3 n° 586. Emphasis added. See also: HR vol. 6 no 68A § 13 ("*dar men des copmans mechtich were*").

against merchants who had purchased them in more remote Russian principalities, where the aldermen did not have the political support necessary to enforce their authority.

In the absence of clear territorial limits to the application of the "German merchant's Law", the aldermen's justice was likely to compete with local authorities in terms of regulating trade. As a result, such jurisdiction could hardly have existed without the support of the respective city councils. Sources from the 1340s and 1350s suggest that some of them did indeed relay the aldermen's statutes, and even used their authority to reach out more effectively to all German merchants. This is illustrated, for example, by the statutes of 22 February 1346, the preamble to which stated that the decision "of the aldermen, wise men and common German merchants" had been taken "at the written and oral request (*na den breven unde den bode*) of the maritime cities outside and within the country (*sted[e] buten landes unde binnen landes bi der see*)".[71] The exact identity of these "maritime cities outside and within the country" is unclear. Lübeck, Visby, Riga, Reval, and Dorpat spring to mind because of their frequent involvement in the regulation of the Peterhof in this time, but the initiative may also have come from only some of these cities, which may have kept their identities vague on purpose.[72] In any case, the fact that the cities in question placed their decisions under the authority of the Peterhof shows that they recognised its legitimacy. Thus, whether or not the Riga City Council had taken part in the statutes of February 1346, it was only after their publication by the Common Merchants in Novgorod that the city registered them in its *bursprake* and brought them to the attention of the other German merchants active in Livonia.[73] The mere fact that these statutes were kept by several towns, including Lübeck and Reval, bears witness to the legal value attached to them.

In Novgorod, this situation was typical for the second third of the fourteenth century. During the thirteenth century, the aldermen of Visby had had authority over the Peterhof, although this had been contested by the city of Lübeck.[74] It is not known under what circumstances this situation came to an end, but the Visby aldermen reasserted their authority over the Common Merchants in Novgorod two

71 Schlüter, Die Nowgoroder Schra, p. 122 (IIIb ms. Ri).

72 Such practices can be traced back to the late thirteenth century, when Lübeck, Visby, and Riga used the seal of the Common Merchants of Gotland to ratify decisions of their own. Boestad, Hansischer Moment, pp. 40–42.

73 A letter from the Council of Riga addressed to the German merchants of Dünaburg (Daugavpils), probably at the end of September 1346, relayed one of the bans adopted by the Peterhof in February, referring to the "statute of the Common Merchant who were then in Novgorod", and specifying that this decision had been announced to the city's burghers in the *bursprake*. (HUB vol. 3 n° 85). On this institution, see: Bolland, Zur städtischen Bursprake.

74 Boestad, Hansischer Moment, pp. 44–50.

final times in the *Third Scra of Novgorod* and in another statute probably adopted in the early fourteenth century.[75] The appearance of statutes adopted by "the alderman and his wise men with the agreement of the Common Merchant who was then at the court of Novgorod" – first in 1318, and then again in 1327, and 1332 –[76] and their subsequent multiplication in the 1340s gives us a rough idea of the time when the Novgorod aldermen managed to consolidate their autonomy and jurisdiction.

Although the sources are less numerous for the other trading posts, some documents show the aldermen in Bruges displaying the same authority as those of the Peterhof. In a letter they sent to Hamburg in 1351, they announced their decision to temporarily transfer their trading post to Ardenburg or Antwerp, and requested that "if any transgressor [of this statute] is found, he be duly punished according to the ordinance of the aforementioned Common Merchant, in the city where he will be found, according to what his offence requires", and that "the fine for his offence be given and passed on for the use of all aforementioned merchants". They added that similar letters had been sent "to all big, renowned or capital cities that exist within our Law (*in nostro jure existentes*)". This surprising expression apparently referred to all cities – or at least the main ones – whose merchants used to visit Bruges and Flanders and placed themselves under the protection of the *judicium et libertas Teutonicorum* there. However, it explicitly excluded the "Lords Masters of Prussia and Livonia", i. e., the Provincial Masters of the Teutonic Order, to whom letters had also been sent, but who were mentioned separately, as if their rank did not allow them to be considered as subject to the justice of the merchants. All this might suggest that the aldermen of Bruges had authority over all cities whose merchants took part in the Law of the Germans – of which no one felt the need to draw up an exact list – for all matters relating to German trade in Flanders. At the same time, the letter's conclusion shows that this authority depended entirely on the cooperation of the cities in question, which were asked "to kindly consent and firmly abide by the aforesaid ordinance, unless you can think of a better ordinance and way".[77]

To sum up, in the mid-fourteenth century, several courts claimed to be ruled by a "Law of the Germans". The previous examples reveal increasing contacts between these jurisdictions. They also illustrate the supporting and controlling role played in the background by some of the merchants' hometowns: in relaying and sometimes initiating the Common Merchants' statutes they contributed decisively to the emergence of the "Law of the Germans" as a network of merchant jurisdictions.

---

75 Schlüter, Die Nowgoroder Schra, p. 116 (IIIa ms. R). On the political context of the elaboration of the *Third Scra*, see: Ibid., p. 21; Yrwing, Visby, pp. 126–130.

76 HUB vol. 3 n° 584–587.

77 HR vol. 1 n° 161.

4.2 The First Hanse Diets and the "German Law"

The emergence of the Hanse Diets in the 1350s meant a limitation of the alderman jurisdictions' autonomy. The very term "Common Cities", which was coined in the late 1350s to designate these assemblies, clearly alluded to the "Common Merchants" and to the intention to unify the "German Merchant's Law" by subjecting the tradesmen who abided by it to the joint authority of their respective city councils.[78] Thus, after the statutes of the Peterhof had been significantly revised by consuls from Lübeck and Visby in 1361, the Lübeck Diet of 24 June 1366 declared that "merchants staying in Novgorod must not adopt any important, major, or serious statutes without the knowledge and agreement of the cities of Lübeck, Visby, and the other cities, to which they must have sent letters beforehand".[79] The city diets also became more closely involved in the administration of the trading posts in Bergen and Bruges from 1366, and in London from 1375 onwards.[80]

These growing interventions of the cities by no means implied that the associations of Common Merchants lost their capacity for action after the 1360s. Their jurisdictional relations to the Diet remained ambiguous, and in London as well as in Bruges, the Common Merchants continued to adopt statutes on their own initiative. This was done without always informing the cities – whereas, as indicated above, many merchant statutes prior to 1360 were adopted under the supervision of cities.[81] There is therefore, no need to exaggerate this evolution by summarising it as the transition from a "Hanse of merchants" to a "Hanse of cities", as has sometimes been done in older literature about the Hanse.[82] The asserted subordination of the Common Merchants to the diets of the Hanse cities may have been above all an attempt to clarify and formalise jurisdictional bonds that were perceived with good reason as ambiguous and unclear, at a time when escalating conflicts with the city of Bruges put the cohesion and solidarity between German merchants and their representative bodies on trial.[83]

These developments are, however, reflected in the terminology used in the sources. From the late 1350s onwards, references to "German Law" almost com-

78 Boestad, Pour le profit, pp. 589–595.

79 Schlüter, Nowgoroder Schra, p. 126 (V § 1); HR vol. 1 n° 376 § 26–1 (ms. Ld). See also Groth, Das Verhältnis.

80 Boestad, Quand une juridiction.

81 Jörn, Money and bloode, pp. 312–313; Boestad, Quand une juridiction.

82 See for example: Dollinger, La Hanse; Wernicke, Die Städtehanse. This model has been contested and most scholars now agree that "Hanse of merchants" and "Hanse of cities" should not be opposed too schematically: Pitz, Bürgereinung und Städteeinung; Hammel-Kiesow, Die Hanse; Stephan Selzer, Die mittelalterliche Hanse. Yet, it is still possible to find remnants of it in some handbooks and other publications.

83 On this conflict, see: Hammel-Kiesow, Die Hanse, pp. 63- 66.

pletely disappeared. On the contrary, from 1379 onwards the use of the – admittedly exceptional – variant "*der stede recht*" – the "Law of the cities" – confirms that the city diets now pretended to be the real custodians of the "Law of the Germans".[84] Essentially, however, two other expressions grew to dominate from the 1360s to the 1380s: on the one hand, the "Merchant's Law" (*copmans recht*), or more rarely the "German Merchant's Law" (*copmans recht van Almanien*); on the other hand, the "German Hanse" (*Dudesche henze*) or sometimes simply the "Hanse" (*henze*).

The earliest references to the "German Hanse" have an adjacent meaning to that of "German Law". They did not designate a permanent organisation based on an alliance of cities.[85] They simply referred to the associations of Common Merchants as a whole, while the "cities of the German Hanse" were the cities whose merchants participated in these associations and who supported them. Thus, when in 1350 the Lübeck merchant Tideman Blomenrod was condemned by the German aldermen in Bruges after having sought justice from the city's magistrates, he was excluded from the Common Merchants for having "offended against the Common Merchant and against the aforementioned ordinances, which state that no merchant should seek justice anywhere else than before us". At first, Blomenrod managed to "remain within the Law of the Germans, as he used to be", by paying a fine. Soon however, he was excluded again, and it was then decided that anyone "belonging to the German Hanse" (*de to der Duschen henze behore*) should avoid any interaction with Blomenrod or be expelled from "the Law of the Germans" (*buten der Duschen rechte*) as well.[86] Both expressions are also closely associated in the famous statute of the "Common Cities of the German Hanse", which was promulgated at the end of an assembly of nine cities held in Lübeck on 20 January 1358:

> *If a city in the German Hanse were to boldly oppose this law and not comply with it, that city will have to remain outside the German Hanse forever and lose [the benefit of] the German Law forever.*[87]

In all these examples, "German Law" and "German Hanse" appear to have been used almost synonymously. It is difficult to draw a clear distinction between the two, especially since early references to the Hanse were flexible depending on the

---

84 HR vol. 2 n° 190 § 7 (*"andere lude, de in der stede recht nicht behoren"*). See also n° 220. There are also slightly more frequent references to "their right" (*"ere recht"*), where the possessive pronoun *"ere"* refers to cities. See for example: HR vol. 2 n° 84 (*"de menen stede, de in der Dudeschen henze sin, mid vulborde der andren stede to ereme rechte horende"*); n° 190 § 1 (*"dat ze de stede in ere recht unde vryheyt nemen unde entfanghen wolden"*).

85 Jahnke, Die Hanse, pp. 26–30.

86 HUB vol. 3 n° 160.

87 HR vol. 1 n° 212 § 10.

political context and the objectives pursued.[88] Generally speaking, the term "Hanse" emphasised German merchants as a group, whereas "German Law" focused on the statutes and liberties that they shared. However, exceptions are easy to find. The Diet of 24 June 1366, for example, stated that "no one shall go to or visit Novgorod unless he is included '*in the Law or Hanse of the Germans*'".[89] In the same year, the archbishop of Lund – who may of course have been unfamiliar with these concepts – addressed a privilege on the right of salvage "to the burghers and merchants of the following cities, that is Lübeck, Rostock, Stralsund, [etc.,] and all and each of those which are included with them '*in their justice, which is properly named German Hanse*' (*justicia, que hanse Theutonica proprie dicitur*)".[90] In both examples, there is no noticeable difference between "German Hanse" and "Law of the Germans".

The distinction between "German Hanse" as a group of merchants and "the Merchant's Law" as the statutes and liberties they shared became more systematic in the 1370s and 1380s, although both expressions were still mentioned side by side in a number of documents. In 1374, as mentioned above, an assembly of cities declared that "those from Brunswick should be expelled from the Hanse and from the Merchant's Law and Liberty".[91] In 1379, Hanse emissaries in Flanders reported how a merchant from Arnhem, carrying letters of safe conduct from the Duke of Guelders, had approached them to tell them "how those from Arnhem had since olden days been part of the Hanse and of the Merchant's Law" and that "they would like to use the Merchant's Law, for they would like to do like the other cities".[92] These examples consistently differentiated between "Hanse" as a group of merchants and "the Merchant's Law" as a set of liberties and statutes – the latter having completely replaced the earlier references to "the Law of the Germans". It should be stressed that throughout this period, the documentation referred much more frequently to "the Merchant's Law" than to "the Hanse", including in turns of phrases such as "the cities appertaining to the Merchant's Law".[93]

However, the difference between both expressions remained slight, so that they were sometimes used interchangeably. For example, the request made by the city of Nijmegen during the Hanse's negotiations with the Duke of Burgundy and the Flemish cities in 1387 is documented by several reports. These reports, however, do not entirely coincide with each other, for whereas the copies kept in Hamburg and Wismar state that the consuls of Nijmegen had asked to "take their burghers and merchants into '*the justice of the Common Merchant of Germany from the German*

88 Behrmann, Über Zeichen, pp. 118–123; Geelhaar, Wendische Städte, here pp. 66–70.
89 HR vol. 1 n° 376 § 13. Emphasis added.
90 HR vol. 1 n° 372. Emphasis added.
91 HR vol. 2 n° 84.
92 HR vol. 2 n° 192 § 19.
93 See for example: HR vol. 2 n° 203, 232 § 24; vol. 3 n° 144.

Hanse '", in the same place, those of Cologne and Torun mentioned a request "to take them into '*the Merchant's Law*', and to let them use with us '*the liberty and privileges that the Merchant has*', since they had since olden days been part of the Empire, and had then also surely taken part in the Merchant's Law, although they had not used it for a long time".[94]

The reasons why the references to "German Law" were abandoned from the late 1350s are not totally clear but seem closely linked to the emergence of the Hanse Diets. The term may well have been considered too ambiguous, since it could be interpreted as benefiting all merchants of the Empire. The request made by the consuls of Nijmegen in 1387 played on this very ambiguity, suggesting that since the city was part of the Empire, it should also be included in "the Merchant's Law".[95] On the other hand, from the 1360s, the diets had endeavoured to limit the effects of "the Merchant's Law" to cities that were genuinely involved in defending it. Thus, as early as the 1360s, several diets sought to explicitly regulate access to the associations of Common Merchants or recalled that the liberties and privileges of the Germans were reserved for those who were "burghers of a city of the German Hanse".[96] Therefore, the Nijmegen consuls' statement was greeted with scepticism by the Hanse emissaries, who noted that "among all of us, no one thought that they had ever been in the Merchant's Law [...]; and even if they had been part of it in the past, which we did not know, they had in any case not respected the cities' and the Merchant's unanimous decision, at the time the Merchant was established in Dordrecht" (as part of a trade blockade against Bruges).[97] All these examples suggest that in the second half of the fourteenth century there was no such thing as "German Law" or "the Merchant's Law" outside the political alliance of the Hanse cities.

5. Conclusion

At the end of this study, we can thus clarify the meaning of the references to "German Law" – and its many variants – in the sources relating to fourteenth-century German merchants. As far as we can judge, these expressions did not refer to a set of unwritten commercial practices that distinguished them from other groups of merchants, but rather to various jurisdictions of German aldermen and Common Merchants disseminated in Northern Europe, the most important of which being located in Visby – despite its decline during the first half of the

94 HR vol. 2 n° 342 § 14. Emphasis added.

95 HR vol. 2 n° 342 § 14.

96 HR vol. 1 n° 376 § 11, 13; 385. See also: HR vol. 1 n° 287 § 9; 296 § 14.

97 HR vol. 2 n° 342 § 14 (ms. T).

fourteenth century – Novgorod, Bruges, London, and later Bergen, as well as to the corpus of statutes and charters that these jurisdictions produced or negotiated with the respective local authorities. When specific sets of rules were involved, these always corresponded to the written charters and statutes enjoyed locally by the different merchant communities and jurisdictions, which were regularly consulted and publicly read out. The tenor of these rules varied from one marketplace to another.

Despite this plurality, the unity of German Law undoubtedly lay in the awareness of the actors within these jurisdictions – not only the merchants and their aldermen, but also the members of the city councils who often supported their action – that they ultimately served the interests of the "common German merchant" and needed to coordinate to act more effectively. This may be why, as early as the thirteenth century, cities like Lübeck made isolated efforts to connect the various jurisdictions of Common Merchants with each other, although it was only from the second third of the fourteenth century that the results of such policies became perceptible. In that time, the Common Merchants strove to ensure that the statutes they adopted would be enforced not only in the city where they were based, but also across large parts of the German merchants' area of activity. Whereas the hierarchical relationship between the various merchant jurisdictions and the cities within the "Law of the Germans" was initially quite horizontal and vague, efforts were made to clarify it with the emergence of the Hanse Diets from the 1350s onwards in order to strengthen coordination between these bodies under the supervision of the so-called "Common Cities". As a result, "the German merchant's Law" tended to become the prerogative of the citizens of the cities recognised as part of this alliance.

Such institutions helped make the German merchants' interactions with other nationalities more predictable. The Common Merchants did not just strive to establish regulations as lasting and advantageous as possible for them by negotiating and defending trading privileges in their favour; they also kept them regularly informed of their rights and duties, as well as of the general trading conditions at the market where they were established. The way German merchants used their charters to assert their rights testifies to the importance they attached to such documents for ensuring predictability. One may think of the desperate request made by the German merchants in Novgorod in 1331, demanding to be "judged according to our charters" as the Peterhof was besieged by a mob after the murder of a Russian.[98] It was probably with similar views to predictability that the interconnectedness between the associations of Common Merchants and their subordination to the Diets were achieved in the course of the fourteenth century. Such responses were meant to

98 HUB vol. 2 n° 505. See Boestad, Pour le profit, p. 616–618.

allow swift reactions to short-term disruptions in trade, either by informing the merchants or by taking common and appropriate decisions. They seem to have counted much more in the German merchants' and cities' efforts to make their trade more predictable than possible attempts to harmonise their legal environments.

Bibliography

BEHRMANN, Thomas, Über Zeichen, Zeremoniell und Hansebegriff auf hansischen Tagfahrten, in: Volker HENN (ed.), Die hansischen Tagfahrten zwischen Anspruch und Wirklichkeit, Trier 2001, pp. 109–124.

BOESTAD, Tobias, Ein erster "hansischer Moment". Lübeck, die "Seestädte" und die Frühformen der hansischen Konsensbildung im späten 13. Jahrhundert, in: Hansische Geschichtsblätter 140 (2022), pp. 31–57.

BOESTAD, Tobias, "Pour le profit du commun marchand". La genèse de la Hanse (XIIe–milieu du XIVe siècle), Genève 2022.

BOESTAD, Tobias, Quand une juridiction marchande mène sa propre politique : le Marchand de Bruges et la Hanse (c. 1360–c. 1460), in: Histoire urbaine, forthcoming.

BOESTAD, Tobias, The "Old Peace" as a Peacemaking Institution in Thirteenth-Century German Russian Trade Treaties, in: Simon LEBOUTEILLER/Louisa TAYLOR (eds.), Peacemaking and the Restraint of Violence in High Medieval Europe (1100–1300), London 2023, pp. 107–128.

BOLLAND, Jürgen, Zur städtischen 'Bursprake' im hansischen Raum, in: Zeitschrift des Vereins für Lübeckische Geschichte und Altertumskunde 36 (1956), pp. 96–118.

BURKHARDT, Mike, Die Ordnungen der vier Hansekontore Bergen, Brügge, London und Novgorod, in: Antjekathrin GRAßMANN (ed.), Das Hansische Kontor zu Bergen und die Lübecker Bergenfahrer, Lübeck 2005, pp. 58–77.

CORDES, Albrecht, Auf der Suche nach der Rechtswirklichkeit der mittelalterlichen Lex mercatoria, in: Zeitschrift der Savigny-Stiftung für Rechtsgeschichte: Germanistische Abteilung 118 (2001), pp. 168–184.

CORDES, Albrecht, "Deutsches Recht", in: Albrecht CORDES (ed.), Handwörterbuch zur deutschen Rechtsgeschichte, [vol. 1], Berlin 2008, col. 1003–1007.

CORDES, Albrecht, Future of the History of Medieval Trade Law, in: American Journal of Legal History 56/1 (2016), pp. 12–20.

DOLLINGER, Philippe, La Hanse (XIIe-XVIIe siècle), Paris 1964.

EBEL, Wilhelm, Deutsches Recht im Osten. Sachsenspiegel, Lübisches und Magdeburgisches Recht, Kitzingen 1952.

EBEL, Wilhelm, Lübisches Recht im Ostseeraum, Lübeck 1971.

FOSSIER, Robert, "Privilège", in: Claude GAUVARD/Alain de LIBERA/Michel ZINK (eds.), Dictionnaire du Moyen Âge, Paris 2012 [2002], pp. 1149–1150.

Frahm, Friedrich, Das Stadtrecht der Schleswiger und ihre Heimat, in: Zeitschrift der Gesellschaft für Schleswig-Holsteinische Geschichte 64 (1936), pp. 1–99.

Frankot, Edda, 'Of Laws of Ships and Shipmen'. Medieval Maritime Law and its Practice in Urban Northern Europe, Edinburgh 2012.

Frensdorff, Ferdinand, Das statutarische Recht der deutschen Kaufleute in Nowgorod. Erste Abteilung, Göttingen 1887.

Geelhaar, Tim, Wendische Städte oder civitates maritimae? Sondierungen zum Sprachgebrauch in den Hanserezessen von 1256–1370, in: Rudolf Holbach/Dietmar von Reeken (eds.), "Das ungeheure Wellen-Reich": Bedeutungen, Wahrnehmungen und Projektionen des Meeres in der Geschichte, Oldenburg 2014, pp. 57–70.

Goetz, Leopold-Karl, Deutsch-russische Handelsverträge, Hamburg 1916.

Gonneau Pierre/Ivanovs, Aleksandrs (eds.), Les plus anciennes chartes russes: le fonds des archives municipales de Riga, xiie–xive siècle, Turnhout 2021.

Groth, Carsten, Hanse und Recht. Eine Forschungsgeschichte, Berlin 2016.

Groth, Eckhard, Das Verhältnis der livländischen Städte zum Novgoroder Handelskontor im 14. Jahrhundert, Hamburg 1999.

Gustafsson, Sofia, Sale of Goods around the Baltic Sea in the Middle Ages, in: Stuart Jenks/Justyna Wubs-Mrozewicz (eds.), The Hanse in medieval and early modern Europe, Leiden/Boston 2013, pp. 129–148.

Hammel-Kiesow, Rolf, Die Hanse, München 2000.

Hammel-Kiesow, Rolf, The Early Hansas, in: Donald J. Harreld (ed.), A Companion to the Hanseatic League, Leiden/Boston 2015, pp. 15–63.

Henn, Volker, Über die Anfänge des Brügger Hansekontors, in: Hansische Geschichtsblätter 107 (1989), pp. 43–66.

Höhlbaum, Konstantin/Hagedorn, Anton (eds.), Das Hansekontor zu Brügge-Antwerpen. Verzeichnis der Urkunden, in: Mitteilungen aus dem Stadtarchiv von Köln 1 (1882), pp. 17–34.

Höhlbaum, Konstantin (ed.), Hansisches Urkundenbuch. Halle an der Saale 1876–1886.

Höhn, Philipp, Kaufleute in Konflikt. Rechtspluralismus, Kredit und Gewalt im spätmittelalterlichen Lübeck, Frankfurt am Main/New York 2021.

Höhn, Philipp, Pluralismus statt Homogenität. Hanse, Konflikträume und Rechtspluralismus im vormodernen Nordeuropa (1400–1600), in: Roland Deigendesch/Christian Jörg (eds.), Städtebünde und städtische Außenpolitik. Träger, Instrumentarien und Konflikte, Ostfildern 2018, pp. 261–290.

Jahnke, Carsten, Die Hanse. Überlegungen zur Entwicklung des Hansebegriffes und der Hanse als Institution resp. Organisation, in: Hansische Geschichtsblätter 131 (2013), pp. 1–32.

Jahnke, Carsten, Handelsstrukturen im Ostseeraum im 12. und beginnenden 13. Jahrhundert. Ansätze einer Neubewertung, in: Hansische Geschichtsblätter 126 (2008), pp. 145–185.

Jahnke, Carsten, "Homines Imperii" und "Osterlinge". Selbst- und Fremdbezeichnungen Hansischer Kaufleute im Ausland am Beispiel Englands, Flanderns und des Ostseeraumes im 12. und 13. Jahrhundert, in: Hansische Geschichtsblätter 129 (2011), pp. 1–57.

Jahnke, Carsten, Livonija no skandinavu un Hanzas perspektivas. Kontakti Baltijas juras telpa viduslaikos, in: Andris Levāns/Ilgvars Misāns/Gustavs Strenga (eds.), Viduslaiku Livonija un tas vesturiskais mantojums, Riga 2022, pp. 64–89.

Jenks, Stuart, Die Carta Mercatoria. Ein "hansisches" Privileg, in: Hansische Geschichtsblätter 108 (1990), pp. 45–86.

Jenks, Stuart, Die Einstellung der Hanse zu den Stadtaufständen im Spätmittelalter, in: Volker Henn (ed.), Die hansischen Tagfahrten zwischen Anspruch und Wirklichkeit, Trier 2001, pp. 75–108.

Jenks, Stuart, Transaktionskostentheorie und die mittelalterliche Hanse, in: Hansische Geschichtsblätter 123 (2005), pp. 31–42.

Jörn, Nils, „With money and bloode". Der Londoner Stalhof im Spannungsfeld der englisch-hansischen Beziehungen im 15. und 16. Jahrhundert, Köln 2000.

Johnson, Tom, Law in Common. Legal Cultures in Late-Medieval England, Oxford 2020.

Kadens, Emily, The Myth of the Customary Law Merchant, in: Texas Law Review 90/5 (2012), pp. 1153–1206.

Kattinger, Detlef, Die Gotländische Genossenschaft. Der frühhansisch-gotländische Handel in Nord- und Westeuropa, Köln/Weimar/Wien 1999.

Koebner, Richard, Deutsches Recht und deutsche Kolonisation in den Piastenländern, in: Vierteljahrschrift für Sozial- und Wirtschaftsgeschichte 25 (1932), pp. 313–352.

Koppmann, Karl (ed.), Die Recesse und andere Akten der Hansetage von 1256–1430, Leipzig 1870–1913.

Kypta, Ulla, Von Brügge nach Antwerpen. Institutionen statt Organisationen, in: Rolf Hammel-Kiesow/Stephan Selzer (eds.), Hansischer Handel im Strukturwandel vom 15. zum 16. Jahrhundert, Trier 2016, pp. 161–182.

Leloux, Herman, Kariche und Caritas im Leben der Genossenschaft des deutschen Kaufmanns zu Brügge, in: Hansische Geschichtsblätter 91 (1973), pp. 34–45.

Mohnhaupt, Heinz/Dölemeyer, Barbara (eds.), Das Privileg im europäischen Vergleich, Frankfurt am Main 1997–1999.

Munzinger, Mark, The Profits of the Cross: Merchant Involvement in the Baltic Crusade (c. 1180–1230), in: Journal of Medieval History 32 (2006), pp. 163–185.

Nicolussi-Köhler, Stephan, Marseille, Montpellier und das Mittelmeer. Die Entstehung des südfranzösischen Fernhandels im 12. und 13. Jahrhundert, Heidelberg 2021.

Petruxin, Pavel, О датировке списка А договора Смоленска с Ригой и Готским берегом, in: E. A. Mišina (ed.), Лингвистическое источниковедение и история русского языка 2012–2013, Moskva 2012, pp. 161–178.

Petruxin, Pavel, О новом издании смоленско-рижских актов, in: Fiodor B. Uspenskij (ed.), Именослов. История языка. История культуры. Moskva 2012, pp. 386–398.

Pitz, Ernst, Bürgereinung und Städteeinung. Studien zur Verfassungsgeschichte der Hansestädte und der deutschen Hanse, Köln/Weimar/Wien 2000.

Puhle, Matthias, “Hüter der alten Ordnung”? Die Hanse und die Große Schicht von Braunschweig 1374–1380, in: Rudolf Holbach/David Weiss (eds.), Vorderfflik twistringhe unde twydracht. Städtische Konflikte im späten Mittelalter, Oldenburg 2017, pp. 197–208.

Quertier, Cedric, Guerres et richesses d'une nation. Les Florentins à Pise au xive siècle, Rome 2022.

Salminen, Tapio, Obscure Hands – Trusted Men. Textualization, the Office of the City Scribe and the Written Management of Information and Communication of the Council of Reval (Tallinn) before 1460, Tampere 2016.

Schirren, Carl, Verzeichnis livländischer Geschichts-Quellen in schwedischen Archiven und Bibliotheken, Dorpat 1861–1868.

Schlüter, Wolfgang (ed.), Die Nowgoroder Schra in sieben Fassungen vom XIII. bis XVII. Jahrhundert Dorpat 1911.

Schlüter, Wolfgang, Zwei Bruchstücke einer mittelniederdeutschen Fassung des Wisbyschen Stadtrechtes aus dem 13. Jahrhundert, in: Mitteilungen aus der livländischen Geschichte 18 (1908), pp. 492–501, 513–516.

Selzer, Stephan, Die mittelalterliche Hanse, Darmstadt 2010.

Selzer, Stephan/Ewert, Ulf Christian, Institutions of Hanseatic trade: Studies on the political economy of a medieval network organisation, Frankfurt am Main/New York 2016.

Sicking, Louis H. J., Introduction: Maritime conflict management, diplomacy and international law, 1100–1800, in: Comparative Legal History 5 (2017), pp. 2–15.

Stein, Walther, Über die ältesten Privilegien der deutschen Hanse in Flandern und die ältere Handelspolitik Lübecks, in: Hansische Geschichtsblätter 14 (1902), pp. 51–133.

Stützel, Peter, Die Privilegien des Deutschen Kaufmanns in Brügge im 13. und 14. Jahrhundert, in: Hansische Geschichtsblätter 116 (1998), pp. 23–64.

Wernicke, Horst, Die Städtehanse 1280–1418. Genesis – Strukturen – Funktionen, Weimar 1984.

Wubs-Mrozewicz, Justyna, The Late Medieval and Early Modern Hanse as an Institution of Conflict Management, in: Continuity and Change 32 (2017), pp. 59–84.

Yrwing, Hugo, Visby – hansestad på Gotland, Stockholm 1986.

Unpublished archival sources

Archiv der Hansestadt Lübeck, Lübeck, 07.1–3.

Historisches Archiv Köln, Köln, Best. 80.

Gijs Dreijer

From *lex maritima* to *iura maritima*

Maritime Law, Legal Pluralism, and Predictability in the Low Countries (15th–16th centuries)

1. Introduction

The maritime sector has shown remarkable resilience in the face of shocks such as pandemics and war.[1] Notwithstanding its ability to adapt when faced with threats, it has historically preferred predictability and security over conflict, even if maritime transport was, and is, crucial in times of upheaval. This was no less the case in the past than it is now. To help ensure this predictability and resolve disputes about cases of maritime law smoothly and quickly, well-functioning legal institutions are, and were, a major prerequisite for the flow of maritime trade.

Somewhat surprisingly, the history of maritime law has been neglected in the history of maritime trade, which is itself the subject of a voluminous body of literature.[2] Moreover, its development has, at times, also been neglected in comparative legal history. This, even in the face of a long-standing tradition of studying Roman maritime law and its dissemination throughout Europe, although this is largely confined to the medieval period.[3] More recently, topics like maritime conflict management and maritime neutrality under the Law of the Sea have been put back on the scholarly agenda, both concerning what we would nowadays characterise as Public Law.[4] How predictability was historically (and legally) ensured for the maritime sector is thus still very much an open question, one that, given the important role of maritime trade for the world economy, should not be neglected.[5] The topic

---

1 See e. g. https://www.economist.com/leaders/2020/05/09/the-global-food-supply-chain-is-passing-a-severe-test, accessed 08/28/2023.

2 See: Lucassen and Unger, Shipping.

3 Even if much of the work is on commercial law, Levin Goldschmidt is often credited with the first "modern" coinage of the idea. See: Goldschmidt, Handbuch des Handelsrechts [vol. 1], p. 335–354 for maritime law. See also for an intellectual history of *lex mercatoria*: De ruysscher, Conceptualizing. See for older works on maritime law : Pardessus, Collection de lois, maritimes antérieures au XVIIIe siècle [6 vols.]. An early modern attempt was made in: Cleirac, Us et coutumes. See for background to the latter: Trivellato, Usages and Customs.

4 See for example: Sicking and Wijffels, Conflict Management. This is also evident in: Blakemore, Law and the Sea.

5 General Average is, for example, still a hotly debated topic among present-day maritime lawyers. See: Kruit, General Average.

is not only of interest to legal historians but also to economic historians, as the importance of legal institutions has increasingly been recognised.[6]

What is problematic in this regard is that much of the scholarship on the development of maritime law has followed a seductive, yet false and teleological story, centred around the idea of a *lex maritima*.[7] This *lex maritima* denotes the idea that an overarching, autonomous law, based on unwritten mercantile custom and private-order conflict resolution, supposedly governed maritime practice in North-Western Europe during the late medieval period. This idea has been put forth as part of, or analogous to, the more famous idea of the *lex mercatoria* applicable to commercial law.[8] While the precise nature of the relationship between *lex mercatoria* and *lex maritima* is debated, I consider them to be analogous to each other, as maritime and commercial law were separate legal fields even in the medieval period, although of course they were closely related as well.

An early argument for the existence of a general maritime law came from the German scholar Levin Goldschmidt, who argued that certain *Rechtskreise* (legal circles) existed in medieval Europe, e. g. a Mediterranean and a Northern European one. Goldschmidt argued that all of these circles had their basis in Roman maritime law, i. e. Justinian's Digest.[9] Whilst being no supporters of this idea, both Albrecht Cordes and Richard Blakemore have noted that the evidence for a *lex maritima* is stronger than that for a *lex mercatoria*. They point out several important compilations of maritime law, e. g. the *Rôles d'Oléron* for the Atlantic area, the *Consolat del Mar* for the Mediterranean and the Wisby Laws for the North and Baltic Sea area, existed in the late medieval period codifying several important principles of maritime law.[10] Arguing against the existence of such a *lex maritima* in North-Western Europe, Edda Frankot's meticulous study clearly pointed out the significant

---

6 North, Law and Economics.

7 For example in: Tetley, The General Maritime Law.

8 The idea of a *lex mercatoria* was popularised by Gerald Malynes in 1622. See: Malynes, Consuetudo. See for an analysis and its influence: De ruysscher, Conceptualising. See for a critical perspective on the "myth" of the *lex mercatoria*: Kadens, The Myth, pp. 1153–1154; Kadens, The Medieval Law. See for supporters: Epstein, Reflections; Trakman, The Evolution; Benson, Spontaneous Evolution; Berman, Law and Revolution.

9 Goldschmidt, Universalgeschichte des Handelsrechts, p. 335–337 and 344.

10 Cordes, Lex Maritima; Blakemore, Law and the Sea. All three collections have been studied extensively in various languages. For the *Rôles d'Oléron* see: Kiesselbach, Der Ursprung; Krieger, Ursprung; Runyan, Rolls of Oleron; Ward, Medieval Shipmaster; Shephard, Rôles d'Oléron. See for the *Consolat del Mar*: Constable, The Problem; Krieger, Entwicklung des Seerechts. See for the Wisby Laws: Frankot, Medieval Maritime Law; Frankot, Die Ehrbaren Hanse-Städte; Goudsmit, Geschiedenis, pp. 142–193; Jahnke, Maritime Law; Jahnke, Seerecht; Landwehr, Seerecht im Ostseeraum; Landwehr, Seerecht der Hanse.

differences in the application of laws in municipalities around the North Sea in the areas of jettison, shipwreck, and salvage.[11]

The framework of the (non-)existence of a *lex maritima* reinforces a simplistic, binary narrative about the development of law. Was it autonomous and developed by merchants, shipmasters, and ship-owners, or was the state the main instigator to develop new legal rules and norms? As many legal historians have emphasised, the jurisdictional and legal situation in late medieval Europe was complex. As such, legal historians working on the development of mercantile law have acknowledged the "jurisdictional complexity" and "pluralistic" nature of law.[12] For maritime law, the situation is perhaps even more complex. Although the compilations of medieval maritime law indeed offered some standard principles for maritime trade, many other sources of law came into play. Rather than framing the discussion as one of the (non-)existence of a *lex maritima*, this chapter aims to go beyond the binary distinction between a harmonised *lex maritima* and an unlimited legal pluralism. As such, a framework discussing the development of maritime law as one of transnational principles with local details or of a law grounded in local practice with some transnational characteristics is more fruitful.[13] Moreover, this allows for a more actor-centric approach that highlights the influence of merchants and shipmasters on the development of maritime law.

Emily Kadens has argued that in late medieval Europe the "'*iura mercatorum*', the laws of merchants: bundles of public privileges and private practices, public statutes and private customs" existed. Accordingly, this chapter argues that a similar concept of *iura maritima* (note the plural) should be applied to the case of maritime law. This means that there were always multiple sources of law – either overlapping, complementing, or sometimes contradicting each other.[14] Through lengthy negotiations, new rules, either formal laws or informal norms, were subsequently formed by the various actors in the maritime sector to address new challenges, such as the rising threat of privateering and/or piracy in the sixteenth century. The relative complexity of the development of law is not a trivial concern for lawyers only, but goes to the heart of questions about how law aided, or hindered, economic development in premodern Europe, and how legal institutions for maritime trade developed.[15]

Whilst private maritime law concerns a number of issues, e. g. jettison, salvage, and shipwreck, to name just three major areas, this article aims to advance the claim that *iura maritima* existed by zooming in on the example of General Average

---

11 Frankot, Ships and Shipmen. See for a similar perspective: Cordes, Lex Maritima.

12 See Donlan and Heirbaut, Patchwork.

13 Ibid.

14 As argued by: Kadens, Order within Law, p. 42.

15 See for example: Gelderblom, Cities of Commerce.

(GA) in the sixteenth-century Low Countries. GA already existed in Roman law and still exists today under the so-called York-Antwerp Rules. GA redistributes extraordinary costs incurred to save ship and cargo across all parties engaged in a maritime venture, for example, when cargo was jettisoned to save a ship and its cargo during a storm.[16] GA has been used by proponents of *lex maritima* as an example of the remarkable stability of maritime law throughout history, although this has also been questioned by Frankot and Jolien Kruit, among others.[17] As such, GA offers an excellent window onto the questions at hand. This chapter argues that *iura maritima* allowed for predictability on basic issues, while permitting for the necessary flexibility in court to solve new cases.

This chapter, drawing on sources from both formal law and legal practice, focuses on the development of GA in the Low Countries in the fifteenth and sixteenth centuries, as during this period the area, particularly its four seafaring provinces Holland, Zeeland, Flanders, and Brabant, was one of Europe's most advanced maritime economies. Merchants from all over Europe were present in the Low Countries, coming from different legal traditions and with their own ideas about how GA should be applied. The Low Countries were thus a legally pluralistic and jurisdictionally complex environment par excellence, making it a highly interesting laboratory to study how merchants dealt with questions of predictability and legal pluralism.

2. Legal Pluralism, Harmonisation, and Predictability

Terms like legal pluralism are often used in different ways by different people. In the legal-historical sense of the word, it denotes the existence of multiple legals systems within a certain geographical area, for example, when state law and religious law exist next to each other. In other words, different forms of law and rules exist beside one another.[18] Some historians, however, have also interpreted legal pluralism as a system of diversified access to courts and the law. In medieval and early modern Europe, for example, common people had different rights and options than the nobility.[19] In this sense, legal pluralism refers to a difference in legal status, which inevitably resulted in a system that accommodated different laws for different

16 For a short history of the instrument: Cornah and Reeder, Lowndes and Rudolf, p. 1–6.

17 For a critical view and historiographical references see: Kruit, General Average; Frankot, Ships and Shipmen.

18 Twining, Normative and Legal Pluralism.

19 See e. g. the case of the Great Council in the Low Countries: van Rhee, Litigation.

people. This arrangement should not be confused with forum shopping, as the two are often conflated in studies on historical legal pluralism.[20]

This frequently confuses studies on legal pluralism, something that is also echoed in debates on *lex maritima* and *lex mercatoria*. Legal pluralism and jurisdictional complexity were not bugs of the system: both *were* the system, and thus the question of *whether* a medieval society was legally-pluralistic is the wrong one.[21] The question is rather, *how* people coped with this system, and *how* change could be realised within this system.[22] Of course, cities or sovereigns sought a certain base level of predictability, but common sense suggested that even within cities or countries full harmonisation would be futile, e. g. as foreign *nationes* had their own, limited, jurisdiction.[23] Conceptions of a unified *lex mercatoria* and *lex maritima* thus rest on a total misunderstanding of how medieval law, including commercial and maritime law, functioned.[24] Many different forms of law existed next to each other, sometimes overlapping, but sometimes also contrasting.[25] Yet, even if laws were different in many areas of Europe, certain legal "*principles*" did exist, GA being a primary example. The relationship between principles and application would thus determine the extent of "legal pluralism" in medieval Europe, coupled with the differences in access to the courts.

3. Maritime Law in the Low Countries

Since maritime trade is almost by definition interregional, it should not be a surprise that compilations setting out basic principles for maritime trade were drawn up to regulate maritime affairs throughout Europe, as well as other regions. Already in the sixth century, Justinian's Digest contained a significant number of rules on maritime law, including the principle that would later become known as GA under the so-called *lex Rhodia de iactu*.[26] Fast forward to the Late Middle Ages, three compilations were of particular importance according to scholars: the *Rôles d'Oléron* (governing the Atlantic zone), the *Consolat del Mar* (governing the Mediterranean zone), and the Wisby Laws (governing the North Sea and Baltic

---

20 See e. g. for examples Wubs-Mrozewicz, Conflict Management.

21 Donlan and Heirbaut, Patchwork.

22 See also the introduction to this volume.

23 For an overview of the foreign merchant communities in the Low Countries see: Blondé, Gelderblom and Stabel, Foreign Merchant Communities.

24 See also Kadens, Order within Law, p. 42.

25 Donlan and Heirbaut, Patchwork.

26 Cornah and Reeder, Lowndes and Rudolf, p. 1–4. See also for the Digest and the so-called *Lex Rhodia*: Aubert, Dealing with the Abyss; Chevreau, La lex Rhodia.

area). These compilations were often published, as were offshoots and translations, for example the *Black of Book of the Admiralty* in England.[27] Yet, this does not give the full picture, as in every region of Europe many other compilations existed; both in the Mediterranean and in Northern Europe, local towns often compiled their own rudimentary legal documents, including rules on maritime law and GA.[28] Most compilations from the late medieval period included, next to maritime labour law, some basic rules on jettison, shipwreck, and salvage, although details differed across the compilations.

The Low Countries were an important node in late medieval Europe.[29] Bruges in the fifteenth, Antwerp in the sixteenth, and Amsterdam in the seventeenth century were among the major commercial centres of North-Western Europe.[30] Economic historians have pointed to various reasons for the ascent of the cities in the Low Countries in the economic system of Europe, of which improvements in maritime technology figure prominently.[31] The Low Countries possessed many natural harbours, for instance that at the mouth of the Zwin river in the Bruges estuary or as well as the Scheldt and Honte in Zeeland and Brabant.[32] From the eleventh century onwards, maritime trade was one of the major economic activities of the Low Countries, at least in the provinces of Flanders, Brabant, Zealand, and Holland, often considered the economic and political core of the Low Countries.[33] As the maritime economy developed, legal rules had to keep up with expanding trade. This was the case particularly during the fifteenth and sixteenth centuries, when Bruges and Antwerp attracted a lot of foreign merchants, legal development gained momentum, as various interested stakeholders in the maritime economy, merchants, shipmasters, but also municipal governments and the central state, sought to bend the rules in their favour.[34]

Early maritime trade in the Low Countries was largely local, focusing on nearby regions such as England, the western Hanseatic cities and northern France. Commercial contacts with France, primarily in the wine trade, introduced the *Rôles d'Oléron* (Judgements of Oléron) to the Low Countries. The *Rôles*, compiled during the twelfth century near Bordeaux, contained rules for the personnel on board,

---

27 Supra, note 10, for the applicable references.

28 Blakemore, Law and the Sea.

29 A classic work on this topic is: van Werveke, Brugge en Antwerpen. More recent works include: Brown and Dumolyn, Bruges; Puttevils, Stabel and Verbist, Een eenduidig pad.

30 Gelderblom, Cities of Commerce.

31 Lucassen and Unger, Shipping; for a later period see also: North, Sources of Productivity.

32 For an overview see: Parmentier, Maritiem-economische schets.

33 Blockmans, Metropolen aan de Noordzee, pp. 649–651; Sicking, Neptune.

34 See e. g. De ruysscher, Maxims.

actions to be taken in case of danger, and rules for loading and unloading ships.[35] Although the *Rôles* were primarily meant to regulate the wine trade in Gascony, the principles drawn from it were transferred rather easily. As a result, translations existed throughout Northern Europe, for example, in England as the *Black Book of the Admiralty*.[36] In the Low Countries, a translation known as the so-called *Vonnisse van Damme*, named after a port town in the estuary system near Bruges, was introduced in the mid-fourteenth century.[37] Different versions of the *Vonnisse* circulated in the Low Countries, each adding some new articles or slightly changing some of the rules.[38]

Yet, as was the case in other parts of Europe, the *Rôles* were not the only source of law to deal with disputes arising from maritime trade. In Amsterdam, for example, the so-called *Ordonnantie* was published around 1413, a copy of which has also been found in Staveren (Friesland).[39] This compilation regulated maritime law in the Zuiderzee area, largely focusing on maritime labour issues. Although some scholars have argued this was an extension of the *Vonnisse*, Frankot has clearly shown that the *Ordonnantie* was a stand-alone collection, with rules different from those found in the *Vonnisse*.[40] In another example, Antwerp compiled its *Keurboeck* in 1419, which included some clauses on maritime labour law.[41] Meanwhile, the city of Kampen used the so-called *Dat Boek van Rechte* and the *Gulden Boeck* during the fourteenth and fifteenth centuries, dealing with various issues including jettison, shipwreck, and salvage.[42] Most interestingly, the *Gulden Boeck* included a clause stating that it only contained local customs, explicitly noting that in other port towns customs could be different.[43] This was a clear acknowledgement of legal pluralism by the town's aldermen, adding support for Frankot's thesis that local application always varied despite the fact that there was agreement on general principles, for example, in the case of GA.[44]

In the fifteenth century, foreign merchants also brought their local rules with them, which they applied in the consular courts for disputes within their so-called *nationes*. The consular courts were courts for disputes that took place within the

---

35 Frankot, Medieval Maritime Law; Krieger, Ursprung und Wurzeln.

36 Runyan, The Rolls of Oleron.

37 Den Tex, Oud-Nederlandsch zeerecht; Kiesselbach, Der Ursprung.

38 van den Auweele, Het Brugse zeerecht, pp. 147–150; van den Auweele, Zeerecht, pp. 221–223; Korthals Altes, Zeerecht.

39 Frankot, Ordinancie van Staveren.

40 Frankot, Ships and Shipmen, pp. 31–35; Goudsmit, Geschiedenis, pp. 121–123.

41 Text printed in: De Longé, Coutumes, pp. 50–51.

42 Frankot, Ships and Shipmen, pp. 31–32; Goudsmit, Geschiedenis, pp. 306–308.

43 Ibid., pp. 307–308: "*Wanneer sie comen tandern havenen in andern lande dar nemen si dat recht alse daer zedelic ende woentlic is.*"

44 Frankot, Ships and Shipmen.

natio, with the consuls acting as judges. One example concerns the early fifteenth-century *Consolat del Mar*, which was introduced in the Low Countries by Catalan-Aragonese merchants based in Bruges (although it is unclear when precisely this process took place).[45] Hanseatic maritime law meanwhile, was known in the Low Countries already during the mid-fifteenth century.[46] The Hanseatic *Kontor* (office) in Bruges first created the so-called *Waterrecht*, a combination of the *Vonnisse*, the Amsterdam *Ordonnantie*, and some decisions drawn from various *Hanserecesse* (written records of Hanse Diets).[47] Around 1500, the Hanseatic aldermen added some provisions from Lübeck municipal law to this collection as well. This collection came to be known as the Wisby Laws, named after the city of Visby on the island of Gotland (Sweden), where they were most likely first printed.[48] It appears to have been the most complete compilation of Hanseatic maritime law in the medieval period, and therefore was used widely.[49]

From the late fifteenth century onwards, the Habsburg sovereigns increasingly sought to regulate maritime issues as well. Between 1488 and 1592, they published no less than eighteen *Ordonnances* which dealt with various aspects of maritime law, for example, insurance, navigation, and the Admiralty.[50] Both the issues of maritime defence and insurance have been well-studied by scholars, as these were the primary subjects of regulation.[51] In both cases, reforms proposed by the Habsburgs were moderately successful, as opposition from merchants, cities, and estates made their implementation difficult. Yet, a lesser studied subject is the role that royal legislation played in catalysing norms on issues like GA; indeed, the 1551 *Ordonnance* was the first source of law to provide an actual definition of the instrument.[52] Both the 1551 and 1563 *Ordonnance*, for example, included the Wisby Laws as the customary maritime laws of the Low Countries; while the 1563 *Ordonnance* regulated all aspects of maritime law, including insurance, GA, and shipwreck.

Following the promulgation of the 1531 *Ordonnance* by the Habsburg sovereign Charles V, all towns and cities were obliged to write down their local customs and send them to the central government to be "homologated" (ratified).[53] Although Antwerp, together with other cities resisted this development, it did in the end

45 SCHWEITZER, Schiffer und Schiffsmann, pp. 19–22 and 28–30.
46 JAHNKE, Seerecht im Hanseraum; FRANKOT, Die Ehrbahren Hanse-Städte.
47 The *Hanserecesse* contain the proceedings of the Hanse Diets – meetings of the Hanseatic towns.
48 FRANKOT, Medieval Maritime Law, p. 153; see also FRANKOT, Die Ehrbaren Hanse-Städte.
49 VAN DEN AUWEELE, Zeerecht, pp. 220–224.
50 DE GROOTE, De zeeassurantie, pp. 28–31.
51 See for example: SICKING, Neptune; DE GROOTE, De zeeassurantie; DE RUYSSCHER and PUTTEVILS, Art of Compromise.
52 KRUIT, General Average, p. 202.
53 GILISSEN, Phases.

comply, compiling four successive versions of its so-called *Costuymen* (Customs) in 1548, 1570, 1582, and 1608.[54] Although none of these was in the end homologated for various reasons, the ones of 1582 and 1608 are considered masterpieces of legal scholarship, and were applied in Antwerp and widely accepted by the mercantile community.[55] Indeed, the latter version of Antwerp municipal law covered almost every element in private law, testifying to its importance.[56] On maritime law, for example, the *Costuymen* of 1608 (called the *Compilatae*) contained over 500 articles.

Bram van Hofstraeten has studied the origin of the rules in the *Costuymen* of 1608, based on the so-called *Memoriën op de Costuymen* (Notes about the Customs).[57] According to those contemporary notes, about half of the rules on maritime law were based on *usus*, i. e. customs or usage, which were often included as rules of thumb in the above-mentioned medieval compilations such as the Wisby Laws.[58] A significant minority of rules on GA were drawn from royal legislation, of which the 1563 *Ordonnance*, issued by Philip II, was clearly the most important.[59] Given the constant tensions between the Habsburg central government and Antwerp, it may come as a surprise that royal legislation was quite influential. Yet, as the 1563 *Ordonnance* closely aligned with legal practice on the subject of GA, this is not necessarily surprising. Another key source was the 1569 *Hordenanzas*, particularly on the subject of insurance and the liability of insurers to pay for GA losses. Learned law, in contrast, was almost neglected, even if most of the compilers of the *Compilatae* were trained jurists.

The so-called *Hordenanzas* of 1569 were a compilation of rules on insurance and GA issued by the Bruges-based Castilian *natio*. Castilian merchants had already settled in Bruges since the early fourteenth century and would leave only in 1705, some two hundred years after most *nationes* had gone to Antwerp.[60] The *Hordenanzas* were based on both royal Castilian legislation and mercantile custom.[61] Charles Verlinden, who studied the *Hordenanzas* in the 1950s, interrogated the text closely and concluded that the *Hordenanzas* indeed encompassed the "costuymen vander borse van Antwerpen" (customs of the bourse of Antwerp), as it stated.[62] More

---

54 van Hofstraeten, Juridisch humanisme, pp. 7–10.

55 Ibid.; De ruysscher, Romeinsch recht, pp. 55–68.

56 van Hofstraeten, Juridisch humanisme, pp. 111–117. Roman law was subsequently considered redundant in Antwerp for commercial and maritime law, as Antwerp municipal law covered all relevant legal issues.

57 Ibid.

58 van Hofstraeten, Recording Customs, pp. 292–293.

59 Ibid.

60 Maréchal, Le depart.

61 Coronas González, La Ordenenza, p. 407.

62 Verlinden, Code d'assurances, pp. 38–46.

recently, authors such as Henry De Groote and Guido Rossi have however disputed this sharply. They have pointed to the fact that these were simply Castilian customs, significantly influenced by Castilian legislation.[63] Most likely, the collection's billing as the customs of Antwerp was a way to present the collection as mercantile custom shared by all merchants, since this may have been the strongest source of law regarding maritime and commercial law. Custom was probably perceived to be the most important source of law for merchants in Antwerp and Bruges, even if it became less fluid during the sixteenth century when it moved from unwritten to written.[64] Yet, references to the "customs of the bourse of Antwerp" were a popular way to gain authority.

4. General Average in the Low Countries (15th–16th Centuries)

Next to shipwreck and salvage, the redistribution of deliberate losses after jettison or mast cutting is among the most long-standing topics in maritime law. It is thus no surprise that General Average (GA), as the instrument is known in the present day, has been used as evidence of *lex maritima*. This is true particularly as today's so-called York-Antwerp Rules, drawn up by the *Comité Maritime International*, govern GA as a largely private-order solution.[65] However, even contemporary lawyers dealing with GA have noted the manifold applications of the instrument throughout history, as Jolien Kruit for example, has written:

> An analysis of the various historic regimes shows that they all incorporated the concept that expenditure and sacrifices made for the common safety of the parties interested in the maritime adventure were to be paid by (some of) the parties who had benefited therefrom. The analysis also makes it clear that each period of time and geographic area had its own regulations and application of the general average principle with specific features. […] There has never been an overall uniform regulation in place. Even today, the YAR have not created a uniform application of the concept of general average.[66]

As all the sources of formal law introduced in the previous section also deal with GA, there is much to gather from a study of those very sources. However, GA's most famous application, jettison, was already known in D.14.2 of Justinian's Digest in the sixth century. This chapter of the Digest was also well-known across medieval

63 De Groote, De zeeassurantie, pp. 52–58; Rossi, Insurance, pp. 20–21.

64 Kadens, Convergence.

65 See for example: Tetley, Maritime Law; Paulsen, Historical Overview. For a more nuanced view of the development of GA see: Mukherjee, Essentials, pp. 24–26.

66 Kruit, General Average, p. 202.

Europe, and rules like the *Rôles d'Oléron* essentially only added procedural rules to the principle mentioned therein. D.14.2.1 was originally noted down by the Roman jurist Julius Paulus in the third century.[67] The rule concerned jettison and stated that

> it is provided by the Lex Rhodia that if merchandise is thrown overboard for the purpose of lightening a ship, the loss is made good by the assessment of all which is made for the benefit of all.[68]

Although the so-called *lex Rhodia de iactu* was cited in the Digest, the original eighth-century BC rule has not survived to present times. As jettison was, and is, the most common way to declare GA, this is the most frequently cited rule and remained the topic of discussion throughout the medieval and early modern period; moreover, it is used as *the* example of continuity of the instrument throughout time.[69] Yet, other options for costs to be redistributed were also cited, for example, mast cutting, and ransoms paid to pirates.[70] As such, the principle was not yet fully developed, as both deliberate actual losses, e. g. jettison and mast cutting, and expenses to prevent greater losses, e. g. ransoms paid to pirates, could lead to a contribution by all in the interest of the community.

In the twelfth-century *Rôles d'Oléron*, and thus in the *Vonnisse van Damme*, the scope of the principle was more focused. Only jettison and mast cutting were mentioned as causes for GA, clearly allowing only direct losses into the contribution by all.[71] Late-medieval sources in the Low Countries however, broadened the application again. The *Rechten van Westcappelle*, an early sixteenth-century translation of the *Rôles*, for example, added the rule of extraordinary pilotage in times of distress.[72] The fifteenth-century *Ordonnantie* of Amsterdam included extraordinary pilotage as well as the use of lighter ships to save cargo when sailing into port.[73] Although the principle of contribution after jettison was well-known

---

67 The edition used for this research is: Corpus Iuris Civilis: tekst en vertaling [vol. III, Digesten 11–24], ed. by Spruit. *Corpus Iuris Civilis*, D.14.2.1: *"Lege Rodia cavetur, ut, si levandae navis gratia iactus mercium factus est, omnium contribution sarciatur quod pro omnibus datum est."* An analysis is provided in: Ashburner, The Rhodian Sea-Law, pp. ccli-cclxxxv.

68 See https://www.oldsaltblog.com/2022/04/the-what-how-why-of-the-ancient-principle-of-general-average/ for the English translation, accessed 03/18/2024.

69 See e. g. Constable, The Problem.

70 See e. g. *Corpus Iuris Civilis*, D.14.2.2.3 and D.14.2.3.

71 Kiesselbach, Der Ursprung, pp. 44–60; *Rôles d'Oléron*, Arts. 8 and 9.

72 Korthals Altes, Ons oudste zeerecht, p. 20.

73 Goudsmit, Geschiedenis, pp. 121–123.

throughout Europe, e. g. in Hanseatic and Mediterranean legal compilations, the exact scope and rules remained a question of local application.[74]

What was clear was that the application in many places broadened from jettison to other procedures, including expenses to prevent greater losses. Thus, up to the sixteenth century there was broad agreement in North-Western Europe on the *principle*, but not on the exact legal rules applying that principle. This may have been called legal pluralism in the legal-historical sense of the word, and indeed the fifteenth-century Kampen *Gulden Boeck* explicitly acknowledged that rules on the contribution after jettison could be different in other ports, a clear recognition that legal pluralism existed at least in the Low Countries.[75] Yet, the actual incorporation of this acknowledgement, I would argue, shows both the predictability as well as the flexibility it granted merchants. They could rely on the application of the broad principle, but had to take into account local differences in application. This, of course, could be as much a problem as an opportunity, as merchants could seek a 'better' option in a nearby town.

The development of GA was really expanded by royal legislation as introduced in the previous section. Both the 1551 and 1563 *Ordonnances* of the Habsburg sovereigns Charles V and Philip II presented significant advances regarding the standardisation of the *principle* of GA. Following the 1550 *Ordonnance*, which was concerned with protection costs and curbing insurance and bottomry, Charles followed up with the 1551 *Ordonnance*, which also included regulations on private maritime law, including GA.[76] According to the 1551 *Ordonnance*, these rules were further regulations adopted to supplement the Wisby Laws, the latter being accepted as the "customary" maritime law of the Low Countries.[77] On GA, the 1551 *Ordonnance* offered both definitions of GA as well as Small or Common Average (SA, the operational expenses of the ship paid for by the contribution of merchants).[78] The *Ordonnance* stated that all damages suffered for the common beneficiary of the ship were to be shared over the ship and cargo according to the "*nae ouder gewoonten van der zee*" (customs of the sea), thereby defining GA.[79]

Besides these definitions, the *Ordonnance* added a new rule on GA, following Castilian and Portuguese lobbying.[80] The expenses incurred while fighting off

74 Schweitzer, Schiffer und Schiffsmann, pp. 180–181; Goudsmit, Geschiedenis, p. 208.

75 Goudsmit, Geschiedenis, p. 307–308.

76 See Sicking, Neptune, pp. 240–280.

77 Surprisingly, this element has been all but neglected in the literature, the exception being: Sicking, Neptune, pp. 247–253.

78 The 1551 *Ordonnance* can be found in: Recueil des ordonnances des Pays-Bas. Deuxième série, 1506–1700 [vol. 6], ed. by Lameere, pp. 163–177.

79 1551 *Ordonnance*, Arts 41 and 42.

80 For this see: Sicking, Les marchands; Sicking, Stratégies de réduction.

pirate attacks could be included in GA. When a seaman was, for example, wounded, hurt, or had died in the fight, all expenses would be shared between all the parties involved in the venture, including the ship owner, the owners of the cargo, and the shipmaster.[81] The 1563 *Ordonnance* of Philip II also subsequently incorporated an expanded rule, where in the case of a dead seaman, his widow would also receive compensation.[82] This was included to bypass curbs on marine insurance established by the Habsburg sovereigns, as they saw insurance as a speculative tool rather than one of risk management.[83]

As compliance with Charles's *Ordonnances* was rather limited, Philip II published his 1563 *Ordonnance* detailing even more on GA, making it one of the most detailed sets of GA rules we possess for the sixteenth century, and offering a clear view of the development of the instrument. Twelve articles on GA were promulgated.[84] Three major categories can be distinguished: first, what could count as GA was clarified; second, the position of the shipmaster was regulated; third, the *Ordonnance* also regulated salvage and shipwreck. In the first category, the *Ordonnance* introduced *strangen* (voluntarily running aground to save ship and cargo, for example in a storm), next to customary *werpen* (jettison) and *kerven* (mast cutting).[85] The *Ordonnance* proclaimed these three actions as "standard" causes for GA but paradoxically subsequently added more rules, including extraordinary pilotage, extraordinary lighter ships, and the aforementioned expenses to fight off pirate attacks.[86] Clearly, this *Ordonnance* mentioned multiple expenses to prevent greater losses, primarily taken from the Amsterdam *Ordonnantie*. Moreover, it contained the rule that large ordinary expenses, above six pounds *Grooten Vlaams*, could be shared as GA among all the parties with an interest in the venture.[87] This meant that besides the merchants and the ship-owner, the shipmaster would also have to contribute to GA when expenses rose above a certain threshold.

The shipmaster was a pivotal figure in sixteenth-century maritime law in the Low Countries.[88] Whereas the *Rôles* still proscribed consultations aboard, merchants increasingly stayed onshore from the fifteenth century onwards. As a result, we can observe a double-edged development in the sixteenth-century sources. On the one hand, masters were given greater freedom to perform an act of GA when necessary, for example, as they only had to liaise with crew members before a jettison. On the

81 1551 *Ordonnance*, Art. 28.

82 The 1563 *Ordonnance* can be found in: Collection de lois [vol. IV], PARDESSUS, pp. 64–102.

83 On this see: DE RUYSSCHER and PUTTEVILS, Art of Compromise.

84 1563 *Ordonnance*, Title IV.

85 Ibid., Art. 6.

86 Ibid., Arts. 2 and 9.

87 Ibid., Art. 10.

88 For general European considerations see: ROSSI, Liability; ROSSI, Polysemi; ROSSI, Approach.

other hand, rules against fraud were established. For example, merchants had the right to inspect the ship before it left port; and when the shipmaster's negligence was proven, merchants did not have to contribute to GA.[89] This linked to the third part on salvage and shipwreck, as the *Ordonnance*, for example, also told masters to repair ships within one month before declaring GA or shipwreck.[90] Although the *Ordonnance* did not define shipwreck, it was clear that the rationale behind the *Ordonnance* was to stimulate GA and not shipwreck.[91]

As saving ship and cargo was the goal, salvage was subsequently emphasised; crew members were, for example, obliged to do their utmost best to save ship and cargo.[92] Moreover, the *Ordonnance* acknowledged the use of *negotiorum gestio* (*zaakwaarneming* in Dutch), a concept from Roman law that allowed spontaneous action on behalf of someone else, for example, when salvaging the cargo of merchants.[93] In short, royal legislation stimulated the use of GA and salvaging cargo over shipwreck, as this also provided an incentive to use insurance less. However, in order to provide this option, merchants also needed to make sure they would not be cheated by the shipmaster.

As a result, the *Ordonnance* offered an expansive view of GA and on salvaging cargo after jettison, besides the strict liability of the shipmaster. For the central government, GA was morally superior to insurance as the instrument did not allow for speculation, but the *Ordonnance* also shows that maritime law always responded to new problems and situations that arose. Thus, many rules drawn from medieval compilations like the *Rôles d'Oléron* were either confirmed in the *Ordonnances* or expanded upon. Some new rules, however, were also added, as developments in practice, e. g. merchants not travelling with their cargo, necessitated this. This was not necessarily legal pluralism, but rather *iura maritima*, as the sources built upon and complemented each other to create a secure legal environment for parties in the maritime sector to deal with new challenges.

Following the publication of the 1563 *Ordonnance*, Quintin Weytsen wrote a treatise to provide intellectual support for the *Ordonnance*.[94] This work was peppered with references to the Digest and glosses, as of course references to both classical Roman law and *Ius Commune* offered significant intellectual capital. However, Weytsen's work did more, in the last part he also offered practical advice on calculations and expanded on difficult cases and noted customs. Customs, in Weytsen's work, did not only include those written down in compilations like the

89 1563 *Ordonnance*, Art. 1 and 2.

90 Ibid., Arts. 3, 12 and 13.

91 Ibid.

92 Ibid., Arts. 12 and 13.

93 Ibid., Art. 12.

94 Dreijer and Vervaart, Een Tractaet.

Rôles d'Oléron, but also customs merchants brought to court.[95] Weytsen allowed for some long-held customs to override *Ius Commune*, such as on the issue of pilotage.[96] Weytsen noted that in France and the Biscay area, shipmasters customarily paid 2/3 of the ordinary pilotage expenses, with the merchants contributing only 1/3.[97]

Following these customs, this case had significant monetary consequences for the master as well, contrary to the relatively kind solution of the 1563 *Ordonnance*. Here, we thus observe an acknowledgement of legal pluralism throughout Europe, i. e. the application of the principle was different in the Low Countries to that in France or Biscay, but also an example of *iura maritima* in which two sources of law offered conflicting solutions. Rather than hinder predictability, I would argue this shows the flexibility of the system and allowed courts to find solutions that fitted each individual case best, without threatening the predictability that the shipmaster would always have to contribute in case of a GA declaration.

In another part of his work, Weytsen sketched the various views on the question whether minted money could be brought into GA. Weytsen summarised a *turbe* (legal inquiry) from 1548 in Antwerp, where some merchants had argued for this rule as Charles V had jettisoned money (i. e. he threw cases with coins overboard) on his way to the Low Countries, whereas others had argued that valuation was so tricky that this should not be allowed. Moreover, as coins were not considered cargo "proper", GA could not be applied.[98] Weytsen, however, appeared to join the 1563 *Ordonnance* in allowing it, but also noted that while the Antwerp municipal court had permitted it, this judgement had been overruled by the Council of Brabant in 1548.[99] The 1563 *Ordonnance* allowed for this,[100] and Weytsen appeared to agree with the *turbe* as well, without necessary advocating a clear solution. As a result, Weytsen thus also added certain customs to the 1563 *Ordonnance*, which partially contradicted royal legislation, even if the work was written to support it in principle. Again, this should not be taken as evidence of an unpredictable situation, but rather of the necessary flexibility of *iura maritima* to adapt to new circumstances. As a merchant manual, the treatise thus offered real problems with various solutions, taken from *Ius Commune*, mercantile practice, and royal legislation.

---

95 Weytsen, Een Tractaet van Avarien, dat is Gemeyne Contributie vande Coopmanschappen ende Goederen indien schepe gevonden om te helpen draghen/'t verlies van eenighe Cooplieden ofte Schippers goeden/ghewillighlijck ghebeurt/om lijf/Schip ende goet te salveeren, 1631. See also: De ruysscher, Maxims.

96 This was not uncommon in *Ius Commune*. See: Jacobs, Ius Patrium, pp. 39–44; Lesaffer, European Legal History, pp. 269–270.

97 Weytsen, Een Tractaet, pp. 9–10.

98 See for the history of *turben*: Waelkens, Origine.

99 Weytsen, Een Tractaet, pp. 4–5.

100 1563 *Ordonnance*, Art. 7. This article was incorporated for a very specific reason, for an extended explanation see: Dreijer, Power, p. 112.

Meanwhile, the *Hordenanzas*, published by the Bruges-based Castilian *natio*, were a compilation of insurance regulations meant to influence the ongoing debate over insurance.[101] However, for our purposes, what is interesting is the link between insurance and GA.[102] Although Weytsen had hinted at the fact that insurers could be held liable for GA payments, thus contradicting the 1563 *Ordonnance*, which explicitly prohibited this, the *Hordenanzas* was the first formal source of law to confirm this. This was primarily taken from various Spanish *Ordonnances*, e. g. the 1538 Burgos, 1556 Seville, and 1560 Bilbao *Ordonnances*, meant to regulate the *Consulados*,[103] although Antwerp legal practice also agreed to the liability of insurers for GA payments since the late 1540s.[104] This again shows that rules could contradict within the same territory, but the Antwerp municipal court consistently ruled in some twenty-five cases against insurers between 1548 and 1575, creating a legal precedent and thus predictability.[105]

On 8 March 1548, the insurer Cornelis de Jonge, for example, filed a case at the municipal court against Joost de Mellar, whose cargo had been jettisoned after the ship carrying his cargo from Dover encountered a storm off the coast of Zeeland.[106] De Mellar claimed the money for GA costs for the remainder of the damage back from De Jonge, who declined to pay and filed a case to avoid liability. De Mellar, in contrast, claimed that the "customs of the sea" (*costuymen vander zee*) allowed him to levy the costs for GA from his insurer. De Jonge claimed protection against payment on two grounds: first, that the master had brought additional cargo on board for his own profit; and second, that the storm had not been heavy enough to justify jettisoning the cargo. This would mean that the conditions of the insurance policy were violated because the necessary measures to protect cargo had not been taken. The court however concurred with De Mellar and forced De Jonge to pay.

As Johan van Niekerk has noted, the liability of the insurer was rooted in the fact that no one could opt out of the interest community.[107] Insurers could be liable in two ways: first, when insured cargo was jettisoned, the remaining loss after

---

101 De Groote, De zeeassurantie, pp. 45–51.

102 See also: van Niekerk, Development, pp. 76–80.

103 See for the links: De Groote, De zeeassurantie, pp. 52–58; Rossi, Insurance, pp. 148–157; Coronas González, La Ordenenza.

104 See: Dreijer, Maritime Averages.

105 See e. g. cases in: Antwerp Municipal Archives (or: BE-SAA), Ancien Régime, Stadsbestuur, Rechtspraak, Raadkamer, Vonnisboeken, V#1241, fol. 283r-v; V#1242, fol. 127r; V#1244, fol. 128r-130r; V#1245, fol. 120r-121r and 174r-v; V#1246, fol. 62r-v; V#1247, fol. 82v-84v, 148r-151r and 269r-v; V#1249, fol. 1r-v, 6v-7v, 130r, 204r-205r; V#1250, fol. 139r, 150v-151r and 241r-v; V#1251, fol. 45v-46v, 71v-72r and 104r-v; V#1252, fol. 78r-v and 168r-v; V#1254, fol. 107r-v and 147v-148v; V#1255, fol. 221v-225r; V#1256, fol. 58v-59v.

106 BE-SAA, Vonnisboeken, V#1241, fol. 283r-v.

107 van Niekerk, Development, pp. 76–80.

reimbursement from the others in the interest community through GA had to be covered by insurers; second, when a merchant had to make a GA contribution to someone else's loss and insured cargo was used to determine the value of the contribution.[108] The *Hordenanzas* included these rules as well, although it appeared that the former was more likely. The compilation included protection of insurers against fraudulent behaviour, but otherwise stipulated that insurers had to be held liable in most instances.[109]

Finally, the Antwerp *Compilatae* of 1608 contained some two hundred rules on GA.[110] Most rules followed the 1563 *Ordonnance* or other common rules, for example, the older compilations of maritime law. This again shows that most sources of law built on each other or complemented older compilations.[111] The contribution of the *Compilatae* to maritime law instead lay in two other areas: first, it codified in Antwerp municipal law the insurability of GA, which explicitly contradicted royal legislation but confirmed long-standing legal practice; and second, it officially acknowledged Particular Average (PA) as a third variety of averages, besides GA and SA: PA concerned cases where no deliberate loss occurred and therefore the loss would fall to the owner of the cargo only.[112] What the *Compilatae* also included were so-called franchise clauses, meaning insurers and insured could agree on the reimbursement of damages only if this concerned a sum larger than 1% of the total loss, so as to prevent disputes over small sums.[113] These therefore allowed "free of average" clauses up to a certain percentage, but the *Compilatae* moreover also permitted full "free of average" (*vrij van averij*) clauses, meaning insurers could opt out of GA liability.[114] Similar clauses were more common in the seventeenth-century Dutch Republic, but were rare in Antwerp.[115] Yet, it also made clear that Antwerp municipal law was plainly allowing for various creative innovations, whereas royal legislation took a very reserved position on the interaction between insurance and GA.

Certain trends can thus be detected in the sixteenth-century Low Countries on GA legislation. All sources, for example, contained expenses to prevent greater

---

108 Ibid.

109 1569 *Hordenanzas*, Title XIII, Art. 12.

110 The text of the *Compilatae* can be found in: De Longé Coutumes [vols. 3/4]. Part 4 of the *Compilatae* deals with maritime law. See vol. 4, Part 4, Title VIII (pp. 86–171) for the chapters on GA and bottomry and vol. 4, Part 4, Title XI (pp. 198–333) for the titles on insurance.

111 *Compilatae*, Part 4, Title VIII, Arts. 28, 74, 77–78, 92–93, 122–123, 127–128, 143, for similar clauses.

112 Ibid., Arts. 66–67, 75, 79 and 153–156 for the varieties of Averages. Ibid., Title XI, Arts. 177–180.

113 van Niekerk, Development, pp. 1040–1043; 1608 *Compilatae*, Part IV, Title XI, Arts. 203–204.

114 van Niekerk, Development, p. 1037; 1608 *Compilatae*, Part IV, Title XI, Art. 210.

115 van Niekerk, Development, p. 1037. From the sixteenth century, only one case is known regarding "free of average". See: Sneller and Unger Bronnen, p. 8 (Nr. 18).

losses, a notable development from the strict principle of deliberate, actual losses found in the *Rôles*. The shipmaster was strictly regulated in both royal legislation and Antwerp municipal law as well. On the insurability of GA, however, there was no agreement. Royal legislation explicitly did not allow for this, as the central government was very sceptical of the use of insurance. Antwerp legal practice, in contrast, licenced it, largely following the rules of the *Hordenanzas*. On other issues, Antwerp municipal law and royal legislation disagreed as well, notably on the issue of large pilotage expenses and on franchise clauses. On most principles, there was substantial agreement between various negotiating parties, but in terms of practical application, differences emerged even within the Low Countries, not to speak of North-Western Europe or all of Europe, making a *lex maritima* impossible. In contrast, the history of GA shows that there were always overlapping sources of law such as, privileges, royal legislation, municipal law, local compilations, and mercantile customs, which governed GA procedure.

5. Conclusion

Maritime law in the Low Countries in the sixteenth century did not develop in a vacuum. Political considerations and extensive negotiations between various stakeholders influenced the evolution of law, and thus also the economic institutions that underpinned the Low Countries' rise as a maritime and economic power. Maritime law should best be analysed by acknowledging the interplay and tension between various sources of law in a jurisdictionally complex and legally-pluralistic society; the latter in the legal-historical sense, although there were also differences in access to courts in the Low Countries for local and foreign merchants.[116] Hence, the supposed existence of an autonomous law like *lex maritima* is not supported by evidence from the sixteenth-century Low Countries. Although the case study on GA shows that there was certainly a harmonisation of rules, laws concerning multiple issues were still evolving. Different sources of law, such as royal legislation and Antwerp municipal law, did not necessarily agree with one another, e. g. on pilotage or the liability of the insurer.

Following Emily Kadens' pointed analysis, this chapter has argued that when we scrutinise medieval law in Europe, we should assume a similar concept analogous to *iura mercatorum*, being *iura maritima*. This broad concept allows scholars to account for the complex nature of legal development in medieval Europe.[117] Legal pluralism existed, but was not particularly problematic for merchants, as there

116 van Rhee, Litigation, pp. 41–42.
117 Kadens, Order within Law, p. 42.

was substantial agreement on *principles*, if not on their exact application. Various sources of law built upon, complemented, and challenged each other, depending on the political, legal, and economic necessities that came up. Predictability was provided by courts that consistently applied the same solutions, as was shown in the case of insurance and GA in Antwerp, and by the fact that merchants throughout North-Western Europe could rely on the general principle being respected. This was the case for GA but also for shipwreck and salvage.[118] Legal pluralism in the legal-historical sense of different rules was openly acknowledged but appears to have been seen as an indicator of the necessarily limited flexibility in applying rules, rather than hindering the facilitation of international trade. In other words, some flexibility did indeed aid predictability rather than hinder it.

As the business environment grew ever more complex, it shaped the need for a new legal equilibrium for both commercial and maritime law. However, the search for legal standards was definitely not finished by the end of the sixteenth century. It is therefore highly unlikely that an autonomous and unified maritime law existed in the sixteenth-century Low Countries. Rather, transnational principles such as GA existed in dialogue with local customs, while concerning the exact application, the latter always took preference over the former. A discussion about the precise relationship between these two in a wider European setting would be more beneficial than discussing the existence of a *lex maritima*, or for that matter, a *lex mercatoria*, as the legally pluralistic and jurisdictionally complex setting of medieval and early modern Europe clearly deserves a better analysis. Acknowledging the existence of *iura maritima*, which allows for understanding this complexity and also potential changes over time, would be only a first step.

Acknowledgements

The author thanks Jake Dyble, Gregor Rohmann, and Ulla Kypta, as well as the participants in the session "Law as a Resource" at the World Economic History Congress 2022 in Paris and the team members of the VICI project "Exploiting the Empire of Others" (Leiden University) for comments on previous versions of this essay. Financial support for the research was provided by the European Research Council under Grant Agreement 724544 (AveTransRisk).

---

118 Frankot, Ships and Shipmen.

Bibliography

Ashburner, William, The Rhodian Sea-Law, Oxford 1909.

Aubert, Jean-Jaques, Dealing with the Abyss. The Nature and Purpose of the Rhodian Sea-law on Jettison (*Lex Rhodia De Iactu*, D 14.2) and the Making of Justinian's Digest, in: John W. Cairns and Paul J. Du Plessis (eds.), Beyond Dogmatics. Law and Society in the Roman World, Edinburgh 2007, pp. 157–172.

Benson, Bruce L., The Spontaneous Evolution of Commercial Law, in: Southern Economic Journal 55 (1989), pp. 644–661.

Berman, Harold J., Law and Revolution. The Formation of the Western Legal Tradition, Cambridge MA 1983.

Blakemore, Richard J., Law and the Sea, in: Claire Jowitt, Craig Lambert and Steven Mentz (eds.), The Routledge Companion to Marine and Maritime Worlds, 1400–1800. London/New York 2020, pp. 388–425.

Blockmans, Wim P., Metropolen aan de Noordzee. De geschiedenis van Nederland, 1100–1650, Amsterdam 2010.

Blondé, Bruno/Gelderbloom, Oscar C./Stabel, Peter, Foreign Merchant Communities in Bruges, Antwerp and Amsterdam, in: Donatello Calabi and Stephen T. Christensen (eds.), Cultural Exchange in Early Modern Europe, [vol. 2], Cities and Cultural Exchange in Europe, 1400–1700, Cambridge 2013, pp. 154–174.

Brown, Andrew/Dumolyn, Jan, (eds.), Bruges, A Medieval Metropolis, c. 850–c. 1550, Cambridge 2018.

Chevreau, Emmanuel, La lex Rhodia de iactu : un exemple de la réception d'une institution étrangère dans le droit romain, in : Legal History Review 73 (2005), pp. 67–80.

Cleirac, Ettinene, Us et coutumes de la mer. Divisées en trois parties, Bordeaux 1647.

Constable, Olivia A., The Problem of Jettison in Medieval Mediterranean Maritime Law, in: Journal of Medieval History 20 (1994), pp. 207–220.

Cordes, Albrecht, Lex Maritima? Local, Regional and Universal Maritime Law in the Middle Ages, in: Wim P. Blockmans, Mikhael M. Krom and Justyna J. Wubs-Mrowewicz (eds.), The Routledge Handbook of Maritime Trade around Europe 1300–1600, Abingdon/New York 2017, pp. 69–85.

Cornah, Richard H./Reeder, Jonathan, Lowndes and Rudolf. The Law of General Average and the York-Antwerp Rules (14th edition), London 2013.

Coronas González, Santa M., La Ordenenza de seguros maritimos del Consulado de la Nacion de España en Brujas, in: Anuario de Historia del Derecho español 54 (1984), pp. 385–407.

De ruysscher, Dave, Conceptualizing *lex mercatoria*. Malynes, Schmitthoff and Goldman Compared, in: Maastricht Journal of European and Comparative Law 27 (2020), pp. 465–483.

De ruysscher, Dave, Maxims, Principles and Legal Change. Maritime Law in Merchant and Legal Culture (Low Countries, 16th century), in: Zeitschrift der Savigny-Stiftung für Rechtsgeschichte. Germanistische Abteilung 138 (2021), pp. 260–275.

De ruysscher, Dave, "Naer het Romeinsch recht alsmede den stiel mercantiel". Handel en recht in de Antwerpse rechtbank (16e–17e eeuw), Kortrijk 2009.

De ruysscher, Dave/Puttevils, Jeroen, The Art of Compromise. Legislative Deliberations on Marine Insurance Institutions in Antwerp (c. 1550–c. 1570), in: BMGN-Low Countries Historical Review 130 (2015), pp. 25–49.

Den Tex, Charles, Oud-Nederlandsch zeerecht. Kritische bewerking van den tekst der Vlaamse Zeeregten, in: Bijdragen tot rechtsgeleerdheid en wetgeving 5 (1830), pp. 33–62.

Donlan, Sean P./Heirbaut, Dirk, "A Patchwork of Accommodations". European Legal Hybridity and Jurisdictional Complexity – An Introduction, in: Sean P. Donlan and Dirk Heirbaut (eds.), The Laws' Many Bodies. Studies in Legal Hybridity and Jurisdictional Complexity, c. 1600–1900, Berlin 2015, pp. 9–34.

de Groote, Henry, De zeeassurantie te Antwerpen en te Brugge in de zestiende eeuw, Antwerp 1975/2000.

Dreijer, Gijs P., Maritime Averages and the Complexity of Risk Management in Sixteenth-Century Anwerp, in: Tijdschrift voor Sociale en Economische Geschiedenis 17 (2020), pp. 31–54.

Dreijer, Gijs P., The Power and Pains of Polysemy. Maritime trade, Averages and Institutional Development in the Low Countries (15th–16th centuries), Leiden/Boston 2023.

Dreijer, Gijs P./Vervaart, Otto, Een Tractaet van Avarien – 1617, in: Pro Memorie 21 (2019), pp. 38–41.

Epstein, Richard A., Reflections on the Historical Origins of Economic Structure of the Law Merchant, in: Chicago Journal of International Law 139 (2004), pp. 1–20.

Frankot, Edda, De "Ordinancie van Staveren" en het Hanzeatisch zeerecht, in: It beaken 77 (2015), pp. 1–23.

Frankot, Edda, Der Ehrbaren Hanse-Städte See-Recht. Diversity and Unity in Hanseatic Maritime Law, in: Justyna J. Wubs-Mrozewicz and Stuart Jenks (eds.), The Hanse in Medieval and Early Modern Europe, Leiden/Boston 2013, pp. 109–128.

Frankot, Edda, Medieval Maritime Law from Oléron to Wisby. Jurisdictions in the Law of the Sea, in: Juan Pan-Montojo/Frederik J.G. Pedersen (eds.), Communities in European History. Representations, Jurisdictions, Conflicts, Pisa 2007, pp. 151–172.

Frankot, Edda, "Of Laws of Ships and Shipmen". Medieval Maritime Law and its Practice in Urban Northern Europe, Edinburgh 2012.

Gelderblom, Oscar C., Cities of Commerce. The institutional foundations of international trade in the Low Countries, 1250–1650, Princeton NJ 2013.

Gilissen, John, Phases de la codification et de l'homologation des coutumes dans les XVII provinces des Pays-Bas, in : Tijdschrift voor Rechtsgeschiedenis 18 (1950), pp. 36–67 and 233–290.

Goldschmidt, Levin, Handbuch des Handelsrecht, [vol. 1], Erlangen 1864.

Goudsmit, Martinus T., Geschiedenis van het Nederlandsche zeerecht, The Hague 1882.

Jacobs, Beatrix C.M., Ius Patrium en Ius Commune: twee zijden van een medaille, in: Pro Memorie 11 (2017), pp. 22–46.

Jahnke, Carsten, Hansisches und anderes Seerecht, in: Albrecht Cordes (ed.), Hansisches und hansestadtliches Recht, Trier 2008, pp. 41–68.

Jahnke, Carsten (ed.), Seerecht im Hanseraum des 15. Jahrhunderts. Edition und Kommentar zur Flandrischen Copiar Nr. 9, Lübeck 2003.

Jahnke, Carsten, The Maritime Law of the Baltic Sea, in: Michel Balard (ed.), The Sea in History. The Medieval World, Woodbridge 2017, pp. 574–582.

Kadens, Emily, Convergence and the Colonisation of Custom in Pre-Modern Europe, in: Olivier Moreteau, Antonio Masferrer and Kjell A. Modéer (eds.), Comparative Legal History, Cheltenham/Northampton MA 2019, pp. 167–185.

Kadens, Emily, Order within Law, Variety within Custom. The Character of the Medieval Law Merchant, in: Chicago Journal of International Law 139 (2004), pp. 39–65.

Kadens, Emily, The Medieval Law Merchant. The Tyranny of a Construct, in: Journal of Legal Analysis 7 (2015), pp. 251–289.

Kadens, Emily, The Myth of the Customary Law Merchant, in: Texas Law Review 90 (2012), pp. 1153–1206.

Kiesselbach, Theodor, Der Ursprung der rôles d'Oléron und des Seerechts von Damme, in: Hansische Geschichtblätter 12 (1906), pp. 1–60.

Korthals Altes, Alexander, Ons oudste zeerecht, Zwolle 1976.

Krieger, Karl-Friedrich, Die Entwicklung des Seerechts im Mittelmeerraum von der Antike bis zum Consolat de Mar, in: German Yearbook of International Law 16 (1973), pp. 179–208.

Krieger, Karl-Friedrich, Ursprung und Wurzeln der Rôles d'Oléron, Cologne/Vienna 1970.

Kruit, Jolien A., General Average – General Principle *plus* Varying Practical Application *equals* Uniformity?, in: Journal of International Maritime Law 21 (2015), pp. 190–202.

Kruit, Jolien A., General Average, Legal Basis and Applicable Law. The Overrated Significance of the York-Antwerp Rules, Zutphen 2017.

Lameere, Jules (ed.), Recueil des ordonnances des Pays-Bas. Deuxième série, 1506–1700, [vol. 6], Brussels 1922.

Landwehr, Gotz, Das Seerecht der Hanse (1365–1614). Vom Schiffordnungsrecht zum Seehandelsrecht, Hamburg 2003.

Landwehr, Gotz, Das Seerecht im Ostseeraum vom Mittelalter zum Ausgang des 18. Jahrhunderts, in: Jörn Eckert/Kjell A. Modéer (eds.), Geschichte und Perspektiven des Rechts im Ostseeraum. Erster Rechthistorikertag im Ostseeraum, 8–12 März 2000, Berlin 2002, pp. 275–303.

Lesaffer, Randall, European Legal History: A Cultural and Political Perspective, Cambridge 2009.

De Longé, Gulliaume P. (ed.), Coutumes du Pays et Duché de Brabant, Quartier d'Anvers. Coutumes de la ville d'Anvers, [vols. 1–4], Antwerp 1890.

MALYNES, Gerald, Consuetudo, vel, Lex Mercatoria. Or, the Ancient Law-Merchant. In three parts, according to the essentials of Traffick. Necessary for Statesmen, Judges, Magistrates, Temporal and Civil Lawyers, Mint-men, Merchants, Mariners, and all other negotiating in any parts of the world, London 1629/1686.

MARÉCHAL, Jos, Le depart de Bruges des marchands étrangers (XVe et XVIe siècle), in: Handelingen voor het Gemootschap "Société d'Émulation" te Brugge 88 (2005), pp. 26–74.

MUKHERJEE, Proshanto K., Essentials of General Average. A Synoptic Overview of an Ancient Maritime Law, in: WMU Journal of Maritime Affairs 6 (2007), pp. 21–36.

NORTH, Douglass C., Law and Economics in Historical Perspective, in: Fabrizio CAFAGGI/Antonio NICITA/Ugo PAGANO (eds.), Legal Orderings and Economic Institutions, London 2007, pp. 46–53.

NORTH, Douglass C., Sources of Productivity Change in Ocean Shipping, 1600–1850, in: Journal of Political Economy 76 (1968), pp. 953–970.

PARDESSUS, Jean-Marie (ed.), Collection de lois, maritimes antérieures au XVIIIe siècle [6 vols.], Paris 1828–1845.

PARMENTIER, Jan, Een maritiem-economische schets van de deltahavens, 1400–1800, in: Maurits EBBEN/Simon GROENVELD (eds.), De Scheldedelta als verbinding en scheiding tussen Noord en Zuid, 1500–1800, Maastricht 2007, pp. 11–26.

PAULSEN, Gordon W., Historical Overview of the Development of Uniformity in International Maritime Law, in: Tulane Law Review 57 (1982–1983), pp. 1065–1091.

PUTTEVILS, Jeroen/STABEL, Peter/VERBIST, Botho, Een eenduidig pad van modernisering van het handelsverkeer. Van het liberale Brugge naar het gereguleerde Antwerpen?, in: Bruno BLONDÉ (ed.), Overheid en economie. Geschiedenissen van een spanningsveld, Antwerp 2014, pp. 39–54.

ROSSI, Guido, Insurance in Elizabethan England. The London Code, Cambridge 2016.

ROSSI, Guido, The Barratry of the Shipmaster in Early Modern Law. Polysemy and *mos Italicus*, in: Tijdschrift voor Rechtsgeschiedenis 87 (2019), pp. 65–85.

ROSSI, Guido, The Barratry of the Shipmaster in Early Modern Law. The Approach of Italian and English Law Courts, in: Tijdschrift voor Rechtsgeschiedenis 87 (2019), pp. 504–574.

ROSSI, Guido, The Liability of the Shipmaster in Early Modern Law. Comparative (and Practice-Oriented) Remarks, in: Historia et Ius 12 (2017), Paper 12, pp. 1–47.

RUNYAN, Thomas J., The Rolls of Oleron and the Admiralty Court in Fourteenth Century England, in: American Journal of Legal History 19 (1975), pp. 95–111.

SCHWEITZER, Julia, Schiffer und Schiffsmann in den Rôles d'Oléron und im Llibre del Consolat de Mar. Ein Vergleich zweier mittelalterlicher Seerechtsquellen, Frankfurt am Main/New York 2007.

SHEPHARD, James W., The Rôles d'Oléron: a lex mercatoria of the Sea?, in: Vito PIERGIOVANNI (ed.), From lex mercatoria to Commercial Law, Berlin 2005, pp. 207–254.

SICKING, Louis H./WIJFFELS, Alain A. (eds.), Conflict Management in the Mediterranean and the Atlantic, 1000–1800. Actors, Institutions and Strategies of Dispute Settlement, Leiden/Boston 2020.

Sicking, Louis H., Les marchands espagnols et portugais aux Pays-Bas et la navigation à l'époque de Charles Quint. Gestion des risques et législation, in : Publications du Centre Européen d'Etudes Bourguignonnes 51 (2011), pp. 253–274.

Sicking, Louis H., Neptune and the Netherlands. State, Economy, and War at Sea in the Renaissance, Leiden/Boston 2004.

Sicking, Louis H., Stratégies de réduction de risque dans le transport maritime des Pays-Bas au XVIe siècle, in : Simona Cavaciocchio (ed.), Ricchezza del mare – ricchezza dal mare, secc. XIII–XVIII: atti della Trentasettesima settimana di studi, 11–15 Aprile 2005, [vol. 2], Florence 2006, pp. 795–808.

Sneller, Zeger W./Unger, Willem S. (eds.), Bronnen tot de geschiedenis van den handel met Frankrijk: supplement, The Hague 1942.

Spruit, Jop E. et al. (ed.), Corpus Iuris Civilis: tekst en vertaling, [vol. III, Digesten 11–24], The Hague 1996.

Tetley, William, The General Maritime Law – the Lex Maritima, in: Syracuse Journal of International Law & Commerce 20 (1994), pp. 105–146.

Trakman, Leon E., The Evolution of the Law Merchant. Our Commercial Heritage, in: Journal of Maritime Law & Commerce 12 (1980), pp. 1–24 and 153–182.

Trivellato, Francesca, Usages and Customs of the Sea. Ettiene Cleirac and the Making of Maritime law in Seventeenth-century France, in: Tijdschrift voor Rechtsgeschiedenis 84 (2016), pp. 193–224.

Twining, William, Normative and Legal Pluralism: A Global Perspective, in: Duke Journal of Comparative and International Law 20 (2010), pp. 473–517.

van den Auweele, Dirk, Het Brugse zeerecht, schakel in een supranationaal geheel, in: Valentin Vermeersch (ed.), Brugge en de zee. Van Bryggia tot Zeebrugge, Antwerp 1982, pp. 145–155.

van den Auweele, Dirk, Zeerecht, in: Gustaaf Asaert et al., Maritieme Geschiedenis der Nederlanden, [vol. 1], Bussum 1976, pp. 220–226.

van Hofstraeten, Bram, Juridisch humanisme en costumiere acculturatie. Inhouds- en vormbepalende factoren van de Antwerpse Consuetudines Compilatae (1608) en het Gelderse Land- en Stadrecht (1620) van het Roermondse Overkwartier, Maastricht 2008.

van Hofstraeten, Bram, Recording Customs in Early Modern Antwerp, a Commercial Metropolis, in: Zeitschrift des Max-Planck-Instituts für europäische Rechtsgeschichte 24 (2016), pp. 288–301.

van Niekerk, Johan, The Development of the Principles of Insurance Law in The Netherlands from 1500 to 1800, [vol. 1], Hilversum 1998.

van Rhee, Christiaan H., Litigation and Legislation. Civil Procedure at First Instance in the Great Council for the Netherlands in Malines (1522–1559), Brussels 1997.

van Werveke, Hans, Brugge en Antwerpen, acht eeuwen Vlaamse handel, Ghent 1941.

Verlinden, Charles (ed.), Code d'assurances maritimes selons la coutume d'Anvers, promulgué par le consulat espangol de Bruges en 1569, in: Handelingen van de Koninklijke

Commissie voor de Uitgave der oude wetten en verordeningen van België 16 (1950), pp. 38–142.

Waelkens, Laurent, Origine de l'enquete par turbe, in: Tijdschrift voor Rechtsgeschiedenis 53 (1985), pp. 337–346.

Ward, Robin, The World of the Medieval Shipmaster. Law, Business and the Sea c. 1350–c. 1450, Cambridge 2009.

Weytsen, Quintin, Een Tractaet van Avarien, dat is Gemeyne Contributie vande Coopmanschappen ende Goederen indien schepe gevonden om te helpen draghen/'t verlies van eenighe Cooplieden ofte Schippers goeden/ghewillighlijck ghebeurt/om lijf/Schip ende goet te salveeren, Haarlem 1631.

Wubs-Mrozewicz, Justyna J., Conflict Management and Interdisciplinary History, in: Tijdschrift voor Sociale en Economische Geschiedenis 15 (2018), pp. 89–107.

Internet links

The Economist, The Global Food Supply Chain is Passing a Severe Test, https://www.economist.com/leaders/2020/05/09/the-global-food-supply-chain-is-passing-a-severe-test, accessed 08/28/2023.

The Old Salt Blog, The What, How, and Why of the Ancient Principle of General Average, https://www.oldsaltblog.com/2022/04/the-what-how-why-of-the-ancient-principle-of-general-average/, accessed 18/03/2024.

Unpublished archival sources

Antwerp Municipal Archives (or: BE-SAA), Ancien Régime, Stadsbestuur, Rechtspraak, Raadkamer, Vonnisboeken, V#1241-V#1256.

Ulla Kypta

Relations without Sanctions

Predictability in Principal-Agent Constellations in Fifteenth- and Sixteenth-century Antwerp

1. Introduction

Representation counts among the most important innovations in economic history, especially the history of trade.[1] Advanced commercial activities hardly seem possible without some concept of representation, and scholars believe that in every period of history, as soon as trade became more than direct exchange, traders began to work with agents who bought goods or collected debts for them.[2] Such agents considerably enhance the scope of action for a merchant. Without them, a merchant could only do one trade at a time. Representation is therefore often connected with the expansionary phases in trading history, for instance during the Late Roman Empire,[3] at the dawn of the Industrial Revolution,[4] and during the High Middle Ages in Europe. During the latter period, commercial activities grew in terms of distance as well as in the volume and range of products being traded.[5] This process, commonly called the Commercial Revolution,[6] presumably relied, at least in part, on merchants who became stationary while working with agents to carry out their trade.[7]

Representation, nonetheless, came with some problems. Researchers have extensively dealt with the relation between merchants and their agents under the heading of the 'principal-agent problem': how can the principal – the merchant – be sure that his agent is acting in the principal's best interests?[8] Economic theory suggests that if a principal cannot be sure that his agent will not cheat him, he will not enter

---

1 Lopez, Proxy, p. 187. Lopez calls it "one of the most important legal innovations of the Middle Ages."

2 Fränkel, Grundsätze der Stellvertretung, p. 291, cites for example the Code of Hammurabi, a Babylonian text from 1750 BC that deals with agents; Ross, Economic theory, p. 134.

3 Müller, Direkte Stellvertretung, p. 16.

4 Hölzl, Stellvertretung, p. 222.

5 Epstein, Economic and social history, chapter 3; Cipolla, Before the Industrial Revolution, p. 162.

6 Lopez, Commercial Revolution.

7 Greif, Reputation and Coalitions, p. 857.

8 Stiglitz, Principal and agent; Ross, Economic theory, pp. 134–139.

into the relationship and will not be able to expand his trade. Yet, principals can seldom directly monitor agents, and this is all the more true for premodern times.[9]

Premodern economic historians thus tend to invoke "trust" as a catch-all term to explain why trading partners worked together: – they supposedly trusted each other. However, the term is often used for quite different concepts, leading to some confusion and to attempts to clarify matters by distinguishing for example between differential and uniform trust in institutions and particularised or generalised trust in persons.[10] Guinnane proposes to use the term "trust" only in cases when the forming of a relationship cannot be accounted for by either information (the parties know a lot about each other) or sanctions (they know that they can punish misbehaviour).[11] Even though this definition is analytically convincing in so far as it makes analysing relationships much easier, it is not yet employed in many empirical studies. Many researchers still use "trust" as a general term for explaining all kinds of relationships. This is probably the case because "trust" just comes with too many connotations that cannot be silenced by any sharp definition.

It is thus perhaps time for a new concept to grasp the foundations of relations where partners did not know much about each other nor could they rely on a sanctioning authority. Predictability, the topic of this volume, might be a promising candidate. The phrase "I trust you" in essence means "I believe you will not behave in a completely unpredictable way".[12] Predictability also lies at the core of institutional theory. Institutions reduce transactions costs because they make the actions of others foreseeable, i. e. I know what to expect of people whose life is shaped by the same institutions.[13] This can result from formal institutions that issue rules and punish wrongdoers, but it also stems from informal institutions like norms or behavioural customs that allow members of a society to predict the actions of others. Predictability can hence explain why relations worked that were neither secured by information the parties shared about each other nor by a sanctioning institution. The concept of predictability furthermore has the advantage that it can be used with more nuance than trust. Trust works as an either-or concept, either I trust a person, or I don't. In contrast, I can predict the behaviour of a person on a curve, to a lesser or higher degree. The concept of predictability allows us to discuss the degree of probability that was necessary to keep trade going. As I will show below, it

9 Jensen and Meckling, Theory of the Firm, p. 3.

10 Ogilvie, Use and Abuse.

11 Guinnane, Trust, pp. 15–52.

12 As Guinnane, Trust, p. 5 phases it: "Trust implies a three-part relationship involving at least two actors and one act. I trust specific individuals or specific institutions to do specific things."

13 Greif for example, defines institutions as "a system of social factors – such as rules, beliefs, norms, and organizations – that guide, enable, and constrain the actions of individuals, thereby generating regularities of behavior", Greif, Fundamental problem, p. 257.

was obviously not necessary that merchants were always completely sure that their partner would act as they expected, rather, merchants entered into relationships with others when they could gauge the risks of their possible misbehaviour to a sufficient degree.

In this article, I want to draw attention to two relationships that are connected to representation and that cannot be explained by information or sanction but instead by predictability. The first of these relationships exists between the agent (*procurator*, *factor*) and the third person, the one the agent had to get in contact with to carry out his tasks on behalf of the principal. For example, if an agent had to collect debts for his principal, he had to deal with the debtor. This third party had to believe the agent was in fact allowed to represent the principal, otherwise, representation would not have been possible. The second relation is the one between the principal (*constituens*) and his sub-agents (also called *procuratores* or *factores*). In premodern trade, many principals entered into formal relations with an agent and allowed the agent to install sub-agents whenever he found it helpful. As far as the sources show, the agent did not tell the principal whom to choose. The principal therefore sometimes did not know who was acting on his behalf. Since agents and third parties, principals and sub-agents, more often than not were not subject to the same jurisdiction, they further also had to deal with the challenges of legal pluralism when trying to ensure predictability.

Both these relationships can be regarded as weak ties according to Mark Granovetter's terminology.[14] Premodern history has so far focused primarily on strong ties between persons from the same hometown, family, or guild. Weak ties, in contrast, link members of different groups. Weak ties allow people to expand their scope of activities and to enhance their exchange relations since they are not restricted to doing business only within their own group of family or friends. Weak ties between groups are important for holding a society together and preventing it from breaking into fractions. What is still missing also from Granovetter's account, however, is an answer to the question of how weak ties hold individuals together at all. People connected by weak ties do not know much about each other, and they are typically not subject to the same sanctioning authority. However, as the analysis below will show, the actors can nevertheless predict each other's behaviour and this strengthens the tie.

Until now, research on agents has rarely discussed these two relations.[15] However, sources from Antwerp, one of the main trading hubs of the late medieval economy in Northern Europe, indicate that premodern merchants were concerned with these

14 Granovetter, Strength.

15 One newer article from the realm of legal history briefly touches upon the relation between principal and third party but only spends one page discussing it, see Amend-Traut, Akteure im Hintergrund, p. 397.

relations. The sources show that merchants often went to a notary or to the city council and asked them to issue procurations, which then served to secure both sides of a relationship. With a letter of procuration, a merchant authorised another person to act on his behalf, in modern terms he gave him the power of attorney. This connection could be established between members of the same company, but it was also common for a merchant to issue a procuration for someone who was not connected to him in any other form of relationship. In one of the few articles written on proxies in economic history, Robert Lopez underlines the importance of procurations for trading history. As he put it, "[i]n Italy and in the West, too, there were almost no business associations and not many transactions that did not involve powers of attorney for some or all of the parties […] *procuratio* was the *bonne à tout faire* of medieval business."[16]

Merchants used procurations when they had to prove that the agent was acting on their behalf, especially when he was authorised to collect debts or represent them in court. In these cases, it was crucial that the third party acknowledged the agent as a legitimate representative of his creditor or the opposing party in court. The relation between agent and third party hence had to be secure for representation to work. In addition, the letters of procuration could be passed on to substitute proxies and thereby create a new connection between principal and sub-agent.

In this article, I will discuss why these two relationships functioned well enough to keep business flourishing in the trading metropolis of the late fifteenth and sixteenth centuries. Firstly, I will sketch why Antwerp is a good example to study the weak ties of representation and explain how I chose the sources I have analysed. Then, I will discuss the two reasons that have so far been most commonly given to explain how premodern business relations functioned, focusing in particular on why one party did not betray the other. Both explain strong ties, but do not suffice to account for the weak ties between agents and third parties and between principals and sub-agents. The following sections will analyse how these two types of relationships could be reliable in the absence of a central public authority or a close-knit group.

Relations between agent and third party were secured by the procuration that the agent carried with him. These letters of procuration looked and worked very similarly, regardless of the issuing authority. Their purpose and operation could thus be predicted by merchants from different backgrounds. Relations between principal and sub-agent, meanwhile, relied on the fact that merchants fulfilled both roles at a different or on occasion even at the same point in time. It made sense for them to act honestly because by doing so they strengthened the idea that parties in a representative relationship should act honestly. They profited in future trades from

---

16 Lopez, Proxy, p. 189.

such a norm. This can be called the principle of abstract reciprocity. Merchants did not act honestly towards other people because they expected to trade with that same person again, but rather because they expected to be in the same role as the other person at some point in the future and thus had an interest in enforcing rules of honest behaviour by complying with them. In general, thus, the merchants analysed here show a tendency not to betray, but instead to cooperate even with colleagues they did not know well. This behaviour made sense because all parties shared the common interest of keeping trade going.

2. Antwerp's Heyday and the Sources

Antwerp's importance for merchants grew steadily from the fourteenth to the sixteenth century after the city began serving as the staple market for English cloth.[17] Then the Peace of Senlis signed in 1493 by the Holy Roman Emperor Maximilian I (r. 1508–1519) and the French King Charles VIII (r. 1483–1498) brought stability that fostered trade. Another major boost came in 1498, when the Portuguese King Manuel I (1495–1521) decided that the first colonial goods such as sugar and spices should be traded via Antwerp.[18] In response, merchants from southern Germany travelled to Antwerp to provide the Portuguese with silver and copper which they needed for their worldwide journeys.[19] Many other merchants followed in their wake, turning the city on the river Schelde, not far away from the North Sea, into a node for trade that was becoming global in scale.[20] Hanseatic merchants sold grain, wax, and ash, silk came from Tuscany, and salt from France. Several hundred merchants from different regions of the continent stayed in Antwerp at the same time.[21]

The merchants in Antwerp obviously must have found ways to make the relationships work between third parties and their agents on the one hand, and the principal and the sub-agent, on the other. Without a working system of representation, merchants could not have achieved the huge scale of trading activities they undertook. Studying how represented and representing parties structured their relations in Antwerp thus offers insight into how premodern merchants dealt with the challenges of organising these volatile relations in light of the uncertainties

17 Davis, Rise of Antwerp.

18 van Houtte, Anvers, p. 253; Harreld, Atlantic sugar.

19 Harreld, High Germans.

20 van der Wee, Trade; van der Wee, Growth; van der Stock, Antwerp; Limberger, Aufstieg; Blondé and Puttevils, Antwerp.

21 van der Wee and Materné, Antwerp, p. 23 f. A contemporary estimate is given by the Florentine merchant Guicciardini, Descrittione, p. 157.

of trade.[22] Of course, it is likely that not all these relationships went smoothly. A further study based on the Antwerp court records could enrich the picture by analysing what kinds of problems arose and how the various parties dealt with obstacles. However, for such disruptions to have occurred, a basic system must have existed.

Fortunately, the documents that formed the basis for the representation system still exist in large numbers. If a merchant wanted to authorise a proxy, he went to the city council[23] or to one of the Antwerp notaries[24] and instructed them to issue a procuration. The council or the notaries recorded these actions in their registry books, of which more than a hundred have survived in the Antwerp archives, each one in turn containing hundreds of procurations. Studying the workings and the general idea of the representation system in place in Antwerp required a qualitative approach that could not include all the procurations in the books.[25] In the study presented here, I thus focus on procurations issued in connection with merchants from German-speaking towns and regions. Relevant sources were identified in two source editions by Strieder and Doehard.[26] Both of these editions give only short summaries of the content of each document and only in a very few cases print the whole text of a procuration. It was therefore necessary to check the original material at the Felix Archief Antwerpen (Antwerp City Archive)[27] and the Rijksarchief Antwerpen-Beveren (National Archive of Antwerpen-Beveren).[28]

In total, I analysed 137 documents in which a person installed an agent. Among these, 75 were written between 1490 and 1515 and appear in the urban registers while 62 were written between 1525 and 1567 and appear in the notarial registers. The style and layout of the procurations did not change between 1490 and 1567. Nine of the 137 procurations analysed here (7 per cent) install an agent for general representation; 32 procurations (23 per cent) allow him to collect all outstanding debts; 63 procurations (46 per cent) authorise him to collect a specific debt from a certain person; in 23 cases (17 per cent) the agent was appointed as a general juridical representative, and in 10 cases (7 per cent) he was allowed to perform some delimited task at court.

22 CIPOLLA, Industrial Revolution, pp. 163 f.

23 EVERAERT, Power.

24 NELIS, Les origins; GORIS, Études, p. 89–93. Notaries were ascendant in this role during the first quarter of the sixteenth century, especially among foreign merchants.

25 124 registry books from the city council survive from the first half of the sixteenth century.

26 STRIEDER, Aus Antwerpener Notariatsarchiven; DOEHAERD, Études.

27 FelixArchief Antwerpen, N # 541, N # 546, N # 2070, N # 2071, N # 2072, N # 2073, N # 2074, N # 2075, N # 2076, N # 2077, N # 3132, N # 3133, N # 4456, CERT # 3, CERT # 4, SR # 97, SR # 102, SR # 104, SR # 106, SR # 108, SR # 110, SR # 112, SR # 114, SR # 116, SR # 118, SR # 119, SR # 122, SR # 123, SR # 126, SR # 127, SR # 129, SR # 131, SR # 133, SR # 135, SR # 143, SR # 145.

28 Rijksarchief Antwerpen-Beveren, Notariaat 522 and 523.

For three reasons, the focus on proxies of or by people from German-speaking towns promises to give a nuanced and varied picture of how representation worked in premodern Antwerp. First, the group consisted of merchants who organised their business activities in varying ways, from the larger trading houses of the Fugger and Welser to the smaller partnerships of Joachim Pruner and the networks of the brothers Luchtmaker.[29] The focus on German merchants thus promises to bring into view different relations between merchants, agents, third persons, and sub-agents. Second, the group contains merchants and agents from the well-known trading cities of Augsburg, Nuremberg, Cologne, Lübeck, and Hamburg, but also from towns that have not featured as prominently in premodern economic research such as Wrocław, Cleve, and Würzburg.[30] Third, the analysis starts with Germans, but also features merchants from other towns who acted as principal, agent, or sub-agent for Germans or entered into relationships with German agents as third parties. These persons came from Antwerp and its surroundings,[31] from London, Spain, France, and Poland.

3. The Limits of Public and Private Institutions for Explaining Representation Relations

The principal-agent problem has been discussed far and wide in economic and social science literature.[32] This is unsurprising since it is hard to imagine how members of any relatively complex society could go about their daily business without employing agents. Researchers concerned with this issue have analysed in particular how to prevent moral hazard (an agent acting against the interests of the principal) and adverse selection (a principal choosing an agent ill-suited for the job).[33] In a modern economy, the problem is mostly supposed to be dealt with inside a company. Managers supervise employees and the company owners in

---

29 Denzel, Kommerzielle Innovationen, p. 69; Jenks, Small is beautiful.

30 Principals and agents also came from Berlin, Gdansk, Dortmund, Frankfurt, Koblenz, Leipzig, Lüneburg, Memmingen, Münster, Tallinn, Stralsund, Ulm, Ravensburg, Vilnius, and Wesel. In a number of cases records indicate merchants coming from northern ("*Hanse*" or "*Osterling*") or southern Germany ("*almanus*"), so obviously it was not crucial for the notarial and urban scribes to locate them precisely.

31 The majority of agents were citizens of Antwerp, but others came from: Amsterdam, Arnemuiden, Bruges, Brussels, Deventer, Dordrecht, Ghent, Haarlem, Hoogstraten, Kampen, Leiden, Leuven, Mechelen, Middelburg, and Veere.

32 For different overviews see for instance: Eisenhardt, Agency theory; Shapiro, Agency theory; Miller, Political Evolution.

33 Richter and Furubotn, Neue Institutionenökonomik, p. 225–266.

turn regulate the work of the managers.[34] Premodern companies, however, rarely possessed bureaucratic surveillance structures.[35] Instead, two other systems are discussed to explain how a premodern principal could be reasonably sure that his agent would not cheat – public authorities on the one hand and close-knit groups on the other.

Douglass C. North has argued most prominently that the main reason why economic actors entered exchange relations was the existence of a state that provided institutions like laws and courts to regulate exchange, enforce regulations, and thereby secure property rights.[36] Sheilagh Ogilvie in her discussion of different types of trust stresses that public institutions at their best are able to generate uniform trust. Uniform trust in an institution prevails if everyone believes that the institution in question will help him or her, and this fosters general trust in every person one does business with.[37] Before the emergence of the nation-state, urban governments played an important role in providing institutions for exchange such as urban courts or brokers who were urban clerks.[38] Such public authorities supposedly enacted laws that governed principal-agent relations and enabled the principal to enforce his claims against his agent.[39]

The second explanation claims that merchants organised their relations in more or less tight-knit groups. In the absence of a strong public authority, they opted for private-order solutions. Avner Greif has argued most prominently that Jewish merchants active in eleventh-century trade in the Levant trusted each other because they could easily punish one another for misbehaviour.[40] If one merchant betrayed another, the harmed merchant would tell all his friends never to do business with the offender again, so the latter would be unable to remain in trade. Since everyone knew this risk, everyone was induced to play fair in the first place. Hence, merchants did not trust everyone, but they trusted their colleagues who belonged to the

---

34 Jensen and Meckling, Theory of the Firm; Fama and Jensen, Separation.

35 For the principal-agent problem in premodern times see Greif, Reputation, p. 857 f. In high medieval Italy and early modern southern Germany, some enterprises might have existed that could be regarded as similar to modern companies, such as the Medici or the Fugger company, see Lopez, Commercial Revolution; Roover, The organisation of trade, in: Postan, Rich and Miller, Cambridge Economic History; Hildebrandt, Georg Fuggerischen Erben; Hildebrandt, Unternehmensstrukturen. However, they can be regarded as exceptions, see Landsteiner, Kein Zeitalter.

36 North, Transaction costs.

37 Ogilvie, Use and Abuse.

38 Gelderblom, Cities of Commerce, p. 6.

39 For merchants in Bruges, Antwerp, and Amsterdam ibid., chapter 5.

40 Greif, Reputation.

same group.[41] Many scholars have questioned Greif's exclusive focus on private-order institutions,[42] recognising that premodern merchants usually used multiple different institutions to solve their problems,[43] and that private solutions were often enforced with the help of a public authority.[44]

Researchers can thus give convincing explanations of how the principal-agent problem was solved in premodern trade. However, neither explanation suffices when it comes to the two other links that emerged in close connection with the principal-agent relation. The first of these joined the agent to the third party, that is, to the person his principal wanted to do business with. For example, the merchant Joachim Pruner, who according to the sources came from Berlin and had settled in Antwerp,[45] traded in gemstones between Lisbon and Venice. Pruner first sent a number of gemstones to Franz von Bombergen, his representative in Venice. Later, Pruner authorised another colleague in Venice, Michael Imhof, to go to Franz von Bombergen and settle accounts with him.[46] When Michael Imhof reached Franz von Bombergen in Venice, the latter had to believe that Imhof had really come on behalf of Joachim Pruner. Otherwise, he would not have agreed to settle the accounts with him, Joachim Pruner would have had to travel to Venice himself, and the whole advantage of a representation system would have been lost. Bombergen could not have relied on a public authority to back up his claims if he had trusted Imhof and it had then turned out that Imhof had not been acting on Pruner's behalf. Indeed, Venetian city officials could prosecute Imhof only if he was still in Venice, and the Antwerp city council had no right to intervene in business matters in Venice. In general, a city council could write to another town and ask for help in prosecuting the offender, this was a lengthy process however, and the outcome depended on the cooperation of the other town council.[47] Bombergen also had no chance to ostracise Imhof because they did not belong to the same group of merchants.

The second connection emerged between the principal and the sub-agents whom the agent installed. For instance, the Augsburg merchant Ambrosius Hochstetter sent an agent of his company to Cologne to collect outstanding debts, and allowed

---

41 Ogilvie, Use and Abuse, calls this "differential trust in institutions" that generates "particularized trust in persons" who are part of the same family, guild etc.

42 Goldberg, Trade and Institutions, p. 149 f.

43 Grafe and Gelderblom, Rise and Fall, p. 478.

44 Gelderblom, Cities of Commerce, chapter 4.

45 Notariaat 522, fo. 87v.

46 Notariaat 522, fos. 87–8.

47 For instance, the council of St Gallen wrote to the council of Nördlingen because someone falsely declaiming that he worked for a trading company from Nördlingen had defrauded a burgher of St Gallen. The dispute ended amicably, but lasted for one and a half years, see Peyer, Leinwandgewerbe und Fernhandel, No. 372, p. 166–167.

the agent to install substitute agents on this behalf.[48] In another case, a merchant living in Antwerp gave three lawyers the power of attorney to represent him at the court in Bruges and allowed them to transfer this power to 'one or more' substitutes.[49] Henrick Proestinck acted in Antwerp as the representative of the Lübeck merchant Hans Vlanwijck and handed his authorisation down to another merchant, Gheert Kunre from Deventer.[50] In such cases the agent did not have to inform the principal about his choice of sub-agents. Thus, a principal might have been represented by a person whose name he did not even know. Kunre was allowed to collect debts for Hans Vlanwijck, but he most probably had never met him.

If Vlanwijck was not satisfied with Kunre's performance, he could hardly make Kunre feel it. Vlanwijck's hometown court in Lübeck was not responsible for dealings in Antwerp. To take Kunre to court in Antwerp, on the other hand, would have required Vlanwijck to travel to Antwerp himself, which he had wanted to avoid by installing a proxy, or to employ another proxy or sub-agent, in other words, to trust in the system that had just failed. Vlanwijck could not ostracise Kunre since the latter was not part of the group of Lübeck merchants. Even if Vlanwijck, or his first agent Proestinck, managed to get his business contacts to cease doing business with Kunre, in a vibrant trading hub such as Antwerp Kunre would find several alternative business partners quite quickly.

In sum, neither a public authority nor the reputation-based system of a private group suffices to elucidate why the third parties recognised the agents and why principals agreed that the agent could install sub-agents whenever he wanted. Both sanction-based regimes cannot be found here. Instead, as the next sections show, it was enough for merchants to be able to predict the behaviour of their colleagues to a certain degree to enter into relationships with them.

4. The Relationship between the Agent and a Third Person

If an agent did not tell his business partner that he was acting as the representative of another person, there was no specific challenge to securing this business transaction since it worked just like any other deal between two parties. But in the Late Middle Ages, agents frequently disclosed that they were working for another person. When an agent met with the business partners of his principal, he had to somehow identify himself as the principal's rightful representative. This was unavoidable in cases

---

48 SR # 97, 35r. He gave him the *"potestas substituendi"* – the power to substitute.

49 N # 2071, fo. 131v.: *"Eene oft meer procureurs In huer stede etc."*

50 SR # 102, fo. 152v.

where the agent had to collect debts or even to represent a merchant at court. The agents had to tell the debtors or the judges and other parties at court that they were acting on behalf of someone else. One of many examples is Hans Hochstetter from an Augsburg trading company, who instructed his servant Lazarus Ravensburger to collect debts from two merchants in Calais. The merchants in Calais probably did not know Ravensburger and had to believe him when he claimed that he was in fact collecting the money for Hochstetter and would be passing the money on to him.[51]

The Antwerp registry books show how an agent usually identified himself: he carried with him a procuration stating that person A had installed him, person B, as his agent, and that he, person B, was allowed to carry out certain tasks in the name of person A. Drafts of these procurations were written down in the registry books before the documents were issued in one or multiple copies,[52] and the later presentation of these copies ensured that the agent would be recognised as a valid representative of the principal.[53] For instance, the brothers Luchtmaker from Hamburg did not form a company,[54] but acted as proxies for one another. Andreas Luchtmaker was stationed in Antwerp, and his brothers Clarus[55] and Matthäus[56] authorised by him to collect debts in their name. Andreas also collected debts for another Hanse merchant named Paul Otte.[57] In turn, Andreas gave another brother, Henning, the power of attorney to collect his debts in Ghent.[58] Continuing the family saga, Matthäus was once installed by a colleague, Peter Elbeck, to go to a fifth brother, Elar Luchtmaker, in London in order to reclaim some goods of Elbeck's that were in Elar's possession.[59] Merchants from southern Germany also

---

51 SR # 114, fo. 236v.

52 Most of the notarial documents include the phrase that the principal asked the notary to issue one or more procurations, see for example Notariaat 523, fo. 193r or N # 541, fo. 53v.

53 Procurations have mostly been regarded as the realm of legal history, see Fränkel, Grundsätze der Stellvertretung; Müller, Direkte Stellvertretung; Hölzl, Stellvertretung; Schmoeckel, Juristische Stellvertretung; Signori, Der Stellvertreter; Amend-Traut, Akteure im Hintergrund; Zimmermann, Law of Obligations, Part I, Chapter 2, II. They were an extremely common feature of late medieval life, however, one could also, for example, authorise another person to receive an inheritance, see for instance in CERT # 3, fo. 397r. In particular, the centralisation of the papal administration which began to unfold in the High Middle Ages could not have been achieved without an elaborate system of procurators, see Heckel, Ständige Prokuratoren; Müller, Urkunden.

54 Lopez points out that the business of Benedetto Zaccaria, "one of the most powerful capitalistic structures of the Middle Ages", was also not designed as a trading company, but rather held together by proxies, Lopez, Proxy, p. 191–194.

55 N # 2071, fo. 3r.

56 N # 2071, fo. 17v.

57 N # 2070, fo. 156 f.

58 N # 2070, fo. 394.

59 N # 2071, fo. 15.

worked with, and as, proxies. Gabriel Steidelin,[60] for example, acted as an agent for a merchant from Aachen, Jan Geldolf. Steidelin travelled to Rouen to deliver wire in Geldolf's name,[61] and there demanded the payment of a letter of exchange owed to him.[62] Steidelin also collected debts in the name of Count Philipp of Eberstein,[63] while he himself gave various agents the power of attorney to exact debts for him in Middelburg,[64] Paris,[65] France,[66] England, and Scotland.[67]

Procurations enabled agents to get in touch with people they had not known before. The third party could in turn gauge the actions of the agent because he had shown his letter of procuration. Letters of procuration did not provide absolute security that the agent was legitimately acting on behalf of another person, and the third party could not be forced to acknowledge his claim, but procurations looked and worked in ways that were predictable. For merchants with some experience in trade, this obviously provided them with enough security to enter into relationships. Procurations were predictable in two regards: first, they were issued by a public authority, and second, the documents were structured and even worded in a very similar way and were thus easily recognisable as procurations.

The fact that the procurations survived in the registry books of the Antwerp city council and its notaries highlights the importance of the authority that these two institutions carried. The city council and the notary invested the document with their official power. All the procurations written by the clerks of the city council ended with the short phrase "*sub Sigillo*" (under the seal), indicating that when the procuration was issued, the urban seal was attached to attest to the authority of the city council. When issuing a procuration, the scribe of the city council added a sentence stating that the mayor, aldermen, and the council of Antwerp proclaimed the procurations.[68]

---

60 It is not certain where Gabriel Steidelin was from, but the records describe him as "*almanus*", which typically indicated a southern German. He once installed his brother-in-law who lived in Memmingen in Swabia as a proxy for a court case, so it is possible he was born in Swabia, Notariaat 522, fos. 197–198.

61 N # 2072, fos. 217–218.

62 N # 2073, fo. 109.

63 N # 541, fo. 103.

64 N # 2070, fo. 249.

65 N # 2073, fos. 12–13, to his son and to Jehan Dhay, and again to a Florentine merchant, N # 2073, fos. 28–29.

66 N # 2073, fo. 12.

67 N # 2073, fo. 13.

68 Some of the procurations issued in Antwerp survive in the Gdansk Archive, see for instance Archiwum Państwowe w Gdańsku, 300, D/71, Nr. 122. It starts: "*Wy Burgermeesteren Scepen ende Raidt vander Stadt van Antwerpen doen cond ende kenlick allen den ghenen die dese litteren sullen seen oft hooren lesen dat […]*".

The notaries authenticated their procurations by drawing their signet onto the issued procuration and by signing it.[69] They stressed that they were "public" (*publicus, openbaer*) notaries and that the document they produced was hence a public instrument. Notaries had to be officially appointed,[70] and some of them further mentioned this fact explicitly.[71]

The jurisdictional and legislative power of a city council ended at the city walls or the boundaries of its hinterland, and no central authority existed that could issue regulations on how procurations had to be drawn up in every European town or that could sanction procurations that had been wrongly issued. Nevertheless, each city council recognised other cities' notaries as public authorities that could legitimise a document. The archives record the Antwerp notaries and city council recognising as valid procurations documents issued by, among others, the city councils of Cologne,[72] Frankfurt/Main,[73] Gdansk,[74] Nuremberg,[75] Lübeck,[76] Sluis,[77] and Augsburg[78] as well as by notaries based in Augsburg,[79] Mechelen,[80] Lisbon,[81] and Goa in India.[82]

Interestingly, it was not necessary that the authority be well known in the jurisdiction where the procuration was presented. The seal of the town council of Cleve or the notary of the Bishop of Augsburg were probably not widely known in Antwerp, but a procuration issued by their offices was nevertheless acknowledged there.[83] Public authorities could thus exert power without being able to impose sanctions. The town councils and notaries, albeit being public institutions, functioned as private institutions are supposed to work, that is, through a common informal agreement among a group of equal partners. City councils and notaries mutually

69 See Archiwum Państwowe w Gdańsku, 300, D/71, Nr. 120, for an example issued by the Antwerp Notary Jacobus de Platea.

70 Goris, Études, p. 90.

71 Cleys van Loemele for example, called himself "public notary by imperial concession, appointed by the estates of Brabant", N # 541, fo. 53.

72 N # 3132, fo. 82r.

73 For example CERT # 3, fo. 378v.

74 For instance N # 2071, fo. 159v.

75 For example SR # 123, fo. 49r.

76 SR # 102, fo. 152v.

77 SR # 104, fo. 133r.

78 For example Notariaat 522, fo. 61r.

79 SR # 143, fo. 93v.

80 Issued by an imperial notary, see N # 2071, fo. 179r.

81 Notariaat 522, fo. 148.

82 Issued by the royal Portuguese notary, N # 2071, fo. 151v.

83 SR # 143, fo. 93r; SR # 145, fo. 117r; SR # 139, fo. 138r. In all three cases it was the Fugger representative Felix Hanolt, who got his procurations from the clerk of the bishop.

approved the official status of each other's documents. The fact that procurations followed a standard form likely assisted with recognition.[84] Persons with experience in trade could predict how a letter of procuration ought to look.

When someone had to assess a procuration issued by an unknown authority, he could not only check for seals and signatures but also examine whether it was worded and arranged like a proper procuration. For example, Ludwig Rem, a merchant from Augsburg trading in Antwerp, came to the Antwerp notary named Zeger Adriaan 's-Hertoghen and produced a power of attorney issued by a Portuguese notary stationed in Goa, which he wanted to transfer to Albert Raetman, a merchant from Berlin living in Lisbon. The Antwerp notary stated in his registry book that he had seen the procuration from Goa and decided to acknowledge the document because of its correct tenor (*ex tenore recti*).[85] When an agent brought a procuration from another town to the Antwerp city council to identify himself, the city council underlined that they had seen the document (*quam vidimus*) which presumably implied that they had checked whether it sounded like a proper procuration.

A procuration typically consisted of five parts: (1) the appointment of the agent (person A installs person B as his agent), (2) an enumeration of the acts the agent was allowed to perform in the name of the principal (A installs B in order to do x), (3) a declaration by the principal that he would abide by everything the agent agreed to in his name (he promises to uphold everything that the agent or the subagents does in this matter), (4) some elements strengthening the legitimacy of the document such as a seal or the names of witnesses, and (5) the effective date.[86] These similarities can be found in all kinds of procurations, whether they authorised an agent to trade on behalf of a merchant, to collect debts for him, or to defend him in court. A procuration allowing an agent to defend his principal in court looked quite similar to a procuration enabling an agent to manage the business in a distant town. The former was longer because several detailed permissions had to be granted for

84 A comparison between procurations from Lübeck, Lisbon, Augsburg, Bolzano, Genoa, Marseille, Seville, Venice, Amsterdam, Cologne, Essen, Danzig, Hamburg, Kiel, Lübeck, Nuremberg, Reval, Stralsund, and Wismar show a number of remarkable similarities which I discuss in Kypta, Urban Legal Boundaries.

85 N # 2071, fo. 151r.

86 To give one very short example in full: A burgher of Cologne gave the power of procuration to a lawyer at the court of Brabant: "*Godevaert Stertken de Jonge burger tot Coelen mechtig Michielen Daems procurator stipulerende inden Raide van Brabant Omme alle zine zaken die hy inden Rait van Brabant voerscreven nu te doene heeft oft naemaels te doene zal hebben het zy in aenleggene oft in verweerene tachtervolgende ter bedringene onde te verantwordene Iegens ende Jegelicken Recht dae af te gevene ende te nemene Ende voorts allet constituit etc. Geloven etc. xiiij d aprilis.*" CERT # 3, fo. 350v.

an individual to act as a representative in court, but the structure remained the same.[87]

Parts (1) and (2) used a standard vocabulary to describe the basic act of representation. For example, many of the notarial procurations stress that the principal had been present at the notarial office when installing the agent. This may have been offered to counterbalance the fact that the principal was not present when the agent presented the document to the third party. Lists of powers were also required and were often quite long and elaborate. This was especially important for representatives in court, since Roman law procedure consisted of several special steps, and the agent had to have the explicit power to act in each of these steps.[88] The long lists seem to have served as an assurance for the third party that the agent was allowed to deal with all the relevant issues. For example, a debt collector was commonly authorised to issue a quittance for a debt.[89] The third party could thus be sure that the principal would not claim afterwards that the agent was not allowed to acquit the debtor and that he, the principal, would not recognise the debtor as quit and would continue to claim his money.

This last point seems to have been quite important, since part (3) of a procuration especially deals with it. In this section, which appears in 88 per cent of the cases studied here (120 of 137), the principal explicitly stated that he would be responsible for everything the proxy did in his name. In half of the procurations, this liability of the principal is addressed in more detail. The constituent, as the principal is called in the procurations, indemnified the agent for all his losses and guaranteed to bail him out with all his movable and immovable goods should something go wrong. Furthermore, he declared he would not contest the acts of the agent in any court.[90]

Part (4) does not feature prominently in the sketches in the registry books but was an important part of the issued procuration. This is of course understandable, since the notaries and city councillors did not need to make the claim that this was an official document written by an official authority in their own records. In the issued procurations, however, the phrases feature more prominently, since the agent had to back up his claim to be a legitimate agent with an official document.[91]

---

87 Sometimes the group of persons who carried out these acts differed, since, for example, at the courts at Brabant a lawyer had to be specially appointed.

88 For example, when Pruner was authorised to collect a debt for Hieronymus Sailer, he was allowed, if necessary, to take the debtor to court and, among many other acts, to file a petition or contest petitions of the opposing party, to call witnesses, or interrogate the witnesses of others and to hear the judgement, see Notariaat 522, fo. 148r.

89 See for instance SR # 145, fo. 68r.

90 See for example in N # 2072, fo. 49r.

91 They can be found in the procurations that have survived in the Gdansk Archive, as shown above. See Archiwum Państwowe w Gdańsku, 300, D/71, Nr. 120, Nr. 121, Nr. 122.

Part (5), the date, appears either at the top or the bottom of the documents. Some notarial procurations even state the date at the beginning and repeat it at the end of the procuration. This was an important element because if a procuration had been issued too long ago, it would no longer be recognised as valid.[92] It is not clear how old was too old, but in one case a procuration was declared void because it was five years old[93] and another was updated after only five month.[94]

In sum, the third party believed that the agent was legitimately acting on behalf of another person because the agent produced a procuration. This document worked on the basis of two fundamental features. First, it was drawn up by a public authority. This public authority, however, did not have to be the one in charge at the place where agent and third party met, or where the agent or the third party conncted. Multiple and diverse public authorities were recognised across Europe. Second, the third party could check the validity of a procuration even if it did not know the authority that had drawn up the document, simply because the procuration looked like it should. Procurations corresponded to a standard common pattern. This pattern, however, was not decreed from above, from one central political authority or one central intellectual reference point such as Roman law. Rather, it emerged through exchanges between public authorities and between merchants.

The third party could hence never be absolutely certain that the agent definitely was a legitimate agent. He could only gauge if the procuration had the right "tenor". The agent, in turn, could not be sure that the third party would recognise him because no central authority or group could force the third party to do so. Apparently however, the process of recognition was successful in most cases, at least in a sufficient number of cases to keep the system running. Public authorities thus played an important role in securing the system of representation even though they had no power to sanction transgressions. They enhanced predictability by issuing procurations that looked similar, and they recognised such documents drawn up by other authorities. They did not do so because some higher authority forced them to, instead it seems that they shared an interest to keep the system of trade running to help enable their citizens to continue their business activities in other towns. This hypothesis will emerge again when we study the other weak tie in the representation system.

---

92 The council of Reval once refused to recognise a procuration because of an incorrect date, but unfortunately, they did not state in what regard the date was wrong, see Revaler Ratsurteile, no. 424, p. 59, 01/10/1543.

93 Ebel, Lübecker Ratsurteile, p. 687.

94 In December 1540, some merchants from Germany came to an Antwerp notary and presented a procuration issued by the Antwerp city council in July 1540. When they came back to install the same colleagues as agents again in January 1542, they did not bring the procuration from July 1540, but a newer one from December 1540. See N # 2071, fo. 4 and fos. 267–268.

5. The Relationship between Principal and Sub-agent

Of the 137 procurations studied here, 99 describe a principal installing an agent. In the other 38 cases, an agent passed his power of attorney to a sub-agent. In 83 of the 99 cases where a principal installed a primary agent, he gave him the power to appoint sub-agents. This right is commonly termed the 'power of substitution'.[95] Georg Timmermann for instance, who authorised his father, Matthäus Timmermann from Gdansk to act on his behalf, installed three lawyers as substitute proxies to defend his father in court.[96] This was a quite typical constellation:[97] A merchant, who was himself not in Antwerp, authorised a proxy from his own hometown. This agent travelled to Antwerp or already had his residence there. When this proxy needed to do something which required specific knowledge, such as debt collection or representation in court, he passed his authorisation on to another person better suited to the task.

Thus, the appointment of a sub-agent created a relation between two persons who in many cases did not know each other. One could argue that the sub-agent was, in fact, acting as an agent of the first agent, so the relation between agent and sub-agent was secured through the same ways and means as the one between principal and agent. For the principal, in theory, it did not matter what the sub-agent did. If problems arose, the principal could resort to the agent, and if the problem had originated with the sub-agent, the agent had in turn to resort to the sub-agent. In practice however, the addition of two principal-agent relations enhanced the level of uncertainty the principal had to face. He had to gauge that his agent would be capable of finding reliable sub-agents. If the agent failed in this, the merchant had to either cut his losses or engage in proceedings that often turned out to be lengthy and costly.

Contemporaries did, in fact, not regard the relation between agent and sub-agent as the same as that between principal and agent. The notarial and urban scribes clearly distinguished between a principal installing an agent and an agent

95 *"potestas substituendi"*, for example in N # 2070, fo. 249v or SR # 114, fo. 44v; *"puissance de substituer"*, for instance in N # 2074, fo. 70v; *"macht eenen oft meer procureurs in zyne stede te stellene"*, for example in N # 2072, fo. 1r. The last phrase is commonly shortened to *"eenen oft meer etc"*, see for instance SR # 127, fo. 293r.

96 N # 2071, fos. 159–160.

97 To name some more examples: An agent of a merchant from Nuremberg installed a sub-agent to collect debts in the Netherlands, see SR # 143, fo. 427v; agents of a Hanse merchant did the same, SR # 143, fo. 431v or SR # 104, fo. 133r; the agent of a merchant from Augsburg did the same, SR # 127, fo. 225r; an agent of a merchant from Augsburg passed on his authorisation to represent the merchant in court to someone from Antwerp, SR # 145, fo. 48r; the agents of merchants from Gdansk authorised sub-agents to represent their principals at the Imperial Court in Mechelen, N # 3132, fo. 52, and at the Court in Brabant, N # 2073, fo. 72.

transferring his power of attorney to a sub-agent. The verb for the first process was "*mechtigt*" or "*constituit*", whereas the second process was phrased "*mechtigt ende substitueerd*"[98] or "*substituit*".[99] The procurations for the sub-agent state that the business the sub-agent was allowed to handle was the business of the principal, not of the first agent. For example, Dierick Prondequin from Antwerp acted as the representative of Georg Rameler from Nuremberg. He passed on his authorisation to represent him in the court of Brabant to Goedenaerde te Hane, a lawyer accredited by this court. The procuration states that Goedenaerde te Hane was now allowed to take care of George's business (not Dierick's).[100] Similarly, when Joachim Pruner transferred his power of attorney to Kilian Rietwieser, the procuration made it clear that Rietwieser now acted in the name of Hieronymus Sailer from Lisbon.[101] In some cases, the principal explicitly declared that he would be responsible for everything his agent or the sub-agents did.[102] The sub-agent hence, represented not the agent, but the principal.

It is hard to gauge why sub-agents did not continuously cheat, since the parties did not explicitly discuss their reasons, for example in their letters.[103] I can only put forward two hypotheses based on a more theoretical line of reasoning. First, the fact that merchants continued to engage in this two-stage representational system suggests that they assessed the gain that would be yielded by allowing an agent to install sub-agents to be higher than the cost of the uncertainty that the sub-agent might rip them off. Representation in general helps trade to expand, and the same is true for the second stage of representation discussed here. If a merchant in Lübeck needed to collect debts in Antwerp, it saved him a lot of time and effort if he could avoid travelling there himself to search for an agent and install him directly. It was much more convenient to commission a colleague or partner from Lübeck who was maybe travelling to Antwerp anyway to look for a suitable agent to collect the debts. Even if the sub-agent did not recover all the funds, this option was probably nevertheless more profitable for the Lübeck merchant than to spend money and time on a journey to Antwerp.

The assumption that merchants employed such a risk assessment is supported by the observation that principals set two limits to the transfer of their authority. First,

---

98 For instance: SR # 104, fo. 66v.

99 For example: N 2071, fo. 151v.

100 SR 126, fo. 269r.

101 Notariaat 522, fo. 149r.

102 For instance in: Notariaat 522, fo. 141v.

103 I'm currently doing a research project analysing the merchants' letters of the Tucher family from Nuremberg in order to find out if and how they talked about their agents and sub-agents or about their behaviour as agents or sub-agents. So far it seems that this was not an important topic of conversation.

they typically allowed the agent to pass on only as much power as he had received from the principal.[104] The agent was not allowed to broaden the assignment. Second, agents were more reluctant to allow sub-agents to appoint sub-sub-agents; whereas 84 per cent of the agreements studied permitted sub-agents, only 26 per cent (10 out of 38 sub-procurations) permitted sub-sub-agents. Seemingly, merchants deemed a third level of representation as too risky to counterbalance possible gains, but not the second level. Even though principals could not be certain what the sub-agent at the second level was doing, they could still, to a certain degree, predict his behaviour since the principal's agent had picked the sub-agent. At the third level, in contrast, the predictability of the agent of one's agent's agent apparently sank too low to form the basis of many relationships.

The second explanation why sub-agents did not cheat to a degree that threatened the functioning of the system can be termed "abstract reciprocity"; they acted towards others as they wanted others to act towards them.[105] It lay in the interest of every merchant that his colleagues followed the norms of how to act as a principal, proxy, or sub-agent. One strategy to strengthen these norms was to follow them himself. Abstract reciprocity, of course, resembles direct reciprocity, a principle that governed the behaviour in close-knit groups. Direct reciprocity entailed that a merchant did something for another because he hoped that the other would then feel induced to do something for him in return.[106] Direct reciprocity only works in relatively small groups, and it was not very likely that merchant A did something for merchant B and then the situation arose that merchant B had the chance to do the same for merchant A among the large groups of merchants in Antwerp. Rather, merchant A likely acted honestly because he thereby strengthened the norm of honest behaviour, a norm from which he profited in general.

Two facts make the assumption of abstract reciprocity plausible. First, the same person took on different roles over time, sometimes acting as a principal and sometimes as a proxy or sub-agent, such as Gabriel Steidelin, who one time authorised one Jehan Dhay to collect debts for him and at another time himself collected debts for one Jan Geldolf.[107] Nearly every merchant installed proxies and worked as a proxy himself, and thus, nearly everyone benefited from a smooth working of the

---

104 For example, in Notariaat 522, fo. 148v, the agent was allowed to pass on the same or lesser powers to sub-agents.

105 A similar concept is employed by Putnam who calls it "generalized reciprocity": "I'll do this for you without expecting anything specific back from you, in the confident expectation that someone else will do something for me down the road". PUTNAM, Bowling Alone, p. 20 f.

106 Hanseatic trade is supposed to have rested on such direct reciprocity, even though it is hard to prove, see EWERT and SELZER, Wirtschaftliche Stärke, p. 44; STARK, Über Handelstechniken, p. 104 f.

107 N # 2073, fos. 12–13; fo. 109.

system. Sub-agents likely acted honestly to enforce the norm that proxies acted honestly. Next time they installed a sub-agent themselves, they would benefit from that norm.

Second, the rule 'do onto others as you would have them do unto you' is not really an exotic one, but rather the normative base of nearly every society.[108] Abstract reciprocity is the typical way informal institutions are strengthened. It therefore seems not too far-fetched to suppose that merchants also followed that rule in their dealings. Furthermore, research has pointed to how merchant apprentices learned the rules and norms of their trade by staying with and working alongside elder merchants.[109] It obviously was a well-known tradition to follow rules others had established. Actions became predictable because everyone was trained in the same norms and according to the same rules. In a setting where roles were swapped regularly, it made sense to enforce norms by following them.

In sum, the relation between principals and sub-agents worked without an authority – be it public or private – capable of enacting sanctions and punishing wrongdoers. Rather, the actors involved could predict the actions of others because they shared the same roles and norms. This result again points to the fact that all the parties involved shared a basic common interest in keeping the system running. Without representation, trade could not flourish. Therefore, merchants showed a general tendency to cooperate.

6. Conclusion

This article discussed two relations that laid the groundwork for agency relations that let premodern trade grow. For representation to work, it did not suffice that the relation between principal and agent was secured. Two other connections also have to be considered. The third party had to recognise the agent, and the principal had to rely not only on the agent, but also on the sub-agents the latter could install. Due to the fundamental legal pluralism inherent to premodern trade, the two explanations typically given to answer the question why cooperation worked in premodern trade do not fit here. Neither could one public authority govern relations between persons from different places, nor did the parties involved belong to the same close-knit group that could threaten to ostracise culprits.

My analysis of 148 procurations leads to an alternative explanation for the resolution of the principal-agent problem. The parties involved could not be sure that

108 Curry et al., "Morality", analysed sixty contemporary societies and found out that cooperation is seen as a norm in all of them.

109 Denzel, Professionalisierung.

they would not be cheated, but they could predict the behaviour of the other parties reasonably well enough to establish relations with them. The first relation discussed here, the one between agent and third party, was based on procurations that worked as a means of recognition, not because some central authority guaranteed their validity, but because they followed a common format that emerged through constant exchange between the trading towns of Europe. Their form and function were thus predictable for everyone involved in trading activities. Notaries and city councils had no power to sanction anyone from outside their sphere of influence who did not recognise them; their authority rested on a common implicit agreement to accept one another's documents. These informal institutions made relations to a certain degree predictable and thus reliable.

The second relation, between principal and sub-agent, was also shaped by a relative level of predictability that resulted from the fact that merchants performed different roles during their business activities and acted as principals as well as agents, third parties, and sub-agents. The assumption that one would at some point be in the same position as one's business partner led to a principle that can be called "abstract reciprocity". It makes sense to assume that parties did not betray their partners, not only because they wanted to do business with the same person in the future, but also because strengthening the norms of cooperation would be in their own long-term business interest. Principals could thus not be completely sure that their sub-agents would not defraud them, but they obviously gauged the profits from installing agents and sub-agents as higher than the risks.

The very concept of "predictability" thus explains why merchants formed not only strong ties with colleagues belonging to the same network or subject to the same authority, but also weak ties with people they hardly knew. It comes as no surprise that the parties involved could predict each other's behaviour if we take into account that they belonged to different small circles of partners, family members, and co-citizens, but they also formed part of the overall society of merchants in the sense that they were the ones responsible for keeping trade going and providing different regions with the means for life. The members of this large and loosely-knit group shared a common aim, they all had an interest in ensuring that trading activities would continue, since otherwise they would lose their profession. Representation formed an important building block of all trading activities. To keep trade going, it was thus important to enable the representation system to prevail, and in order to do that, it made sense to play by the (written and unwritten) rules.

Hence, such interconnected trade relationships worked, even though no public or private authority could convincingly threaten to sanction everyone who did not abide by the norms of cooperation. Weak ties could hold because the persons connected by them acted predictably enough. Not formal, but informal institutions made weak ties stable enough to keep trade moving. Merchants "trusted" their various partners in the sense that they could gauge with a high degree of probability how they would act in the future.[110] They believed with a sufficient probability that their colleagues would share their aim of keeping trade going.[111]

All in all, it seems that weak ties such as the ones between agent and third party and between principal and sub-agent worked because everyone supposedly had an interest in continuing cooperation. In trade, maybe especially in premodern trade, individual aims and cooperation seldom came into conflict, instead they went hand-in-hand in most cases.[112] The merchants analysed here cooperated even with colleagues they did not know well because it lay in their individual interest to do so. They acted as cooperative individualists.[113]

Bibliography

AMEND-TRAUT, Anja, Akteure im Hintergrund. Die Rolle der Faktoren in kaufmännischen Netzwerken und die Genese ihres rechtlichen Handlungsspielraums (Heiliges Römisches Reich Deutscher Nation und Deutsches Reich), in: Tijdschrift voor Rechtsgeschiedenis, 90 (2022), pp. 387–418.

AXELROD, R., The evolution of cooperation, New York 1984.

BLONDÉ, B./PUTTEVILS, J., Antwerp in the Renaissance, in: B. BLONDÉ/J. PUTTEVILS (eds.), Antwerp in the Renaissance, Turnhout 2020, pp. 9–28.

CIPOLLA, C. M., Before the Industrial Revolution. European society and economy 1000–1700, New York 1993.

CURRY, O. S./MULLINS, D. A./WHITEHOUSE, H., Is it good to cooperate? Testing the theory of morality-as-cooperation in 60 societies, in: Current Anthropology 60 (2019), pp. 47–69.

DAVIS, R., The rise of Antwerp and its English connection, 1406–1510, in: D. C. COLEMAN/A. H. JOHN (eds.), Trade, government and economy in pre-industrial England, 1976, pp. 2–20.

110 Premodern merchants did not calculate the probability of future events with mathematical models, but of course expectations about the future played an important role in their business decisions. These have been studied for instance at Antwerp University by Jeroen Puttevils and team in their ERC project "Back to the Future: Future expectations and actions in late medieval and early modern Europe, c. 1400–c. 1830".

111 This kind of trust falls between the two categories of personal trust which Ogilvie defined: Merchants did not only place particularised trust in persons who belonged to the same group; and they did also not show generalised trust in everyone they met, see OGILVIE, Use and Abuse, p. 18. Rather, they presumed that everyone inside the vague and large society of merchants could be trusted within certain limits because everyone wanted trade to continue.

112 Similar hypotheses have already been put forward, see for example FRANK, Passions, p. 69: "We can benefit from a predisposition to cooperate"; or AXELROD, Evolution of cooperation, p. 190: "The key to doing well lies not in overcoming others, but in eliciting their cooperation".

113 I discuss this term in more detail in my forthcoming book KYPTA, Kooperative Individualisten.

de Roover, R., The organization of trade, in: M. M. Postan/E. E. Rich/E. Miller (eds.), Cambridge Economic History of Europe, [vol. 3], Cambridge 1963, pp. 70–105.

Denzel, M. A., Professionalisierung und sozialer Aufstieg bei oberdeutschen Kaufleuten und Faktoren im 16. Jahrhundert, in: G. Schulz (ed.), Sozialer Aufstieg. Funktionseliten im Spätmittelalter und in der frühen Neuzeit, München 2002, pp. 413–42.

Denzel, M. A., Kommerzielle Innovationen für den Hanseraum? Ein Beitrag zum Strukturwandel des internationalen Handels des 15. und 16. Jahrhunderts, in: R. Hammel-Kiesow/S. Selzer (eds.), Hansischer Handel im Strukturwandel vom 15. zum 16. Jahrhundert, Trier 2016, pp. 67–99.

Doehaerd, R., Études Anversoises. Documents dur le commerce international à Anvers, 3 volumes, Paris 1963.

Ebel, W. (ed.), Lübecker Ratsurteile, Band 3. 1526–1550, Göttingen 1958.

Eisenhardt, K. M., Agency theory: An Assessment and Review, in: Academy of Management Review, 14 (1989), pp. 57–74.

Epstein, Stephen A., An Economic and Social History of Later Medieval Europe, 1000–1500, Cambridge 2009.

Everaert, J., Power in the metropolis. The impact of economic and demographic growth on the Antwerp city council (1400–1550), in: Urban History, 47 (2020), pp. 589–609.

Ewert, U. C./Selzer, S., Wirtschaftliche Stärke durch Vernetzung. Zu den Erfolgsfaktoren des hansischen Handels, in: M. Häberlein/C. Jeggle (eds.), Praktiken des Handels. Geschäfte und soziale Beziehungen europäischer Kaufleute in Mittelalter und früher Neuzeit, Konstanz 2010, pp. 39–69.

Fama, E. F./Jensen, M. C., Separation of ownership and control, in: Journal of Law and Economics, 26 (1983), pp. 301–325.

Frank, R.H., Passions within reason. The strategic role of the emotions, New York 1988.

Fränkel, R., Die Grundsätze der Stellvertretung bei den Scholastikern, in: Zeitschrift für vergleichende Rechtswissenschaft, 27 (1912), pp. 289–391.

Gelderblom, Oscar, Cities of commerce. The institutional foundations of international trade in the Low Countries, 1250–1650, Princeton 2013.

Goldberg, J. L., Trade and institutions in the medieval mediterranean. The Geniza merchants and their business world, Cambridge 2012.

Goris, J. A., Études sur les colonies marchandes méridionales (Portugais, Espagnols, Italiens) à Anvers de 1488 à 1567. Contribution a l'histoire des débuts du capitalisme modern, Louvain 1925.

Grafe, R./Gelderblom, Oscar, The Rise and Fall of the Merchant Guilds. Re-thinking the Comparative Study of Commercial Institutions in Premodern Europe, in: Journal of Interdisciplinary History, 40 (2010), pp. 477–511.

Granovetter, M. S., The strength of weak ties, in: American Journal of Sociology, 78 (1973), pp. 1360–1380.

Greif, A., Reputation and coalitions in medieval trade: evidence on the Maghribi traders, in: Journal of Economic History, 49 (1989), pp. 857–882.

Greif, Avner, The fundamental problem of exchange: A research agenda in Historical Institutional Analysis, in: European Review of Economic History, 4 (2000), pp. 251–284.

Guicciardini, Lodovico, Descrittione di tutti i Paesi Bassi, altrimenti detti Germania Inferiore, Antwerp, 3rd edn., 1588.

Guinnane, T. W., Trust: a concept too many, in: Jahrbuch für Wirtschaftsgeschichte, 46 (2005), pp. 77–92.

Harreld, D. J., Atlantic sugar and Antwerp's trade with Germany in the sixteenth century, in: Journal of Early Modern History 7 (2003), pp. 148–163.

Harreld, D. J., High Germans in the Low Countries. German merchants and commerce in golden age Antwerp, Leiden 2004.

Heckel, R., Das Aufkommen der ständigen Prokuratoren an der päpstlichen Kurie im 13. Jahrhundert, in: Scritti di Storia e Paleografia, 2 (1924), pp. 290–321.

Hildebrandt, R., Die „Georg Fuggerischen Erben". Kaufmännische Tätigkeit und sozialer Status 1555–1600, Berlin 1966.

Hildebrandt, R., Unternehmensstrukturen im Wandel. Personal- und Kapitalgesellschaften vom 15.–17. Jahrhundert, in: Hans Jürgen Gerhard (ed.), Struktur und Dimension. Festschrift für Karl-Heinrich Kaufhold zum 65. Geburtstag. Band 1, Mittelalter und Frühe Neuzeit, Stuttgart 1997, p. 93–110.

Hölzl, F. J., Friedrich Carl von Savignys Lehre von der Stellvertretung. Ein Blick in seine juristische Werkstatt, Göttingen 2002.

Jenks, S., Small is beautiful. Why small Hanseatic firms survived in the late Middle Ages, in: J. Wubs-Mrozewicz/S., Jenks (eds.), The Hanse in medieval and early modern Europe, Leiden 2013, pp. 191–214.

Jensen, M. C./Meckling, W.H., Theory of the firm: managerial behavior, agency costs and ownership structure, in: Journal of Financial Economics, 3 (1976), pp. 305–360.

Kypta, U., Kooperative Individualisten. Gesellschafter, Diener und Bevollmächtigte deutscher Kaufleute im Antwerpen des 15. und frühen 16. Jahrhunderts, Stuttgart 2025.

Kypta, U., Crossing Urban Legal Boundaries. Merchants' agents and the process of bottom-up harmonization between European towns, 14th to 16th century, in: Urban History (2024), pp. 1–16.

Landsteiner, Erich, Kein Zeitalter der Fugger: Zentraleuropa im langen 16. Jahrhundert, in: F. Edelmayer/P. Feldbauer/M. Wakounig (eds.), Globalgeschichte 1450–1620. Anfänge und Perspektiven, Wien 2002, pp. 95–123.

Limberger, Michael, Der Aufstieg einer neuen Weltregion. Nordwesteuropa, in: P. Feldbauer/J.-P. Lehners (eds.), Die Welt im 16. Jahrhundert, Wien 2008, pp. 31–51.

Lopez, R. S., Proxy in medieval trade, in: W. C. Jordan/B. McNab/T.F. Ruiz, Order and innovation in the middle ages. Essays in honor of Joseph R. Strayer, Princeton 1976, pp. 187–194.

Lopez, R. S., The commercial revolution of the Middle Ages 950–1350, Cambridge 1976.

Miller, G. J., The political evolution of principal-agent models, in: Annual Review of Political Science 8 (2005), pp. 203–225.

MÜLLER, Ulrich, Die Entwicklung der direkten Stellvertretung und des Vertrages zugunsten Dritter. Ein dogmengeschichtlicher Beitrag zur Lehre von der unmittelbaren Drittberechtigung und Drittverpflichtung, Stuttgart 1969.

MÜLLER, Harald, Die Urkunden der päpstlichen delegierten Richter. Methodische Probleme und erste Erkenntnisse am Beispiel der Normandie, in: R. HIESTAND (ed.), Hundert Jahre Papsturkundenforschung, Göttingen 2003, pp. 351–371.

NÉLIS, Hubert, Les origins du notariat public en Belgique (1270–1320), in : Revue belge de philologie et d'histoire 2 (1923), pp. 267–277.

NORTH, D. C., Transaction costs in history, in: Journal of European Economic History 14 (1985), pp. 557–576.

OGILVIE, S., The use and abuse of trust. Social capital and its deployment by early modern guilds, in: Jahrbuch für Wirtschaftsgeschichte 1 (2005), pp. 15–52.

PEYER, H. C., Leinwandgewerbe und Fernhandel der Stadt St. Gallen von den Anfängen bis 1520, unter der Benützung der Vorarbeiten von Alfred SCHELLING und Hektor AMMANN, Band 1: Quellen, St. Gallen 1959.

PUTNAM, R. D., Bowling alone. The collapse and revival of American community, New York 2000.

RICHTER, R./FURUBOTN, E. G., Neue Institutionenökonomik. Eine Einführung und kritische Würdigung, translated by M. STREISSLER, Tübingen 4th edn. 2010.

ROSS, S. A., The economic theory of agency. The principal's problem, in: American Economic Review 63 (1973), pp. 134–139.

SCHMOECKEL, Mathias, Die Entwicklung der juristischen „Stellvertretung" im Kontext theologischer und juristischer Begrifflichkeiten, in: O. CONDORELLI/, F. ROUMY/M. SCHMOECKEL (eds.), Der Einfluss der Kanonistik auf die europäische Rechtskultur, Band 1: Zivil- und Zivilprozessrecht, Köln 2009, pp. 107–136.

SHAPIRO, S. P., Agency theory, in: Annual Review of Sociology 31 (2005), pp. 263–284.

SIGNORI, Gabriela, Der Stellvertreter. Oder: Wie geht eine Anwesenheitsgesellschaft mit Abwesenheit um?, in: Zeitschrift der Savigny-Stiftung für Rechtsgeschichte, Germanistische Abteilung 132 (2015), pp. 1–22.

STARK, Walter, Über Handelstechniken auf dem Brügger Markt um die Wende vom 14. zum 15. Jahrhundert, in: N. JÖRN/W. PARAVICINI/H. WERNICKE (eds.), Hansekaufleute in Brügge 4. Beiträge der internationalen Tagung in Brügge, Frankfurt/Main 2000, pp. 97–107.

STIGLITZ, J. E., Principal and agent, in: J. EATWELL/M. MILGATE/P. NEWMAN (eds.), Allocation, information and markets, London 1989, pp. 241–253.

STRIEDER, Jakob, Aus Antwerpener Notariatsarchiven. Quellen zur Deutschen Wirtschaftsgeschichte des 16. Jahrhunderts, Stuttgart 1930, ²Wiesbaden 1962.

VAN DER STOCK, Jan (ed.), Antwerp, story of a metropolis 16th–17th century, Gent 1993.

VAN DER WEE, H., The growth of the Antwerp market and the European economy (fourteenth-sixteenth centuries), 3 volumes, Den Haag 1963.

van der Wee, H., Trade in the southern Netherlands, 1493–1587, in: H. Van der Wee (ed.), The Low Countries in the Early Modern World, translated by L. Fackelman, Aldershot 1993, pp. 87–114.

van der Wee, H./Materné, J., Antwerp as a world market in the sixteenth and seventeenth centuries, in: Jan van der Stock (ed.), Antwerp, story of a metropolis 16th–17th century, Gent 1993, pp. 19–31.

van Houtte, J. A., Anvers aux xve et xvie siècle, in : Annales 16 (1961), pp. 248–278.

Williamson, O. E., Markets and hierarchies. Analysis and antitrust implications, New York 1975.

Zimmermann, Reinhard, The Law of Obligations. Roman Foundations of the Civilian Tradition, Cape Town 1990.

Unpublished archival sources

Archiwum Państwowe w Gdańsku, 300, D/71, Nr. 120, 121, 122.

FelixArchief Antwerpen, N # 541, N # 546, N # 2070, N # 2071, N # 2072, N # 2073, N # 2074, N # 2075, N # 2076, N # 2077, N # 3132, N # 3133, N # 4456, CERT # 3, CERT # 4, SR # 97, SR # 102, SR # 104, SR # 106, SR # 108, SR # 110, SR # 112, SR # 114, SR # 116, SR # 118, SR # 119, SR # 122, SR # 123, SR # 126, SR # 127, SR # 129, SR # 131, SR # 133, SR # 135, SR # 143, SR # 145.

Rijksarchief Antwerpen-Beveren, Notariaat 522 and 523.

Leslie Carr-Riegel

Reprisals Gone Wrong

English Cases of Mercantile Dispute, 13th–15th Centuries

1. Introduction

This article explores reprisals gone wrong – cases of mercantile dispute involving Englishmen between 1250 and 1450, which for a variety of reasons failed to achieve a satisfactory conclusion for the plaintiff.[1] To set the stage, the right of reprisal was a customary law, common across Europe during the Late Middle Ages, which followed the principal of collective liability. With a writ of reprisal, individuals from one community were legally granted the right to seek redress from members of another community for a wrong done by one of their compatriots. This right authorised merchants to seize the person and or property of traders from a different locality, in retribution for acts committed by members of the offending community. These offences usually took the form of unpaid debt or theft.[2]

Given that this volume centres on predictability in legal pluralism, the inclusion of a chapter exploring exceptional cases of failure might appear out of place. Yet, while this article looks at exceptional events – times when the stately progress of a reprisal went wrong, I will argue that they show predictable problems which occurred frequently with reprisals because of the system's inherent design. Given that the initial workshop which inspired this volume focused on Northern Europe, the case studies presented are all from England and events that occurred along the Celtic Sea, the North Sea, and the Baltic Sea. They represent a sampling of a larger set of examples encompassing hundreds of reprisals taken from all across Europe which demonstrate a pattern of predictable failures of reprisals.

The sources for this study come primarily from English documents, in particular the Close and Patent Rolls which were the administrative records produced by

---

1 This publication was made possible by a fellowship from the Käte Hamburger Kolleg "Legal Unity and Pluralism" at the University of Münster, funded by the German Federal Ministry of Education and Research (BMBF).

2 The fundamental works on reprisals include: del Vecchio and Casanova, Le rappresaglie; Tanzini, Le rappresaglie; Cassandro, Le rappresaglie; Tai, Honor; Maccioni, La giustizia; Chavarot, La Pratique; Timbal, Les lettres; Eiglier, Etude Historique; Maccioni, L'utilizzo; Fabrega, Marques i represàlies; Mutgé i Vives, La marca; Tanzini, Rappresaglie tra Toscana; Clark, The English Practice; Wink and Sicking, Reprisal and diplomacy; Planitz, Deutscher Arrestprozess.

the royal chancery starting around the year 1200, and are helpfully published in their entirety.[3] These documents contain a wide variety of letters, privileges, safe conducts, charters, court decisions, and royal mandates, which at times also include reference to reprisal cases. Added to this are also selected documents transcribed by Hubert Hall, from the as yet unpublished records of the King's Bench, which offer more detailed description of particular cases.[4]

To first look at an example of a "perfect reprisal"; one that, at least according to the merchants enacting it, went right. The year is 1313 and David Cotesbrok, merchant of London, seeks to sell 48 marks worth of goods in Norway. His goods, however, are detained amongst others belonging to merchants from England without apparent cause. Angered at this injustice, David protests to the king of England, who sends a letter of complaint, requesting the goods be returned, but the king of Norway fails to do so. Whereupon the king of England commands his sheriffs to seize goods belonging to merchants from Norway to the value of 48 marks for David's damages. Soon after, the unlucky ship of Ivar Sherfhunger and his fellows, merchants of Norway, put into the English port of King's Lynn. They immediately have their goods (lumber, oil, and fish) seized to the amount of 48 marks. The goods are sold, and the proceeds handed over to David as compensation.[5]

This, according to the order of the day, was what should happen when a reprisal was granted and executed. The English merchant David Cotesbrok, who had been robbed while abroad, had been denied justice as the local authorities in the foreign jurisdiction had failed in their duty to protect him and perpetuated the wrong through inaction. These were the grounds upon which a reprisal could be legitimately granted according to the jurisprudential theory of the day, expressed most succinctly by the famous Italian law professor, Bartolus de Saxoferrato (b.1313–1357), just a few years after the events described above. Bartolus, who would come to be acknowledged as one of the most influential Roman legal scholars of the Middle Ages, had a major impact on how reprisals were viewed.

Reprisals have frequently been characterised by scholars as "legal piracy"; but this misrepresents the case.[6] Such reprisals were rather a form of debt security

3 Calendar of the Close Rolls [henceforth CCR], Edward I: Vol. 1, 1272–1279; CCR Edward I: Vol. 5, 1302–1307; CCR Edward II: Vol. 1, 1307–1313; CCR, Edward II: Vol. 2, 1313–1318; CCR, Edward II: Vol. 3, 1318–1323; CCR, Henry III: Vol. 1, 1227–1231; CCR, Richard II: Vol. 3, 1385–1389, London 1921; Calendar of the Patent Rolls [henceforth CPR] Edward II: Vol. 5, 1324–1327; CPR, Edward III: Vol. 1, 1327–1330; CPR, Edward IV, Edward V, and Richard Ill: 1476–1485; CPR, Henry III: Vol. 1, 1216–1225; CPR, Henry IV: Vol. 4, 1408–1413.

4 Select Cases Concerning the Law Merchant A.D. 1293–1633, Vol. 2: Hall, Central Courts.

5 CCR Edward II: Vol. 2, 1313–1318, p. 2.

6 Lloyd, Alien Merchants, p. 20; Tai, Honor, p. 9; Dick, Framing Piracy, p. 87; Part of the reason for this assessment has been due to the confusion between medieval reprisals, or letters of marque, and the later privateering letter of marque which became popular during the early modern period.

enforcement and guarantee of protection for citizens abroad which was based on the principle of collective responsibility.[7] Under this principle, individuals were responsible for the behaviour of their fellow citizens. This flies in the face of modern legal theory which stresses the culpability solely of an individual for their own actions. In premodern times however, the application of collective responsibility was a common means by which societies sought to curtail bad behaviour and promote social harmony.

Jurists even at the time were uneasy about such matters, but eventually came around to characterising them as a necessary evil.[8] Bartolus de Saxoferrato himself admitted in his short treatise dedicated to reprisals, the *Tractatus Repressaliarum*, that they appeared both according to biblical teachings and under Roman law to be "illegal in the forum of conscience and repugnant to natural reason".[9] In typical scholastic fashion however, he then seeks to undermine this initial assertion,

---

While related, these two legal institutions are entirely different. Medieval reprisals were issued only in times of peace, for a private claim of a specified sum, and only after a full legal case had been mounted and several attempts made to reach a settlement of the claim. On the other hand, privateering licences, while often confusingly referred to as letters of marque, were very different. These licences to plunder were issued in times of war, with an open clause to harass a lord's enemies; and any prize claims or judicial oversight handled after the fact and usually adjudicated by an admiralty court. Both followed the principle of collective reprisal, but were distinctly different in purpose and execution. For more on this see: Carr-Riegel, Letter of Marque, pp. 60–62.

7 For more on collective responsibility as a means by which to alleviate the fundamental problem of exchange through the judicious use of reprisals, see the game theory-based analysis of: Greif, Fundamental problem.

8 Bartolus's predecessor, Italian jurist Odofredus, argued strongly that reprisals were unjust and should be abolished. He wrote that *"Et auth. ita dicit: Si tibi anglico vel hispano mutuo pecuniam vel sum spoliatus in Anglia vel Hispania, vel Tuscia, non propterea si invenio alios anglicos vel hispanos vel tuscos, debeo eos pignorare in civitate ista (Bononia). Nec licet mihi hoc facere, imo omnino prohibeor hoc facere: et si contra facio, debeo puniri et condemnari in quadruplum eius quod pignoravi, insuper cadam ab actione mea. Hoc dicit ista authentica"* (Anyone who has lent money to an Englishman or Spaniard or has been robbed in England, Spain or Tuscany has no right to make up for the damage he has suffered by seizing a countryman of the debtor or the culprit who is not responsible for the damage), in: Odofredus, Codicis Praelectiones lib. IV, 12, p. 203. And further that *"certum est ex alterius obligatione neminem debere conveniri et omnimodo qui convenit alium pro alio, ita puniatur"* (it is certain that no one should be approached for the obligation of another and he who approaches one instead of another is always punished accordingly), in: Odofredus, Commento al Codice, p. 318. For more on Odofredus see: Schaube, Handelsgeschichte, p. 757. See also del Veccio, and Casanova, Le rappresaglie, p. XVI.

9 *"quod alius pro alio non potest capi. Praeterea non licet in foro conscientiae facere id quod repugnat naturali rationi."* Saxoferrato, Omnia Quae Exstant, p. 120, 1.1. Bartolus referenced Ezekiel 20:18, demonstrating Biblical prohibitions against collective responsibility. Collective responsibility for debt is further prohibited in three articles of the *Digesta* of the *Corpus Iuris Civilis* – Laws 11.57.1, 11.59.16, and 12.60.4 – and in three of the Novellae Constitutiones – Novel 52, Novel 128, Cap. 14, and Novel 134, Cap. 4.

eventually producing a clear and concise work defending reprisals and describing their proper procedure. Bartolus and the jurists who followed him managed this feat by equating reprisals with just war, invoking arguments made by Augustine and Thomas Aquinas.[10] By linking reprisals to private just war and protection of property and self, Bartolus neatly hedged the issue. So long as a significant injury was suffered, over which a manifest denial of justice could be proven, then a superior authority, such as a sovereign lord or his judicial representative, could legitimately issue a reprisal.[11] Thus, late medieval jurists justified the use of reprisals legitimating a practice which was continuously ongoing, frequently regardless of learned opinions.

On the ground, merchants and sovereigns, however, also sought at times protections from reprisals, with merchants seeking to acquire charters of privilege which exempted them from collective liability, and sovereigns granting such protections together with letters of safe conduct to individuals. The jockeying between seeking to enforce reprisals against others while protecting your own interests was a constant push and pull affair that predictably made collecting reprisals a more complicated and frequently drawn-out affair.

The case of the English merchant David Cotesbrok met all the requirements put forward by Bartolus and thus, according to judicial theory of the era and common legal practice across Europe at the time, he was granted just recompense through the taking of articles from compatriots of those who had harmed him. By the fourteenth century, reprisals were a standard part of medieval judicial procedure. Merchants travelling from the far reaches of Ireland to Hungary, from the boot of Italy to the Norwegian fjords, could expect to run into reprisal proceedings. This ubiquity makes reprisals an interesting piece of medieval jurisprudence. As a part of mercantile and burgeoning international law, it was one of the rare pieces of law which travellers could predictably expect to run into in nearly every European jurisdiction.[12]

However, as we shall see in the following cases, the commonality of this practice did not mean that frequently things couldn't go horribly awry. Reprisal cases were

10 Saxoferrato, Omnia Quae Exstant, p. 120, 1.1–2. Bartolus cites: Augustine, Contra Faustum, XXII.74, Viginti Unius Sententiarum Sive Quaestionum Liber Unus, VI, and Thomas Aquinas, Summa theologiae, Secunda secundae partis, Q. 40, art. 1. For a fuller explanation of the medieval theory of just war see: Russel, Just War.

11 This view was adopted by numerous later writers including Bartolus, Giovanni de Legnano, Baldus de Ubaldinus, Honoré Bonet, and Christine de Pizan, to name just a few. Saxoferrato, Omnia Quae Exstant, pp. 119–125; Legnano, pp. 307–9; Ubaldinus, Sed omnino post Cod. 4.12.4, f. 23vb, n. 8 in Fedele, The Medieval Foundations of International Law, p. 570; Bonet, L'arbre, pp. 192–196.

12 For an exploration of the widespread practice of reprisals from the medieval to the early modern era, see my forthcoming volume: Carr-Riegel, The Right of Reprisal, forthcoming 2026.

often complicated; they involved merchants from multiple jurisdictions, languages, long travel times, extensive debts, pirate actions, international politics, human ingenuity, and greed. This potent mix meant that such cases were ripe for conflict and error. Upon reviewing a large number of English reprisals which occurred between 1250 and 1450, I have identified five primary ways in which things could go wrong from the point of view of a claimant. Instead of an orderly progression from complaint to payment, something caused the process to be disrupted and the claimant to lose time or their money entirely. The following sections of this article address each failure in turn.

2. Failure to Follow Proper Procedure

The way a reprisal was to work itself through the justice system in England was clearly defined by the fourteenth century.[13] Reprisal cases might be presented to a fair court or local jurisdiction; but they eventually made their way before the King's Bench. There, the case, with extensive paperwork and witnesses, was reviewed and a decision made to release or withhold a writ of reprisal. If the claimant's suit was deemed justified, then a writ of reprisal was released, and the king informed his local officials, sheriffs or bailiffs, to begin collection of the registered amount from the compatriots of the named parties. However, while this path was relatively straightforward, a number of kinks could appear as it was tread. These failures could take several forms.

The first stumbling block might be a process error, the original suit not having been filed properly due to the negligence of the claimant.[14] As part of reprisal proceedings, a significant good will effort to recover their property through normal

---

13 The English system of reprisal administration was particularly well elaborated and robust. Similar centralised arrangements can be seen, for example, in the Kingdom of Aragon and the Kingdom of Hungary while far more ad hoc arrangements where the collection of reprisal terms were undertaken by the claimants themselves can be seen in the Italian city states, the Low Countries, the coastal cities of France and throughout the Holy Roman Empire. Carr-Riegel, The Right of Reprisal.

14 An example of such a case from 1305 involving English and Flemish merchants: King Edward I awarded Bernard Maillekyn and Reymund de Mountinas, merchants of Bayonne [then within the domains of the king of England] a reprisal against merchants from Flanders for goods worth 312 marks that they had been robbed of while in Flanders. However, having received new information, showing that the two merchants had not properly made out their original suit for restitution of their goods, the seizure was ruled improper. Consequently, all that had so far been taken in reprisal from the merchants of Ypres was to be released and restored to its owners (Dec. 1305.) About half a year later however (June 1306), goods from Flemish merchants were again being taken to restore the debt of Bernard and Reymund. CCR Edward I: Vol. 5, 1302–1307, pp. 358–9, 455–6.

channels was generally expected of all claimants. Reprisals were to be utilised as a last resort and only after ample proof was provided that justice had been denied. For justice to be denied, it had to be sought in the first place. Merchants who failed in this critical initial step would be refused reprisals further down the line.

Second, an error could be made by the reigning authorities in mistakenly granting a reprisal in violation of existing law. Such cases were frequently complicated and pitted local law against mercantile and international norms. In this event, local law tended to prevail as we shall see in further detail anon.

The third and final procedural failure occurred when overzealous merchants attempted to extract reprisals themselves, rather than leaving it to the proper authorities.[15] This form of self-help had been commonplace in earlier times and was still practised in other parts of Europe. However, in England, the Crown had reserved a monopoly for itself on this type of action and so merchants were forbidden to attempt such vigilante justice. Instead, goods were to be seized and held by the king's designated officials – sheriffs and bailiffs, who then handled its redistribution to the claimants. This system had its own pitfalls as will be described below, but it was the official procedure and deviation from it could result in the forfeit of the claim.

In all these cases, the problem was revealed upon appeal by foreign merchants who were upset that their goods had been taken. English examples demonstrate that foreign merchants making such an appeal stood a good chance of winning the argument if they proved in court that the plaintiffs had made an error, usually through a lack of proper documentation, or if they could prove that the law had been misapplied. The third option, of merchants seeking to take reprisal into their own hands, appears surprisingly infrequently in English sources; but a few instances do appear.[16] This point has actually attracted considerable scholarly de-

---

15 Clark, English Practice.

16 An example of such a case from 1260 involved English and Rouen merchants. William of Tangham sought restitution for 11 marks sterling, owed to him by Robert Crocket. He brought his case before the court in Rouen and the bailiffs there, finding no movable goods owned by Robert, awarded William the rents of property owned by Robert in the city. William didn't like the judgement however, and returning to England, sought reprisal and return of the money owed. In pursuit of this, he seized 4 bags of wool worth 30 marks from merchants from Rouen in Harwich in Essex, and further imposed upon three other men: Richard Josep, John Horn and William of Howell, for debts they supposedly owed to Robert [the debtor of my debtor owes me money principle]. The three men denied ever having been to Rouen, or owing Robert money, and no one had any evidence to the contrary, so they were excused. Robert was by now greatly inconvenienced by this sequestration; as goods he had then been trading in Rouen were in turn taken into custody for the now 30 marks owed. He protested that while he admitted to the 11 marks he owed to William, the rest of the money gained from the sale of the wool taken from men of Rouen should be returned to them. The court found that this was correct and further granted Robert 40 solidi in damages.

bate as until recently it was taken as gospel that unilateral reprisals undertaken by wrong merchants were a constant plague. The great English historian Reginald Marsden believed that frequently in the thirteenth and into the fourteenth century, "reprisals were made without authority. With or without formal letters of reprisal there is no trace in the records of any systematic check having been placed upon the proceedings of those who redressed their own wrongs by captures made at sea."[17] Marsden was, however, focused on English Chancery records which did not present the whole picture of events and rather overrepresented the issue. My own research and recent work by Jurriaan Wink and Louis Sicking underscore this error.[18]

While process errors usually occurred in the early stages of a plea and might be remedied with better documentation, as stated, self-help reprisals were rare. Cases in which a reprisal was shown to violate existing law were complex and deserving here of further exploration. To take an example, in 1321, Thomas Seaman, the Bailiff of Westminster Fair, took into possession the goods of Henry Mays, France of Cologne, William Herynt, and Nicholas de Ulteme, among others. This seizure was done at the behest of John Prior, who claimed them as part of a suit against the Duke of Brabant. This was done presumably using the debtor of my debtor owes me money rule whereby cash could be collected from those who owed funds to the indebted merchant as if they were the merchant themselves. This, even though they assured they were not sureties of the duke. The merchants claimed their injury amounted to £500 in goods sequestered and damages. Thomas claimed that everything had gone according to custom between John Prior and the plaintiff merchants at the fair; and produced a quitclaim document, supposedly given to him by the merchants, exonerating him of all debts and obligations. The merchants claimed this was a fake and demanded that an inquiry be made into its authenticity. An attempt was then made to certify the document; but then Thomas did not show up for the next court hearing, the merchants cried foul, and the court agreed with them. The Sheriff of Middlesex was therefore assigned to collect the debt from Thomas; but upon inspection, he claimed that Thomas held no property in his shire. The merchants, having no way now to collect their due from Thomas, switched tactics and instead sought to charge the Abbot of Westminster, who was in charge of the fair, to stand surety for Thomas's behaviour and debts, as he was acting in the capacity of his

---

The case is particularly interesting for the fact that William claimed that he had the right to take the goods of merchants from Rouen *"secundum legem mercatorum"* (according to merchant law). The court apparently saw no problem with this assertion; but they disliked the way he went about collecting it. Records of this case bolster the argument made by some scholars that there existed an unwritten code of law applicable to merchants, a *lex mercatura*, that was common across Europe during the medieval period. Hall, Select Cases, Nr. 4.

17 Marsden, Early Prize, p. 682.

18 Wink and Sicking, Reprisal and diplomacy, p. 61.

bailiff. The abbot however, upon being brought to the court, claimed that under English law he could not be held responsible for the bad behaviour of another individual.[19] This was a direct attack against the collective responsibility rule which underlay the issuing of reprisals. The merchants maintained that this defence was poppycock and, as the authority in charge of and responsible for the jurisdiction of the fair, the abbot was very much accountable. The judge however disagreed, finding in favour of the abbot and instead of the return of the money they had sought they were charged with raising a false claim.[20] This example demonstrates the difficulties merchants might have faced in a foreign court against a formidable adversary, even when their case was watertight. Knowledge of local law, but all the more of social circumstances were key to a successful prosecution.[21] Cases such as this, where the claimants sought damages against a powerful individual or at a delicate political moment predictably ended in failure.

3. Failure of Enforcement

The second means by which reprisals might be botched was through a failure of enforcement. In such cases all proper procedures were followed, and the reprisal was released, but at the enforcement stage, local officials failed to properly carry

19 *"abbas quod predictum breve originale super quo dictus processus fundatur indebite emanavit, cum nullus per legem et consuetudinem regni Anglie teneatur respondere de personali facto alterius"* (the abbot says that the aforesaid original writ upon which he said process is founded was issued improperly, since none by the law and custom of the realm of England is bound to answer for the personal act of another.) Hall, Select Cases, p. LXVI, Nr. 39.

20 Hall, Select Cases, p. LXVI, Nr. 39.

21 Another extremely interesting case which falls outside of our sphere of inquiry but deserves mention here demonstrates that foreigners with a good knowledge of local law could also turn it to their advantage, thereby avoiding a reprisal. An example of such a case from 1280 involved English and Florentine merchants. In the wake of political upheavals in Florence between the Guelf and Ghibelline factions, who were battling for control of the city, property damage had occurred. Hugh la Pape requested of King Edward I that he require the Florentine authorities to reimburse him for the destruction wrought on some of his property there. The king sought this intervention to no avail, so a series of arbitrations were arranged in London with 24 Florentine merchants resident in the city, who appointed three men to help settle the dispute. The Florentine merchants however, eventually refused to offer payment, as they argued "by the custom of England they were not bound to answer in England for anything done in another kingdom. They also denounced the deed of arbitration with the approval of one of the two acting arbitrators." The court agreed with the Florentine merchants, stating that, due to this reason and other errors made during the suit, the original arbitration judgement could not be executed. The Florentines resident in London were thereby spared having to pay restitution for damages wrought upon Hugh la Pape's property in their country of origin. Hall, Select Cases, Nr. 15.

out their duties. Here, four malfunctions were possible. Number one, we have a blunder when the authority in English cases, usually the local bailiff but sometimes also a sheriff, handed over materials which should have been collected for reprisals back to their original owners and let them go freely away. Although how often this was a "mistake" might be questioned. Such events might be put down to human error or perhaps payments made under the table, encouraging officials to look the other way as evidence suggests transpired in some instances.

An example of such a case occurred in 1270 and involved English and Flemish merchants. In that year, Jacob the Slick, merchant of England, claimed he was owed £86 at the Boston Fair by merchants from Brussels for a wool shipment he was never paid for. The Fair Court approved Jacob's claim and right to reprisal; and 23 sacks of wool belonging to the commune of Brussels were taken into custody. The goods were to be held for a year and a day, at the end of which time, if Jacob's debtors had not paid him, he would be permitted to sell the wool as he saw fit in recompense. However, Roger, the bailiff of the fair, ignored this order and delivered the wool sacks instead back to the merchants from Brussels, ignoring the king's writs and denying Jacob justice. The two were later ordered to appear before the King's Bench with security and pledges.[22]

Obviously, the sovereign might seek to punish such behaviour by his representatives, but even in a comparatively centralised kingdom such as England was at the time, the centre often lacked sufficient local power to enforce all it might desire in provincial zones. The second type of enforcement failure was similar to the first, but more obviously contemptable. This type occurred when local officials simply refused to obey the order to collect a reprisal despite a royal writ commanding them to do so.[23] A third variation on this theme would be when officials outright stole the reprisals themselves.[24] The king was far away; and mistakes and the potential for illicit profits were constant companions.

22 Hall, Select Cases, Nr. 7.

23 An example of such a case from 1309 involved English and Flemish merchants. Gilbert of Chesterton, merchant, had received a writ of reprisal from the king and sought to enact it at the annual Boston Fair for £60, owed to him by John of Messines. The Boston Fair Bailiff, Richard de Bernyngham, however refused, in contempt of the king's order, *"in Regis contemptum manifestum"* to hand over wool he had previously collected from Flemish merchants in response to another claim of reprisal. Of the amount sequestered, 6 bales of wool worth £200 remained. The court maintained that Richard ought to hand over the 6 bales to Gilbert. However, first Richard and then Gilbert failed to appear properly in court, Richard was eventually told to hold onto the bales of wool until a proper settlement could be reached. Hall, Select Cases, Nr. 30.

24 Such a case can be seen in that discussed above in section one where Thomas Seaman, the Bailiff of Westminster, absconded with Flemish merchant goods. Authorities routinely sought to curtail such behaviour. The Venetian Great Council for example, ordered banishment for customs officers caught abusing their positions. Tai, Marking Water, pp. 212–213.

The fourth enforcement failure was a bit more complex and involved local officials colluding with foreign merchants to evade the reprisal in return for a bribe. For example, in 1307, Walter le Keu and other merchants of Lincoln, England, claimed that Geoffrey Drew, the former Mayor of King's Lynn, had conspired with merchants from Hainault to avoid a reprisal that had been rightly granted against them. The Lincoln merchants had lost nearly £900 worth of goods when their ship was attacked by men from Zeeland on its way to Brabant. The ship had been hauled to the port of Gerfelt, where the stolen goods were sold off. The Lincoln merchants complained of this outrage to the King of England, who requested justice from the Count of Hainault. Nothing was done, so a letter of reprisal was released. However, *"mandatorum Regis predictorum contemptum et illusionem manifestam"* – in manifest contempt and evasion of the king's mandate, Geoffrey Drew, the Lincoln merchants claimed, took goods from the Hainault merchants, and in return for a kickback, vouched for the goods as his own property. The Lincoln merchants were therefore unable to collect upon their reprisal and so brought suit. Geoffery Drew denied all charges and a jury was called to decide the question.[25]

Here, we see one of the difficulties premodern (and modern) attempts to regulate commerce run into – human ingenuity in the face of possible profit. An order or reprisal forestalled a trade otherwise desired by both parties; and so individuals resorted to illegal activities to accomplish it – smuggling in other words. Reprisals raised transaction costs. Indeed, this was part of their purpose as a means to encourage foreign malfeasants to pay reparations, thereby deterring similar bad behaviour. Thus, due to their very nature, reprisals opened wide the doors for parties to enrich themselves by facilitating trade which had been rendered illegal or highly costly. Where there is property ownership there is the possibility for theft; and where there are limits on trade there will be those who profit by finding ways to breach those limits. In this sense, all reprisals which failed due to a lack of enforcement did so thanks to a quirk of human nature. The case of Geoffery Drew was not an isolated incident. Such forms of graft were likely even more common than the record indicates; as the ones we have knowledge of are only the ones where the parties were caught.[26] This type of failure was thus as predictable as human error and human greed, two factors which have gone down through the ages as a regular feature of commerce and personal interaction.

---

25 Hall, Select Cases, p. LXVI, Nr. 31; Marsden, Law and Custom of the Sea, pp. 56–59.

26 "In the case of John Burton, refusal of the Ostend court to grant a hearing was shown to be the result of the judges' partiality toward one Adrian Clark, burgomaster of the town, into whose hands the pirates had delivered the ships and goods of which John had been robbed." CPR Edward IV, Edward V, and Richard III, 1476–1485, pp. 369–370.

4. Failure due to Protected Status

Moving on to the third type, we have a failure due to protected status. Here, the reprisal was released, properly enforced, and then it was discovered that either the reprisal violated an existing treaty, or the merchant whom officials sought to take goods from had a special status. In the latter case, the merchant held a special charter, protecting him from reprisals, or the merchant held a letter of safe conduct. This last was an extremely common case and while of great benefit to the merchant, was no doubt unendingly frustrating to deal with for the officials and merchants holding the writ of reprisal.

Treaties and agreements made between governments had been a part of the European political landscape since ancient times. During the medieval period, these documents frequently included friendship clauses and trade agreements. Under these headings also fell reprisals, which in stronger treaties were limited in scope or outright abolished between the two signees.

Charters of protection and letters of safe conduct on the other hand were more limited in scope, applying to a particular town, group, or individual, and commonly valid for a restricted timeframe. These documents were renegotiated on a regular basis. They were dependent to some extent upon the current attitude of the ruler, who could negate them at will, although admittedly not without political consequence. Protection against reprisals while in the sovereign's domain was a prized privilege to obtain in such documents. Foreign merchant groups and individual purveyors within the Kingdom of England lobbied hard to have it included in their charters.[27] Those with privileged status arising from charters or individual letters of safe conduct might still be arrested for reprisals, as we shall see, but upon presentation of their documents their goods were returned to them, and they were set at liberty.

Let us look at examples of the two types of protected status, starting with a treaty violation.[28] In 1412, John Penkeston, citizen of Dublin, and John Parys, together

27 English kings offered charters of protection against reprisals to merchants from Cologne, starting in 1157. Merchants from other German towns were granted various privileges over the next century: Gotland (1237), Lübeck (1238), and Hamburg (1252). By 1281 however, these diverse sets of merchants from various German-speaking towns had united into a single Hanse, and thereafter sought always to be acknowledged as a group – the German Hanse of London. Meanwhile, in France and the Low Countries, protections were extended to: Ypres (1216–1272), St Omer (1255), Ghent (1259), Douai (1260), Flanders (1294), and Dinant (1352). Lloyd, England and the German Hanse, pp. 15–22; CCR Henry III: Vol. 1, 1227–1231, p. 456; Koch and Kruisheer, Oorkondenboek van Holland, p. 2928.

28 For further cases involving treaty violations see one from 1388 involving England and Portugal. King Richard II of England ordered the mayor and bailiffs of the town of Dartmouth to set free the men and goods belonging to a recently landed Portuguese ship. They had detained the men and

with other lieges of the King of Ireland, seized a ship loaded with salt and other goods worth 700 marks, belonging to a group of Breton Merchants near Dublin. However, it was determined by the King of England that the reprisal, which had been granted by Thomas Boteller, deputy of the king's son Thomas, Duke of Clarence, Lieutenant of Ireland, was in error, because it violated a treaty between the King of England and the Duke of Brittany. The two Johns were ordered to return the merchandise and make restitution to the Breton merchants immediately.[29]

This case is particularly interesting as it demonstrates that the King of England was not the only individual within the British realms who could legally release a writ of reprisal, as is usually held to be the case, but that he continued to hold sway in larger "international" disputes. Further, it demonstrates that treaties trumped grants of reprisal; and that those who did not do their homework, would be out of luck should the case be brought to court.

As stated above, the second type of protected status was where "individuals" were granted a privilege. As an example: in 1309 Adam, the Clerk of King's Lynn, received a right of reprisal against merchants from the towns of Greifswald, Stralsund, and Lübeck, because his ship, loaded with £300 worth of goods, had been attacked on route to Perth, Scotland, by Henry of Rithinghouse and others from these towns. They had killed many of Adam's crew and highjacked the ship, taking it to Aberdeen and then Stralsund, where they sold the goods and kept the ship. Adam complained, and many letters were sent to the towns, seeking justice. Nothing, however, was done, so the King of England issued him a reprisal. Bailiffs in various ports in England thus took possession of the goods of merchants from the said towns. However, a number of them claimed to be part of the Hanse of London and thus exempt; as their charter included the provision that they were free from reprisals if they were not the principal debtor or a surety. Adam disputed this, maintaining that at the time of the taking, these merchants had not been part of the Hanse of London, having only recently joined, and so should not be exempted. To decide the question, the king summoned a jury of 24 knowledgeable men, 12 expert locals, and 12 foreign merchants, to look into the matter, and it was eventually decided that the said merchants were indeed members of the London Hanse, always had

---

distrained their goods despite the fact that a long-standing treaty between England and Portugal (1373) named them friends and free from reprisals. This was done at the behest of Dionysus, the Infante of Portugal, brother of the current king; CCR Richard II: Vol. 3, 1385–1389, p. 518; a year later, King Richard II of England ordered the Mayor and Bailiffs of Lynn to release cloth owned by Matthew Thurgarde, merchant of Prussia, which had been taken in reprisal for goods which had apparently been taken from English merchants by locals in Prussia. Due to the king's treaty agreement with the Teutonic Order, reprisals were not to be taken against the region's merchants, and the cloth had to be handed back, CCR Richard II: Vol. 3, 1385–1389, p. 574.

29 CPR Henry IV: Vol. 4, 1408–1413, p. 474.

been, indeed still were, and so their goods should be returned.[30] This stands as one among a number of such cases where members of the London Hanse took refuge behind their charter of privilege.[31] Numerous other similar cases could be cited. Some involved large-scale agreements, such as the charter between England and the Hanse, while others involved individual letters of safe conduct.[32]

This case squarely demonstrates the frequent difficulty in collecting a reprisal, given that numerous categories of individuals were exempted from its application. This list included: clergy, ambassadors, students, anyone selling food, and merchants from selected communities who had received a charter of privilege granting them a right of exemption.[33] By the early 13th century this included most of the major trading cities within Britain, the Hanse of London, and selected merchants from communities on the continent.[34] This must have been incredibly frustrating for the traders seeking redress through reprisal; as it meant a good chunk of potential arrivals were off limits, and was a regular cause for reprisals failing in their aims. It was also a highly predictable outcome for many attempts at reprisal collection as merchants had great incentive to work to protect themselves while seeking to ensure others could be held collectively liable. Foreknowledge of ship owners, merchant cargos, and their affiliations would have to some extent informed in advance if an attempt at collection would be successful, but as the record shows, attempts were frequently made to collect from individuals who held special privileges with predictably futile results.

5. Failure Due to Mistaken Jurisdiction or Identity

The fourth type of failure involved a mistaken jurisdiction or identity. Here, officials sought to enforce a reprisal that belonged to another jurisdiction or misidentified

---

30 CCR Richard II: Vol. 3, 1385–1389, p. 2; Hall, Select Cases, p. XCI.

31 Charters protecting all members of the German Hanse from reprisals were granted in 1303, and renewed in 1324, 1327, 1338, and 1340. For more on the importance and usage of this privilege by Hanse merchants in England see: Lloyd, England and the German Hanse, pp. 15–50; Faber, Carta mercatoria, p. 148; Jenks, Carta Mercatoria. pp. 77, 78, 82–83, 84–85.

32 CPR Henry III: Vol. 1, 1216–1225, p. 299; CCR Edward I.: Vol. 1, 1272–1279, p. 306; Hall, Select Cases, Nr. 36.

33 Ballard, British Borough Charters, 1042–1216, pp. LXIV–LXV; Colbert, Retaliations, p. 41.

34 For an example of an individual letter of safe conduct protecting a merchant from reprisals in England see: CPR Henry IV: Vol. 4, 1408–1413, p. 234. For a case demonstrating a failed reprisal where an individual had their goods arrested in London in 1361 and was then released because they were trading edible provisions see: CPR Edward III: Vol. 1, 1327–1330, pp. 169–70; For more general restrictions on reprisals related to individual English towns see: Ballard, British Borough Charters, pp. LXIV–LXV.

those they sought to take reprisals against as coming from the location for which the reprisal was released. The first instance is rather unusual, while the second is the most common type of failure to be found in the records. Let us look more closely at these two categories of events.

Cases of mistaken jurisdiction were uncommon but did occur. They were usually caused by simple ignorance of Englishmen who lacked an understanding of political orderings abroad. For example, in 1309, Wynand Moran of Beverly complained before the king of debts owed him by Alard Papyn and Swether Papyn, together with others from the town of Groningen, who owed Wynand a considerable sum totalling £263. Although Wynand and the king himself had sent numerous letters to the Bishop of Utrecht, complaining about the debts owed, nothing had been done. So a letter of reprisal was released and the bailiff of Kingston upon Hull, undertaking the duty, impounded considerable goods from two merchants from Groningen – Bernard and Ralph. These merchants however, then complained to the king that the sequestration was unjust, as the Bishop of Utrecht was only their spiritual lord, but their temporal lord was the German King. Wynand maintained that this was false, and the case was paused while the question was looked into. The goods of the two Groningen merchants were to be released to them if they could offer sufficient security. Meanwhile, to answer the issue, the Sheriff of London and 24 German merchants from the City were sent for to assist. There, together with a jury of men from England and others from Brabant chosen by the litigants, an oath was sworn by all with the outcome that indeed Groningen was held under the German king, not the Bishop of Utrecht. At this, the court asked Wynand if he could show further proof of his debt claims, and he could not. The case was sent back to the Chancery Court and the goods of Bernard and Ralph returned to them.[35] Such mistaken jurisdictions were frustrating for all concerned but seemingly an inevitable part of doing business in a world where knowledge of more distant lands was at a premium, and borderlines and political ties were in continual flux.

Far more common than mistaken jurisdiction, however, was mistaken identity. Here, foreign merchants were accused of being from an entirely different political entity, one to which a reprisal might be applied. This was an extremely common error, as means of properly identifying individuals was limited, and frequent assumptions were made. To look at a specific case, in 1385, merchants from the Hanse town of Wismar complained to the King of England that their ship, *le Marieknyght*,

35 The case is actually somewhat unclear as to why the Bishop of Utrecht was considered ultimately responsible, rather than the merchants from Groningen, unless the ones mentioned in the case were acting all on his behalf? This remains unclear. Hall, Select Cases, pp. LXVI–LXVII; For further cases involving claims that the Bishop of Utrecht was merely a spiritual and not a temporal overlord, and reprisals were therefore invalid, see: CCR Edward II: Vol. 1, 1307–1313, pp. 68–69,150, 211, 228, 238, 247, 278.

and its goods had been impounded in King's Lynn, due to a reprisal standing against men of Prussia (*Sprucia*). The crew of the *Marieknyght* declared to the local authorities that they were not in fact from Prussia, and the case was referred to the king. Upon review, the king acknowledged that Wismar was in fact not in Prussia and ordered the local bailiffs to release the ship. A year later (1386), the bailiffs succeeded in arresting an actual merchant of Prussia and another the year following.[36]

These sorts of misidentifications are incredibly common in the sources and speak to the difficulties people had during the period before passports, identity papers, and even literacy, in accurately ascertaining from whence an individual came. The identity of an individual was usually assessed by means of an oath, witness testimony, and other documentation, including letters of recommendation, guild affiliation, or personal privileges. The merchant markings applied to goods aboard a ship (lead or wax seals, painted or carved emblems on barrels and chests) might also be used as a means to divine the origin of cargo and individuals; but here mixed ownership could cause even greater confusion.[37] This all the more at a time when such identifications were important in a pluri-legal society; as they determined what legal regime those individuals would be assessed under. The proper execution of a reprisal thus frequently ran into such roadblocks, disrupting trade with little gain for the aggrieved parties. The clear difficulties of identifying the origin and therefore legal regime – liabilities, privileges, and exemptions – under which an individual ought to be considered led to predictable difficulties in executing a reprisal successfully.

6. Failure due to Meritorious Conduct

The final type of failure was one that was occasioned by meritorious conduct. In such rare cases, an individual from the location under reprisal was forgiven, due to their previous good conduct and reputation as a merchant.

For such a case we look to 1326; when King Edward II of England negated an ongoing reprisal against the French town of Besatz [Bazas] by ordering that the goods of John and Gillard de Gout of Besatz, amounting to thirteen tons of wine and one pipe, be released. For, although the king had ordered a reprisal against the merchant of Bazas, John and Gillard had been furnishing the king with wine for years and had "always borne themselves faithful towards the king and his subjects". They had been, in fact, active in England during the most recent times.[38]

---

36 CCR Richard II: Vol. 3, 1385–1389, pp. 2, 24, 55, 358.

37 Tai, Honor, pp. 212–213; Girling, English merchants' marks.

38 The Gascon Rolls Project (1317–1468) GSR C61 32; Calendar of the Close Rolls Edward II: Vol. 3, 1318–1323, p. 618; CPR Edward II: Vol. 5, 1324–1327, p. 312.

In total, King Edward II would pardon four merchants, all hailing from Gascony in Aquitaine, which at the time was disputed territory between the King of England and the King of France.

The larger context for this case was that in 1324 a small war had broken out in the region – the War of Saint-Sardos (August 1324–May 1325), which the French more or less won. The merchants who received the pardon were all from the same town – Bazas, and traded in wine. At least one of them sold wine directly to the King of England.[39] While we have very few details about the case itself, it seems that the reprisal which was granted (which we very sadly not have a record of) covered those areas which were taken under the control of the French king during the war, and specifically not those still loyal to the King of England. Bazas, however, appears to have wound up under the French. This fact, it was argued in the release from reprisal, was not important because the merchants in question, despite being from Bazas, were both full of merit and had been in England rather than in Gascony during the recent upheavals. That these merchants directly supplied the English king with wine cannot be overlooked. It helped to have friends in high places.

To offer further protections and ensure the continued arrival of wine to the royal palace, after the merchants were released from the reprisal, they were then granted additional letters of safe conduct.[40] What is perhaps revealing, is that two other people were granted similar safe conduct letters at the same time. One of them happened to be Bernard Faver, the factor of Raymond Durand, a noble, lawyer, and the King of England's representative in Gascony. It seems likely that the merchants were extremely well-connected, which helped them gain this special grant of favour and release from reprisal. Otherwise, the records only indicate that "the king learns upon trustworthy testimony" that the merchants were meritorious, and no further details were given.[41]

Thus, foreign merchants who had served well in a country might, through the power of their personal reputation and private connections, avoid punishment, while by all rights according to the law they should have received it. Instead, the executive power of the king waived punishment, moulding the regular legal process to suit justice and his own desires in light of individual circumstances. This underscores the power of reputation during the medieval period and its extreme importance in both trade and legal disputes. It further highlights the power of sovereign authority invested in the hands of the king, who might choose to render the spirit of justice when and how he saw fit, however the letter of the law might quibble.

---

39 The Gascon Rolls Project (1317–1468) GSR C61 32.

40 CPR Edward II: Vol 5, 1324–1327, p. 41.

41 Ibid.

7. Conclusion

To conclude, in the examples here discussed, one can see that in a multitude of ways, the inherent design of the system of reprisal opened the way for failures. Yet, such systemic failures were simultaneously by and large predictable. In terms of how frequently such reprisal cases occurred in comparison with regular shipping rates, statistics for this period are difficult to come by. To give a small sense of volumes with the evidence available from a slightly later period, between 1464 and 1465, 51 ships arrived and departed from King's Lynn, 32 of which were foreign with trade value amounting to £2,560.[42] Meanwhile, the number of reprisal cases arising in a particular port in a given year was rarely more than two to three and frequently none at all. Reprisals were thus rare, yet common enough that merchants were certainly aware of the possibility. Claimants were likely also then knowledgeable about the numerous failure points and sought means to avoid them.

Procedural failures, then as now, occurred when paperwork and proof of claim were submitted poorly; or where the powers that be bungled their own procedure. Failures of enforcement where local officials failed to properly carry out their duties were perhaps less predictable in specific instances, but unsurprising in the aggregate. Human error mixed with a dollop of maleficence were to be expected, as merchants always had to be wary. Failures due to protected status were actively sought by foreign merchants, as they worked to acquire charters of privilege and protection which would inoculate them from reprisal claims. These charters and treaty agreements were not hidden; and interested locals might have readily found out about them and planned their trading ventures accordingly. If they feared running into an issue that might lead to a desire to acquire a writ of reprisal, then they could have avoided working with merchants from those protected communities. In this, failures due to mistaken jurisdiction or identity, given the then current state of identification technology, were also only to be expected. This particular fault in the system was systemic, difficult to alter, and thus unavoidable but also therefore highly predictable. When requesting a reprisal, merchants would know that, however frustrating the event might be, it was likely they would encounter this problem during their case's execution. Finally, a failure due to meritorious conduct, on the other hand, was highly unusual and stands as a counterpoint to the rest in that it would have been all but impossible to foresee and protect against. Such events, however, were also exceedingly rare and so stand as the exception that proves the rule that plaintiffs would be able to predict the likelihood of most types of reprisal failures. Yet, for all the many issues inherent to the institution and imposition of reprisals, they remained an important feature of international

---

42 Burwash, English Merchant Shipping, p. 214.

trade, both by sea and on land, into the early modern period. While the many cases presented in this study demonstrate that failure was always an option, in the main, reprisal cases were successful, and claimants eventually received the funds owed to them.

Bibliography

BALLARD, Adolphus (ed.), British Borough Charters, 1042–1216, Cambridge 1913.

BURWASH, Dorothy, English Merchant Shipping: 1460–1540, Toronto 2016.

Calendar of the Close Rolls, Edward I: Vol. 1, 1272–1279, London 1900.

Calendar of the Close Rolls, Edward I: Vol. 5, 1302–1307, London 1908.

Calendar of the Close Rolls, Edward II: Vol. 1, 1307–1313, London 1892.

Calendar of the Close Rolls, Edward II: Vol. 2, 1313–1318, London 1893.

Calendar of the Close Rolls, Edward II: Vol. 3, 1318–1323, London 1895.

Calendar of the Close Rolls, Richard II: Vol. 3, 1385–1389, London 1921.

Calendar of the Patent Rolls, Edward II: Vol. 5, 1324–1327, London 1904.

Calendar of the Patent Rolls, Henry III: Vol. 1, 1216–1225, London 1901.

Calendar of the Close Rolls, Henry III: Vol. 1, 1227–1231, London 1902.

Calendar of the Patent Rolls, Edward III: Vol. 1, 1327–1330, London 1891.

Calendar of the Patent Rolls, Edward IV, Edward V, and Richard Ill: 1476–1485, London 1901.

Calendar of the Patent Rolls, Henry IV: Vol. 4, 1408–1413, London 1909.

CARR-RIEGEL, Leslie, The Right of Reprisal, forthcoming 2026.

CASANOVA, Eugenio, Le rappresaglie nei comuni medievali e specialmente in Firenze, Bologna 1894.

CASSANDRO, Giovanni Italo, Le rappresaglie e il fallimento a Venezia nei secoli 13.–16.: con documenti inediti, Torino 1938.

CHAVAROT, Marie-Claire, La Pratique des Lettres de Marque d'apres les Arrets du Parlement (XIII e-debut XV siecle), in: Bibliothèque de l'École des Chartes (1991), pp. 51–89.

CLARK, Groves, The English Practice with Regard to Reprisals by Private Person, in: American Journal of International Law 27.4 (1933), pp. 694–723.

COLBERT, Evelyn Speyer, Retaliations in international law, New York 1948.

DA LEGNANO, Giovanni, Tractatus De Bello, De Represaliis et De Duello, ed. by James BROWN SCOTT, Washington 1917.

DE UBALDINUS, Baldus, 'Sed omnino' post Cod. 4.12.4, f. 23vb, n. 8 in Dante Fedele, The Medieval Foundations of International Law, Leiden 2021.

DEL VECCIO, Alberto/CASANOVA, Eugenio, Le rappresaglie nei comuni medievali e specialmente in Firenze, Bologna 1894.

DICK, Bryan, Framing "Piracy": Restitution At Sea in the Later Middle Ages, University of Glasgow Dissertation, 2010.

EIGLIER, Joseph, Etude Historique sur le droit de marque ou de represailles a Marseille aux XIIIe et Xve siecles, Marissels 1888.

FABER, Richard, Die Entstehung des Agrarschutzes in England: Ein Versuch. I. Die Carta mercatoria Eduard's I. von 1303, Berlin 1888.

FEDELE, Dante, The Medieval Foundations of International Law. Baldus de Ubaldis (1327–1400), Doctrine and Practice of the Ius Gentium, Leiden 2021.

GIRLING, Frank Aldous, English merchants' marks: a field survey of marks made by merchants and tradesmen in England between 1400 and 1700, in: Transactions of the Historic Society of Lancashire and Cheshire 62 (1901), pp. 1–34.

GREIF, Avner, The fundamental problem of exchange: a research agenda in historical institutional analysis, in: European Review of Economic History 4.3 (2000), pp. 251–284.

HALL, Hubert (ed.), Select Cases Concerning the Law Merchant A.D. 1293–1633, Vol. 2: Central Courts, London 1909.

JENKS, Stuart, Die Carta Mercatoria. Ein 'hansisches' Privileg [The Carta Mercatoria. A 'Hanseatic' Charter], in: Hansische Geschichtsblätter 108 (1990), pp. 45–86.

KOCH, A. C. F./KRUISHEER, J. G., Oorkondenboek van Holland en Zeeland tot 1299 [The Charter Book of Holland and Zeeland until 1299], The Hague 1970.

LLOYD, Terence Henry, Alien Merchants in England in the High Middle Ages, Brighton 1982.

MACCIONI, Elena, La giustizia mercantile a Genova fra XIV e XV secolo: la gestione delle rappresaglie tra normativa, istituzioni politiche e diplomazia, in: Archivio storico italiano 179.2 (2021), pp. 259–308.

MACCIONI, Elena, L'utilizzo della rappresaglia nella Corona d'Aragona alla fine del Trecento: dai registri Marcarum di Giovanni I il Cacciatore, in: Archivio storico italiano 171.2 (2013), pp. 229–272.

MARSDEN, Reginald Godfrey (ed.), Documents Relating to Law and Custom of the Sea: AD 1205–1648, [vol. 1], London 1915.

MARSDEN, Reginald G., Early Prize Jurisdiction and Prize Law in England, in: English Historical Review 24, No. 96 (1909), p. 675–697.

MARTÍN FABREGA, Maria Rosa, Marques i represàlies a la Corona de Aragó al etapa final del regnat de Pere el Cerimoniós (1373–1386), in: Butlletí de la Societat Catalana d'Estudis Històrics (2003), pp. 179–188.

MUTGÉ I VIVES, Josefina, La marca d'en Bernat Melhac, la corona catalano-aragonesa i el Llenguadoc (1327–1336), in: XIIe Congrès d'Histoire de la Couronne d'Aragon, Montpellier 1985, [vol. 1] (1987), pp. 175–188.

NYS, Ernst (ed.), Honoré Bonet, L'arbre des batailles, London 1883.

ODOFREDUS, Codicis Praelectiones lib. IV, 12, London 1550.

ODOFREDUS, Commento al Codice, e precisely al Cod. 4, 12, in: Philippine Christina VAN DEN BRANDE (ed.), Remedium repraesaliarum': The Medieval and Early Modern Practice and Theory of Reprisal within the Just War Doctrine, Grotiana 41.2, Leiden 2020.

PLANITZ, Hans, Studien zur Geschichte des deutschen Arrestprozesses. Der Arrest gegen den fugitivus, in: Zeitschrift der Savigny-Stiftung für Rechtsgeschichte/Germanistische Abteilung 34 (1), pp. 49–140.

RUSSEL, Frederick H., The Just War in the Middle Ages, Cambridge 1975.

SAXOFERRATO, Bartoli a, Omnia Quae Exstant Opera T. 10 Consilia Quaestines Et Tractatus, Venice 1590.

SCHAUBE, Adolf, Handelsgeschichte der Romanischen Volker, Munich 1906.

TAI, Emily Sohmer, Honor Among Thieves: Piracy, Restitution, and Reprisal in Genoa, Venice, and the Crown of Catalonia-Aragon, 1339–1417, Harvard University 1996.

TAI, Emily Sohmer, Marking Water. Piracy and Property in the Premodern West, in: Jerry H. BENTLEY/Renate BRIDENTHAL/Kären WIGEN (eds.), Seascapes. Maritime Histories, Littoral Cultures, and Transoceanic Exchanges, Honolulu 2007, pp. 205–220.

TANZINI, Lorenzo, Le rappresaglie nei comuni italiani del Trecento: il caso fiorentino a confronto, in: Archivio storico italiano 167.2 (620) (2009), pp. 199–252.

TANZINI, Lorenzo, Rappresaglie tra Toscana e Catalogna nei registri Marcarum dell'Archivio della Corona d'Aragona, in: Lorenzo TANZINI/Sergio TOGNETTI (eds.), Mercatura è arte: uomini d'affari toscani, in Europa e nel Mediterraneo tardomedievale, Collana 2012, pp. 205–224.

The Gascon Rolls Project (1317–1468) GSR C61 32, (https://www.gasconrolls.org/edition/calendars/C61_32/document.html#it032_12_01f_438), accessed 09/18/2022.

TIMBAL, Pierre-Clément, Les lettres de marque dans le droit de la France médiévale, in: John GILISSEN (ed.), L' Étranger, [vol. 2], Bruxelles 1958.

WILLARD, Charity Cannon/WILLARD, Sumner (eds.), Book of Deeds of Arms and of Chivalry by Christine de Pizan, Philadelphia 2010.

WINK, Jurriaan/SICKING, Louis, Reprisal and diplomacy: conflict resolution within the context of Anglo-Dutch commercial relations c1300–c1415, in: Comparative Legal History 5.1 (2017), pp. 53–71.

Matthias Berlandi

Cities as Centres of Innovation?

Institutional Change in Late Medieval Scotland

1. The Cultural Transformation Hypothesis: The Decline of Feudalism

It is almost commonplace that cities, and especially the merchants within these cities, were innovative and the motor transforming the feudal economic system into a capitalist one. This picture is widely accepted, since the two opposing dominant schools of thinking fostered this view. Marxists, on the one hand, needed the urban merchants as having been successful to fit their teleological model of political and social development. Early capitalists had to be more successful and innovative than their feudal counterparts because these were the key attributes of capitalism Marx identified for its success, "*Alles Ständische und Stehende verdampft*" (All that is solid melts into air).[1] The Liberal tradition on the other hand, started from the same premise, explaining the need for the further empowerment of the captains of industry at the expense of old aristocratic families in the 19th century.

Taking a closer look at the social and economic realities in the cities, it becomes clear that not "*Alles Ständische*" (all that is solid) was melted. Inequality and thus unfreedom persisted within the urban communities. It is even hard to spot significant differences between successful merchant and noble families regarding their economic decision-making, as Stollberg-Rilinger has pointed out.[2] What is additionally opposing the narrative of economic success of the cities is the fact that, for example, most German cities were bankrupt at the end of the Holy Roman Empire in 1806.[3]

Still, the intuition that urban societies developed a market-based economy earlier than other places, is of course manifoldly confirmed. This development is attributable, among other reasons, to the fact that many cities developed around marketplaces, and the correspondingly denser population enabled the emergence of demand in the first place. However, there are numerous additional reasons cited by research for the market economy's innovative capacity within urban societies. Oscar Gelderblom has convincingly shown how the competition between cities for attracting trade led to the development of institutions and the legal framework

---

1 Marx and Engels, Selected Works, [vol. 1], p. 111.
2 Stollberg-Rilinger, Barbara, Gut Vor Ehre, p. 45.
3 Nipperdey, Deutsche Geschichte, p. 20.

for free market access.[4] Maarten Prak and Jan Luiten van Zanden also regard urbanisation and commercialisation as the prime factors inspiring economic growth in the late medieval Netherlands.[5] Other potential factors where scrutinised by van Zanden in *The Long Road to the Industrial Revolution: The European Economy in a Global Perspective 1000–1800*. Despite controversial discussion,[6] this study convincingly justified the assumption that there were preconditions for the "Great Divergence"[7] dating back to the Middle Ages.[8]

The fact that even renowned experts in the field struggle to agree on factors for the socio-economic changes of the Late Middle Ages is a clear indication that the transformation of the nature of economic activity and the organisation of society during the period has been insufficiently researched. Institutional historical research with a focus on economic and social history has focused on the Middle Ages in order to explain the Great Divergence. In this process, the outcome of this development, namely a market-based, bourgeois society, was projected back onto the period, and the precursors of this development were posited as its causes. This focus however has obscured the view of causes that lie beyond urban societies. Instead of looking at regions, which followed a more or less successful economic path from 1400 to 1800, which is apparently the case for the Low Countries, but definitely not for Tudor England,[9] it might be also worthwhile to include regions where there were extraordinarily low rates of urbanisation and simultaneously extensive institutional development. In this most-different-case design, hypotheses

---

4 GELDERBLOM, Cities of Commerce, p. 3.

5 PRAK and VAN ZANDEN, Pioneers of capitalism, pp. 66 f.

6 Some scholars hold the European Marriage Pattern to be less relevant for European economic development than VAN ZANDEN, see: SZOŁTYSEK and ZUBER-GOLDSTEIN, Historical Family Systems; Attila MELEGH, Historical Demography, pp. 309 f.; a quantitative refutation can be found in: DENNISON and OGILVIE, European Marriage. An overemphasis on Protestantism can also be traced in the underlying hypothesis: HAJNAL, European Marriage, p. 132: "A full explanation of the background of European marriage patterns would probably lead into such topics as the rise of capitalism and the protestant ethic", and also VAN ZANDEN's conclusions end up referring to the significance of protestant ethics, see: VAN ZANDEN, Long Road, p. 292.

7 The Great Divergence refers to the period, beginning in the late 18th century, during which Western Europe and parts of North America experienced rapid industrialisation, economic growth, and technological advancement, leading to a significant economic gap between these regions and much of the rest of the world, see e. g.: ALLEN, Great Divergence.

8 "the accumulation of useful knowledge in Western Europe the centuries before 1800 was closely linked to the growth of human capital that began during the Middle Ages […] due to improved institutions, new technologies, Protestantism and the growing demand for skilled labour in the […] cities. […] in fact, this made it possible to successfully 'predict' the performance of countries during the 'Great Divergence' in the nineteenth century", VAN ZANDEN, Long Road, p. 292.

9 "However, the Tudor monarchy of Henry VIII, supposedly about the time the Little Divergence began, seems not to fit the model", see: HARLEY, Review, p. 795.

that have been developed based on the more urbanised contexts of the Low Countries and England could be tested. Furthermore, factors contributing to institutional development, but originating from rural aristocratic societies rather than urban societies, could be identified. One of these regions, with low urbanisation but high institutional development, can be found in Scotland. The Kingdom of Scotland underwent a substantial institutional transformation during the Late Middle Ages while maintaining a low urbanisation rate of an estimated 10% while having an overall population of about between 350,000 and 400,000.[10] The findings from Scotland may indicate that urbanisation was perhaps a necessary, but insufficient, explanation for the transition from a feudal to a market economy. In studying this phenomenon in other regions, Bas van Bavel has emphasised that institutional change can be initiated through various developments, of which urbanisation constitutes only one.[11] The observation presented here also indicates that a planned collective action with the aim to foster institutional change or market access was also not a necessary condition. Institutional change could also be the unintentional result of an attempt to solve practical problems with a short-term perspective.

Looking to the model for institutional change developed by Avner Greif, Paul Milgrom, and Barry R. Weingast, they have suggested that this change was enforced by – in their example – the bargaining power of merchants who collectively imposed trade bans on the ruler who would not provide basic security and legal property rights.[12] Since the common explanations seem not to be suitable for the Scottish example, it is even more interesting to ask what might have been the common structural problem that motivated institutional change in all these cases?

In this chapter, I will examine the prospects of this explanation for the institutional change in the world of the lower nobility in later medieval Scotland. Firstly, I will give an overview of the current explanations for the rapid change in Scottish writing culture in the fifteenth century. In a second step, I will propose a fresh interpretation of a type of document, called "bonds", which emerged during this period. The emergence of the different forms of this type can be explained by institutional changes in the Scottish legal system.[13]

---

10 This constitutes a rough estimate for the fifteenth century, see: ORAM, Worst disaster, p. 231.

11 VAN BAVEL, Invisible Hand, p. 23 f.

12 GREIF, MILGROM and WEINGAST, Coordination.

13 The argument was further developed by Daron Acemoglu and James Robinson and synthesised into a grand thesis: sustained economic growth is primarily due to inclusive institutions, while extractive institutions concentrate resources in the hands of the elite. However, it remains unclear how and under what conditions extractive institutions transform into inclusive ones. The ideas brought together here could contribute to this question, see: ACEMOGLOU and ROBINSON, Why Nations Fail, pp. 31 and 35.

Finally, I will argue that the institutional transformations under discussion opened up novel legal pathways, facilitating the effective enforcement of ownership rights. Such advancements, in turn, significantly improved predictability for individual participants within the economic framework, thereby reducing the uncertainty and risk associated with investment. Remarkably, evidence suggests that these developments extended opportunities to non-noble actors, allowing them to participate in land market investments previously dominated by the aristocracy. This broadening of investment opportunities indirectly stimulated a surge in capital deployment across the land market. Consequently, these collective changes played a crucial role in bolstering Scotland's economic infrastructure and contributed substantially to its economic resurgence in the fifteenth century.

2. Current Explanations for the Change in Scottish Writing Culture

In order to understand the Scottish research discussion, and the current interpretation of innovations in the manuscript culture of the Scottish nobility in the fifteenth century, it is necessary to look at the development of Scottish medieval studies.

The discipline emancipated itself from English-dominated British studies in the 1970s. Previously, it was claimed that Scotland was a barbaric country with low centralisation and constitutional development, which only became civilised after the Union of the Crowns in 1603.[14] Starting from the 1950s a new Scottish nationalism arose, which reached universities in the 1970s and drew a very different picture of the time of Scottish independence. Alexander Grant and Jenny Wormald were mainly concerned with contesting that Scotland had had no development deficit in comparison with England, and that Scottish society had actually been peaceful and not as violent as the Unionist perspective had claimed.

Michael Brown has labelled a particular counter-narrative within Scottish historiography as the "New Orthodoxy".[15] This perspective reinterprets the events of the 15th century, casting them within a specific interpretative framework that often overlooks or minimises internal discord. Such a re-evaluation has reached a point where segments of Scottish academic research seemingly negate the existence of severe internal conflicts entirely. This stance is maintained despite historical incidents that starkly suggest otherwise; notably the assassination of James I in 1437 and the battlefield death of James III in 1488, as well as the killing of an heir apparent, the Duke of Rothesay, in 1402, all of whom fell victim to violence perpetrated by their

14 Robinson, Development, p. 35.

15 Brown, Scotland Tamed.

own subjects. This contradiction highlights the complexity and contentiousness of interpreting Scotland's historical narrative.[16]

It is not surprising that the current interpretation of the Scottish *"bonds of manrent"* also echoes this research bias. A bodn of manrent according to Wormald's definition, was a special private contract in which a laird bound himself to a greater lord without receiving any material reward for his offered services. He only could expect the vague promise of "good lordship" in return. In the Scottish sources, good lordship was translated into "maintenance".

According to Wormald, this development was explicable by two variables. Firstly, the classic feudal contract would have lost its function to create meaningful, personal relationships between both parties, especially because of subinfeudation. This is why Scottish society would have preferred a way to create 'true' loyalty between the parties involved and thereby ensure reliable behaviour of both parties in the future. Secondly, through the web of personal loyalties which tied together all parts of Scottish society, conflicts would have been internalised before they escalated into violence. This is why Scottish society was pacified without a comparable constitutional development as can be observed in England.[17]

Scottish research at this point has acknowledged that there are some inconsistencies in Wormald's interpretation. As Stephen Boardman has pointed out, bonds of manrent appeared before and after conflicts without having a measurable effect on the course of that conflict. This hints at the fact that bonds of manrent might not have been an independent variable in the explanation of conflicts.[18] Grant meanwhile, has shown that over 80% of Scottish charters were still occupied with land and economic interests, and that a cultural shift to a mere exchange of loyalty promises seems unlikely.[19] Furthermore, if bonds of manrent would have had such a pacifying influence on society, we would expect to see indicators hinting at the internalisation of conflicts, but the opposite is the case. For example, Scottish kings issued remissions in cases of manslaughter to settle a conflict after compensation payments had been paid to the victim's family.[20] In the reign of James III, when the

---

16 Grant, Crown and Nobility, p. 35: "disputes are natural within all societies [...] the main characteristics of Scotland's domestic politics were peace and stability", see: Grant, Independence and Nationhood, pp. 196 f.

17 Wormald, Taming the magnates; Wormald, Laisser-fair government; Wormald, Bloodfeud, p. 57; Duncan argued that feudal land transactions were not apt to create hierarchical relationships within the Scottish nobility because of wide spreading subinfeudation, see for a summary of this position: Grant, Service and Tenure, p. 156; Oram, Gold into lead. This led to Wormald's idea that the *"bond of manrent"* were necessary to recreate the alleged loss of hierarchy in Scottish society, see: Wormald, Lords and Men, pp. 11–13, 46–51.

18 Boardman, Politics, p. 55.

19 Grant, Service, pp. 175 f.

20 Grant, Murder Will Out, p. 214.

bonds of manrent was already a well-established instrument, royal revenues from remissions skyrocketed and even Parliament urged the king to abstain from issuing remissions and settle the widespread conflicts in a more substantial way.[21] This seems to indicate that the latter half of the fifteenth century was struck by severe internal conflicts and the bonds of manrent did not contribute to pacifying Scottish society.

Further difficulties arise when analysing the formula of the bonds of manrent. There is no plausible explanation for the fact that there is a significant difference between the terms "manrent" and "homage", even though both terms were frequently used interchangeably. An example can be found in a charter of the 5th Earl of Douglas to Thomas Kirkpatrick dating from 1428. The Earl demands *"litteras homagii et retinencie"* of Kirkpatrick, which equals the formula in Scots *"lettres, becummys men of speciale retinew"*.[22] The equivalent use of both terms was also observed by Wormald in the corpus of the Maxwell family charters. The Maxwells lived in the Anglo-Scottish borderlands and used both terms as synonyms. Sometimes the lord's promise of good lordship was expressed in a separate document that is denoted as a bond of maintenance.[23] This makes it even harder to support the assumption that there was a fundamental cultural change in the way the band of loyalty had been understood in the fifteenth century. Obviously, there was a quid pro quo in issuing bonds of manrent, although the reward for loyalty was sometimes not mentioned within the *bond* itself but in supplemental documents like a bond of obligation or a bond of maintenance.

This already signifies a part of the problem. There were many different bonds in Scotland, but current research is focused primarily on the bond of manrent, which played, in comparison to other types of bonds, only a minor part in the institutional transformation of Scotland in the fifteenth century. In order to understand this transformation, the functions of the various bonds first have to be analysed and categorised accordingly. Then, the observed changes in the manuscript culture of the Scottish nobility have to be interpreted in the framework of the institutional innovations of the fifteenth century. This in turn will reveal why the bonds of obligation in particular were growing in popularity.

---

21 TA i, 1–12; APS ii, p. 207 f., 122; cf. the complaints in Parliament from 1473 and 1478: RPS, 1473/7/10; RPS, 1478/6/80; Sutton, Hector Boethius, Appendix chapter 51, 63; MacDougall assessed the royal income from remissions at £686 13s 4d, see: MacDougall, James III, pp. 136 f., 142.

22 NRS AD1/41; see also: Fraser, The Douglas Book, [vol. iii], no. 82.

23 Wormald, Lords and Men, pp. 14 f., 20, 24.

3. Functions of the Various Scottish *Bonds* and their Links to Legal Institutions

Since cultural studies explanations for the bonds of manrent have proven to be unsustainable, a functional explanation is proposed here. To start, the contexts and legal function of the various bonds will be examined. To determine the functions of the Scottish bonds, a corpus of 157 documents classified as bonds located in the Scottish Record Office was utilised. There are three primary classes of bonds in this corpus: (1) bonds of manrent, (2) bonds of friendship and (3) bonds of obligation.[24]

The much-discussed bonds of manrent are the second largest group in the sample presented here, encompassing only 31 out of 157 documents. In contrast to previous assumptions, the bonds of manrent do mention economic compensations for services offered by the hierarchically lesser noble. These compensations could be as simple as the lord's acceptance to build a house for his man, as Alexander Forbes promised to Alexander Ogisstoun on 10 May 1430.[25] In another case, Archibald Campbell, Earl of Argyll, promised Patrick Blackadder to appoint him as his *baillie* in Culros, if he agreed to enter into a bond of manrent with him.[26] This promise was made in a separate notarial instrument and was not articulated in the *"bond"* itself, which casts of course a different light on those bonds, as we do not have the context for how recompense was arranged. The correlating document might be lost or simply not found yet, since service and maintenance were not always mentioned in the same document.

Other bonds of manrent do not discuss economic compensations since they were already tied to existing loyalty relations. In 1442, Hugh Fraser of Lovat entered into a bond of manrent with Alexander MacDonald, Lord of the Isles.[27] Current interpretations of this bond neglect to consider the fact that there was already a loyalty relationship between Fraser of Lovat and the Lord of the Isles that had existed since at least 1336 onwards.[28] Since the Fraser of Lovat family had an extensive network of kin and possessions in Moray, Aberdeenshire, and Angus, MacDonald probably felt the need to ensure Hugh Fraser's loyalty due to possible

24 I will here only summarise my findings published in: Berlandi, Birthplace.

25 NRS RH1/2/196; this example is open to debate. Since the document is a modern transcript, it is uncertain whether the receipt for building the house has something to do with the previously issued bond of manrent. For the sake of this argument it is assumed that both documents were bound together for a reason.

26 NRS GD15/153.

27 Hugh Fraser enfeoffed the Lord of the Isles with land that had previously been taken from him. This unusual act suggests a loyalty relationship that existed even before the Lovat-Ross bond, see: Munro and Munro, Acts of the Lords, pp. 57 f.

28 Ibid., pp. 38 f.

double obligations. Interestingly enough, Fraser excluded the Earl of Moray and the king from his oath of loyalty. The bonds of manrent did not therefore create a form of 'true' loyalty, in fact, it did the contrary; the bond limited Fraser's loyalty towards the Lord of the Isles to certain terms. This was necessary due to the complexity of family networks and double loyalties created by concentration tendencies within the feudal economy.

Bonds of manrent could not only specify the terms of pledged loyalty but could also define services to be provided by an individual. Bonds which demanded administrational duties had of course to specify the lands and properties that should be administered.[29] Services could be formulated very concretely as in the already cited bond of Ogisstoun and Forbes, wherein the former promised to serve his lord with three horses, and after the death of his father with six.[30] In this regard, bonds offered the possibility for specialisation, which was not feasible within the formula of the classical feudal contract, which demanded services in an unspecific way. Bonds of manrent instead offered a possibility to employ specialists for specific tasks and thus optimise lordship with limited resources.

Still, there are 20 bonds in the sample which do not mention any form of compensation for swearing manrent, because these documents do not supplement or substitute feudal contracts but were issued in the context of dynastical structures. Bonds of manrent between nobles from the same family network dealt with the challenges of the joint administration of certain lands or how to deal with the families' landed property in phases of tutelage or in cases of inheritance.

Examples might be found in the various bonds of the Douglas of Dalkeith family. In 1468 James Douglas, 1st Earl of Morton, and Hugh Douglas of Granton exchanged bonds, as is noted in a notarial instrument. Hugh Douglas gave up all his claims to Dalkeith, while James Douglas promised to protect Hugh's lands of Moffat in Annandale and Borgue in Kirkcudbright.[31] A superficial interpretation of this document would indicate that Hugh Douglas had offered manrent without any material reward, despite the vague promise of protection of his lands. However, there was also a family relation between both men. Hugh and James Douglas were cousins. James Douglas, Lord of Dalkeith, the father of the mentioned 1st Earl of Morton, had been declared incapable of administering his lands. For that reason, James Gifford of Sheriff Hall, the brother-in-law of the mentioned 1st Earl of Morton,

29 Fraser, Scots of Buccleuch, vol. ii, pp. 70–72; also quoted in: Boardman, Politics, p. 114.

30 NRS GD52/1077.

31 NRS GD150/142; Boardman, Politics, pp. 104 f., also mentioned this inheritance plan, while providing a different interpretation. Boardman assumes a feud between both branches of the family, while the documents can also be interpreted as an indicator of cooperation between both branches as was argued here.

had been assigned as administrator of Dalkeith.[32] Henry Douglas, the said Lord's brother, had then claimed the right to administer Dalkeith for himself, and started a blood feud against James Gifford. In 1442, King James II declared Dalkeith to be forfeit, since the feud between Henry Douglas and James Gifford had caused so many casualties amongst the king's vassals.[33] Nevertheless, Henry Douglas kept the title Lord of Dalkeith, and from 1452 onwards, Henry and his brother James issued charters as Lords of Dalkeith, keeping the title jointly.[34] Hence, the bond between both cousins, namely Hugh Douglas and the 1st Earl of Morton, was agreed upon to restore the intended property situation and make sure that Henry would not lay claim to Dalkeith because of the former responsibilities of his father. In return, the 1st Earl of Morton bound himself to respect Hugh's share of the family property by protecting exactly those lands which were given to Henry Douglas according to the inheritance plan of both men's grandfather, James, Lord of Dalkeith.[35]

The oath of manrent in this context only signified that Hugh Douglas was ready to submit to the new head of the family, the 1st Earl of Morton, and would abstain from challenging the property situation as it had been intended in James Douglas's inheritance plan. This is why it was not necessary to transfer lands in return for manrent, because technically, the exchange of bonds in this case only repaved the pre-existing power structure within the Douglas of Dalkeith family, thus clearing an inchoate situation, with multiple family members laying claim to the title, Lord of Dalkeith.

Many other bonds of manrent, which do not agree upon material reward, were issued in the context of cases of inheritance within family networks. In order to assure the land was kept within their own circles, to ensure smooth power transitions, and at times to acknowledge the dynastic power structure and subdue side branches of the family, heads of these family networks demanded written oaths of loyalty from the heir during their lifetime.[36]

As Boardman rightly pointed out, bonds of manrent did not pacify conflicts. What can be added to this assessment is that they can be interpreted as feudal or family contracts to deal with complicated situations. Still, their success was dependent on the willingness of the involved parties to reach a conclusion with respect to their mutual interests.

---

32 Mort. Reg. ii, pp. 207–209.

33 NRS RH6/307.

34 RMS ii, no. 515.

35 The charter of confirmation by James III has survived. It was issued after the exchange of the *"bonds"* on 3 September 1473. A manipulation of the inheritance plan cannot be ruled out for that reason, see: RMS ii, no. 1138.

36 See e. g.: the *"bond of manrent"* between the branches of the Kennedys of Dunure, NRS GD25/1/59; for more examples see: Berlandi, Birthplace, pp. 282–284.

Still, there was a type of bond that explicitly dealt with conflict resolution – the bond of friendship. Numerically, within the sample from the Scottish Record Office, the bond of friendship is the smallest class, only encompassing seven documents. Fortunately, there is a quite convincing explanation for why this is the case given by the Scottish chronicler Walter Bower.[37] After a detailed narration of some infamous feuds in the year 1413, Bower reminds his audience of just behaviour in such cases by describing the usual form to end violent conflicts,

> *I say this therefore because when in former days men were enemies, they swore to a perpetual and friendly bond as a means of making peace, and as a confirmation of this they participated in the communion of the sacrament of Christ's body.*[38]

In most cases, the bond of friendship was a written record of mutual oaths of peace exchanged in front of an altar which had the practical value of preventing the use of violence in a conflict without solving it. Both parties agreed to pursue their contradicting interests at court and not on the battlefield. This is why Bower condemned the murder of Patrick Graham, Earl of Strathearn, by John Drummond of Concraig, as most despicable, since he had issued a bond of friendship beforehand:

> *They had made an alliance of perpetual friendship at the time of the marriage of the said knight to the earl's sister, and what is worse they had together taken communion in the breaking of the sacrament of the body of Christ to strengthen the indissoluble character of their bond.*[39]

There are a number of other legal documents demanding the issue of bonds of friendship between feuding parties to end their violent conflicts. In 1492 Robert, Lord Lyle, ordered as *justiciar* that "*letteris of slanis and friendship, according to the use in siclike thingis*" should be issued in the context of a major feud.[40] Other legal disputes, like the one conducted by Robert, Lord Fleming, and Gilbert Kennedy over the lands of Kirkintilloch, assessed at 40 merks in the Barony of Lenzie, used

---

37 Boardman, Politics, p. 76 on the basis of various "*bonds of friendship*" comes to a similar conclusion.

38 Watt (ed.), Walter Bower, pp. 82 f.: "*Hec propterea dico quia cum ante inimici extiterant, in composicione pacis perpetuam juraverunt amicabilem fidelitatem, et ad confirmacionem huius participaverunt de communione sacramenti corporis Christi.*"

39 Watt (ed.), Walter Bower, pp. 82 f.: "*quod ante hoc erant per literas et juramenta assecurati, et de perpetua amicicia confederati data in matrimonium dicto militi sorore dicti comitis ac de fraccione sacramentis corporis Christi ad firmiorem federis indissolubilitatem ad invicem communicati.*"

40 Atholl Muniments, Blair Castle, Blair Atholl, 1/1/22; quoted after Boardman, Politics, p. 76.

the bond of friendship in this sense. Both parties agreed to cease using violence until the case could be settled by a court.[41]

Some rare examples even anticipate a potential conflict. Robert Erskine lost lucrative incomes as Keeper of Edinburgh and Stirling Castle and Sheriff of Edinburgh, which were transferred to various princes in 1372, 1373, and 1374. Despite these losses, the Erskines were an important local family in Fife, and Robert's second born son, Robert, Earl of Fife and Menteith, agreed upon a bond of friendship with Robert Erskine to ensure him that the royal family would not transfer even more property of his to their own members. At the same time, Erskine promised not to pose an obstacle to Robert Stewart's lordship in Fife.[42]

By far the largest category of bonds in the here presented sample are the bonds of obligation, with 85 individual documents. These encompass a variety of different topics, ranging from leasing land (to pay a debt) to marriage treaties, from ensuring free passage areas protected by castles to addenda to already existing treaties. However, they all have in common that they monetise everything and also contain a *poenatio* to be paid in money. A usual component of the formula of such a bond was that the agreement should be conducted *"in the most sickerest form"*.[43] This might already hint at the fact that the increasing use of the bonds in the fifteenth century had some institutional foundation and it is worthwhile to note that most of the bonds openly and clearly dealt with economic interests.

Still, three main functions of the bonds of obligation can be observed: (1) marriage contracts took this form or were accompanied by them, (2) the sale of land or its exchange was also conducted this way, and (3) "bonds of obligation accompanied all kinds of agreement providing additional securities and financial penalties.

An example of a marriage contract in the form of a bonds of obligation can be found in the contract concluded between Hugh, Lord Montgomery, and Archibald Edmonston of Duntreath, who agreed upon the terms of their children's alliance, John Montgomery and Bessie Edmonston.[44] Sometimes, the negotiations were centred on the question of how the bride should be provided with a *"witum"* in case of an early death of her bridegroom. This also influenced the amount of the dowry. John Ramsay of Colluthi was ready to pay a comparably high dowry of 300

41 Although this attempt ultimately failed, because Fleming accused Kennedy of preventing him from having the opportunity to speak before the *justiciar* in person. The feud escalated into violence in 1466, see: Boardman, Politics, pp. 80–84.

42 NRS GD124/7/1; Erskine also lost the barony of Ednam and the guardianship of Margaret Barclay, the heiress to lands in Brechin, see: Boardman, Early Stewart Kings, pp. 43, 52–54.

43 Variation: *"sall mak sekerneß in the sekrest form that can be dimisyt"*, see: NRS GD16/41/3.

44 NRS GD3/2/1/16.

merks, under the condition that his daughter would be provided with lands worth 20 merks p.a. by the family of her future husband.[45]

High dowries had to be paid in instalments over decades and a marriage had huge implications for inheritance and the future land claims of both families involved. This is why marriage agreements were, at times, flanked by complex bonds of obligation to cope with all implications to the property involved.

This was also true for other occasions when land was transferred from one noble family to another. In March of 1393, William Keith exchanged three minor lordships near Petindreich for annual payments from Dunnottar, which the family intended to make their principal residence. Although an early example, the exchange of these lands was conducted by a bond of obligation.[46]

Later, when the use of the bonds of obligation had become widespread, it served as an additional security to flank all kinds of agreements. Archibald Campbell, Earl of Argyle, for example in a bond of obligation promised Patrick Blackadder to appoint him as his *baillie* in Culros Abbey, if he would swear manrent to him.[47] The Scottish Record Office classifies this as a bond of manrent, which is not quite accurate, since the contractors only agreed upon issuing a bond of manrent in the future.

To understand why the bonds of obligation became so popular in the land transactions of the Scottish nobility, it is necessary to describe the greatest flaws of the judicial system of the time. Since Scotland was a decentralised kingdom, local jurisdiction could easily be monopolised by local elites. For nobles outside these local power structures, even if they were powerful magnates, it was highly attractive to circumvent local jurisdiction and let their case be settled by Parliament. Such was the case even when such individuals held only a small lordship at some distance from their home, where their influence was lessened. This was especially possible in those cases in which the claimant could prove that the defendant had broken an oath given beforehand. This is what the bonds of obligation provided – a proof that both parties had agreed upon a certain matter. The rights and claims of both parties supported by this could then be negotiated, even before Parliament, giving these agreements the highest form of legal backing.

The feasibility of this development can be attributed to a multifaceted institutional transformation in fifteenth-century Scotland, a topic that has only recently begun to garner attention. Until now, this shift had not been linked to the evolution of Scottish writing culture and the predominance of the bond in the majority of legal transactions. By taking a closer look at this institutional development, it becomes

45 NRS GD430/170.

46 HMC Report iii, p. 405.

47 NRS GD15/153.

obvious that these changes had a far greater impact on Scottish diplomatic charters than any alleged cultural change within noble society.

4. The Institutional Transformation of the Kingdom of Scotland in the Fifteenth Century

The advantages of using bonds alongside classical feudal contracts are obvious. They allowed for adjusting feudal relationships, they gave the opportunity to hire experts for administrative or military tasks by paying money or offering a form of provision, without the necessity to give out land to one person with limited expertise. They also could solve the problem of divided loyalties and could organise smooth transitions within a family network in cases of inheritance. Still, most of these problems existed throughout the Middle Ages and the question remains, why these bonds (especially the bonds of obligation) were more frequently used only in the fifteenth century. Part of the explanation might be found in the massive institutional transformation of the Kingdom of Scotland in this period, the extent of which becomes apparent in the case *Wemyss v Forbes* from 1543.

Patrick Wemyss of Pittencrieff proceeded against Arthur Forbes of Reres due to a dispute concerning lands in Fife. The complaint was heard at the session, the court of the Lords of Council, which was located at the Tolbooth in Edinburgh. Forbes' lawyer, Master Thomas Marjoribanks, argued that the Session was not the right place to hear the complaint, since according to Scottish common law only the *justiciar* could decide matters concerning land property, which has to be issued by the *brieve of right*. He supported his argument with "*quhilk ground rycht of auld aucht be act of parliament.*"[48]

Although Marjoribanks' argument was completely in line with written Scottish common law and various acts of parliament dating from the fifteenth century, the Lords of Council dismissed his concerns. They declared themselves competent to decide the matter since the brieve of right had fallen out of use, and the Lords of Session had already decided like matters repeatedly in the past:

> *The lords of [session] notwithstanding found themselves to be competent judges in this matter. For they had been in the habit of calling such matters before them over many years, and of giving many interlocutors on the point – as in the cause of the Lord of Sanquhar and*

48 Murray and Dolezalek, Sinclair's Practicks, cn. 308. In modern English: "which rightful ground, of old, ought [or rightfully belongs] by act of parliament […]" (Translation by the Author); the following sources were also quoted by Simpson and Wilson, Scottish Legal History, pp. 108 ff.

> *the cause of a certain Pringle of Torsonce and of diverse others. Also, the lords made this decision because the brieve of right has not been used in this realm for many years.*[49]

The Scottish legal system during the later Middle Ages was decentralised. Lords in the localities could easily monopolise jurisdictions leading to constant complaints against incompetent and/or biased judges. Additionally, increasing literacy made it easier for claimants to review and assess legal proceedings. Since records were kept privately, courts had no ready access to all necessary documents involved in the case. Withholding documents could delay or even influence court decisions damaging claimants, who started issuing complaints at the only place where false judgments could be revised – this was Parliament.

In 1450, the number of complaints exceeded every capacity of the Scottish Parliament, which started to form institutions to deal with the complex matter of reviewing judgements from local courts. The first court was basically a committee formed by Parliament, which elected legal experts from its own ranks as Lord Auditors. The second court was formed by advisors chosen by the Crown. These were usually men sitting in the daily council and were called Lords of Council for that reason. Sources refer to both courts as the Sessions. The two sessions (parliamentary and council) eventually were transformed into the Court of Session in 1532, which was Scotland's first centralised and institutionalised highest court.[50]

This development was by no means linear. Local powerholders feared losing their grip on local land transactions and used their weight in Parliament to make sure that the competencies of the Sessions remained limited. As late as 1497, Parliament enforced local jurisdiction and at the same time issued the *Education Act*, which forced all holders of hereditary judicial offices to provide for educating their heirs in common law.[51] The success of these regulations was limited. The hereditary Sheriff of Bute was still illiterate in 1549.[52] Competences of the Sessions were also restricted by the *"fee and heritage rule"*, which prohibited cases concerning landed property under feudal law and heritage to be heard at the Sessions, thus strengthening local powerholders and the local jurisdiction.

---

49 Murray and Dolezalek, Sinclair's Practicks, cn. 308; in modern English: "such as they were in various years in the habit of calling such matters before them and various such interlocutors given, as in the case of the Lord of Sanquhar and in the case of a certain Pringill of Torsounis and various others, and also because the brief of right is (nor has it) not yet been used for many years in this realm." (Translation by the Author).

50 For a detailed description of this development see: Simpson and Wilson: Scottish Legal History, pp. 108–111; Godfrey, Civil Justice.

51 RPS 1487/10/14; Simpson and Wilson: Scottish Legal History, pp. 117 f.

52 HMC xi, app. 6, p. 24, translated in: Simpson and Wilson: Scottish Legal History, pp. 109 f.

This was of course only a Pyrrhic victory for the old legal system. As soon as there was an alternative forum that could revise false judgements of local courts, people found a way to bring their complaints before this. Arthur Forbes, for example, brought action against the Wemyss brothers. He sued them for *spulzie* of oxen and corns, since robbery of goods could be heard at the Sessions.[53] Still the complaint was dismissed:

> *because the landis that the said gudis was takin of is clamyt fee and heretage be baith the said parties and the questioun of the richt dependis apoun heritage.*[54]

This decision of the *Session* implies that *Wemyss v Forbes* was actually a dispute concerning the ownership of the land. Since Forbes could not make his complaint heard by suing the Wemyss brothers for property rights, he argued to have been robbed of the income the land produced.

Regarding the institutional setup of the Scottish legal system, it is no surprise that bonds and especially bonds of obligation were used more frequently. A common feature of these private contracts was that they all agreed upon compensation payments in case of a breach of the agreement. Disregarding the underlying conflict, the Sessions usually decided according to the agreements made in a bond of obligation. This is why these regularly claimed that the agreements made were conducted *"in the most sickerest form"* – which meant that it enabled both parties to issue complaints at the Sessions with a good chance of success.

The Scottish economy struggled during the fourteenth century. After the 1st and 2nd Wars of Independence (1296–1328 and 1332–1357), huge parts of Scotland were devastated. Things became worse when several pandemics, the Black Death among others, hit Scotland from the 1350s onwards. Added to this, the Dantean Anomaly made it impossible to grow grain in several parts of the Scottish Highlands.[55] Agricultural output broke down, incomes decreased, and the struggle among the nobility for the remaining valuable land became more desperate and bloodier. This is also the reason why local jurisdictions were so susceptible to corruption, finally resulting in claimants enforcing institutional change by flooding Parliament with complaints.

---

53 RPS 1485/3/3, the *"lords of council"* should only exercise these competences for a certain period; for the term spulzie, see: "Spulyie v., n.", Dictionary of the Scots Language, 2004. Scottish Language Dictionaries Ltd., http://www.dsl.ac.uk/entry/snd/spulyie, accessed 09/10/2023.

54 MacQueen, Common Law, p. 227; In modern English: "because the lands from which the said goods were taken are claimed as fee and heritage by both of the said parties, and the question of the right depends upon [a matter of] heritage." (Translation by the Author).

55 Oram, Climate Change, p. 228; Mayhew, Scotland, pp. 109 f.

The new form of central jurisdiction conducted by the Sessions gave rise to a new contract form, the bond of obligation, which, in essence, made all kinds of land transactions legally binding and much safer in comparison to the old system. The written form, and the possibility to archive these documents, would safeguard landed property even beyond the lifetime of individuals. It is obvious that the new types of documents emerging in the second half of the fifteenth century can be interpreted as a response to the institutional changes within the Scottish legal system. This is a much more plausible explanation than the older claim that the bonds were a sign of the degeneration of the feudal system. Although it is true that the observed institutional changes are only one puzzle piece within the transformation of the Scottish feudal system into a market-oriented one, these were obviously not initiated by innovative merchants improving their economic performance, but by the elites trying to adapt the feudal system to new challenges. At the heart of these challenges lay the necessity to increase Crown revenues, due to the specific environmental, military, and economic challenges Scotland faced in the fifteenth century. There were violent conflicts within Scottish society, there was also a very destructive asymmetrical war with England in the 1480s, a civil war in 1483, and another in 1488. Rapid inflation, higher military costs due to the invention of artillery, and the climatic condition in the aftermath of the Dantean Anomaly all combined to hinder the Scottish economy.

5. Economic Consequences of the Institutional Change in Late Medieval Scotland

The introduction of new legal regulations and the establishment of a central court system in fifteenth-century Scotland enabled landowners to bypass potentially biased local jurisdictions. This legal pluralism enhanced the security of land property rights, promising more objective enforcement in theory, and thus enhancing the predictability of investments on the land market. These modifications also facilitated access to the land market, significantly impacting not only landowners, but also the broader social and economic landscape. The reduction of uncertainty and risk associated with investments was particularly noteworthy. Furthermore, this legal evolution opened up investment opportunities to non-noble actors, challenging the aristocracy's previous dominance in land market investment.

The gradually growing independence of the land market from local noble networks offered the opportunity for burghers and merchants to buy into the land market. Coincidently, this started to happen precisely in the middle of the fifteenth century, when the central jurisdiction started to stabilise as an institutionalised body. A quite interesting example is the Menzie family, burghers from Aberdeen, who bought land in the earldom of Kincardineshire, south of Aberdeen. At that time, the Arbuthnot family as baillies of the Keith family still controlled access to the land market in Kincardineshire. They were the ones who had to conduct the legal procedures to introduce the new owner to the land. They also mediated minor conflicts and were present as witnesses in most land transactions within the shire.

In 1443, Gilbert Menzie, a citizen of Aberdeen, faced difficulties recovering a loan of £160 from a minor noble landowner of the region, John Touch. Consequently, the estates of Ochterdtoun and Portertoun, valued at £8, were leased to Gilbert Menzie. The proceeds from this arrangement were intended to settle the debt.[56] However, there was apparently disagreement as to whether the rents were actually paid to the Menzies. Moreover, during the long lease period, the Touch family attempted to reclaim the estates on grounds of inheritance, but these efforts failed due to the strong documentation of the case, including various obligations. In 1453, the Lords of Council confirmed the Menzies' rights to the contested lands.[57]

Nevertheless, the Menzie family faced difficulties enforcing their monetary claims against the Touch family. In 1483, Alexander Menzie transferred the relevant lands to Robert Arbuthnot and had to promise in another bond of obligation to issue a letter of reversion in favour of Walter Touch, declaring the debts settled.[58] However, the land did not revert to the Touches. Robert Arbuthnot was installed into these lands with an instrument of sasine.[59] It is conceivable that Robert Arbuthnot took over the remaining debts of the Touches and took possession of the lands for that, or it was a sale of the Menzies' land use rights because they had difficulties collecting the rents from the lands. Mathematically, the debts should have been paid off by the annual nominal rental income of £8 by 1463. This could indicate that the Menzies, although the royal judiciary had repeatedly recognised their debt title, had difficulties enforcing their claims.

This example illustrates how the increasing professionalisation of the central courts provided upwardly mobile families like the Menzies with the opportunity to assert themselves legally against local noble networks. However, in practice, these local networks still played a significant role. In 1461, the Touch family attempted to secure the support of Andrew Ogilby through a bond of manrent, in which Ogilby promised, in return, to assume the Touch family's debts and redeem the estates.[60] This effort, however, appears to have been unsuccessful. Ultimately, the estates ended up in the possession of the regionally influential Arbuthnot family, suggesting that the Menzies struggled to exercise lordship in Kincardine without the support of such prominent families.

---

56 Ms. 2764 2 34.

57 Ms. 2764 2 42.

58 Ms. 2764 2 69.

59 Ms. 2764 2 70.

60 Menzie iii, no. 47; I am grateful to Sebastian Weil for hinting at this bond of manrent.

Obviously, the opening of the land market also opened the opportunity to shake up local power structures. That said, some of the local families such as the Arbuthnots still had a huge amount of informal power, which they used to dominate the region. Although it was also in the interest of local families to gain legal protection for their properties, which is why they supported the new institution of the "*Sessions*" in the first place, the new central jurisdiction also resulted in unintended consequences, against which they sought to protect themselves. Among these unwanted consequences was the possibility for newcomers to buy into the ranks of the lower nobility. The first consequence of the establishment of a central jurisdiction was therefore an emergence of social mobility resulting in new social conflicts.

There were also economic consequences. After an economic breakdown, due to the 1st and 2nd War of Independence (1296–1328 and 1332–1357), the Black Death, and the harsh climatic conditions brought on by the Dantean Anomaly, as well as a several other pandemics in the fourteenth and the beginning of the fifteenth century, the Scottish economy shrank significantly. Although data is scarce, the assessment of lands for taxation purposes to pay the ransom of King David II in 1366, known as the Verus Valor, revealed a 40% decrease in land values in comparison to prewar assessment of these lands.[61]

To the surprise of many scholars, land assessments started to rise again at the end of the fifteenth century. This new boom can be found in retours to the exchequer. These retours were issued on the occasion of new enfeoffments due to inheritance, marriage, or the sale of land, assessing the involved land in the Old and New Extent. This land valuation formed the basis for the Crown's primary source of revenue, the right to demand Ward and Relief following the death of a vassal. Ward consisted of semi-annual rents to be paid until the new landowner was installed into the affected lordship or reached the age of majority. Relief described the annual income of a land which was to be paid to the Crown as an entry payment. The installation procedure required that the heir demand a brieve of succession from the Crown, which then instructed the sheriff to determine which lands, rents, or similar were to be inherited and, simultaneously, whether the applicant was entitled to inherit and of legal age. This allowed for the final assessment of the annual value of the concerned lands and the feudal services associated with them. Additionally, it was necessary to ascertain who was the direct feudal lord of the lands in question and whether certain lands claimed by the heir were already in the possession of other landowners, and if so, on what legal basis the current ownership stood. The outcome of this investigation was thereafter returned to the royal chancery.[62]

---

61 RPS, 1424/25; RPS, 1424/26.

62 Thomson, Inquisitionum Ad Capellam, p. 1.

Unfortunately, Oliver Cromwell had the records of the sheriff courts shipped to London and then sent back to Edinburgh. On their way home in 1661, one of the ships sank in the North Sea, resulting in a catastrophic loss of Scottish land assessments conducted at the Sheriff Courts.[63] The retours only survive in a sixteenth-century copy containing documents dating from 1544 onwards. The retours contain an Old Extent and a New Extent, whereas the Old Extent is not dated. A comparison with rare fifteenth-century rentals suggests that the Old Extent refers to fifteenth-century land assessments. For ecclesiastical lands, the situation is more complicated, since they were not assessed in terms of Ward and Relief and thus there were no Old Extent reports, leaving only sixteenth-century extent.[64]

Scottish research is, for various reasons, highly suspicious of the Old Extent, mainly because many cases show a significant increase in land assessment. The New Extent is regularly four times the Old Extent, a fact which has even led some scholars to believe that there was no economic growth, but only a numerical increase of land assessments due to the heavy inflation during the fifteenth century.

This argument seems to be less convincing since official documents most of the time used currencies of account, which then had to be translated into a certain amount of coins during the payment. More of the inflated coins, with a lower quota of silver, simply had to be paid. Still, there is no way to be absolutely certain, since the retours do not render their numbers officially in a currency of account. This said, even if we assumed the increase in land assessments to be explicable partly in terms of inflation, the numbers are still too high.

The most serious coinage crisis was the Black Money crisis under James III in 1480–1482, which got its name because of the black copper farthings coined at a nominal silver value not backed by the material of the coin. While the Crown covered its expenses with inflationary copper coins, James III hoarded coins made of precious metals. It is estimated that by doing so, James III earned £29,000, almost twice as much as the regular annual income of the Crown, which amounted to approximately £16,000.[65] After substantial protests, the copper coins were denounced, but the financial damage was done. It contributed to the violent uprising against James III leading to his death in the aftermath of the battle of Sauchiburn in 1488.[66]

Contemporaries already mention the lack of bullion as the main reason for the rising prices (and hence also land values). However, the coinage was probably not the only cause driving this. According to Blakeway, the metal content of Scottish coins dropped by 87% between 1456 and 1603, thus far exceeding the European

63 Grant, Service, p. 145.

64 Berlandi, Birthplace, pp. 80–84.

65 ER ix, pp. 286, 480; MacDougall, James III, p. 186.

66 APS ii, p. 204; MacDougall, James III, p. 347.

average of 51%.[67] A more recent study of Scotland's economic performance made by Ball, is inconclusive about the reasons for Scottish inflation in the fifteenth century, while generally agreeing that it was very high. Ball also pointed out that probably 50% of the coinage circulating in Scottland was actually English coins.[68]

If inflation driven by devalued coinage was the prime cause for the increase in land values, we should observe a much higher increase in retours than is the case. Also, given the variety of coins circulating in Scotland, it is more plausible to interpret the extents given in the retours as factored in currencies of account.

Therefore, it seems plausible to assume that land values did increase during the fifteenth century, but as yet, there are few convincing explanations for this. First and foremost, there is a demographic argument: The Scottish population recovered during the fifteenth century and therefore labour costs decreased, labour became more available, and the demand for agricultural products grew. Increased demand and lower labour costs may have resulted in a rising value of arable land. However, we do not in fact have any evidence that agricultural productivity grew in the fifteenth century. Contrarywise, contemporary accounts of foreign diplomats paint the state of Scottish agriculture only in the darkest colours.[69] We also have no data which would confirm the hypothesis of a slow recovery of the Scottish population in the fifteenth century, although this is highly plausible given the demographic patterns in other European countries, which showed a steady increase after the catastrophic events of the fourteenth century.

Another explanation refers to the freeing of the bondmen as reason for the increase in agricultural productivity. Accordingly, during the fifteenth century, landowners started to lease their lands to 'free' tenants instead of having their lands cultivated by serfs, the so-called bondmen. It is assumed that tenants with inheritable or long-running tenancies (20 years or longer), in comparison to bondmen without property rights or tenants with shorter tenancies, had a higher incentive to invest in the land on which they were working. This idea was also brought up by contemporaries, who interpreted one-year tenancies as especially harmful for economic development. Yet, looking at the tenancy contracts of the monastery Cupar Angus reveals that in 1516 still 418 tenancy contracts were limited to only three years. This indicates that long-running tenancies were not widespread, thus the incentive for tenants to invest in their leased lands remained low.[70]

67 Blakeway, Sixteenth-century Price Rise, pp. 181, 183.

68 Ball, Role of Demographic, pp. 85, 93–94, 136, and especially p. 345: "For Scotland, the evidence of mint output driving prices was difficult to discern."

69 Brown, Early Travellers, pp. 39, 44: "*The corn is very good, but they do not produce as much as they might, because they do not cultivate the land.*"

70 Constable and Mackay, Greater Britain, pp. 30 f.; Sanderson, Scottish Rural Society, p. 46.

There are a couple of problems with this assessment. First of all, the freeing of the serfs was still far from complete around 1500. In many charters, the words describing serfdom/bondage are still frequently used and the rare ecclesiastical account books, which give some insight into the social structure of their workforce, still show a mixture of 'free' tenants and unfree bondmen. What is especially intriguing is that 'free' tenants had to pay remarkably higher rents than bondmen, who however, also had to render unpaid services of all kinds to the monastery. The higher rent of tenants obviously compensated for the loss of unpaid labour resulting in very similar standards of living for 'free' and unfree. This is why we should not overinterpret the legal status of the 'free', as long as economically speaking, tenants were still completely dependent on their lords.[71] They even had to bear higher risks and could fall into absolute poverty easily as soon as they could not pay the high rents, e. g. following a sudden loss of workforce within the farmer's family by illness or death, which usually also resulted in painful additional payments to the landlord.

The potential threat to economic existence posed by these burdensome death duties can be illustrated by the speech of a poor man in David Lindsay's play, "A Satire of the Three Estates". In a dialogue with the personified Diligence, a poor man describes the circumstances of his impoverishment. He recounts that after having worked hard to support his elderly father and mother, the death duties eventually deprived him of his economic foundation. Furthermore, shortly thereafter, his wife died, making the burden of the duties unbearable. As a result, he was forced to start begging in order to sustain himself.[72]

Still, for wealthier peasants, the new system offered a chance for social mobility. They had the financial resources to lease greater chunks of land and sub-lease it to smaller tenants. This, allegedly, lead to the emergence of a new social group in the Scottish Highlands, the so-called tacksmen, who grew some wealth out of sub-leasing small pieces of land, 'tacks', to sub-tenants, who had to meet the high rents demanded by the land owner and probably had to pay also for the profits of the tacksmen. Unfortunately, this cannot be assessed in detail, since to my knowledge, there is no surviving example of such a sub-leasing contract. Although there was a degree of social mobility, the majority of 'free' tenants likely found themselves in a less favourable position compared to their unfree counterparts.[73]

Although it is hard to tell where the money should have come from that enabled the ordinary tenant to invest in his land, the possibility and the incentives the new system offered might have had an effect, but this should again, not be overestimated.

---

71 Kießling, Konsersmann and Troßbach, Agrargeschichte, [vol. 1].

72 "*Now haue I tald ȝow the blak veritie/How I am brocht into this miserie*", see: Lindsay, Ane Satyre, pp. 150 f.; see also pp. 479 f.

73 Coldingham Corresp., pp. lxxxv–civ; McKerral, The Tacksman, pp. 15–17.

Maybe the new legal securities also gave the landowners more incentive to develop their property. In comparison to the other social groups, the lower nobility also had some financial resources to invest. Although there is as little evidence for this explanation as for the others, I would argue it is still more plausible. The lower nobility could also control who worked on their land, and for which purpose the land was used. This enabled them to shift production to less labour-intensive pasturage or fishery, which would increase productivity even without heavy investment policies. These strategies are well documented in England, when landlords had to adapt to the demographic crisis of the fourteenth century, and there is no reason to believe that Scottish landowners would not have used the same techniques.[74] Of all the ideas circulating so far, it seems most plausible to explain the increase in land values with higher incentives for tenants and landlords to invest in their properties. Landlords had more institutionalised property rights since they had more financial resources and more possibilities to develop their estates, and this might have been more important than the possible incentives mentioned above.

Further evidence for this can be found in the rentals of the Douglas of Dalkeith family. Only a few rental books of the lay nobility have survived, and the Dalkeith rental book, which was written at the beginning of the fifteenth century, before the development of the legal system had begun, in most cases shows the same land values as the Old Extent, which can be found in the early modern retours.[75] Although there are not enough rentals to make a proper quantitative analysis, this more or less anecdotal evidence still indicates that the increase in land values took place in the second half of the fifteenth century, when property rights enjoyed additional protection by a newly emerging central jurisdiction.

6. Was Scotland's Development Unique?

It seems odd. Scotland had an urbanisation rate of only 10% in the Late Middle Ages, there lived at best 400,000 people dispersed over roughly 30,081 square miles. At the beginning of the fifteenth century the Scottish economy was more or less shattered, and due to inflation, there was a steady decrease in real wages observable throughout the fifteenth century. At the same time, we can detect an opening of the land market, which presumably attracted investment resulting in the growth of land values during the same period.

In Scotland, this development was obviously not triggered by a process of urbanisation or commercialisation. Instead, it can be seen as an unintended consequence

74 Behringer, Kulturgeschichte des Klimas, pp. 139 f.

75 Kelham, Bases of Magnatil Power, pp. 312–316.

of solving practical problems of the nobility's land transactions. These attempts ultimately led to significant legal and institutional reforms, including the introduction of new legal statutes, and the establishment of a centralised court system. This in turn led to an increase in legal pluralism. These reforms allowed landowners to circumvent local judicial systems, which were often perceived as biased. This critical development not only enhanced the security and enforceability of land property rights but also aimed at a more impartial application of the law. As a result, a more accessible and open land market emerged, profoundly affecting both landowners and the wider societal and economic realms.

These institutional changes created new legal avenues that effectively protected property rights, thereby fostering a more predictable and stable environment for economic participants. This predictability was crucial in reducing the risks and uncertainties traditionally associated with investments, making the market more attractive to a broader array of investors. Notably, these legal advancements extended investment possibilities to include non-aristocratic players, thereby disrupting the traditional monopoly held by the nobility over land investments. This shift towards a more inclusive model of land ownership catalysed a significant increase in investment across the land market, facilitating broader economic engagement and investment.[76]

Judging from the more common examples forwarded to explain institutional change, this is surprising. Other regions in Europe experiencing an opening of factor markets, such as for capital, labour, or land, like the Low Countries or Northern Italy, had experienced a phase of urbanisation and commodification before this opening, which was not the case in Scotland.[77] Besides that, neither the Crown nor the nobility seems to have been consistent or foresighted about what they were doing. This is indicated by the resistance burgher families met when they tried to benefit from the new legal securities offered for land properties. In the case of the Menzie family, local authorities consistently ignored the sentences of the newly emerging central court. At the same time, noble families tried to benefit from the new court, striving to circumvent possibly biased local courts. For the Crown, it was just a matter of coping with the complaints issued at Parliament and delegating the pleas to a group of experts. There was also no coordinated collective action by the lower nobility. They just issued complaints about the dysfunctional local jurisdiction.

---

76 This development may be analogous to the risk management strategies employed by actors in late medieval marine insurance, though adapted for the terrestrial market. Broadly speaking, new legal forms were devised to render economic transactions more secure and predictable, cf. SCHELLER, Experten des Risikos.

77 VAN BAVEL already questioned the direct connection between urbanisation and the opening of factor markets, see: VAN BAVEL, Manors and Markets, p. 163–167.

So, was the common element which motivated the actions of the Scottish kings and their subjects solely a financial one? The lower nobility's and also the tenants' interest was to enjoy their leased or owned land with greater predictability and legal security. The Scottish kings wanted to reduce administrative costs to extract taxation from their subjects by outsourcing complaints to the Council and Parliamentary Sessions. The magnates wanted to stay in charge of local jurisdiction, which had enabled them to dominate land transactions for a century. This is why they lobbied for the fee and heritage rule, which was intended to prevent the newly emerging courts from interfering in most of the judicial cases concerning land.

The necessary conditions for the Scottish development can be found in the increase of literacy among the nobility and the increased use of notarial instruments in business activities. This can be seen in the increased use of bonds accounts, but also by the existence of grammar schools in most of Scotland's greater cities.[78] Greater literacy enabled parties to archive contracts and remember specifics such as expiration dates or certain conditions in leasing contracts. It opened the possibility for various economic activities including the permanent or temporary transfer of land property. Besides this, notaries, in some cases, also acted as advocates, which indicates that the judicial system, as such, had also started to become more specialised and run by experts, while the older system had relied on oral traditions and the memory of aldermen in a region.[79]

With these findings, this investigation aligns itself with a broader sequence of outcomes within the realm of recent institutional history. Evidently, an enhancement in the efficiency of institutional performance took place in fifteenth-century Scotland. A transformation which was not characterised by urbanisation and commercialisation, contrary to initial conjectures by Norton and earlier institutional history.[80] This leads to further research queries, such as: what were the causal factors driving this shift? Plausibly, this could be attributed to the intrinsic logic of feudalism rather than to allegedly already existing proto-capitalist structures. Conceivably, a development may have unfolded within smaller circles of experts, serving as a functional elite, exerting influence over the institutional trajectory of the fifteenth century.[81] In

78 Although a significant campaign to increase literacy is only traceable in Scotland after the Reformation. In the eighteenth century, Scotland's universities would count amongst the best in Europe, see: Houston, Literacy, pp. 39 and 88 f.

79 The significance of experts and expert knowledge in the development of economic institutions was recently examined at the Göttingen Graduate School's program on "Expert Cultures of the 12th to 16th Centuries", see: Füssel, Knäble and Elsemann, Wissen und Wirtschaft.

80 van Zanden, Long Road, p. 17: "Typically, new contributions to this literature have suggested that institutions that were previously considered 'conservative' and 'inefficient' [...] were surprisingly efficient, if the functioning of these institutions were examined more closely."

81 This has preliminarily been considered by Knäble, albeit with a methodological focus on cultural studies, as referenced in: Knäble, Einleitung, pp. 18 f.

any event, the Scottish example presented here contributes to the identification of new interconnections in the evolution of institutions, prompting future endeavours to similarly encompass so-called structurally weak regions characterised by limited urbanisation.

Bibliography

ACEMOGLOU, Daron/ROBINSON, James A., Why Nations Fail. The Origins of Power, Prosperity, and Poverty, New York 2013.

ALLEN, Robert C., The Great Divergence in European Wages and Prices from the Middle Ages to the First World War, in: Explorations in Economic History 38 (2001), pp. 411–447.

BALL, Katherine, The Role of Demographic and Monetary Factors in the Late Medieval Economies of England, Scotland and the Southern Low Countries (1351–1530), Oxford 2018.

BEHRINGER, Wolfgang, Kulturgeschichte des Klimas. Von der Eiszeit bis zur globalen Erwärmung, München 2007.

BERLANDI, Matthias, Birthplace of Valour. Landvergabe und Gewaltbewältigung im schottischen Spätmittelalter, Affalterbach 2024.

BLAKEWAY, Amy, The sixteenth-century price rise: new evidence from Scotland, 1500–85, in: Economic History Review 68,1 (2015), pp. 167–190.

BOARDMAN, Stephen, Politics and the Feud in Late Mediaeval Scotland, St Andrews 1989 (unprinted).

BOARDMAN, Stephen, The Early Stewart Kings Robert II and Robert III 1371–1406, East Linton ^{2}1996.

BROWN, Michael, Scotland Tamed? Kings and Magnates in Late Medieval Scotland: a review of recent work, in: The Innes Review, vol. XLV, 2 (1994), pp. 120–146.

BROWN, Peter Hume (ed.), Early Travellers to Scotland, Edinburgh 1891.

CONSTABLE, Archibald/MACKAY, Aeneas J. G (eds.), A History of Greater Britain As Well England As Scotland, compiled from the Ancient Authorities by John Major 1521, Scottish History Society, 10, Edinburgh 1892.

DENNISON, Tracy/OGILVIE, Sheilagh, Does the European Marriage Pattern Explain Economic Growth?, in: The Journal of Economic History 74, No. 3 (2014), pp. 651–693.

DICKSON, T./PAUL, James Balfour (eds.), Accounts of the Lord High Treasurer Scotland, Edinburgh 1877–1916.

FRASER, William (ed.), The Douglas Book, 3 vols., Edinburgh 1885.

FRASER, William (ed.), The Scots of Buccleuch, 2 vols., Edinburgh 1878.

FÜSSEL, Marian/KNÄBLE, Philip/ELSEMANN, Nina (eds.), Wissen und Wirtschaft. Expertenkulturen und Märkte vom 13. bis 18. Jahrhundert, Göttingen 2017.

GELDERBLOM, Oscar, Cities of Commerce: The Institutional Foundations of International Trade in the Low Countries, 1250–1650, Princeton 2013.

Godfrey, A. Mark, Civil Justice in Renaissance Scotland, Leiden 2009.
Grant, Alexander, Crown and Nobility 1450–1509, London 1976.
Grant, Alexander, Independence and Nationhood, Edinburgh 1984.
Grant, Alexander, Murder Will Out: Kingship, Kinship and Killing in Medieval Scotland, in: Steve Boardman/ Julian Goodare (eds.), Kings, Lords and Men in Scotland and Britain, 1300–1625. Essays in Honour of Jenny Wormald, Edinburgh 2014, pp. 193–226.
Grant, Alexander, Service and Tenure in late medieval Scotland, 1314–1475, in: Anne Curry/Elizabeth Matthew (eds.), Concepts and Patterns of Service in the Later Middle Ages, Woodbridge 2000, pp. 145–179.
Greif, Avner/Milgrom, Paul/Weingast, Barry R., Coordination, Commitment, and Enforcement: The Case of the Merchant Guild, in: The Journal of Political Economy vol. 102, 4 (1994), pp. 745–776.
Hajnal, John, European Marriage Patterns in Perspective. The uniqueness of the European pattern, in: David Viktor Glass/David Edward Charles Eversley (eds.), Population in History. Essays in Historical Demography, Volume I: General and Great Britain, Chicago 1965, pp. 101–143.
Harley, Knick, Review: Jan Luiten van Zanden, The Long Road to the Industrial Revolution: the European Economy in Global Perspective, in: Economic History Review vol. 65, 2 (2012), pp. 794–795.
Historical Manuscripts Commission. Eleventh Report Appendix Part VI. The Manuscripts Of The Duke Of Hamilton, K.T., London 1887.
Historical Manuscripts Commission. Third Report Of The Royal Commission On Historical Manuscripts, London 1872.
Houston, Robert Allan, Literacy in Early Modern Europe, London 2002.
Innes, Cosmo (ed.), Registrum Honoris de Morton. A Series of Ancient Charters of The Earldom of Morton with Other Original Papers in Two Volumes, Edinburgh 1853.
Kelham, Charles Adrian, Bases of Magnatil Power in Later Fifteenth-Century Scotland, Edinburgh 1986.
Kießling, Rolf/Konsersmann, Frank/Werner Troßbach, Grundzüge der Agrargeschichte, [vol. 1], Göttingen 2016.
Knäble, Philip, Einleitung, in: Marian Füssel/Philip Knäble/Nina Elsemann (eds.), Wissen und Wirtschaft. Expertenkulturen und Märkte vom 13. bis 18. Jahrhundert, Göttingen 2017, pp. 9–32.
Lindsay, David, Ane Satyre of the trie Estats, in Commendation of Vertew and Vitvperation of Vyce, Edinburgh 1602.
MacDougall, Norman, James III, Edinburgh 2009.
MacIntosh, Gillian H./Mann, Alastair J./Tanner, Roland J. (eds.), The Records of the Parliaments of Scotland to 1707, St Andrews, https://www.rps.ac.uk/, accessed 06/30/2025.
MacQueen, Hector L., Common Law and Feudal Society in Medieval Scotland, Edinburgh 1993.
Marx, Karl/Engels, Friedrich, Selected Works in three volumes, [vol. 1], Moscow 1973.

MAYHEW, Nicolas J., Scotland: Economy and Society, in: S. H. RIGBY (ed.), A Companion to Britain in the Later Middle Ages, Oxford 2009, pp. 107–124.

McKERRAL, Andrew, The Tacksman and His Holding in the South-West Highlands, in: SHR 26 vol. 101,1 (1947), pp. 10–25.

MELEGH, Attila, Historical Demography, in: D. MISHKOVA/B. TRENCSÉNYI (eds.), European regions and boundaries: A conceptual history, New York 2017, pp. 300–321.

MUNRO, J./MUNRO, R. W. (eds.), The Acts of the Lords of the Isles, Edinburgh 1986.

MURRAY/DOLEZALEK (eds.), Sinclair's Practicks. Law reports Edinburgh, Court of Session, 1540–1549, 2000, https://home.uni-leipzig.de/jurarom/scotland/dat/sinclair.html, accessed 06/30/2025.

NICHOLS, J., The Correspondence, Inventories, Account Rolls and Law Proceedings of the Priory of Coldingham, Edinburgh 1841.

NIPPERDEY, Thomas, Deutsche Geschichte 1800–1866. Bürgerwelt und starker Staat, München 1983.

ORAM, Richard D., 'The worst disaster suffered by the people of Scotland in recorded history': climate change, dearth and pathogens in the long 14th century, in: ProcSocAntiqScot 144 (2014), pp. 223–244.

ORAM, Richard D., Gold into lead? The state of Early medieval Scottish history, in: Terry BROTHERSTONE/David DITCHBURN (eds.): Freedom and Authority, East Linton 2000, pp. 32–43.

PAUL, James Balfour (ed.), Registrum Magni Sigilli Regum Scotorum. The Register of the Great Seal of Scotland A.D. 1424–1513, [vol. 2], Edinburgh 1882.

PRAK, Marten/VAN ZANDEN, Jan Luiten, Pioneers of capitalism: The Netherlands 1000–1800, Princeton 2023.

Howard ROBINSON, The Development of the British Empire, Cambridge 1922.

SANDERSON, Margaret H.B., Scottish Rural Society in the Sixteenth Century, Edinburgh 1982.

SCHELLER, Benjamin, Experten des Risikos. Informationsmanagement und Wissensproduktion bei den Akteuren der spätmittelalterlichen Seeversicherung, in: Marian FÜSSEL/Philip KNÄBLE/Nina ELSEMANN (eds.), Wissen und Wirtschaft. Expertenkulturen und Märkte vom 13. bis 18. Jahrhundert, Göttingen 2017, pp. 55–78.

SIMPSON, Andrew R. C./WILSON, Adelyn L.M., Scottish Legal History. Volume 1: 1000–1707, Aberdeen 2017.

STOLLBERG-RILINGER, Barbara, Gut vor Ehre oder Ehre vor Gut? Zur sozialen Distinktion zwischen Adels- und Kaufmannsstand in der Ständeliteratur der Frühen Neuzeit, in: Johannes BURKHARDT, Augsburger Handelshäuser im Wandel des historischen Urteils, Berlin 2015, pp. 31–45.

STUART, John/BURNETT, George (eds.), Rotuli Scaccarii Regum Scotorum. The Exchequer Rolls of Scotland, 23 vols., Edinburgh 1878–1908.

SUTTON, Dana F. (ed.), Hector Boethius, Scotorum Historia (1575 Version), Irvine 2010, http://www. philological.bham.ac.uk/boece/, accessed 06/14/2020.

Szołtysek, Mikołaj/Zuber-Goldstein, Barbara, Historical Family Systems and the Great European Divide: The Invention of the Slavic East, in: Demográfia 52, 2 (2009), pp. 5–47.

Thomson, Thomas/Innes, Cosmo (eds.): Acts of the Parliaments of Scotland, 12 vols., Edinburgh 1814–1875.

Thomson, Thomas, (ed.): Inquisitionum Ad Capellam Domini Regis Retornatarum Quae in Publicis Archivis Scotiae Adhuc Servantur, Abbreviatio, 3 vols., London 1840.

van Bavel, Bas, Manors and Markets: Economy and Society in the Low Countries 500–1600, Oxford 2010.

van Bavel, Bas, The Invisible Hand? How Market Economies Have Emerged and Declined Since AD 500, Oxford 2016.

van Zanden, Jan Luiten, The Long Road to the Industrial Revolution: The European Economy in a Global Perspective, 1000–1800, Leiden 2009.

Watt, Donald E.R. (ed.) et al., Walter Bower, Scotichronicon, vol. viii., Edinburgh 1987–1998.

Wormald, Jenny, Bloodfeud, Kindred and Government in Early Modern Scotland, in: Past & Present 87 (1980), pp. 54–97.

Wormald, Jenny, Lords and Men, Edinburgh 1985.

Wormald, Jenny, Laisser-fair government and local patronage: Scotland, sixteenth to Early seventeenth century, in: Maczak Antoni (ed.), Klientelsysteme in Europa der Frühen Neuzeit, München 1988, pp. 159–175.

Wormald, Jenny, Taming the magnates?, in: Gordon Menzies (ed.), The Scottish nation. A History of the Scots from Independence to Union, London 1972, pp. 46–59.

Archival Sources

Atholl Muniments, Blair Castle, Blair Atholl, 1/1/22

Aberdeen Special Collections

Ms. 2764 2 34

Ms. 2764 2 42

Ms. 2764 2 69

Ms. 2764 2 70

National Records of Scotland

NRS AD1/41

NRS RH1/2/196

NRS GD15/153

NRS GD52/1077

NRS GD150/142

NRS RH6/307

NRS GD16/41/3

NRS GD3/2/1/16

NRS GD430/170

NRS GD15/153

NRS GD25/1/59
NRS GD124/7/1

Anna Maleszka

Merchants and Law in Anglo-Norman Towns in Plantagenet Ireland[1]

1. Introduction

On 20 September 1220, the King of England, Henry III, was petitioned by his subjects – *"mercatorum veniencium in Hybernia et proborum hominum Dubline"* (merchants frequenting Ireland and the good men of Dublin) – with a problem that had evidently been growing for some time. They explained that the royal officials, led by the justiciar, made *"indebitis exactionibus"* (undue exactions) and claimed *"prisas cum per mutua vinorum et pannorum, victualium et rerum suarum aliarum"* (prisage (from Old French *prise*, meaning "requisitioning, taking") describing the forced loan of wine, clothes, victuals, and other articles). The practice was so prevalent that the plaintiffs suffered impoverishment. Moreover, *"[c]ivitas et ipsa nostra Dublin et alie parcium illarum ita jam hac violenta mutacione et capcione omnibus mercatoribus diversarum regionum facte sunt exose, quod non est aliquis qui jam cum mercandisis suis ad eas velit descendere, unde plurimum sumus dampnificati"* (the city itself, our Dublin, and other parts of those regions have become so detested by all merchants from various countries due to this violent upheaval and capture that there is no one who now wishes to approach with their merchandise, which has caused us great harm).[2] Indeed, a royal representative (not necessarily a justiciar by the way), by virtue of his position, was entitled to collect two barrels of wine from each ship which visited Dublin's port. Merchants trading in wine who travelled to Dublin at the time had to reckon with this, but they had it calculated – unless there was malpractice, such as that described above, which went beyond the pale. Whatever predictability had worked in favour of the merchant movement earlier,

---

1 This article was produced within the collaborative project "BARMER. From the ship to the market. Economic activity, social relations and armed conflicts in the cities and port towns of late medieval Atlantic Europe" no. PID2020- 118105GBI00. The article was prepared as part of my research stay at the University of Cantabria (Santander) and financed by Nicolaus Copernicus University's Research University – Initiative of Excellence, no. 90-SIDUB.6102.7.2022.MP5, dec. no. 13/2022/ Mobilności.

2 Translated as "the city of Dublin and other Irish cities were so hateful to merchants of various countries that none will go thither" in Sweetman, Calendar of Documents, no. 971. For the original see Hardy, Rotuli litterarum clausarum, p. 431 (4 Henry III, Memb. 3) and a more legible version in Gilbert, Historic and Municipal Documents of Ireland, p. 74.

it was apparently nullified by the actions of this particular justiciar. The situation came to require the intervention of the legislative and executive power, the king of England. The king decided not to tolerate this harm to burgesses and merchants, he indicated that the justiciar could no longer carry out expropriations of this kind and that future loans incurred from Dublin burgesses should be repaid within 40 days, while those from foreign merchants immediately.

Considering cases such as that above, this article discusses how the situation and activity of merchants in Anglo-Norman towns and cities in Ireland was designed and affected by means of legislation, as well as documents and correspondence of legal and administrative nature. In its scope, the article largely reflects both the abundance and deficiencies of the source base. The aim is, primarily, to present how the English legal and economic system introduced in Ireland applied to merchant activity, what was the interrelatedness of trade and towns in Ireland, how the nature and character of the law influenced the formation of merchant-urban relations, to what extent legal instruments were intended to stabilise the situation of merchants and whether they did so effectively. Ultimately, we should reflect on the extent to which trade in Anglo-Norman towns in Ireland was predictable and how the issue of predictability could have been ensured when a new legal and economic framework was introduced in a colonised region such as Ireland.

Until now, the literature on trade in medieval Ireland has mostly discussed it in terms of its structure and volume against a background of economic and political trends, the origins of merchants visiting Ireland, and the destinations travelled to by Irish merchants, merchant guilds, and the operation of ports. A virtually comprehensive discussion on the structure of Irish trade in the Middle Ages and Early Modern Period has been made primarily by Timothy O'Neill and Wendy Childs.[3] They study the problem of overseas trade mainly in terms of Ireland's networking in European trade, the structure of trade, and the organisation of overseas trade.[4] O'Neill has also recently written more generally on Irish trade in the Middle Ages, mainly in terms of structure, problems encountered by merchants at sea, and the direction of sea routes,[5] whereas Childs has provided accurate statistics on trade involving Irish ports, as well as the emigration of Irish merchants and seafarers to English cities and their relationship with the English.[6] Meanwhile, the timber trade has been studied by Peadar Slattery,[7] trade in the Dublin region by Margaret Murphy and Michael Potterton,[8] and there is a fairly extensive literature on mer-

3 O'Neill, Merchants.
4 Childs and O'Neill, Overseas trade.
5 O'Neill, Trade.
6 Childs, Irish Merchants.
7 Slattery, Woodland management.
8 Murphy and Potterton, The Dublin region.

chant guilds in Ireland, particularly the Dublin Merchant Guild.[9] A very important work for the subject of Italian merchants and bankers, their administrative role for the English Crown, also discussing sources relating to their activities in medieval trade in Ireland, has been published by Mary Donovan O'Sullivan.[10] The concept of *lex mercatoria* – the Law Merchant, has been critically discussed in recent years by Emily Kadens, Richard A. Epstein, and Stephen E. Sachs.[11] Referring to this concept, my article applies the findings of these inquisitive researchers. My article contributes to the existing literature on the subject by addressing, more broadly than in previous studies, the issue of urban regulation of merchant activity and trade in the towns of Anglo-Norman Ireland on the basis of available sources.[12] The topic has once been shortly commented on by John J. Webb,[13] and more recently, Kevin Down has discussed urban commerce in Ireland from a general perspective.[14] In addition, an overview of trade, its organisation, structure, and statistics, but also the risks and challenges of being a merchant in medieval Leinster were presented very accurately by Karina Holton, whose study corresponds very well with mine.[15] Regarding the links between economy, commerce, and urban administration, an interesting and inspirational take, focused on the English zone, is presented in an article by Charles Angelucci and Simone Meraglia.[16] All in all, the considerations presented in my article primarily revolve around the opportunities to provide predictable frameworks for cooperation between Anglo-Norman towns and merchants through the use of various sources of law.

2. The Urbanisation of Trade

The situation recounted above occurred fifty years after Anglo-Norman lords and knights had invaded Ireland, eager to help the dethroned and despised Diarmait Mac

9 Becker, An Analysis; Eggerer, Guild Merchant; Clarke, Fraternities; as well as an article relating to the issue of guild membership by Coleman, Urban elite. Among the older publications on the Merchant Guild and the historical sources it left behind, see: Berry, The Merchant; id., The Records of the Dublin Gild of Merchants; Gross, The Gild Merchant.

10 O'Sullivan, Italian Merchant; see also Down, Colonial society, pp. 483–485.

11 Kadens, Medieval Law (the author also quotes further important literature in this regard); Epstein, Reflections; Sachs, From St Ives.

12 I have dealt with the issue of merchants in cities and towns, more generally, in a comparative view of Ireland, Prussia, and Livonia in my PhD thesis Maleszka, Urbanizacja, pp. 679–687.

13 Webb, Municipal Government, pp. 51–59.

14 Down, Colonial society, pp. 482–484. Anglo-Norman commerce is briefly presented also in de Courcy Ireland, Ireland, pp. 74–84.

15 Holton, From charters to carters.

16 Angelucci/Meraglia, Trade. (https://ideas.repec.org/p/tse/wpaper/27726.html.)

Murchada,[17] and even more eager to carve out estates for themselves in Ireland at the expense of the local overlords and elite.[18] Richard de Clare (Strongbow) managed to snatch Dublin, whose inhabitants attempted to stand up to the attackers.[19] Two years later, Dublin was granted its first charter by the King of England, Henry II – although in fact, as scholars have correctly observed, it was Bristolian merchants who were granted the right to settle or, should we say, to colonise Dublin.[20] Over the next twenty years, a lot changed in Ireland, both on an island-wide scale and in the city of Dublin itself.[21] Indeed, it is the situation in Dublin that well illustrates the changing nature of the Anglo-Norman presence in Ireland. Over twenty years, Dublin developed a new position for itself in the new system, no longer the object, but the subject of charters and donations, as confirmed by Prince John's charter of 1192, the addressees of which were *"hominibus et amicis suis Francus et Anglicis Hiberniensibus et Walensibus"* (to men and friends, French and English, Irish and Welsh), and then *"proborum virorum de Civitate ipsa"* (worthy men of the city).[22] As Howard Clarke describes it, "[t]he charter established the city of Dublin as a formal independent municipality and accorded the citizens of the city a range of judicial, financial and property rights".[23]

One might be tempted to see a certain analogy to this situation in the region of the German legal tradition. In 1211, Bishop Albrecht of Riga granted privileges to merchants visiting the newly founded town at the mouth of the Daugava River concerning, e. g. exemption from customs duties, relief from the burdens of coastal law, and the fixing of the value of the local coinage.[24] Only in the 1220s did local

17 Crooks, Mac Murchada; Martin, Diarmait Mac Murchada.

18 There is extensive literature on the Anglo-Norman settlement in Ireland. For the general view see: Graham, Anglo-Norman; Hartland, English Landholding. See also publications by Annette J. Otway-Ruthven, such as Otway-Ruthven, History of medieval Ireland, pp. 33–65 and ead., Character of Norman; also publications by Empey, Conquest and Settlement; id., Anglo-Norman settlement; id., Settlement of the kingdom; id., County Waterford (and see also other books of the "History and society" series); id., County Kilkenny; see also e. g. Colfer, Arrogant trespass; and for more specific studies see the bibliographies of the works by John Bradley and Brian J. Graham. The comprehensive study of territorial divisions in medieval Ireland by MacCotter, Medieval Ireland is also very valuable. I quote and review extensive literature regarding the medieval Anglo-Norman settlement in Ireland in Maleszka, Urbanizacja.

19 As above, there is a huge literature on the subject. I will only quote here an introductory article with numerous references to this literature: Martin, Allies and an Overlord.

20 Irish Record Commissioners, Chartae, Privilegia et Immunitates, p. 1; Clarke, The 1192 Charter, at p. 8; Duffy, Town and Crown, pp. 101–102.

21 Clarke, The 1192 Charter, p. 8; also: Frame, Colonial Ireland, pp. 22–110; Martin, Overlord; id., John, Lord of Ireland; Lydon, Ireland and the English Crown; Otway-Ruthven, The native Irish .

22 Clarke, IHTA Dublin, p. 31.

23 Clarke, The 1192 Charter, p. 9.

24 Höhlbaum, Hansisches Urkundenbuch I, no. 88.

merchants (*manentes*) gain a dominant position in Riga and become the subject of further trade regulations as Riga's citizens.[25]

The 1192 charter for Dublin is a tangible tool for introducing a new system of power and socio-economic relations. It would be untrue to say that conquest and colonisation brought trade to Ireland. What emerges from the available sources is a picture of the eleventh- and twelfth-century Irish trade in which the prominent position belonged to the Hiberno-Norse hubs.[26] The fact that other inland settlements that evolved alongside early medieval monasteries while the seats of rulers functioned as centres of trade and service has, moreover, contributed to an important debate on the origins of towns in medieval Ireland.[27] Hence, while the English brought their framework of social and economic life, they obviously did not originate trade in Ireland; but, on the other hand, the framework they brought was significant for the later conduct of trade.[28]

One should note that the system introduced to Ireland was actually also relatively new to England.[29] It had developed out of two different legal systems fused into one – the Anglo-Saxon and the Norman-French. In this plurality of two legal systems, the most prominent role belonged to the monarch, who, through the principles of the feudal system, sought to assert his control over the land and all its tenants. The system retained some old Anglo-Saxon laws and categories of tenures in various forms, including one known as socage.[30] The characteristic feature of socage was also what was the essence of the burgess condition in England – personal freedom and the obligation to pay rent in lieu of personal service, due for the use of a small plot of land.[31] In Ireland, the plot of land usually amounted to between 3–12 acres, with a frontage of twenty feet. The burgesses were inevitably predisposed

---

25 Benninghoven, Rigas Entstehung, pp. 36–37; Leimus, Einige Spekulationen, pp. 69–70; Schlau, Sozialgeschichte, p. 42.

26 See a recent publication by Horne, Viking market kingdom, passim. See also: Byrne, The trembling sod, p. 11; Down, Colonial society, pp. 481–482; Ó Cróinín, Early medieval Ireland, passim; Downham, Medieval Ireland, pp. 23–60 and 181–210.

27 Among the scholars who have postulated the theory of an indigenous and evolutionary origin of towns in Ireland, the most notable are Leo Swan and Charles Doherty; see: Swan, Monastic proto-towns; Doherty, The monastic town. This theory was also referred to by Brian J. Graham, indicating that in his view towns in Ireland also took their beginnings from secular centres, see: Graham, Secular Urban Origins. An exchange of views on defining towns was made at one time by Graham, Clarke and Simms in the pages of Journal of Historical Geography 13, 1 (1987). See also: Graham, Definition and Classification.

28 Down, Colonial society, p. 482.

29 Glasscock, Land and people, pp. 233–236.

30 Joy, Sokeright, passim; Hemmeon, Burgage tenure, pp. 4–10. On the changes introduced to trade after the Norman conquest see Miller and Hatcher, Medieval England, pp. 42–43.

31 On the origins of socage and burgage alike there is no consensus among scholars, see: Hemmeon, Burgage tenure, p. 4; Russo, Town Origins, passim; Simpson, History of the Land Law, pp. 10–14.

to engage in trade or crafts – it would have been difficult for them to live off only such a small acreage and earn enough to pay the rent. The law introduced and transformed in England by the Plantagenet dynasty was rehashed in practice in Ireland. This was accomplished first through the use of charters, with which the king granted land to his noble subjects; then, the new landowner introduced an elaborate, yet adjustable economic model into their estates, namely the manor.[32] The landowner in his manor could then implement the fashionable formula of burgage tenure[33] to encourage settlers to come to Ireland, by whom the implied features of burgage tenure (personal freedom) were seen as an opportunity to improve their own fortunes. Finally, the right to organise regular, weekly markets remained a royal *regalium*[34] but the king granted it to the landowners, who usually attached it to the towns within their manors. Legally and historically, however, burgage tenure and the right to hold a weekly market seem not to have been as unambiguously connected as was the case, for example, in the circle of German law, i. e. Prussia.[35] Technically, an English borough created by a landlord would not have been a designated place of trade, had not the same lord had a royal privilege of a weekly market at the ready; likewise, the burgess was not necessarily strictly a merchant, as far as the origins of this social condition are concerned.

In the period of our interest, it was already clear that if there were to be merchants coming and trading in Ireland, they were supposed to do so in towns. It had, after all, been explicitly stated long before, by the Anglo-Saxon kings of the tenth century, that this was to be the case,[36] and the Plantagenet kings of England embraced this practice. I will invoke an example of an early fourteenth-century petition by the burgesses of one Welsh town, Llanbadarn, as it captures well how the intention of the legislator and the functions attributed to chartered towns in the context of the conduct of trade were understood:

> *they were accustomed to have a market day each Monday weekly, for which they are enfranchised by the Charter of our most honourable lord the King, Edward, the grandfather, and by your confirmation, this is taken from them by the great ones of the country. […] Besides […], the people of the Country hold [? sell] various merchandise, in their houses and hamlets, of Meth [? Methe-glyn] and Ale and they hold balances, weights, measures and all other merchandise of oxen, cows, sheep, wool and iron and all other merchandise, to your*

32 Murphy, Manor centres; Keegan, The archaeology, pp. 17–18.

33 Prestwich, Plantagenet England, p. 469; Wilson, Plan Analysis, pp. 21–29.

34 Gross's Introduction in Gross, Select cases, p. xvi; Jamroziak, Networks, pp. 41–44.

35 Zientara, Źródła i geneza.

36 Ballard's Introduction in Ballard, British Borough Charters 1, p. lxvi: "[…] Athelstan added, 'Let every market be in a city,' and the concentration of commerce would hinder the sale of stolen property and facilitate the collection of tolls".

great damage and the impoverishment of your Burgesses, concerning whose grievances [...] they pray your remedy."[37]

What is of particular interest to us here is precisely the town's function of centralising the venue and circumstances of trade. Merchants were expected to come to towns that had previously been granted the appropriate charter allowing them to organise trade within their boundaries, benefiting both the burgesses and, apparently, the lawgiver.[38] The franchise for organising trade was understood as the right to monopolise activities related to trade in a particular area. Such an arrangement, on the one hand, constrained the merchants,[39] but on the other, arguably created the conditions for better organised security, by virtue of the greater ability to control all parties involved. It created an infrastructure that could be brought under a particular law.[40]

The new system of socio-economic activity related to trade and merchantry in Ireland under Anglo-Norman rule was to be closely linked to the English type of urbanity based on charters. New towns were founded "*in cruda radice*" (in raw root) or, much more often, they were established in places with consolidated settlement continuities.[41] The king would grant such towns the right to hold markets and, therefore, to monopolise the commercial activity of the area. In this regard, however, a separate discussion pertains to the uniqueness of the large post-Hiberno-Norse centres in Ireland. In these locations, trade had long been operating,[42] and after twenty years of English presence on the island, they were entering the new system on their own terms. It was these centres themselves, not any landlords above them, who were granted liberties relating to trade and merchants in charters.

The newly introduced system, therefore, was placed into the pre-existing socio-economic reality. Even if in theory the king of England could now decide on the

---

37 Rees, Calendar of Ancient Petitions, p. 398. This petition has reached my attention thanks to Louisa Taylor and Rhun Emlyn of Aberystwyth University, Wales, who cited it in their presentation entitled "Identity, Community, and Connections in Medieval Aberystwyth" at the conference "'Race', divisive law and group identity in Medieval Europe" in Swansea, Wales, held on 7–8 Sept. 2023.

38 Kadens, Medieval Law, p. 260. For a commentary on the royal policy of licencing markets in England, see: Britnell, The Proliferation, p. 211.

39 On prohibiting unlicenced markets also in Ireland, see Holton, From charters to carters, p. 25.

40 As a commentary to fair and marketplaces in the sacral areas, the legal consequences of them, and their liquidation in the early fourteenth century, see ibid., pp. 21–24.

41 Graham, Anglo-Norman Settlement; id., Towns in medieval Ireland; id., Urbanisation in Ireland; see also: Bradley, Planned Anglo-Norman towns in Ireland; Otway-Ruthven, The medieval Irish town.

42 See note 26; see also: Clarke, Dooley and Johnson, Dublin and the Viking World, pp. 26, 95–97; Doyle, Telling the dancer from the dance, p. 35.

distribution of markets, in practice, this authority only applied to new town and market foundations. Apart from the obvious divisions between lands conquered by the Anglo-Normans and those held by Gaelic rulers, in a rather complex proprietary patchwork, various forms of Anglo-Norman ownership and authority over land were at work from the outset. This could make it difficult to navigate for the English kings who in their judgement depended on officials and lords playing out their own ends. The dispute – well known in scholarly literature[43] – between Waterford, a grand old port distinguished by a royal charter, and New Ross, a lordly port, which competed for the same bay, can be seen as an example of the risks involved in adding new markets to a certain established order. The founding of New Ross (c. 1200) was the result of Lord Marshal's rivalry with the king and was rooted in the Lordship of Leinster being deprived of its main port, Waterford.[44] The competition between the two cities was the result of their consistent implementation, with the support of their overlords, of their new powers to organise trade. This was to disrupt the status quo, which had been in Waterford's favour. It is difficult to say whether the creation of New Ross actually caused the impoverishment of Waterford's port, or whether this was just fearmongering on the part of Waterford, which tried to persuade the king to impose a ban on trade in New Ross to protect its interests. Foreign merchants may not have even felt the difference in terms of customs,[45] and the possibility of choice. The royal solution to the conflict rested on a distinction between ships from the Lord Marshal's lands sailing to Leinster and therefore able to enter New Ross directly, and ships of other merchants, who were obliged to visit Waterford. In the 1260s, the conflict escalated, and the king began to penalise bypassing Waterford, while New Ross even started to hijack ships,[46] creating, as we can infer, a potentially dangerous situation for merchants. For, even wishing to comply with the law, they could not be sure that they would be able to. Overall, however, according to McEneaney, in this case, the royal rule was respected and at the same time did not noticeably weaken merchant movement.[47]

43 Lydon, Expansion and consolidation, pp. 166–167; McEneaney, Waterford; Bradley and Halpin, Topographical Development, p. 113.

44 Empey, Evolution of the demesne, p. 52.

45 McEneaney, Waterford, p. 19.

46 Ibid., p. 17.

47 Ibid., p. 19. For examples of similar rivalries between towns in England see Miller and Hatcher, Medieval England, pp. 161–162.

3. Sources of Law and Means of Control

As the example above shows, various interests and various means of pursuing them had to be taken into account as far as trade in a town was concerned. Apart from territorial rulers, local merchants in their own town also had their expectations, while foreign merchants coming to the town, and Irish burgesses trading outside their own town, had theirs. Generally, three sources of law regulated merchants, trade, and the relationship between the various agents of economic life. These sources included first, legal instruments issued by the king or territorial ruler that were created individually for each town, primarily being charters, but also various other rolls with which the king responded to petitions, concerns, and irregularities. A second source of laws was intra-urban communal legislation. The fact that these types of legislation were intended specifically for a particular town does not mean that they were devoid of far-reaching similarities, as discussed below. Third, the English king and Parliament had the means to influence the situation of merchants and organise trade at a general, supra-local level, through the issuing of royal decisions relating to larger communities and through parliamentary ordinances and statutes. Those relating to trade in Ireland are primarily, but not exclusively, the Statute and the Ordinance of the Staple, widely discussed in literature.[48]

3.1 Charters

Charters provided the basic framework for the functioning of an urban community. Charters also meant that the burgesses, as free people, had access to royal courts, as can be seen from the quite numerous surviving petitions of individual burgesses and entire urban communities to the monarch.[49] Enquiries to the king were addressed, it can be said, especially at times when predictability was disturbed, when a solution could not be fully ascertained, and this applied not only to commercial matters. Without delving into the systematics of the charters,[50] it suffices to mention here that those of smaller Irish towns, whose charters were based mainly on the town law of Breteuil-sur-Iton, rarely and very briefly referred to commercial issues.[51] The latter were, in fact, mainly addressed by the charters of the large cities, which had been planned as port cities and were already engaged in trade. Charters related

48 Liddy, War, Politics and Finance, pp. 110–130; Hall, Select cases concerning the law merchant, p. xxvii-xxix; Strickland, The ancient official seals, pp. 170–171; Musson, Second English Justinian, pp. 83–84.

49 Maleszka and Stevens, Maintaining a special relationship.

50 Which was undertaken by Buldorini, Drogheda; on Irish charters related to Bristol see: Gwynn, Medieval Bristol and Dublin; Duffy, Town and Crown, p. 102; Clarke, The 1192 Charter, p. 7.

51 Buldorini, Drogheda, p. 103; Ballard, The Law of Breteuil; Bateson, The Laws of Breteuil.

to Bristol and London, which in Ireland were usually patterned after the 1192 charter of Dublin, show a great deal of similarity in the way they regulated the relationships that arose from trading. From the point of view of the commercial activity of Dublin and other large cities in Ireland, which were extending the reach of their contacts by entering the orbit of protection by the kings of England, it was certainly perceived as a more advantageous step to have charters similar to the ones applicable in English towns. This legal affinity provided, at the most basic level, predictability for merchants arriving from England.

Simultaneously, in the charters of large Anglo-Norman towns in Ireland the right to organise trade as such was not even separately specified.[52] Instead, they usually listed a number of standard privileges very generally defining how a town could act towards local traders and foreign merchants. The majority of the provisions were intended to enforce protection for the business activity of locals, and the protection of citizens' rights against any exploitation by foreign merchants.[53] If there was to be long-distance trade in the town, local merchants and other burgesses were guaranteed an advantage.[54] Control of compliance with these provisions was delegated to the municipality. Therefore, the municipality's main focus was to uphold this protection and not allow foreign merchants to wriggle out of existing laws, whether concerning trade or other matters. This is particularly relevant and interesting in the context of the colonial centres. The idea behind these centres – in the light of the observation of the contents of the charters – was therefore not (as was still the case with Dublin in 1172) to create markets for sale of supplies with all the privileges and advantages for English (and therefore foreign) merchants, but to create local markets with local merchants who were to participate in trade on an equal footing with merchants living in English towns. It was common in Ireland for charters to limit the trading activities of foreign merchants in a given town to forty days. However, the restriction very often applied only to the retail trade in linen and the sale of wine in taverns. Foreign merchants were prohibited from purchasing wool, grain, leather, and Irish linen from other foreign merchants visiting the towns.[55] The charter of Dublin of 1192 and other royal ports allowed

52 It is probably because the charters for large urban post-Hiberno-Norse centres in Ireland were based on Bristol and London charters in their most contemporary versions, which did not repeat these privileges. The markets that existed in Dublin and were confirmed by royal grants might have operated in these places before, cf. Clarke, IHTA Dublin, pp. 26–27.

53 See the text of the charter of Dublin, Clarke, IHTA Dublin, p. 31; see also texts of the charters of other medium and large cities: MacNiocaill, Na buirgéisí; Irish Record Commissioners, Chartae, passim.

54 Clarke, The 1192 Charter, p. 5 and 9.

55 Drogheda in Meath in 1247, MacNiocaill, Na buirgéisí, p. 174: "*et quod nullus extraneus mercator aliquam mercandisam faciant in predicto burgo nostro de Drogheda aliter quam extranei mercatores faciunt in civitate nostra Dublinie*"; Drogheda in Louth in 1229, ibid., p. 187: "*nullus extraneus*

foreign merchants to retail linen only during fairs, and to run a wine tavern only on board a ship. However, unlike charters of other royal ports, the charter of Dublin imposed a very broad restriction against foreign merchants – they could not stay with any goods in the city for more than forty days.[56] This was undoubtedly a very generous privilege, and so exceptional must its application have been that it caused protests from merchants visiting Dublin, as eloquently described by Seán Duffy:

> John's 1192 charter, for example, was quite clear that "no alien merchant shall delay in the town with his merchandise, to sell his merchandise, beyond forty days". But thirty years later the government of Henry III had no knowledge of this: in 1223 the king wrote to his justiciar to the effect that "very many merchants of England, Poitou and Gascony […] have complained that when they arrive at Dublin they are not permitted to remain beyond forty days unless they unlade their merchandise." What is more, the government thought the idea preposterous, adding that "the king does not believe that the bailiffs and burgesses of Dublin obtained a warrant to do so from himself or his predecessors, and the king commands the justiciar to cause them to desist from this harassing of or exaction from merchants."[57]

Therefore, available sources show that foreign merchants were neither without opportunities to secure facilities and guarantees, nor did they give up trying to circumvent various constraints, especially, as in the example above, when these constraints seemed atypical. Alongside complaints addressed to the king, such as the one above, another such means was through association.

Two aforementioned episodes from the 1220s explain the growing popularity of the Guild Merchant in Dublin. The right to have a merchant guild was granted to urban municipalities in charters.[58] It has often been assumed that it was the guilds that constituted the first intra-urban decision-making bodies in which urban self-government could mature.[59] We have little information about guilds in towns in Ireland, especially in the thirteenth and fourteenth centuries, as references are very

mercator pannos in predicto burgo ad decisionem vendat vel vina ad brocham nisi in grosso"; Wexford in 1317, ibid., p. 233: "*Nulli mercatori extraneo liceat decisionem pannorum facere vel tabernam vinorum vel aliorum mercimoniorum habere in villa de Weiseford nisi ex consensu superioris et communitatis ville predicte nisi fuerit burgensis ibidem*"; Kilkenny in 1202–1210, ibid., p. 136: "*Nulli mercatori extraneo liceat decisionem pannorum facere vel tabernam vinorum habere in villa de Kilkennie nisi per quadraginta dies, et si amplius huiusmodi habere voluerit tantum faciant per communionem burgensium ad proficuum ville quod remaneat*", etc. See also Holton, From charters to carters, p. 35.

56 Clarke, IHTA Dublin, p. 31.

57 Duffy, Town and Crown, pp. 113–114.

58 See note 53.

59 Ó Súilleabháin, Mormaors, pp. 11–12; see also Oexle, Gilde und Kommune.

few and relate to only a small number of towns.[60] The Dublin merchant guild was certainly in the vanguard. Over the course of several decades of the first half of the thirteenth century, many merchants from Wales, England, and from Anglo-Norman towns in Ireland enrolled in the guild.[61] On this basis, one can map the commercial network of early Anglo-Norman dominion in Ireland, and indeed the commercial influence of Dublin. Guild affiliation in English towns which had the right to form such a community entitled the merchant to enjoy those privileges which were provided for local merchants, i. e. burgesses, in the body of the charter, and removed from him the restrictions imposed on the trade of foreign merchants.[62] We may be sure that in Anglo-Norman towns in Ireland the way guilds operated was identical. The record of Drogheda, to which King Henry III granted the following right in a privilege in 1229, can be used as confirmation here: "*Et quod nullus qui non sit de gelda illa mercandisam aliquam in predicto burgo faciat, nisi de voluntate eorundem burgensium*" (And that no one who is not of that guild may trade in the aforesaid town, except at the will of the said burgesses).[63] Guild membership, as one might surmise, made the conduct of trade more predictable by virtue of the access to networks that associations of this type were designed to provide.

Merchants in their own town were most commonly exempt from fees and taxes that the founder of the town and market in Ireland had the right to impose. The charters usually contained a list of financial obligations from which the burgesses were exempted: first and foremost *murage* – a levy on goods brought in, earmarked for the construction or repair of ramparts; *pavage* – a levy for the paving of roads; *pontage* – a fee for crossing a bridge; *lestage* – a fee for the right to trade at a particular place, market or fair, also for loading a ship; *tallage* – a general tax on the use of immovable property; *stallage* – a levy on the use of a market stall, earmarked for the erection of such stalls.[64] However, merchants who, as burgesses of a particular town, were granted a charter, became foreign merchants themselves outside their own town. It was in this respect that there was an element of a certain unpredictability. In the *Liber Primus Kilkenniensis*, a surviving document from 1329, the king confirmed the acquired right of the burgesses of Kilkenny to be excluded from taxes in all towns

60 Surely in Drogheda in Louth and Limerick, see: MacNiocaill, Na buirgéisí, p. 185; O'Flaherty, IHTA Limerick, p. 28.

61 Becker, An Analysis, p. 21–27. Miller and Hatcher, Medieval England, p. 293 indicate that such guilds which included not only merchants and foreigners were important instruments of ensuring "that trade was carried on there within a known and consistent framework of regulations".

62 Fryde, Guilds in England, pp. 219–220.

63 Gilbert, Historic and municipal documents, p. 93.

64 Cf. Sweetman, Calendar of Documents, pp. 583–585; Ballard, British Borough Charters 1, p. lxix. The broader, English context for these exemptions from tolls is shown by Liberman Cuenca, The making of borough customary law, pp. 140–141.

in the Leinster area – being the territory belonging to the lord who had granted the charter to the Kilkenny burgesses.[65] However, problems arose when another town in the area acquired the right to levy a tax – most often a *murage*. There are numerous sources preserved in Irish archives documenting the *murages*, thanks to which we know that this was generally levied on merchants as they brought the taxed goods into the towns for trade.[66] It is clear from the king's document in Kilkenny that there were disputes over which law took priority – whether the exemption from taxation or the permission to levy taxes in another town, which included mainly merchants. In the case of Kilkenny, the king decided that burgesses using an exemption by virtue of their charter should remain exempt from taxes on goods in Leinster towns even when entering those towns where *murage* was allowed to be levied.[67] As can be seen, in the event of a controversy, referral to the king was used as a way of addressing legal uncertainty.[68]

It is in the context of merchants' taxes and tolls that the major difference between royal and lordly towns became apparent. For, while a lord, having *team and toll* over his territory, he could of course release his subjects, including burgesses, from all sorts of fees and taxes, the extent of this exemption did not reach beyond the region of his authority. In contrast, the English monarch had the right to exempt burgesses from taxation throughout the area subject to his sovereignty, not only in the entirety of Ireland but also in England and Wales. Kings did not hesitate to single out their burgesses in this way, thus guaranteeing them a significant advantage over private town merchants.[69]

One other controversy concerning this issue, involving burgesses and the merchants of Kilkenny, is particularly interesting. We learn of it from a document dating from around 1390. This is a petition from the burghers and authorities of Waterford to the king and royal council, the senders of which complained about the practices of the Kilkennians. In their view, "Richard Marshal, by his charter, granted to the sovereign and burgesses of the town of Kilkenny several franchises and liberties which he did not have power or authority to grant".[70] As the wording of the petition indicates, the beneficiaries of the charter granted to Kilkenny claimed exemptions from taxes and fees guaranteed to them by their lord, but they also did so outside the area over which his authority extended.[71] According to the Waterfordians, the

65 McNeill, Liber Primus Kilkenniensis, pp. 10–11.

66 Kreem, Kwiatkowski and Maleszka, Military Affairs, p. 188; Down, Colonial society, p. 483.

67 McNeill, Liber Primus Kilkenniensis, pp. 10–11.

68 Other such cases were invoked by Karina Holton, see: Holton, From charters to carters, p. 34.

69 Jamroziak, Networks, p. 44.

70 Dryburgh and Smith, Handbook and Select Calendar, p. 163.

71 On the area granted to Marshals in Leinster, see: Orpen, The Song of Dermot, pp. 190–191, verses 2613–2622; Orpen, Ireland under the Normans, pp. 319–377; Empey, The evolution, pp. 42, 50–51.

manipulation occurred because of the arbitrariness of the burgesses to add their own liberties to the royal document approving the lord's charter. There is much to suggest that the Waterfordians' allegations are plausible, as late as 1329 the king approved the exemption of the Kilkennians from taxes levied in the towns of Leinster, whereas in an *inspeximus* (a confirmation and reaffirmation of one or several royal grants) of 1 December 1383, King Richard II approved, among numerous "liberties claimed by the burgesses", a provision proclaiming: "*Item superior et burgenses uille predicte tales libertates clamant habere quod quieti sint de tholonio lastagio passagio pontagio muragio et de omnibus aliis consuetudinibus et custumis per totum regnum et dominium domini nostri regis Anglie sicus burgenses de Glowcestre sunt uirtute honoris dicti Gloucestre*" (The sovereign and burgesses are to be quit of toll, lastage, passage, pontage, murage and all other customs and dues throughout the realm and lordship of the king of England, just as the burgesses of Gloucester are by virtue of the said honour of Gloucester).[72] The burgesses of Kilkenny did not indicate that they had received this privilege from their lord, but stated that it was their internal legislation which they had submitted to the monarch for legitimisation. This situation, which can be presumed to have been initiated in 1383 and, within a few years, to have been met with a reaction by the Waterfordians vigilant against any case of undermining their own mercantile hegemony, was, on the one hand, the result of inequalities affecting merchants hailing from the various towns in Ireland, and, on the other, an example of an attempt to exploit the English Crown's desire, just initiated in the 1380s, to control and stabilise the legal status of towns. Edward III's and Richard II's chancellery issued *inspeximus* to towns on the basis of the different types of documents and charters the latter presented.[73] Leaving aside who committed the greater offence – the shrewd burgesses or the careless royal officials who allowed them to do so – one might be tempted to conclude that the Kilkenny merchants, while obtaining confirmation of the town's charters, were attempting to take advantage of the fact that these bore a strong resemblance to each other and based their ploy on this attribute. After all, each town might have anticipated that merchants from large trading cities were usually exempt from taxation. In Kilkenny's case it was invoking an affinity with Gloucester, which was used to justify these very broad tax exemptions.

---

72 McNeill, Liber Primus Kilkenniensis, p. 81; CIRCLE: A Calendar of Irish Chancery Letters, c. 1244–1509, on Virtual Record Treasury of Ireland, Patent Roll 7 Richard II, Item 7, 1 Dec. 1383, [62]. (https://virtualtreasury.ie/item/CIRCLE-6-7-1-7).

73 E. g. CIRCLE, Patent Roll 2 Richard II, 9 Jan. 1379, Item 8, (https://virtualtreasury.ie/item/CIRCLE-6-2-1-8); Patent Roll 4 Richard II, 20 Jul. 1380, Item 2,(https://virtualtreasury.ie/item/CIRCLE-6-4-1-2); Patent Roll 11 Richard II, 4 Jun. 1388, Item 2, (https://virtualtreasury.ie/item/CIRCLE-6-11-1-2).

3.2 Intra-urban Legislation

There is no doubt that issues within the urban economy were included in the intra-urban regulations composed in Anglo-Norman towns in Ireland. Significantly, from the very outset, during the introduction of English law into Ireland, there were prerequisites conducive to making intra-urban regulations similar to English municipal laws. If we dwell on the formulas used, for example, in the charter of Dublin of 1192, we are presented with a certain vagueness that can be interpreted in two ways. Based on the laws of London and Bristol, Dublin's charter allowed citizens to *"habeant omnes libertates et liberas consuetudines subscriptas"* (have all liberties and free customs written below), which Prince John then meticulously listed below.[74] However, at three points in the body of the privilege (12, 13, and 26 in the edition in the Dublin Atlas), including the one about debt handling in the city, John did not specify the procedures to be followed, but ordered Dubliners and anyone else in Dublin to proceed according to an undefined *consuetudo civitatis* (custom of the city).[75] The phrase used here is noteworthy. Each of the points referred to what should be understood as customary urban laws. Such phrasing, and the nature of its occurrence in the body of the charter, raises questions about the nature of this Dublin's law.

The pre-Norman laws that Dublin could have used are not known,[76] and it is also not known whether it was actually possible for the city to use them under the new rule, given that the Plantagenet monarchy from an early date had dictated that only English law was to be applied throughout Ireland under Anglo-Norman rule.[77] Perhaps the old customs used in pre-Anglo-Norman Dublin were also to give way to the new ones known to the English settlers, who were supposed to treat them as Londoners or Bristolians treated their customary laws.[78] In view of this, the English law in Ireland, although intended to function as a single entity, carried over its resultant heterogeneity by indicating in the wording of the charter the need for the "new" urban centre to have its own customs. The influence of Anglo-Saxon law on the customs and social order of Anglo-Norman towns was, therefore, of a deeper, more "subliminal" nature, in that it organised a particular way of thinking about law, its mechanisms, and modes of enforcement, even if the Anglo-Saxon law, as such, was never introduced into Ireland. This is, therefore, a very interesting

74 Clarke, IHTA Dublin, p. 31.

75 Ibid.

76 Ó Súilleabháin, Mormaors, p. 108.

77 Brand, Common Law; Hand, English Law, pp. 1–5.

78 Just as the old authorities were about to give way to the new ones, see: Gwynn, Medieval Bristol and Dublin, p. 277; cf. Ó Súilleabháin, Mormaors, pp. 108–110.

example of how the law presupposes the pre-existence of certain customs by virtue of its heterogeneity, or plurality.

The solution to these presuppositions had to be the composition of the town's own regulations, taking into account the challenges that undoubtedly arose just as the newly established towns began to attract merchants. As comparative studies of urban *custumals*, particularly the invaluable Bateson edition,[79] demonstrate, burgesses and municipal authorities did not hesitate to borrow regulations from other towns, and this also applied to the rules of trade and the treatment of merchants. The standards adopted by these towns were not too different from those applicable in English towns.[80] Late medieval Irish *custumals* which address merchants and trade come primarily from Dublin (the oldest known),[81] but also from Waterford,[82] Kilkenny,[83] Cork,[84] and Galway,[85] i. e. port cities. These regulations emphatically inform on the socio-economic situation, undoubtedly tense at times, of the major cities of Anglo-Norman Ireland. The growth of similar regulations over time, especially in the fifteenth century, on the one hand, resulted from a strengthening of the tendency to codify the rules of communal life,[86] while on the other hand, in the Irish context, it can be arguably linked to the declining involvement of the English kings in Irish matters and the need for local communities themselves to take charge of their own affairs. Assuming that the very elaborate provisions, taking into account various scenarios and exceptions, served to eliminate the frequently occurring or recurring circumvention of the law, the similarity of the problems faced by municipalities in attempting to clarify various issues related to trade operations is striking. This also allows us to infer a similarity in the content of municipal customs themselves.

3.3 Trading as a Social Practice

On the basis of the available legislation, one can reconstruct the application of town law and privileges to merchant activity, as well as the expected behaviour of a merchant in town. A medieval foreign merchant arriving in an Anglo-Norman

79 Bateson, Borough customs, [vol. 1 and 2].

80 Watt, The Anglo-Irish colony, pp. 367–368.

81 Gaffney and de Pontfarcy Sexton, The laws and usages of Dublin; On this and other Dublin custumals see: Maleszka and Możdżeń, Urban Legislation, pp. 95–96.

82 MacNiocaill, Na buirgéisí, pp. 3–59.

83 Ibid., 135–149; also in: McNeil, Liber Primus Kilkenniensis, pp. 74–82; and English edition in CIRCLE, Patent Roll 7 Richard II, 1 Dec. 1383, Item 7, (https://virtualtreasury.ie/item/CIRCLE-6-7-1-7).

84 MacNiocaill, Na buirgéisí, pp. 60–70.

85 Only a few entries from the late fifteenth and then mostly from the sixteenth century: Gilbert, Archives of the Town of Galway, pp. 384–457.

86 Maleszka and Czaja, Law, p. 39.

town in Ireland with goods on a ship or with carts overland was well aware of its laws and his resulting rights and obligations, but also equally well aware of how to circumvent them. First of all, when entering the port with commodities, merchants had to pay customs, and when entering the town through its gates they were obliged to pay tolls.[87] Early Modern entries from Dublin's city book include a tabular listing of customs payable for a variety of goods.[88] The values of tolls and customs, on the other hand, were established, or at least reviewed, by the Crown and communicated to the public.[89] We might expect that if a merchant enjoyed an exemption from tolls or customs he was expected to produce the evidence for that. In 1312, for example, the king, in response to a complaint from Bristolians, instructed the Dublin authorities that it was his will that those merchants should not pay customs in the city.[90] From as early as the second-half of the fourteenth century (1378), records in Dublin provided that only citizens should have the franchises of the city; in this instance there was also information on cases of citizens colluding with strangers who sought to avoid paying customs.[91] In the fifteenth century, the conditions for obtaining these franchises became more stringent.[92] This meant that in Dublin, the basis for exemption from at least part of the charges was one's status as a franchisee. A seafaring merchant was expected to register with the municipal or harbour clerk his name and the names of his crew members, and to declare the goods he brought into the harbour for sale to the burgesses.[93] In Dublin, the standard forty days during which a merchant was allowed to interact commercially were counted from that moment onwards.[94] The city had already warned in the early *Provisiones* that the merchant could not start unloading the commodities before the customs had been paid.[95] It seems that in the second-half of the fourteenth century some towns tightened up – perhaps arbitrarily, given that the cited record is taken from Kilkenny customs – the conditions for foreign merchants to engage in trading, ordering them to obtain the licence of the town authorities and citizens on each occasion.[96]

87 Webb, Municipal Government, p. 37.

88 Gilbert, Calendar of Ancient Records of Dublin, pp. 243–247, 262–263.

89 Berry, Statutes and Ordinances, [vol. I: King John to Henry V], p. 71 and 479.

90 CIRCLE, Close Roll 5 Edward II, 18 June 1312, Item 81 (https://virtualtreasury.ie/item/CIRCLE-4-5-2-81).

91 Gilbert, Calendar of Ancient Records, p. 237.

92 Ibid., p. 283.

93 Bateson, Borough customs 1, p. 173.

94 Gilbert, Calendar of Ancient Records, p. 220.

95 Ibid., p. 220 and in 1452–4, p. 278.

96 CIRCLE, Patent Roll 7 Richard II, 1 Dec. 1383, Item 7, (https://virtualtreasury.ie/item/CIRCLE-6-7-1-7).

According to the law, foreign and local merchants could carry out trade transactions in designated market areas. This could be a single room or a venue specifically dedicated to trade in certain goods, such as a fish or cattle market, as in Dublin.[97] In the fourteenth century, the community of Kilkenny even claimed the right to change the site of the market if that was the will of the public,[98] which technically was beyond their prerogatives. On the venues of commerce in towns, numerous records have been preserved in the *custumals*, testifying to two main tendencies: firstly, foreign merchants and citizens alike, in an effort to circumvent certain prohibitions, engaged in acts of commerce outside the designated places; secondly, the control of the municipality over the venue designated for commerce must therefore have been quite effective. The insistence on controlling the place of trade was perfectly justified, for the medieval community it had a hygienic dimension and, in this context, can be compared with the control of the food producers.[99] In addition, there were devices in the market supposed to ensure that the correct weights and measures, introduced by the English Crown and controlled by officials, were observed.[100] The centralisation of trade in one place was therefore intended to counteract the fraud reported extensively in the *custumals* of the various towns, the common denominator of which was mostly operating in secret from the municipality and officials. Dubliners countered incidents such as the buying up of goods in the neighbouring port of Dalkey to speculate among Dublin's burgesses,[101] as well as the sale of salt from ships' decks.[102] In 1355, at a time when the British Isles were struggling to cope with the Black Death, the citizens of Dublin reported on how the covert export of fish from Ireland was organised, and informed about the manipulation of the quality and the price of fish in the city. Dishonest merchants would "*buy them and by night and dawn or twilight bring them to the city and salt them secretly in their houses, or put them in casks and convey them at night to places where the King is at war*".[103] In 1316–1318, at a time of grave crisis in the city caused by the threat of attack by the rebel army of Edward de Bruce, the brother of Robert de Bruce King of Scots, and the High King of Ireland since 1315, Dublin's commoners formulated a petition

97 Clarke, IHTA Dublin, p. 26–27.

98 CIRCLE, Patent Roll 7 Richard II, 1 Dec. 1383, Item 7, (https://virtualtreasury.ie/item/CIRCLE-6-7-1-7).

99 Holton, From charters to carters, p. 29 and 37; Maleszka and Możdżeń, Urban Legislation, p. 106.

100 Holton, From charters to carters, pp. 26, 38–39. See especially "Tractatus de Ponderibus et Mensuris" and "Bushels and Weights shall be made and sent into every County", in: Ruffhead, Statutes at Large, pp. 148–149 and 227; see also Berry, Statutes and Ordinances, pp. 15, 36 ff.

101 Gilbert, Calendar of Ancient Records, p. 220.

102 Ibid., p. 220 and 221. See also other examples described by Holton, From charters to carters, p. 37.

103 CIRCLE, Close Roll 29 Edward III, 2 June 1355, Item 39, (https://virtualtreasury.ie/item/CIRCLE-5-29-2-39).

to the city authorities, within which they drew attention to abuses on the part of merchants. These alleged abuses included: merchant partnerships monopolising the buying up of the freight of ships arriving in, trading outside designated places, making purchases on behalf of foreign merchants, and forestalling.[104]

Among towns in Ireland, Cork stands out in the context of countering mischief. In 1339, the city dealt very extensively with the various abuses that foreign merchants and citizens were guilty of. It was very precisely detailed how to secure the access of all townspeople to purchase food and other commodities. A local merchant who had bought a load of grain from a foreign merchant was not allowed to refuse to sell the grain to other townspeople who wanted to purchase it. It was forbidden to carry out transactions in secret and or hide from officials; in the event that demand for a commodity exceeded supply, the volume of the commodity was to be divided so that each class of citizens could make a purchase.[105] In doing so, however, foreign merchants were guaranteed a very important decision-making power, "And the delivery of corn shall be made to all sufficient persons, from whom the merchants, buyer or seller, are willing to trust to get payment on the day of covenant of payment, and not to others without good security upon which they are willing to trust."[106] This is an important clause, indicating that despite consistent efforts to regulate the way trade was conducted and to control the practices of foreign merchants, urban communities were aware that a merchant needed the appropriate conditions to initiate a transaction. Stability of regulation was one thing, merchants in Irish towns encountered relatively convergent rules, very similar to those in English towns, but they needed to be guaranteed a degree of flexibility that would not at the same time amount to a breach of the law.

3.4 The Judiciary

Hence, the market provided the visibility and flexibility of transactions to the extent which Emily Kadens describes,[107] and therefore also enabled the availability of justice. This brings us to the problem of the judiciary approachable for merchants in Ireland. According to the legal order which the Anglo-Normans inherited from the Anglo-Saxon system of justice and brought to Ireland, alongside the royal judiciary promoted by the Plantagenets there was a local judiciary, including the hundred courts.[108] In urban settings, it was a court for all burgesses of the town, to whom

104 Gilbert, Calendar of Ancient Records, pp. 132–135.

105 Bateson, Borough customs 1, pp. 173–175.

106 Ibid., p. 176.

107 Kadens, The Medieval Law Merchant, pp. 264–265.

108 Baker, Introduction to English Legal History, pp. 15–43.

charters guaranteed the right to appear before it.[109] It was the basis of franchise – and, therefore, freedom from land courts and estates – granted along with a certain amount of responsibility. Municipal courts were given the power to decide on cases involving merchants, with some authors indicating that special tribunals were also set up to settle ongoing issues during fairs[110] or even at markets, as indicated by English sources especially from the fifteenth century and later.[111] The functioning of the courts in relation to merchants and debt cases mainly in English towns has been described from available sources by Charles Gross,[112] and more recent findings have been made in particular by Stephen E. Sachs.[113]

The much less eloquent medieval sources on commercial disputes and court cases in Anglo-Norman towns in Ireland sketch a picture similar to that given for English towns. The inventories preserved in Dublin's *Liber Albus* indicate that Dubliners kept registers recording merchant and burgess debts and liabilities.[114] We can be sure that such records – private as well as public – were common in the merchant towns of Ireland. From the point of view of a foreign merchant, two issues were the most important: the possibility of quick and efficient recovery of a debt and the possibility of a quick trial. It seems that the functioning of the court in merchant cases involving foreigners in the towns necessarily had to be pragmatic and hence the staffing of the court, its terms of office, or its formula (municipal or dedicated only to merchants, etc.), may have been adaptable.[115] By virtue of the location privileges granted to large commercial cities, debt matters also had to be dealt with according to the customs of the town. The burgesses of Dublin and other towns and cities, including those of Leinster, which were granted a related form of charter, were exempt from liability for the debts of other townsmen whether in or out of the town. At the same time, any townsman trading in a foreign place was responsible for his own debts – in accordance with the procedures of the town in question, which was also provided for in the town charter.[116] The surviving record of the legal proceedings of a Dubliner, Andrew Larcedekene, against the city of Cork in 1338–9 contains a declaration by the Cork authorities that "*citizens of Cork*

---

109 Clarke, IHTA Dublin, p. 31.

110 For the existence of such a court in Kilkenny see: Bateson, Borough customs 1, p. 187.

111 Gross, Select cases 1, pp. xvii–xviii, xx.

112 Ibid.

113 Sachs, From St Ives, passim.

114 See e. g. Gilbert, Calendar of Ancient Records, pp. 130–131.

115 According to Charles Gross, such courts may have replaced the ordinary municipal court for the duration of the fair/market, probably primarily in situations where municipal judges had to officiate in a temporary court. Merchant cases may have been decided before the municipal court, sometimes with a panel fed by representatives of the town lord or the holder of the right to the fair/market, see: Gross, Select cases 1, pp. xxii–xxiii.

116 Clarke, IHTA Dublin, p. 31.

from time beyond memory had liberty to arrest all persons convicted before them of debt". Larcedekene was therefore imprisoned in Cork, which he perceived as an acute injustice for which he demanded compensation.[117] In the following year, the time of proceedings in cases before the municipal court involving foreigners was regulated in Cork – perhaps as a result of the action mentioned. If the defendant was someone from outside town, the trial had to be held the same day before the evening bell (in winter) or dusk (in summer); if this was not possible, the stranger was obliged to wait under guard until the next day.[118]

In Dublin and Waterford, the custumal of the early fourteenth century focused on regulating the timing of the payment of debts – namely, it was accepted that if a foreign merchant was to await payment for goods, the citizen should bear in mind that the final deadline for such a payment to the merchant, who "*est pres vers sun pays dela la mer*" (is ready to return to his land beyond the sea), was after three ebbs and three flows of the tide. If the debtor nevertheless failed to pay, the amount due was to be refunded by the municipal bailiffs, who would then collect the debt from the debtor on their own, in accordance with municipal law.[119] Earlier, in the mid-thirteenth century, an agreement had been made between Dublin and Drogheda whereby the officials of both cities were enabled to enforce debts against Dubliners in Drogheda and Droghedans in Dublin respectively.[120]

The similarity of the rules for dealing with commercial disputes, especially debts incurred with foreign merchants trading in the towns, contributed to the historiographical myth of the alleged functioning of a supra-local, autonomously emerging "law merchant" In the sources explicitly mentioning this, the term law merchant is used in particular to describe a way of securing debts and resolving disputes through a procedure that we can nowadays describe as "fast-track litigation", which was also supposed to exhibit similarities at a supra-local level. As Sachs in his erudite dissertation, and Kadens in her brilliant article indicate, however, the law merchant lawas neither a legal product of the merchants themselves, nor did it replace the application of common or municipal laws, as demonstrated also in the sources cited above, because it did not exist as an independent legal creation. Rather, it was merely a set of standards derived from the application of similar legal norms in towns involved in long-distance trade.[121] In the English legal system, there was no place for the operation of a law over which the king would have had such limited control. Besides, there was no need for it – the regulation of procedures

117 Gilbert, Calendar of Ancient Records, p. 168.

118 Bateson, Borough customs 1, p. 185.

119 MacNiocaill, Na buirgéisí, p. 38; Gaffney and de Pontfarcy Sexton, The laws and usages, p. 194.

120 Gilbert, Calendar of Ancient Records, p. 89.

121 Kadens, The Medieval Law Merchant, p. 254.

and, consequently, the dissemination of them in a standardised version, securing the interests of foreign merchants in English towns and Anglo-Norman towns in Ireland, were provided by royal statutes and acts of parliament.

3.5 Royal and Parliamentary Legislation

During the thirteenth and fourteenth centuries, the English Crown made repeated efforts to ensure that the principle of convergence of the laws running in Ireland with those of England remained known and effective. The *Magna Charta Hiberniae*, issued in 1216, included guarantees of freedom of trade extending also to all those operating in Ireland.[122] In the event of hostilities, reciprocity was envisaged – merchants from the enemy country were to be detained until it was known how merchants under the protection of the king of England would be treated in the enemy country. Ireland also enacted the Statute of Acton Burnell, promulgated in 1283 and reenacted in 1285 as the Statute of Merchants. The provisions of municipal law in Ireland were in concordance with these; and it can be seen that they quoted or paraphrased norms drawn from the same sources of law. In these statutes, the king legislated the efficient recovery of debts incurred with merchants regulated on a central level. The various stages of the procedure for declaring a debt, confirming it with officials, the method of settlement, and the method of enforcement in the event of late payment or inability to pay were very strictly laid down.[123]

Although town charters forbade foreign merchants from trading with other foreigners,[124] this principle was waived in certain respects in the fourteenth century for selected ports under the staple rights. Of the Irish ports, initially, in 1326, three – Dublin, Cork, and Drogheda[125] – and in 1353 four – Dublin, Cork, Drogheda, and Waterford[126] – were designated as staple ports with the right to assemble explicitly designated goods. The goods, destined for Irish ports, were to include wool and sheepskin products, cowhides, and tin. Foreign merchants could purchase these goods from local merchants and trade with each other in the designated ports. However, only after obtaining confirmation of the purchase in the staple port and waiting fifteen days could they transport these goods to other markets where all people could purchase them freely.[127] Merchants in staple ports were placed under royal protection, and the townspeople of these ports who entered into

122 Berry, Statutes and Ordinances, pp. 13–19.

123 Ibid., pp. 101–103. For examples of invoking the rules introduced by the statutes, see a confirmation of a debt from 1323–27, Dryburgh and Smith, Handbook and Select Calendar, p. 147.

124 Clarke, IHTA Dublin, p. 31, no. 15.

125 Berry, Statutes and Ordinances, p. 314.

126 Ruffhead, Statutes at Large, ed. by Owen, p. 275.

127 Berry, Statutes and Ordinances, pp. 314–317.

transactions with the merchants were obliged to comply with rules known indeed as law merchant. Towns and their citizens were made responsible for the safety of merchants in staple ports.[128]

The parliamentary documents of the fourteenth century indicate that the issue of trade was close to the heart of the English kings. Statutes referring strictly to the Irish situation were issued in 1310, 1323, 1331, 1366, and 1380.[129] These were intended, in part, to remedy the issues related to trade and merchants, although they show more of what the royal circle's idea of the needs of merchants in Ireland were, assumptions which were not always accurate. They usually affirmed guarantees for merchants or banned trade with territories at war with England (or restored trade traffic).

An analysis of the structure and volume of trade in Ireland, as well as the political situation of Anglo-Norman towns in the second half of the fourteenth century, indicates that not all the wishes of the English Crown could be realised, even if they were expressed in a normative document. The prohibitions on contact and trade with the Irish must have remained a dead letter and legislative idealism, as Anglo-Norman towns relied on their Irish rural hinterlands for both the so-called small, local merchant traffic, and for the acquisition of goods that town merchants allocated for long-distance trade.[130] Nor did all the Crown's decisions on the general organisation of trade anticipate the effects they would have in Ireland. For example, in a petition of 1378, Dubliners gave voice to a complication that the staple ports legislation had caused. They saw the law as significantly undermining their ability to make a living; interestingly, the petition made very clear what Dublin merchants considered to be a key export commodity and what they had to import into Ireland from other ports:

> *Under an ordinance recently made [...] the citizens of Dublin are bound to bring their merchandise, namely old cloth, wool, hides and other exempted goods, which are very unlike and different from the merchandise of other lands, to the town of Calais, where they can with difficulty sell such goods for any proper value, or obtain wines, iron, salt, or other merchandise fit for Ireland; and the citizens of Dublin, having disposed of their goods at a low price at Calais, are necessitated to take a new freight to England, Gascony or elsewhere, to obtain merchandise suitable for their country, and they have thus to incur two freights instead of one, to their great loss and manifest impoverishment.*[131]

---

128 Ibid., pp. 319–321.

129 Ibid., pp. 265, 293, 330, 430–469, 477–479.

130 Childs and O'Neill, Overseas trade, p. 501; Hoare, The Evolution, p. 101; Watt, The Anglo-Irish colony, p. 370; Clarke, Decolonization, pp. 174 and 179.

131 CIRCLE, Patent Roll 1 Richard II, 8 Apr. 1378, Item 15, (https://virtualtreasury.ie/item/CIRCLE-6-1-1-15).

The Dublin authorities, moreover, identified another problem arising from the abuse of the staple ports legislation by foreign merchants; namely, by invoking the rights, they proceeded to ignore the Dublin charter and trade all goods in retail on an equal footing with local merchants while not participating in taxation.

Problems with complying with the rules of the staple ports law were also reported by the burgesses of Youghal in 1375. It obliged them to make frequent visits to Cork to pay customs on hides, which only then could be sold in other markets. Problematic for Youghal merchants was the need to cross the treacherous bay they shared with Cork.[132] Three years later, in turn, staple port officials in Cork saw the need to establish representation in Youghal and Kinsale, to which merchants carried wine, to avoid encountering the need to pay customs in Cork.[133]

Analysing the fourteenth-century correspondence between municipal authorities and the king and his council, as well as the resulting normative royal documents, inevitably one notices a certain recurrence of motives, among which trade and merchants were a frequent argument used by communities and municipal authorities in their attempts to arouse the monarch's interest in problems of importance beyond temporary local concerns.[134] After all, one cannot deny their sincerity in seeing their fortunes as depending largely on trade. The ability to raise funds from trade may indeed have been a condition for a city such as Waterford being able to pay the fee farm (*firma burgi*) due to the Crown.[135] On the other hand, the reference to the problems of attracting merchants was, in the eyes of the urban community, a justification for increasing the chance of royal favour from King Edward I. The community of Limerick reported a similar problem in 1378. The burgesses complained that they had borne enormous physical and financial burdens to defend their city from Irish and English enemies and rebels alike, nevertheless, they had been unable to ensure the safety of merchant traffic and thus suffered greatly for this reason. They wrote that "*consequently they are at present in such poverty and debility that they cannot in any way defend the city any longer against the malice and plots of those enemies without aid from the King in fortifying and repairing the city walls*".[136]

Urban communities in Ireland began to rely on the predictability provided by merchants' presence and activity, but also on the law relating to merchants and

---

132 CIRCLE, Patent Roll 49 Edward III, 4 July 1375, Item 131, (https://virtualtreasury.ie/item/CIRCLE-5-49-1-131).

133 Sayles, Documents, p. 247.

134 Watt, The Anglo-Irish colony, p. 370.

135 Citizens of Waterford to King: Grievances, c. 1272 – c. 1307, London, The National Archives, SC 8/78/3865.

136 CIRCLE, Patent Roll 1 Richard II, 26 March 1378, Item 12, (https://virtualtreasury.ie/item/CIRCLE-6-1-1-12).

trade in towns. However, just as by a whim of fate the merchant influx could fade, the mere availability of legal instruments did not always guarantee the effectiveness of rule enforcement. An escalating food crisis in the last quarter of the fourteenth century, which forced the authorities in some towns to intensify their control over bakers and butchers,[137] also meant that some merchants attempted to obtain and trade goods in illegal or informal ways. In such a situation, the municipal authorities resorted to the usual instrument of petitioning the king. An example of such a petition is the 1375 complaint of the Dublin burgesses, which outlined the problem of forestallers buying grain at village fairs or, presumably, directly from farmers and hoarding it in disguise in order to induce price increases in the city. To counter this crime, the king equipped the Dublin authorities with an additional instrument of pressure:

> *the king has appointed Nicholas Serjaunt, Mayor of Dublin, Thomas Mareward and John More, to search all granaries and places where grain has been deposited, and in what way and from whom the corn was bought (corn for their households excepted); and they are further to proclaim in the said town that no citizen or merchant or anyone else is to buy grain in any fairs except those markets in the said town, nor to store grain in granaries under threat of forfeiture of the said grain; and all bribers (imbraciatores), forestallers or baggers who act contrary to the said proclamation shall be imprisoned until the K. orders for their release.*[138]

4. Conclusions

An analysis of the legislation, legal and administrative documents, and correspondence reveals that, in legal terms, the situation of merchants in Anglo-Norman Ireland was intended to be an extension of the situation that had been created in England. This legal affinity provided the basis for predictability for merchants arriving from England. The rules of trade and the treatment of merchants in the Plantagenet state remained largely convergent and stable over the decades.

What is interesting are the mechanics of the transfer of the legal system within which the merchants were to operate. This was essentially an originally heterogenous system which was supposed to function as a homogenous one in Ireland. At the same time, this inherent heterogeneity did not impede the development of certain predictable standards. On the contrary, this feature allowed for the development of

137 Maleszka and Możdżeń, Urban Legislation, pp. 112–118.

138 CIRCLE, Patent Roll 49 Edward III, 20 March 1375, Item 207, (https://virtualtreasury.ie/item/CIRCLE-5-49-1-207).

a system where responsibility for trade and merchants was distributed between the king and local self-governing communities. Moreover, the heterogenous elements of the law transferred to Ireland presupposed the pre-existence of urban customs and rules regarding trade and merchants. Therefore, privileged local communities tended to adopt similar rules and procedures, also inspired by those in England, and expect similar ones, because these offered a sufficient degree of predictability that would attract the merchant and benefit the towns. It is also important to highlight here the fact that this was a favourable strategy in an environment where the majority of merchants visiting Ireland were either from England or did most of their business in England; such conditions were certainly an incentive to create and apply legal solutions familiar to them.

The specificity of Ireland as a region, stemming from the structure of its trade and also the constantly changing socio-political situation of frontier regions, affected most strongly the manner of implementation and the effects of the application of at least some of the general, state-wide legislation. This can be seen particularly in the application of principles arising from the Statutes and Ordinance of the Staple, but also, beyond the purely mercantile context, in the failure of the Statutes of Kilkenny and other legislation targeting the assimilation of English and Irish. Law shaped in the towns, locally, was, supposedly, more practical, befitting the actual needs of the various parties involved in the act of trade.

What can be observed from an even cursory comparison of Ireland to other regions is that the Anglo-Irish legal system developed for the purpose of managing trade and merchant relations, from the outset explicitly introduced the principle of protecting local merchants. In general, in terms of the sources of law and the mechanism of their introduction in Ireland, it can be said that compared to other regions subjected to urban conquest and colonisation, the relationship between the conquering country and the conquered country was closer than in analogous regions, for example, in Teutonic Prussia. On the other hand, the features of this very law, this heterogeneity and the norms and responsibilities it provided for, ensured that a thoroughly colonial relationship was not fully established.

Bibliography

ANGELUCCI, Charles/MERAGLIA, Simone, Trade, Self-Governance, and the Provision of Law and Order, with an Application to Medieval English Chartered Towns, Toulouse School of Economics Working Papers 13-443 (2013), https://ideas.repec.org/p/tse/wpaper/27726.html, accessed 05/30/2025.

BAKER, John H., Introduction to English Legal History, Oxford 2019.

BALLARD, Adolphus (ed.), British Borough Charters, [vol. 1: 1042–1216], Cambridge 1913.

BALLARD, Adolphus, The Law of Breteuil, in: The English Historical Review 30, 120 (1915), pp. 646–658.

BATESON, Mary (ed.), Borough customs, [vol. 1], London 1904.

BATESON, Mary (ed.), Borough customs, [vol. 2], London 1906.

BATESON, Mary, The Laws of Breteuil. Part III. Draft of the Laws, in: The English Historical Review 15 (1900), pp. 754–756.

BECKER, Patricia, An Analysis of the Dublin Guild Merchant Roll, c. 1190–1265, MA Thesis, Trinity College Dublin 1995.

BENNINGHOVEN, Friedrich, Rigas Entstehung und der frühhansische Kaufmann, Hamburg 1961.

BERRY, Henry F. (ed.), Statutes and Ordinances, and Acts of the Parliament of Ireland, [vol. I: King John to Henry V], Dublin 1907.

BERRY, Henry F., The Merchant Tailors' Gild: That of St John the Baptist, Dublin, 1418–1841, in: The Journal of the Royal Society of Antiquaries of Ireland 8, 1 (1918), pp. 19–64.

BERRY, Henry F., The Records of the Dublin Gild of Merchants, Known as the Gild of the Holy Trinity, 1438–1671, in: The Journal of the Royal Society of Antiquaries of Ireland 10, 1 (1900), pp. 44–68.

BRADLEY, John, Planned Anglo-Norman towns in Ireland, in: Howard B. CLARKE and Anngret SIMMS (eds.), The comparative history of urban origins in non-Roman Europe: Ireland, Wales, Denmark, Germany, Poland and Russia from the 9th to the 13th century, vol. 2, Oxford 1985, pp. 411–467.

BRADLEY, John and HALPIN, Andrew, The Topographical Development of Scandinavian and Anglo-Norman Waterford, in: William NOLAN and Thomas P. POWER (eds.), Waterford History and Society: Interdisciplinary Essays on the History of an Irish County, Dublin 1992, pp. 105–129.

BRAND, Paul, Common Law, in: Seán DUFFY (ed.), Medieval Ireland: An Encyclopedia. New York 2005, pp. 101–102.

BRITNELL, Richard H., The Proliferation of Markets in England, 1200–1349, in: The Economic History Review 34, 2 (1981), pp. 209–221.

BULDORINI, Chiara, Drogheda as a Case Study of Anglo-Norman Town Foundation in Ireland, 1194–1412, PhD Thesis, Trinity College Dublin 2009.

BYRNE, Francis J., The trembling sod: Ireland in 1169, in: Art COSGROVE (ed.), A New History of Ireland. 2: Medieval Ireland 1169–1534, Oxford 2012, pp. 1–42.

CHILDS, Wendy, Irish Merchants and Seamen in Late Medieval England, in: Irish Historical Studies 32, 125 (2000), pp. 22–43.

CHILDS, Wendy and O'NEILL, Timothy, Overseas trade, in: Art COSGROVE (ed.), A New History of Ireland. 2: Medieval Ireland 1169–1534, Oxford 2012, pp. 492–524.

CIRCLE: A Calendar of Irish Chancery Letters, c. 1244–1509, on Virtual Record Treasury of Ireland, Close Roll 5 Edward II, 18 June 1312, Item 81, https://virtualtreasury.ie/item/CIRCLE-4-5-2-81, accessed 05/30/2025.

CIRCLE: A Calendar of Irish Chancery Letters, c. 1244–1509, on Virtual Record Treasury of Ireland, Close Roll 29 Edward III, 2 June 1355, Item 39, https://virtualtreasury.ie/item/CIRCLE-5-29-2-39, accessed 05/30/2025.

CIRCLE: A Calendar of Irish Chancery Letters, c. 1244–1509, on Virtual Record Treasury of Ireland, Patent Roll 1 Richard II, 26 March 1378, Item 12, https://virtualtreasury.ie/item/CIRCLE-6-1-1-12, accessed 05/30/2025.

CIRCLE: A Calendar of Irish Chancery Letters, c. 1244–1509, on Virtual Record Treasury of Ireland, Patent Roll 1 Richard II, 8 Apr. 1378, Item 15, https://virtualtreasury.ie/item/CIRCLE-6-1-1-15, accessed 05/30/2025.

CIRCLE: A Calendar of Irish Chancery Letters, c. 1244–1509, on Virtual Record Treasury of Ireland, Patent Roll 2 Richard II, 9 Jan. 1379, Item 8, https://virtualtreasury.ie/item/CIRCLE-6-2-1-8, accessed 05/30/2025.

CIRCLE: A Calendar of Irish Chancery Letters, c. 1244–1509, on Virtual Record Treasury of Ireland, Patent Roll 4 Richard II, 20 Jul. 1380, Item 2, https://virtualtreasury.ie/item/CIRCLE-6-4-1-2, accessed 05/30/2025.

CIRCLE: A Calendar of Irish Chancery Letters, c. 1244–1509, on Virtual Record Treasury of Ireland, Patent Roll 7 Richard II, 1 Dec. 1383, Item 7, https://virtualtreasury.ie/item/CIRCLE-6-7-1-7, accessed 05/30/2025.

CIRCLE: A Calendar of Irish Chancery Letters, c. 1244–1509, on Virtual Record Treasury of Ireland, Patent Roll 7 Richard II, 1 Dec. 1383, Item 7, https://virtualtreasury.ie/item/CIRCLE-6-7-1-7, accessed 05/30/2025.

CIRCLE: A Calendar of Irish Chancery Letters, c. 1244–1509, on Virtual Record Treasury of Ireland, Patent Roll 7 Richard II, 1 Dec. 1383, Item 7, https://virtualtreasury.ie/item/CIRCLE-6-7-1-7, accessed 05/30/2025.

CIRCLE: A Calendar of Irish Chancery Letters, c. 1244–1509, on Virtual Record Treasury of Ireland, Patent Roll 7 Richard II, Item 7, 1 Dec. 1383, [62], https://virtualtreasury.ie/item/CIRCLE-6-7-1-7, accessed 05/30/2025.

CIRCLE: A Calendar of Irish Chancery Letters, c. 1244–1509, on Virtual Record Treasury of Ireland, Patent Roll 11 Richard II, 4 Jun. 1388, Item 2, https://virtualtreasury.ie/item/CIRCLE-6-11-1-2, accessed 05/30/2025.

CIRCLE: A Calendar of Irish Chancery Letters, c. 1244–1509, on Virtual Record Treasury of Ireland, Patent Roll 49 Edward III, 20 March 1375, Item 207, https://virtualtreasury.ie/item/CIRCLE-5-49-1-207, accessed 05/30/2025.

CIRCLE: A Calendar of Irish Chancery Letters, c. 1244–1509, on Virtual Record Treasury of Ireland, Patent Roll 49 Edward III, 4 July 1375, Item 131, https://virtualtreasury.ie/item/CIRCLE-5-49-1-131, accessed 05/30/2025.

Citizens of Waterford to King: Grievances, c. 1272–c. 1307, London, The National Archives, SC 8/78/3865.

Clarke, Howard B., and Simms, Anngret, Analogy versus theory: a rejoinder, in: Journal of Historical Geography 13.1 (1987), pp. 57–60.

Clarke, Howard B., Decolonization and urban decline in Ireland, 1300–1500, in: Terry R. Slater (ed.), Towns in decline, AD 100–1600, London/New York 2017, pp. 157–192.

Clarke, Howard B., Dooley, Sheila, and Johnson, Ruth, Dublin and the Viking World. Dublin 2018.

Clarke, Howard B., Fraternities and Guilds, in: Seán Duffy (ed.), Medieval Ireland: An Encyclopedia, New York 2005, p. 184.

Clarke, Howard B., Irish Historic Towns Atlas (IHTA), no. 11, Dublin, Part I, to 1610, ed. by Anngret Simms, Howard B. Clarke, Raymond Gillespie, J. H. Andrews, and Sarah Gearty, Dublin 2002.

Clarke, Howard B., The 1192 Charter of Liberties and the Beginnings of Dublin's Municipal Life, in: Dublin Historical Record 46, 1 (1993), pp. 5–14.

Coleman, B., Urban elite: the county and civic elite of later medieval Dublin, in: Seán Duffy (ed.), Medieval Dublin XV: Proceedings of the Friends of Medieval Dublin Symposium 2013, Dublin 2016, pp. 293–304.

Colfer, Billy, Arrogant trespass: Anglo-Norman Wexford 1169–1400, Enniscorthy 2002.

Crooks, Peter, Mac Murchada, Diarmait, in: Seán Duffy (ed.), Medieval Ireland: An Encyclopedia, New York 2005, pp. 299–302.

de Courcy Ireland, John, Ireland and the Irish in Maritime History, Glendale 1986.

Doherty, Charles, The monastic town in early medieval Ireland, in: Howard B. Clarke and Anngret Simms (eds.), The comparative history of urban origins in non-Roman Europe: Ireland, Wales, Denmark, Germany, Poland and Russia from the 9th to the 13th century, vol. 2, pp. 45–75.

Down, Kevin, Colonial society and economy in the high Middle Ages, in: Art Cosgrove (ed.), A New History of Ireland. 2: Medieval Ireland 1169–1534, Oxford 2012, pp. 439–491.

Downham, Clare, Medieval Ireland, Cambridge 2018.

Doyle, Ian W., 'Telling the dancer from the dance': the archaeology of early medieval Wexford, in: Ian W. Doyle and Bernard Browne (eds.) Medieval Wexford. Essays in Memory of Billy Colfer, Dublin 2016, p. 35–61.

Dryburgh, Paul and Smith, Brendan (eds.), Handbook and Select Calendar of Sources for Medieval Ireland in the National Archives of the United Kingdom, Dublin 2005.

Duffy, Seán, Town and Crown: the Kings of England and their City of Dublin, in: Michael Prestwich, Richard H. Britnell, and Robin Frame (eds.), Thirteenth Century England X. Proceedings of the Durham Conference 2003, Woodbridge 2005, pp. 95–117.

Eggerer, Elmar W., The Guild Merchant of Dublin, in: Seán Duffy (ed.), Medieval Dublin VI: Proceedings of the Friends of Medieval Dublin Symposium 2004, Dublin 2005, pp. 144–159.

Empey, C. Adrian, Conquest and Settlement: Patterns of Anglo-Norman Settlement in North Munster and South Leinster, in: Irish Economic and Social History 13 (1986), pp. 5–31.

EMPEY, C. Adrian, County Kilkenny in the Anglo-Norman period, in: William NOLAN and Kevin WHELAN (EDS.), Kilkenny: History and Society. Interdisciplinary Essays on the History of an Irish County, Dublin 1990, pp. 75–95.

EMPEY, C. Adrian, County Waterford 1200–1300, in: William NOLAN and Thomas P. POWER (EDS.), Waterford History and Society: Interdisciplinary Essays on the History of an Irish County, Dublin 1992, pp. 131–146.

EMPEY, C. Adrian, The Anglo-Norman settlement in the Cantred of Eliogarty, in: John BRADLEY (ed.), Settlement and Society in Medieval Ireland. Studies Presented to F.X. Martin, Kilkenny 1988, pp. 207–228.

EMPEY, C. Adrian, The evolution of the demesne in the lordship of Leinster: the fortunes of war or forward planning?, in: John BRADLEY, Cóilín Ó DRISCEOIL, and Michael POTTERTON (eds.), William Marshal and Ireland, Dublin 2017, pp. 39–77.

EMPEY, C. Adrian, The settlement of the kingdom of Limerick, in: James F. LYDON (ed.), England and Ireland in the Later Middle Ages. Essays in Honour of Jocelyn Otway-Ruthven, Dublin 1981, pp. 1–25.

EPSTEIN, Richard A., Reflections on the Historical Origins and Economic Structure of the Law Merchant, in: Chicago Journal of International Law 5, 1 (2004), pp. 1–20.

FRAME, Robin, Colonial Ireland, 1169–1369, Dublin 2012.

FRYDE, Natalie, Guilds in England before the Black Death, in: Berent SCHWINKEKÖPER (ed.), Gilden und Zünfte: Kaufmännische und gewerbliche Genossenschaften im frühen und hohen Mittelalter, Sigmaringen 1985, pp. 215–229.

GAFFNEY, Phyllis and DE PONTFARCY SEXTON, Yolande, 'The laws and usages of Dublin': a complete translation of Les leys et les usages de la cite de Diveline, in: Seán DUFFY (ed.), Medieval Dublin XVII, Dublin 2019, pp. 174–203.

GILBERT, John T., Archives of the Town of Galway, in: Historical Manuscript Commission, Tenth Report, Appendix, Part V. The Manuscript of the Marquis of Ormonde, the Earl of Fingall, the Corporations of Waterford, Galway, &c., London 1885, pp. 380–520.

GILBERT, John T. (ed.), Calendar of Ancient Records of Dublin, in the possession of the Municipal Corporation of that City, Dublin 1889.

GILBERT, John T. (ed.), Historic and municipal documents of Ireland, A.D. 1172–1320, London 1870.

GLASSCOCK, Robin E., Land and people, c. 1300, in: Art COSGROVE (ed.), A New History of Ireland. 2: Medieval Ireland 1169–1534, Oxford 2012, pp. 205–239.

GRAHAM, Brian J., Analogy and theory: Some further thoughts, in: Journal of Historical Geography 13.1 (1987), pp. 61–63.

GRAHAM, Brian J., Anglo-Norman Settlement in County Meath, in: Proceedings of the Royal Irish Academy. Section C: Archaeology, Celtic Studies, History, Linguistics, Literature, 75 (1975), pp. 223–249.

GRAHAM, Brian J., Anglo-Norman Settlement in Ireland, in: Irish Settlement Studies 1 (1985), pp. 2–40.

GRAHAM, Brian J., Secular Urban Origins in Early Medieval Ireland, in: Irish Economic and Social History 16 (1989), pp. 5–22.

GRAHAM, Brian J., The Definition and Classification of Medieval Irish Towns, in: Irish Geography 21 (1988), pp. 20–32.

GRAHAM, Brian J., Towns in medieval Ireland, in: John LUDLOW (ed.), Medieval Ireland: the Barryscourt Lectures I–X, Cork 2004, pp. 291–310.

GRAHAM, Brian J., Urban genesis in early medieval Ireland, in: Journal of Historical Geography 13.1 (1987), pp. 3–16.

GRAHAM, Brian J., Urbanisation in Ireland during the High Middle Ages, c. 1100 to c. 1350, in: James MULDOON (ed.), The North Atlantic frontier of medieval Europe: Vikings and Celts, Farnham 2009, pp. 285–300.

GROSS, Charles (ed.), Select cases concerning the law merchant, A.D. 1270–1638, [vol. 1: Local Courts], London 1908.

GROSS, Charles, The Gild Merchant, vol. II, Oxford 1890.

GWYNN, Aubrey, Medieval Bristol and Dublin, in: Irish Historical Studies 5 (1947), pp. 275–286.

HALL, Hubert (ed.), Select cases concerning the law merchant A.D. 1251–1779, Vol. 3: Supplementary Central Courts], London 1932.

HAND, Geoffrey J., English Law in Ireland, 1290–1324. Cambridge 1967.

HARDY, Thomas D. (ed.), Rotuli litterarum clausarum in Turri Londinensi asservati, [vol. 1: 1204–1224], London 1833, https://www.digitale-bibliothek-mv.de/viewer/image/PPN848631250/489/, accessed 05/30/2025.

HARTLAND, Beth, English Landholding in Ireland, in: Michael PRESTWICH, Richard H. BRITNELL, and Robin FRAME (eds.), Thirteenth Century England X. Proceedings of the Durham Conference 2003, Woodbridge 2005, pp. 119–129.

HEMMEON, Morley de Wolf, Burgage tenure in mediaeval England, Cambridge 1914.

HOARE, Kieran, The Evolution of Urban Oligarchies in Irish Towns, 1350–1534, in: Lud'a KLUSÁKOVÁ and Laure TEULIÈRES (eds.), Frontiers and identities: cities in regions and nations, Pisa 2008, p. 87–108.

HÖHLBAUM, Konstantin (ed.), Hansisches Urkundenbuch I, Halle 1876.

HOLTON, Karina, From charters to carters: aspects of fairs and markets in medieval Leinster, in: Denis A. CRONIN, Jim GILLIGAN, and Karina HOLTON (eds.), Irish fairs and markets: studies in local history, Dublin 2001, pp. 18–44.

HORNE, Tom, A Viking market kingdom in Ireland and Britain, Abingdon/New York 2022.

Irish Record Commissioners (ed.), Chartae, Privilegia et Immunitates, being Transcripts of Charters and Privileges to Cities, Towns, Abbeys, and other Bodies Corporate. 18 Henry II. to 18 Richard II. (1171 to 1395), Dublin 1889.

JAMROZIAK, Emilia, Networks of Markets and Networks of Patronage in Thirteenth-Century England, in: Michael PRESTWICH, Richard H. BRITNELL, and Robin FRAME (eds.), Thirteenth Century England X. Proceedings of the Durham Conference 2003, Woodbridge 2005, pp. 40–49.

Joy, C. A., Sokeright, PhD Thesis, University of Leeds 1975.

Kadens, Emily, The Medieval Law Merchant: The Tyranny of a Construct, in: Journal of Legal Analysis 7, 2 (2015), pp. 251–289.

Keegan, Mark, The archaeology of manorial settlement in west county Limerick, in: James Lyttleton and Tadgh O'Keeffe (eds.), The Manor in Medieval and Early Modern Ireland, Dublin 2005, pp. 17–39.

Kreem, Juhan, Kwiatkowski, Krzysztof, and Maleszka, Anna, Military Affairs and Community in Prussian, Livonian and Irish Towns, 13th–16th Centuries, in: Matthew F. Stevens and Roman Czaja (eds.), Towns on the Edge in Medieval Europe. The Social and Political Order of Peripheral Urban Communities from the Twelfth to Sixteenth Centuries, Oxford 2022, p. 165–189.

Leimus, Ivar, Einige Spekulationen über die münzberechtigte Autorität auf Gotland in der 2. Hälfte des 12. Jahrhunderts, in: Ilgvars Misāns and Horst Wernicke (ed.), Riga und der Ostseeraum: Von der Gründung 1201 bis in die frühe Neuzeit, Marburg a. d. Lahn 2005, pp. 64–75.

Liberman Cuenca, Esther, The making of borough customary law in medieval Britain, PhD Thesis, Fordham University 2019.

Liddy, Christian D., War, Politics and Finance in Late Medieval English Towns, Woodbridge 2005.

Lydon, James F., Ireland and the English Crown, 1171–1541, in: Peter Crooks (ed.), Government, war and society in medieval Ireland, Dublin 2008, pp. 65–78.

Lydon, James, The expansion and consolidation of the colony, 1215–54, in: Art Cosgrove (ed.), A New History of Ireland. 2: Medieval Ireland 1169–1534, Oxford 2012, pp. 156–178.

MacCotter, Paul, Medieval Ireland: Territorial, Political and Economic Divisions, Dublin 2008.

MacNiocaill, Gearoid, Na buirgéisí: XII–XV aois, Dublin 1964.

Maleszka, Anna and Czaja, Roman, Law, legislation and social impact as three factors shaping the political order of urban communes in Prussia and Ireland (13th–15th c.), in: Jesus A. Solórzano Telechea and Jelle Haemers (ed.), Normativa y autoridad en la ciudad medieval atlántica (y más allá), Logroño 2022, p. 25–42.

Maleszka, Anna and Możdżeń, Julia, Urban Legislation as an Instrument for the Formation and Regulation of Socio-Economic Life in 14th-Century Prussian and Irish Towns, in: Matthew F. Stevens and Roman Czaja (eds.), Towns on the Edge in Medieval Europe, Oxford 2022, pp. 93–119.

Maleszka, Anna and Stevens, Matthew, Maintaining a 'special relationship'? Petitions to the Crown from Irish and Welsh towns, 13th–16th centuries, in: Matthew F. Stevens and Roman Czaja (eds.), Towns on the Edge in Medieval Europe. The Social and Political Order of Peripheral Urban Communities from the Twelfth to Sixteenth Centuries, Oxford 2022, pp. 208–235.

Maleszka, Anna, Urbanizacja na obrzeżach łacińskiej Europy. Studium komparatystyczne rozwoju miast i krajobrazów miejskich w Irlandii, Prusach i Inflantach w XII–XIV wieku, Toruń 2024.

Martin, Francis X., Allies and an Overlord, 1169–72 in: Art Cosgrove (ed.), A New History of Ireland. 2: Medieval Ireland 1169–1534, Oxford 2012, pp. 67–97.

Martin, Francis X., Diarmait Mac Murchada and the Coming of the Anglo-Normans, in: Art Cosgrove (ed.), A New History of Ireland. 2: Medieval Ireland 1169–1534, Oxford 2012, pp. 43–66.

Martin, Francis X., John, Lord of Ireland, 1185–1216, in: Art Cosgrove (ed.), A New History of Ireland. 2: Medieval Ireland 1169–1534, Oxford 2012, pp. 127–155.

Martin, Francis X., Overlord becomes feudal lord, 1172–85, in: Art Cosgrove (ed.), A New History of Ireland. 2: Medieval Ireland 1169–1534, Oxford 2012, pp. 98–126.

McEneaney, Eamonn, Waterford and New Ross trade competition, c. 1300, in: Decies: Journal of the Waterford Archaeological and Historical Society 12 (1979), pp. 16–24.

McNeill, Charles (ed.), Liber Primus Kilkenniensis, Dublin 1931.

Miller, Edward and Hatcher, John, Medieval England: Towns, Commerce and Crafts, 1086–1348, London and New York 1995.

Murphy, Margaret, Manor centres, settlement and agricultural systems in medieval Ireland, 1250–1350, in: Margaret Murphy and Matthew Stout (eds.), Agriculture and settlement in Ireland, Dublin 2015, pp. 69–100.

Murphy, Margaret and Potterton, Michael, The Dublin region in the Middle Ages: settlement, land-use and economy, Dublin 2010.

Musson, Anthony, Second 'English Justinian' or Pragmatic Opportunist? A Re-Examination of the Legal Legislation of Edward III's Reign, in: James S. Bothwell (ed.), The Age of Edward III, New York 2001, pp. 69–88.

Ó Cróinín, Dáibhí, Early medieval Ireland: 400–1200, London 1995.

O'Flaherty, Eamon, Irish Historic Towns Atlas (IHTA), no. 21, Limerick, ed. by Anngret Simms, Howard B. Clarke, Raymond Gillespie, Jacinta Prunty, Sarah Gearty, Dublin 2010.

Ó Súilleabháin, Niall, Mormaors, mayors and merchants: the early development of municipal government in Dublin, in: Seán Duffy (ed.), Medieval Dublin XIII: Proceedings of the Friends of Medieval Dublin symposium, 2011, Dublin 2013, pp. 108–115.

Oexle, Otto G., Gilde und Kommune. Über die Entstehung von 'Einung' und 'Gemeinde' als Grundformen des Zusammenlebens in Europa, in: Otto G. Oexle, Bernhard Jussen, Andrea von Hülsen-Esch, and Frank Rexroth (eds.), Die Wirklichkeit und das Wissen: Mittelalterforschung, historische Kulturwissenschaft, Geschichte der Theorie der historischen Erkenntnis, Göttingen 2011, pp. 569–594.

O'Neill, Timothy, Merchants and Mariners in Medieval Ireland, Dublin 1987.

O'Neill, Timothy, Trade, in: Seán Duffy (ed.), Medieval Ireland: An Encyclopedia, New York 2005, pp. 449–451.

Orpen, Goddard H., Ireland under the Normans, Oxford 1911.

Orpen, Goddard H. (ed.), The Song of Dermot and the Earl, Oxford 1892.

O'Sullivan, Mary D., Italian Merchant Bankers in Ireland in the Thirteenth Century: A Study in the Social and Economic History of Medieval Ireland, Dublin 1962.

Otway-Ruthven, Annette J., A history of medieval Ireland, London 1980.

Otway-Ruthven, Annette J., The Character of Norman Settlement in Ireland, in: James Muldoon (ed.), The North Atlantic frontier of medieval Europe. Vikings and Celts, Farnham 2009, pp. 247–256.

Otway-Ruthven, Annette J., The medieval Irish town, in: Seán Duffy (ed.), Medieval Dublin X, Dublin 2010, pp. 299–311.

Otway-Ruthven, Anette J., The native Irish and English law in medieval Ireland, in: Peter Crooks (ed.), Government, war and society in medieval Ireland, Dublin 2008, pp. 141–154.

Prestwich, Michael C., Plantagenet England: 1225–1360, Oxford 2004.

Rees, William (ed.), Calendar of Ancient Petitions Relating to Wales: Thirteenth to Sixteenth Century, Cardiff 1975.

Ruffhead, Owen, Statutes at Large, from Magna Charta to the End of the Last Parliament, 1761, [vol. 1], London 1763.

Russo, Daniel G., Town Origins and Development in Early England, c. 400–950 A.D., Westport 1998.

Sachs, Stephen E., From St. Ives to Cyberspace: The Modern Distortion of the Medieval 'Law Merchant', in: American University International Law Review 21 (2006), pp. 686–812.

Sayles, Geoffrey O. (ed.), Documents on the Affairs of Ireland before the King's Council, Dublin 1979.

Schlau, Wilfried, Sozialgeschichte der baltischen Deutschen, Köln 1997.

Simpson, Alfred W. B., A History of the Land Law, Oxford 1986.

Slattery, Peadar, Woodland management, timber and wood production, and trade in Anglo-Norman Ireland, c. 1170 to c. 1350, in: The Journal of the Royal Society of Antiquaries of Ireland 139 (2009), pp. 63–79.

Strickland, W. G., The ancient official seals of the City of Dublin, in: Howard B. Clarke (ed.), Medieval Dublin 2: The living city, Dublin 1990, pp. 163–171, 223–225.

Swan, Leo, Monastic proto-towns in early medieval Ireland: the evidence of aerial photography, plan analysis and survey, in: Howard B. Clarke and Anngret Simms (eds.), The comparative history of urban origins in non-Roman Europe: Ireland, Wales, Denmark, Germany, Poland and Russia from the 9th to the 13th century, vol. 1, Oxford 1985, pp. 77–102.

Sweetman, Henry S. (ed.), Calendar of Documents, relating to Ireland, preserved in Her Majesty's Public Record Office, London, [vol. 1: 1171–1251], London 1875.

Watt, John A., The Anglo-Irish colony under strain, 1327–99, in: Art Cosgrove (ed.), A New History of Ireland. 2: Medieval Ireland 1169–1534, Oxford 2012, pp. 352–396.

Webb, John J., Municipal Government in Ireland: Mediaeval & Modern, Dublin 1918.

WILSON, Marion L., Plan Analysis of the Medieval Boroughs of Northumberland, PhD Thesis, University of Edinburgh 1989.

ZIENTARA, Benedykt, Źródła i geneza "prawa niemieckiego" (ius Teutonicum) na tle ruchu osadniczego w Europie zachodniej i środkowej w XI–XII w., in: Przegląd Historyczny 69, 1 (1978), pp. 47–74.

Notes on Contributors

MATTHIAS BERLANDI is a medieval historian specializing in the economic and social history of the Middle Ages. His research focuses on institutional change, resource regimes, and the political economy of high and late medieval Scotland and the Holy Roman Empire.

TOBIAS BOESTAD is an assistant professor in medieval history at the University of La Rochelle. He has dedicated his thesis to the beginnings of the Hanse and now specializes in the study of coastal societies.

LESLIE CARR-RIEGEL is a historian of the European Late Medieval period focusing on Environmental, Social, and Legal history.

GIJS DREIJER is a postdoctoral researcher working on a Gerda Henkel Foundation scholarship on Dutch entrepreneurs in nineteenth-century Africa. His research interests span maritime, business, economic and colonial history between the sixteenth and nineteenth centuries.

PHILIPP HÖHN is an assistant pdrofessor of Medieval History at the University of Halle-Wittenberg. His research focuses on the social and economic history of Northern and Western Europe in the later Middle Ages. His current project examines practices of maritime violence and its criminalization in relation to state formation and the formation of markets in late Medieval England.

OLGA KOZUBSKA is a research fellow at the Institute for Comparative Urban History (IStG) in Münster, Germany. Her research interests include history of towns in the medieval and early modern time, long-distance trade and development of multi-religious urban centers, adoption of Magdeburg law in the historical lands of present-day Ukraine.

ULLA KYPTA is professor for late medieval and early modern history at the University of Hamburg. She specialized in economic history and the history of the Late Hanse.

ANNA MALESZKA is an adjunct at the Faculty of History of the Nicolaus Copernicus University. She specializes in medieval history Ireland and Prussia and urban history.

Dr. Alexandr Osipian is a Research Fellow at the Leibniz Institute for the History and Culture of Eastern Europe (GWZO), Leipzig. His research focuses on late medieval and early modern long-distance trade and cultural transfer between the Middle East and Eastern Europe operated by Armenian merchant networks.

Gregor Rohmann is a professor of regional history at the University of Rostock. He specializes in medieval history and the history of the Hanseatic League.